About This Book

"Professor Oldmeadow's excellent anthology provides the reader with direct and immediate access to the writings of a large number of the exponents of the 'Perennial Philosophy,' including such leading figures as René Guénon, Frithjof Schuon, Ananda Coomaraswamy, and Titus Burckhardt. It is a major convenience to have so many profound philosophical and religious writings within the covers of one book."
—**William Stoddart**, editor of *The Essential Writings of Titus Burckhardt*

"Professor Oldmeadow brings together penetrating intellectual essays, personal reflections upon lived religious practices, and heartfelt calls for harmony and understanding. This book is a worthy companion to Professor Oldmeadow's magnificent *Journeys East* and a valuable anthology in its own right."
—**Timothy Scott**, author of *The Symbolism of the Ark*

"This companion to *Journeys East* offers to the serious reader a marvelous pilgrimage through the truly primordial wisdom of Asia and a most pristine opening toward the *Religio Perennis*, 'the underlying religion.' After introductory articles by the three lights of the Traditionalist School and authoritative spokesmen of 'intrinsic orthodoxy,' Dr. Oldmeadow allows authentic spiritual seekers and prominent scholars to speak with their own voice of their own encounter with the Eastern Light."
—**Renaud Fabbri**, editor of the online journal *Vincit Omnia Veritas*

World Wisdom
The Library of Perennial Philosophy

The Library of Perennial Philosophy is dedicated to the exposition of the timeless Truth underlying the diverse religions. This Truth, often referred to as the *Sophia Perennis*—or Perennial Wisdom—finds its expression in the revealed Scriptures as well as the writings of the great sages and the artistic creations of the traditional worlds.

Light from the East: Eastern Wisdom for the Modern West appears as one of our selections in the Perennial Philosophy series.

The Perennial Philosophy Series

In the beginning of the twentieth century, a school of thought arose which has focused on the enunciation and explanation of the Perennial Philosophy. Deeply rooted in the sense of the sacred, the writings of its leading exponents establish an indispensable foundation for understanding the timeless Truth and spiritual practices which live in the heart of all religions. Some of these titles are companion volumes to the Treasures of the World's Religions series, which allows a comparison of the writings of the great sages of the past with the perennialist authors of our time.

Cover: Nicholas Roerich, *Sangacheling*, 1924
Courtesy of the Nicholas Roerich Museum, New York

LIGHT FROM THE EAST

Eastern Wisdom
for the
Modern West

Edited by

HARRY OLDMEADOW

World Wisdom

Light from the East: Eastern Wisdom for the Modern West

Library of Congress Cataloging-in-Publication Data

Light from the east : eastern wisdom for the modern west / edited by Harry Oldmeadow.
p. cm. -- (The perennial philosophy series)
Includes bibliographical references and index.
ISBN-13: 978-1-933316-22-2 (pbk. : alk. paper)
ISBN-10: 1-933316-22-5 (pbk. : alk. paper) 1. Asia--Religion. 2. Asia--Religious life and customs. 3. Religion and culture--Asia. 4. Spirituality--Asia. 5. Religions--Relations. 6. East and West. I. Oldmeadow, Harry, 1947-
BL1033.L54 2007
200.95--dc22

2006032736

Printed on acid-free paper in Canada.

For information address World Wisdom, Inc.
P.O. Box 2682, Bloomington, Indiana 47402-2682

www.worldwisdom.com

CONTENTS

Harry Oldmeadow — Introduction *vii*

I. Principles: The Formal Diversity and Inner Unity of Traditions

Frithjof Schuon — What Can the East Offer to the West? 3
René Guénon — Oriental Metaphysics 8
Ananda Coomaraswamy — The *Vedanta* and Western Tradition 23
His Holiness the Dalai Lama — A Wish for Harmony 44
Whitall Perry — Anti-Theology and the Riddles of Alcyone 50

II. In the Tracks of Eastern Wisdom

Marco Pallis — The Tibetan Tradition: Its Presiding Idea 69
Huston Smith — Taoism 95
Philip Kapleau — The Private Encounter with the Master 118
Lynna Dhanani — An Introduction to Jainism 139
Swami Abhishiktananda — *Sannyasa* 165
John Paraskevopoulos — The Absolute in the Mahayana and the Pure Land Way 174

III. Art, Symbolism, and the Language of Silence

Titus Burckhardt — Hindu Art 193
Thomas Merton — The Buddha Figures at Polonnaruwa 199
Anagarika Govinda — Tibetan Sacred Music 201
Jean Cooper — The Symbolism of the Taoist Garden 205
Gustie Herrigel — The Substance of the Teaching 217
Jean Biès — Sacredness 220

IV. Eastern Light on Modern Predicaments

Ananda Coomaraswamy	Sri Ramakrishna and Religious Tolerance	229
Rama Coomaraswamy	Who Speaks for the East?	238
Aldous Huxley	Reflections on Time	245
Thomas Merton	Gandhi and the One-Eyed Giant	249
Ian Watson	Hindu Cosmology and Modern Science	272
Gary Snyder	On the Path, Off the Trail	277
Diana Eck	The Imagined Community	286

Sources and Acknowledgments 321
Notes on Contributors 325
Biographical Note 331
Index 333

INTRODUCTION

One of the most remarkable figures of recent times was Ananda Kentish Coomaraswamy, born in Sri Lanka in 1877 of a Tamil father and an English mother. He was educated in England but returned often to Sri Lanka where he founded the Ceylon Reform Movement of which he was the inaugural President. The Society dedicated itself to the preservation of traditional arts and crafts and to resisting "the thoughtless imitation of unsuitable European habits and customs." In 1905, mindful of the destructive consequences of European imperialism, Coomaraswamy wrote these prophetic words:

> Why do we not meet the wave of European civilization on equal terms? . . . Our Eastern civilization was here 2000 years ago; shall its spirit be broken utterly before the new commercialism of the West? Sometimes I think the Eastern spirit is not dead, but sleeping, and may yet play a greater part in the world's spiritual life.[1]

Coomaraswamy went on to become a peerless authority on Asian art and, in his later years, one of the most influential exponents of the perennial philosophy which informs the world's great traditions. Given that he belonged by nativity and temperament to both the East and the West, it is appropriate that we introduce this volume with some considerations taken from his writings.

In one of his essays Coomaraswamy refers to the "impotence and arrogance" implicit in the well-known refrain, "East is East and West is West, and never the twain shall meet." This proposition, he writes, is one "to which only the most abysmal ignorance and the deepest discouragement could have given rise."[2] As an art historian, philosopher, linguist, and hermeneutist, Coomaraswamy himself undertook a massive labor to dispel the West's "most abysmal ignorance" about Eastern traditions. The present volume moves through a terrain charted by such trail-breakers as Coomaraswamy and René Guénon,

[1] Manifesto of the Ceylon Reform Society, quoted in Roger Lipsey, *Coomaraswamy: His Life and Work* (Princeton: Princeton University Press, 1977), p. 22.

[2] "The Pertinence of Philosophy," in Ananda Coomaraswamy, *What is Civilisation?* (Cambridge, UK: Golgonooza, 1989), p. 19.

the French metaphysician who, early in the last century, gave us the first authoritative European exegesis of some of the pivotal doctrines and texts of both India and China. In the half-century since their passing, various clichés about the East have circulated in the West, perhaps the most pervasive of these turning on the well-worn contrast of a "materialistic" West and a "spiritual" East—but let us not forget that clichés, no matter how facile, usually have some foundation. The contemporary debate about East and West is swarming on one side with advocates for Western-style "Progress," and on the other with those prone to romanticize the "East" as the last bastion of an ill-defined "spirituality." In order to dispel some of the confusion and the rhetorical fog which has accumulated around this subject, we can do no better than turn to Coomaraswamy and Guénon.

The now familiar tropes about "East" and "West" sometimes imply a series of immutable differences between essentialized geo-cultural monoliths. It is not always understood that the contrasts to which attention is so often drawn arise, largely, from the preservation of tradition in the East, and its destruction in the West. As Coomaraswamy remarks,

> "East and West" imports a cultural rather than a geographical antithesis: an opposition of the traditional or ordinary way of life that survives in the East to the modern and irregular way of life that now prevails in the West. It is because such an opposition as this could not have been felt before the Renaissance that we say that the problem is one that presents itself only accidentally in terms of geography; it is one of times much more than of places.[3]

If it indeed be the case, as Coomaraswamy and Guénon insisted, that the spiritual malady of the modern world is to be explained by its indifference or hostility to the lessons of tradition, then it follows that the East may have a vital role to perform in any remedy. As is clear from "Oriental Metaphysics," one of the opening essays in this collection, Guénon believed that it was only in the East that various sapiential traditions remained more or less intact. It was to these, particularly Advaita Vedanta as the fullest possible expression of metaphysical

[3] "East and West," in Ananda Coomaraswamy, *The Bugbear of Literacy* (Bedfont: Perennial Books, 1979), p. 80. See also Letter to Sidney Gulick, July 1943, in *Selected Letters of Ananda Coomaraswamy*, ed. Alvin Moore, Jr. and Rama P. Coomaraswamy (Delhi: Oxford University Press, 1988), p. 69.

doctrine, that the West must turn to recover its sense of timeless truths which have been obscured in modern times. Guénon also stressed that any traditional society, such as still survived in the East, is oriented to spiritual ends whilst any anti-traditional society, found everywhere in the modern West, is necessarily governed by values inimical to our spiritual welfare. T.S. Eliot somewhere remarked that the health of any civilization can be gauged by the number of saints it nurtures. We should be in no doubt that, whatever contaminations modernity might have brought to Asia in the last two centuries, the East preserves something of the spiritual effulgence which has characterized it since primordial times—one need only mention Paramahamsa Ramakrishna and Ramana Maharshi, to restrict ourselves to India and to leave aside the Tibetan adepts, Chinese sages, and Zen masters of the Far East.

It is important not to confuse the Eastward-looking stance of figures like Guénon and Coomaraswamy with the sentimental exoticism nowadays so much in vogue. Coomaraswamy reminds us that

> If Guénon wants the West to turn to Eastern metaphysics, it is not because they are Eastern but because this is metaphysics. If "Eastern" metaphysics differed from a "Western" metaphysics, one or the other would not be metaphysics.[4]

One of Guénon's translators made the same point in suggesting that if Guénon turns so often to the East it is because the West is in the position of the

> foolish virgins who, through the wandering of their attention in other directions, had allowed their lamps to go out; in order to rekindle the sacred fire, which in its essence is always the same wherever it may be burning, they must have recourse to the lamps still kept alight.[5]

In other words, a turn to the spiritual heritage of the East need not signal an abandonment of the West but might, rather, prefigure the recuperation of those riches in our own traditions which have been neglected but which can never truly be destroyed. It is sometimes only with the aid of traditions much less ravaged by the onslaughts of modernity that we can appreciate what lies closer to hand. Furthermore,

[4] "Eastern Wisdom and Western Knowledge," in *The Bugbear of Literacy*, pp. 72-73.

[5] Quoted in Gai Eaton, *The Richest Vein* (London: Faber & Faber, 1949), p. 199.

such a rediscovery will help us to understand that metaphysical wisdom, the *sophia perennis*, is indeed always fundamentally the same, albeit that the vestments in which it is clothed will vary from religion to religion. Again, recall the prescient words of Coomaraswamy:

> The only possible ground upon which an effective entente of East and West can be accomplished is that of the purely intellectual wisdom that is one and the same for all times and for all men, and is independent of all environmental idiosyncrasy.[6]

Somewhat paradoxically, the diversity of religious doctrines and practices only goes to prove the point. Properly understood, this multiplicity will be seen as a function of the diversity of mankind and of those manifold Revelations in which all traditions originate, each being attuned to the receptivities and affinities of the human collectivity in question. From each Divine dispensation—the descent of the Koran or the revelation of the Vedas, to choose an example from each hemisphere—issues a doctrine and a method. The doctrine provides an adequate but not exhaustive account of the nature of Reality, and the method marks out a spiritual way whereby, through an alchemy of the soul, we may conform ourselves with the one Reality (by whatever name it might be called). The inter-relationships of the world's integral religious traditions, and the interplay of their esoteric and exoteric dimensions, was the principal concern of the third of the "great triumvirate" of twentieth century perennialists, Frithjof Schuon, another contributor to the volume at hand. Schuon's work ranges through the vast domain of religious forms from all parts of the globe, and he too has had a decisive role to play in bringing the spiritual heritage of the East within a Western purview.

The outlook espoused by Guénon, Coomaraswamy, and Schuon, and by many of the other contributors to this volume—an outlook still very much alive in parts of the East—stands at right angles to the prevailing ideologies of the modern West. One illustration must suffice. For the modern mind, shaped by a profane scientism, the words "matter" and "reality" are often more or less synonymous. Furthermore, in common parlance the word "reality" is generally without gradations; the notion that something might be "relatively

[6] "The Pertinence of Philosophy," p. 19.

real," and that this kind of "reality" is as nothing in the face of the Absolute, is more or less incomprehensible to the modern mind. In the East, and for anyone who understands the first thing about Tradition, nothing could be more absurd. To take as Real that ambiguous tissue of fugitive relativities which constitutes the spatio-temporal world is indeed to be ensnared in *maya*!

* * *

The present volume is structured in four parts. In the first will be found commanding essays by the three figures already mentioned, each throwing into sharp relief the fundamental principles which must be kept in view in any consideration of the spiritual intercourse between East and West. Without such principles to guide us we are likely to succumb to foolishness of one kind or another. From a myriad of possibilities might be adduced two examples of the sort of thing one has here in mind. The corrosive lucubrations of "post-colonial" academics who argue that the entire East-West encounter is to be explained in terms of an "Orient" that is a fabric of ideological fictions to confirm the West's sense of identity and to legitimize Western cultural and political superiority, exhibit the foolishness of deracinated intellectuals for whom the appalling slogan "nothing outside politics" has become a totalitarian rubric. On the other hand, we find another variety of foolishness in the credulous enthusiasm of Western seekers for self-styled Eastern "gurus" whose teachings, as often as not, are a farrago of half-understood doctrines, bizarre syncretisms, and modernistic prejudices, all festooned in a way most likely to seduce those who are understandably disillusioned with both the profane ideologies of modern Western societies and with what is often served up to them in the guise of "religion." The Gospel adage about figs and thistles has lost none of its point! Whitall Perry's essay in this section anatomizes the phenomena of the counterfeit spirituality to be encountered on all sides in the modern world. Also to be found in this section is the transcript of a talk on religious harmony by His Holiness the Dalai Lama, one of those Eastern luminaries whose vocation has included the "spiritualizing of politics," if one may so put it. Gandhi and Thich Nhat Hanh come readily to mind as other exemplars. In the West, Thomas Merton fulfilled something of the same function and it is appropriate that later in the anthology we should come across the Trappist's reflections on the Mahatma.

The second part of the anthology encompasses articles and excerpts which focus more directly on particular traditions, including Jainism and Pure Land Buddhism, here representing those several Eastern traditions of which the modern West still remains largely ignorant.

The third section presents a small sample of writings on Eastern expressive forms which have themselves been vehicles for a Truth which is essentially formless. Needless to say, these fragments can do no more than offer a tantalizing glimpse into the boundless treasure-house of Eastern iconography and symbolism. (Since the death of Ananda Coomaraswamy, no one has been more eminently qualified to elucidate these subjects than the late Titus Burckhardt whose essay on Hindu art opens this section.)

The last segment finds our contributors exploring a range of salient issues in the modern encounter of East and West, pointing up some of the lessons of which we are in the most urgent need. Here we find several figures who, in various ways, have helped to bring the doctrines and practices of Eastern traditions to the attention of the West, and who have been concerned with fostering a global community which respects differences but which affirms the spiritual vocation which is the patrimony of all humankind. Names such as Aldous Huxley, Thomas Merton, Gary Snyder, and Diana Eck will be familiar to readers who have already ventured into this territory. They provide a variety of perspectives on some of our central themes.

World Wisdom recently published *Journeys East: 20th Century Western Encounters with Eastern Religious Traditions*; that book traced the story of the momentous Western engagement with Eastern spirituality. The present work is intended as a companion volume, allowing some of the figures who played a prominent part in that narrative to speak here in their own voices. (By way of an aside it should be noted that neither *Journeys East* nor this volume brings the world of Islam within its orbit, though from certain points of view that branch of the Abrahamic tree belongs as much to the Orient as to the Occident. Nor are these books concerned with the Asian reception of European ideas and influences.)

* * *

Collected in this anthology, then, are the experiences and insights of a variety of people—poets, philosophers, monks, scholars, teachers, pilgrims—who have turned Eastwards in search of spiritual nourishment and intellectual illumination. Amidst the destructive pathologies and the spiritual sterility of modernity, cutting through the profane din and clutter of modern life, here are the voices of men and women who not only searched but who found in the ancient well-springs of the East a sense of the spiritual destiny which alone confers the dignity, freedom, and responsibility of that human condition "hard to obtain." It is my hope that their writings may help each of us in our journey, by whichever path, towards that Light which is of neither East nor West.

Harry Oldmeadow
Bendigo, Australia

I

PRINCIPLES: THE FORMAL DIVERSITY AND INNER UNITY OF TRADITIONS

Agni is One, only kindled in many places.
One is the Sun mightily overspreading the world.
One alone is the Dawn beaming over all this.
It is the One that has severally become all this.

Rig Veda

There is no deity that I am not, and in case any man be
truly a worshipper of any deity whatever,
it is I that am the cause of his devotion and its fruit. . . .
However men approach Me, even so do I welcome them,
for the path men take from every side is Mine.

Bhagavad Gita

WHAT CAN THE EAST OFFER TO THE WEST?*

Frithjof Schuon

Assuredly there are no such things as "problems of our time" in the philosophers' sense of the expression, that is to say there is no thought that one could describe as "new" in its very foundations; there are however some questions that arose from the moment when "science" and "faith" began to part company and which "belong to our time" because they have never ceased to engage people's attention.

Faith is the accepting of that which we do not see, or rather, of that which transcends the experience of the average man; science is the experience of that which we do see, or at least of that whereof we can have an empirical knowledge. Traditional faith has been shaken or lost for reasons that are both subjective and objective; the "intellectual worldliness" inaugurated at the time of the Renaissance and voiced by Descartes brought as its consequence a general weakening of contemplative intelligence and of the religious instinct, while new facts, all manner of discoveries and inventions, came in to profit from this weakening and seemed to inflict a more or less flagrant contradiction upon the propositions of faith. Otherwise put, modern man was not—and is not—"intelligent" enough to offer intellectual resistance to such specious suggestions as are liable to follow from contact with facts which, though natural, normally lie beyond the range of common experience; in order to combine, in one and the same consciousness, both the religious symbolism of the sky and the astronomical fact of the Milky Way, an intelligence is required that is more than just rational, and this brings us back to the crucial problem of intellection and, as a further consequence, to the problem of gnosis and esotericism.

However, the modern skepticism, in order to take root, does not always require the prior misdeeds of Cartesianism; every sort of "worldliness" is a breach open to admit the spirit of doubt and the denial of the supernatural, aided by circumstances. Experience goes to prove that no people, however contemplative, is able in the long run to withstand the psychological effects of the modern discoveries, a fact that

* Editor's Note: from *The Language of the Self* (1959 edition).

clearly demonstrates their "abnormality" in relation to human nature generally; in Europe the hostility of the mediaeval Church towards the new astronomical theses does not appear, in the light of subsequent events, to have been altogether unreasonable, to say the least of it. It is evident that no kind of knowledge is bad in principle or in itself: but many forms of knowledge can be harmful in practice as soon as they cease to correspond to the hereditary experience of man and are imposed on him without his being spiritually prepared to receive them; the human soul finds difficulty in coping with facts that are not offered to its experience in the ordinary course of nature. The same holds true of art: the latter has need of limits imposed by nature, at least in so far as it is the appanage of a collectivity, such being "passive" and "unconscious" by definition; one has but to put at the disposition of a people or a caste the resources of machinery and the chemical industry, and their art, regarded in the broadest sense, will be corrupted, not in its every manifestation of course, but in so far as it belongs to all. This does not mean to say that the majority of an artistic people is totally lacking in discernment, but that the seductive attraction of novel possibilities proves in the long run more powerful than hereditary taste; fineness of soul yields to the clamor of what is easy and offered in quantity, just as happens on the intellectual plane and other planes besides. Human nature is weak and prone to corruption; it is not possible for a whole people to be holy or even simply clear-sighted.

Howbeit, the tragic dilemma of the modern mind results from the fact that the majority of men are not capable of grasping *a priori* the compatibility of the symbolic expressions of tradition with the material observations of science; these observations incite modern man to want to understand the "why and wherefore" of all things, but he wishes this "wherefore" to remain as external and easy as scientific phenomena themselves, or in other words, he wants all the answers to be on the level of his own experiences; and as these are purely material ones, his consciousness closes itself in advance against all that might transcend them.

One of the great errors of our time is to speak of the "failure" of religion or the religions; this amounts to imputing to the truth our own refusal to accept it and at the same time to denying man both his liberty and his intelligence. The latter depends, in large measure, on his will, therefore on freewill, in the sense that the will can contribute towards rendering intelligence effective or else towards paralyzing it; it is therefore not without good reason that mediaeval theologians situated heresy in the will. Intelligence can in fact slip into error, but its own nature is such as not to allow it to resist truth indefinitely; for this to happen the intervention of a volitional factor is required or, to be more precise, of a passional factor, namely prejudice, a sentimental interest, individualism under its many forms. Every error contains an element of irrational "mysticism," a tendency that has nought to do with concepts but which uses concepts or invents them. Behind every philosophical opinion is to be found some particular "savor" or "color"; errors are born of psychic "hardenings," "dissipations," "explosions," or "heavinesses" and these are, each in its own way, obstacles to the shining forth of Intellect and to the vision of the "Eye of the Heart."

The darkening of our world—whether it be a matter of the West properly speaking or of its extensions into the East or elsewhere—is apparent also in the fact that mental nimbleness for the most part goes hand in hand with intellectual shallowness: people are in the habit of treating concepts like mental playthings that commit one to nothing; ideas no longer "bite" on the intelligence and the latter "glides" over concepts without giving itself time to "grasp" them. The modern spirit proceeds "along the surface," hence a continual toying with mental images without awareness of the part these really play; the traditional spirit, on he other hand, proceeds "in depth," whence arise doctrines that may be apparently "dogmatic" but which none the less remain fully satisfying and effective.

* * *

From the doctrinal point of view, the most urgent need at present is to rediscover the spiritual science of exegesis, that is to say the metaphysical and mystical interpretation of the Scriptures. The principles of this science, which for its handling presupposes on every count a highly intuitive intelligence and not simply a mental acuteness, have been expounded, for Christendom, by Origen and others, and put into practice by the Fathers and the greatest Saints. In other words, what the West lacks is an intellectuality founded, not on academic erudition and philosophic skepticism, but upon intellectual intuition as actualized by the Holy Spirit on the basis of an exegesis that takes into account all levels of reality and understanding; this exegesis itself implies the science of symbolism which, for its part extends into all the realms of formal expression and especially into sacred art; the latter includes the liturgical art, in the broadest sense, as well as art properly so-called. Since the traditional East has never departed from this manner of regarding things, a proper comprehension of its metaphysical teachings, its commentaries, its symbolisms, and its arts would be, for the West, of vital interest.

But there is yet another level on which the East is rich in teachings—this is the level of spiritual life, of the "techniques" of realization; we are referring not to those which are exclusively bound up with a given traditional form, but to those which lend themselves to harmonious integration in any perspective or symbolism, this, thanks to the unity of truth itself and the homogeneity of the human species. We are thinking especially, on the one hand, of a more "organic" influence exerted by intellectual knowledge on spiritual life and, on the other hand, of a renewal of incantatory methods, such as are described for instance in the "Way of a Pilgrim";[1] this does not differ, in a final analysis, from the way of the Desert Fathers. From the above example it will be seen that what we have in mind, for the Christian, is a return to his own sources and not an "orientalization" of the West.

Lastly, on the most external plane, there is the conception of life, of social facts, of civilization in general: here again, the Oriental conception agrees with that of the ancient West and of every other traditional society. In all these questions it is important to bear in mind the following: there is no question, for the West, of turning "backwards" purely and simply, for one can never rejoin one's point of departure. On the contrary, what is needed is to combine the normal attitudes, which are timeless like truth itself, with such experiences of modern times as may be utilizable.

On the other hand, it should be pointed out that if the West needs the East, the latter also has need of the West—not of the West as such, of course, but of such few Westerners as have managed to integrate their experiences of the modern world in a traditional and spiritual outlook that might, if one likes, be described as "oriental" or "mediaeval." When in contact with the West, Orientals generally display an astonishing lack of suspicion and this can be explained by the fact that the modern world, while being a "necessary evil," is not a normal possibility. Now the Western elite to which we are referring is

[1] Anonymous Russian works of the mid-nineteenth century which afford a vivid insight into the workings, at a popular level, of *japa yoga* under its Christian form. An English translation (two volumes) has been published by S.P.C.K. in 1954.

endowed with a "discernment of spirits" and a sense of proportion that often are lacking in Orientals; the latter, however, today stand greatly in need of these particular qualities, not on the still uncontaminated soil of their own civilization, where they understand what they are doing, but outside it in a chaotic world that violates every framework and insinuates itself everywhere.

It will be readily understood that when we speak of gifts from the East to the West, we do so without any illusions, since one does not have to be a prophet to foresee that the West is not going to be saved as a whole; nor do the prospects of the East look much more hopeful, at least during the present cycle of humanity. On the other hand the individual both of East and West—together with the spiritual collectivity on which he depends—still keeps all his interior liberty and, with it, must accept his full share of responsibility.

ORIENTAL METAPHYSICS*

René Guénon

For the subject of this essay I have taken Oriental metaphysics. Perhaps it would have been better to have said simply metaphysics unqualified, for in truth, pure metaphysics being essentially above and beyond all form and all contingency is neither Eastern nor Western but universal. The exterior forms with which it is covered only serve the necessities of exposition, to express whatever is expressible. These forms may be Eastern or Western; but under the appearance of diversity there is always a basis of unity, at least, wherever true metaphysics exists, for the simple reason that truth is one.

If this be so, what need is there to deal specifically with Oriental metaphysics? The reason is that in the present intellectual state of the Western world metaphysics is a thing forgotten, generally ignored, and almost entirely lost, while in the East it still remains the object of effective knowledge. Thus it is to the East that one must look if one wishes to discover the true meaning of metaphysics; or even if one's wish is to recover some of the metaphysical traditions formerly existing in a West which was in many respects much closer to the East than it is today, it is above all with the help of Oriental doctrines and by comparison with them that one may succeed, since these are the only doctrines in the domain of metaphysics which can still be studied directly. As for these, however, it is quite clear that they must be studied as the Orientals themselves study them and one must certainly not indulge in more or less hypothetical interpretations which may sometimes be quite imaginary; it is too often forgotten that Eastern civilizations still exist and still have qualified representatives from whom it is possible to enquire in order to discover the exact truth about the subject in question.

I have said "Eastern metaphysics" and not merely Hindu metaphysics, for doctrines of this order, with all they imply, are not only to be found in India, as some people believe who, moreover, barely

* Editor's Note: The text of a lecture given at the Sorbonne in Paris on 12 December, 1925.

grasp their true nature. The case of India is by no means exceptional in this respect; it is precisely that of all civilizations which possess what might be termed a traditional basis. On the contrary, what are exceptional and abnormal are civilizations without such a basis, and to tell the truth, the only one known to us is that of the modern West. To take only the principal Eastern civilizations: the equivalent of Hindu metaphysics is found in China (in Taoism) and is also to be found elsewhere in certain esoteric schools of Islam; it should be understood, however, that this Islamic esotericism has nothing in common with the overt philosophy of the Arabs, which is for the most part Greek-inspired. The only difference is that except in India these doctrines are reserved for a relatively restricted and closed elite. This was also the case in the West in the Middle Ages, in an esotericism comparable in many respects to that of Islam and as purely metaphysical as the Islamic one; of this the moderns, for the most part, do not even suspect the existence. In India it is not possible to speak of esotericism in the true sense of the word, because there is no doctrinal dualism of exoteric and esoteric; it can only be a matter of natural esotericism, in the sense that each goes more or less deeply into the doctrine and more or less far according to the measure of his abilities, since there are, for certain individualities, limitations which are inherent in their own nature, and which it is impossible to overcome.

Naturally, forms differ from one civilization to another; but though more accustomed myself to the Hindu forms, I have no scruple in employing others when necessary, if they can contribute to the understanding of certain points; there are no objections to this since they are only different expressions of the same thing. Once again, truth is one, and it is the same for all those who, by whatever way, have attained to its understanding.

This said, it should be made clear in what sense the word "metaphysics" is used, all the more so since I have frequently had occasion to state that everyone does not understand it in the same way. I think the best course to take with words that can give rise to ambiguity is to reduce them, as far as possible, to their primary and etymological meaning. Now, according to its composition, this word "metaphysics" means literally "beyond physics," taking the word "physics" in the accepted meaning it always had for the ancients, that is as the "science of nature" in its widest sense. Physics is the study of all which appertains to the domain of nature; metaphysics, on the other hand, is the study of what lies beyond nature. How then can some claim that metaphysical knowledge is natural knowledge, either in respect of its object, or with regard to the faculties by which it is obtained? There we have a complete misconception, a contradiction in terms; and, what is more amazing, this confusion affects even those who should preserve some idea of the true metaphysics and know how to distinguish it clearly from the pseudo-metaphysics of modern philosophers.

But, one might say, if this word "metaphysics" gives rise to such confusion, would it not be better to abandon it and substitute something more suitable? Plainly, this would not be advisable, since, by its formation, this word meets the exact requirements; also it is hardly possible, since Western languages have no other word equally adapted to this usage. Simply to use the word "knowledge," as is done in India, because this is indeed knowledge *par excellence* and that which alone can be dignified by that name, is out of the question, for it would only make things more confusing for Occidentals who habitually associate knowledge with nothing beyond the scientific and rational. Also is it necessary to concern ourselves with the abuse to which a word is put? If we rejected all such, what would be left? Is it not sufficient to take precautions to avoid misunderstandings and misrepresentations? We are not any more enamored of the word "metaphysics" than of any other, but since a better term cannot be suggested to replace it we will continue to use it as before.

Unfortunately one comes across people who claim to "judge" that which they do not know, and who, because they apply the name "metaphysics" to a purely human and rational knowledge (which for us is only science or philosophy), imagine that Oriental metaphysics is no more and no other than that; from which they arrive logically at the conclusion that this metaphysics cannot in reality lead to any particular results. They fail to see that it is an effective guide just because it is something quite other than they suppose. What they envisage has really nothing to do with metaphysics since it is only knowledge of a natural order, an outward and profane scholarship; it is not of this that we wish to speak. Can one then make "metaphysical" synonymous with "supernatural"? We are prepared to accept such an analogy, since if one does not go beyond nature, that is to say the manifest world in its entirety (and not only the world of the senses, which is only an infinitesimal part of it), one is still in the realm of the physical. Metaphysics is, as we have already said, that which lies beyond and above nature; hence it can properly be described as "supernatural."

But an objection will undoubtedly be raised here: Is it possible to go beyond nature? We do not hesitate to answer plainly: Not only is it possible, but it is a fact. Again it might be said, is this not merely an assertion; what proofs thereof can be adduced? It is truly strange that proof is demanded concerning the possibility of a kind of knowledge instead of searching for it and verifying it for one's self by undertaking the work necessary for its acquisition. For those who possess this knowledge, what interest can there be in all this discussion? Substituting a "theory of knowledge" for knowledge itself is perhaps the greatest admission of impotence in modern philosophy.

Moreover, all certitude contains something incommunicable. Nobody can truly attain to any knowledge other than by a strictly personal effort; all that one can do for another is to offer him the opportunity and indicate the means by which to attain the same knowledge. That is why it would be vain to attempt to impose any belief in the purely intellectual realm; the best argument in the world could not in this respect replace direct and effective knowledge.

Now, is it possible to define metaphysics as we understand it? No, for to define is always to limit, and that with which we are concerned is, in itself, truly and absolutely unlimited and cannot be confined to any formula or any system. Metaphysics might be partly described, for example, by saying that it is the knowledge of universal principles, but that is not a definition in the proper sense, and only conveys a rough idea. Something can be added by saying that the scope of these principles is far greater than was thought by some Occidentals who, although really studying metaphysics, did so in a partial and incomplete way. Thus when Aristotle envisages metaphysics as a knowledge of being *qua* being, he identifies it with ontology, that is to say he takes the part for the whole. For Oriental metaphysics, pure being is neither the first nor the most universal principle, for it is already a determination. It is thus necessary to go beyond being, and it is this which is of the greatest significance. That is why, in all true metaphysical conceptions it is necessary to take into account the inexpressible: just as everything that can be expressed is literally nothing in comparison with that which surpasses expression, so the finite, whatever its magnitude, is nothing when faced with the Infinite. One can hint at much more than can be expressed, and this is the part played by exterior forms. All forms, whether it is a matter of words or symbols, only act as a support, a fulcrum for rising to possibilities of conception which far outstrip them; we will return to this later.

We speak of metaphysical conceptions for lack of any other term whereby to make ourselves understood, but it is not to be concluded from this that there is here something comparable to scientific or philosophic conceptions; it is not a question of any "abstractions," but of attaining an intuitive and immediate supra-rational knowledge. This pure intellectual intuition, without which there is no true metaphysics, has, moreover, no connection with the intuition spoken of by certain contemporary philosophers, which is, on the contrary, infra-rational. There is an intellectual intuition and a sensible intuition; one lies beyond reason, but the other is situated on its hither side; the latter can only know the world of changing and becoming, that is to say nature, or rather, an inferior part of nature. The domain of intuition, on the contrary, is the province of eternal and immutable principles; it is the realm of metaphysics.

To comprehend universal principles directly the transcendent intellect must itself be of the universal order; it is no longer an individual faculty, and to consider it as such would be contradictory, as it is not within the power of the individual to go beyond his own limits and leave the conditions which limit him *qua* individual. Reason is a specifically human faculty, but that which lies beyond reason is truly "non-human"; it is this which makes metaphysical knowledge possible, and that knowledge, one must again emphasize, is not a human knowledge. In other words, it is not as man that man can attain it, but because this being which is human in one of its aspects is at the same time something other and more than a human being. It is the attainment of effective consciousness of supra-individual states which is the real object of metaphysics, or better still, of metaphysical knowledge itself. We come here to one of the most vital points, and it is necessary to repeat that if the individual were a complete being, if he made up a closed system like the monad of Leibnitz, metaphysics would not be possible; irremediably confined in himself, this being would have no means of knowing anything outside his own mode of existence. But such is not the case; in reality the individuality represents nothing more than a transitory and contingent manifestation of the real being. It is only one particular state amongst an indefinite multitude of other states of the same being; and this being is, in itself, absolutely independent of all its manifestations, just as, to use an illustration which occurs frequently in Hindu texts, the sun is absolutely independent of the manifold images in which it is reflected. Such is the fundamental distinction between "Self" and "I," the personality and the individuality; as the images are connected by the luminous rays with their solar source, without which they would have neither existence nor reality, so the individuality, either of the human individual or of any other similar state of manifestation, is bound by the personality to the principial center of being by this transcendent intellect of which we are speaking. It is impossible, within the limits of this exposition, to develop these lines of thought more completely, or to give a more exact idea of the theory of multiple states of being;* but I think I have said enough to show the extreme importance of all truly metaphysical doctrine.

I said "theory," but here it is not a question of theory alone; this is a point which needs further explanation. Theoretical knowledge, which is only indirect and in some sense symbolic, is merely a preparation, though indispensable, for true knowledge. It is, moreover, the only knowledge which is communicable, even then only in a partial sense. That is why all statements are no more than a means of approaching knowledge, and this knowledge, which is in the first place only virtual, must later be effectively realized. Here we find another discrepancy in the more limited metaphysics to which we referred earlier, for example that of Aristotle. This remains theoretically inadequate in that it limits itself to being, and its theory seems to be presented as self-sufficient instead of being expressly bound up with a corresponding realization, as is the case in all Oriental doctrines. However, even in this imperfect metaphysics (we might be tempted to say this demi-metaphysics), sometimes statements are encountered which, if properly understood, would lead to totally different conclusions; thus, did not Aristotle specifically state that a being is all that it knows? This affirmation of identification through knowledge is the same in principle as metaphysical realization. But here the principle remains isolated; it has no value other than that of a merely theoretical statement, it carries no weight, and it seems that, having propounded it, one thinks no more about it. How was it that Aristotle himself and his followers failed to see all that here was implied? It is the same in many other cases, where apparently other equally essential things are forgotten, such as the distinction between pure intellect and reason, even after having defined them quite explicitly; these are strange omissions. Should one see in this the effect of certain limitations inherent in the Occidental mind, apart from some rare but always possible exceptions? This might

* Editor's Note: See Guénon's later work dedicated to this subject, *The Multiple States of Being* (New York: Larson, 1984).

be true in a certain measure; nevertheless it is not necessary to believe that Western intellectuality has always been as narrowly limited as it is in the present age. But after all, we have been speaking only of outward doctrines, though these are certainly superior to many others since, in spite of all, they comprise a part of the true metaphysics. For our part we are certain that there has been something other than this in the West during the Middle Ages and in olden times; there certainly have existed amongst an elite purely metaphysical doctrines which could be called complete, including their realization, a thing which, for most moderns, is barely conceivable. If the West has lost the memory of this completely it is because it has broken with its proper tradition, which explains why modern civilization is abnormal and deviationist.

If purely theoretical knowledge were an end in itself and if metaphysics went no further, it would still assuredly be worth something, but yet it would be altogether insufficient. In spite of conferring the genuine certainty, even greater than mathematical certainty, which belongs to such knowledge, it would yet remain, though in an incomparably superior order, analogous to that which, at an inferior level, constitutes terrestrial and human, scientific and philosophical, speculation. That is not what metaphysics is meant for; if others choose to interest themselves in a "mental sport," or suchlike, that is their affair; these things leave us cold, and moreover we think that the curiosities of psychology should be completely indifferent to the metaphysician. What he is concerned with is to know what is, and to know it in such fashion as to be oneself, truly and effectively, what one knows.

As for the means of metaphysical realization, we are well aware of such objections as can be made by those who find it necessary to challenge its possibility. These means, indeed, must be within man's reach; they must, in the first stages at least, be adapted to the human state, since it is in this state that the being now exists which subsequently will assume the higher states. Thus it is in these formal means, appropriate to this world as presently manifested, that the being finds a fulcrum for raising itself beyond this world. Words, symbolism, signs, rites, or preparatory methods of any sort have no other reason for existence and no other function; as we have already said, they are supports and nothing else. But some will ask, how is it possible that merely contingent means can produce an effect which immeasurably surpasses them and which is of a totally different order from that to which the instruments themselves belong? We should first point out that these means are, in reality, only fortuitous. The results they help to attain are by no means consequential; they place the being in the position requisite for attainment and that is all. If the above-mentioned objections were valid in this case they would be equally so for religious rites, for the sacraments, for example, where the disproportion between the means and the end is no less; some of those who have raised the above objections might have thought of this too. As for us, we do not confuse a simple means with a cause in the true sense of the word and we do not regard metaphysical realization as an effect, since it is not the production of something which does not yet exist, but the knowing of that which is, in an abiding and immutable manner, beyond all temporal succession, for all states of the being, considered under their primary aspect, abide in perfect simultaneousness in the eternal now.

Thus we see no difficulty in recognizing that there is nothing in common between metaphysical realization and the means leading to it, or, if preferred, which prepare for it. This is why, moreover, no means are strictly or absolutely necessary; or at least there is only one indispensable preparation, and that is theoretical knowledge. This, on the other hand, cannot go far without a means which will play the most important and constant part: This means is concentration. This is something completely foreign to the mental habits of the modern West, where everything tends towards dispersion and incessant change. All other means are only secondary in comparison; they serve above all to promote concentration and to harmonize the diverse elements of human individuality in order to facilitate effective communication between this individuality and the higher states of being.

Moreover, at the start, these means can be varied almost indefinitely, for they have to be adapted to the temperament of each individual and to his particular aptitudes and disposition. Later on the differences diminish, for it is a case of many ways which all lead to the same end; after reaching a certain stage all multiplicity vanishes, but by that time the contingent and individual means will have played their part. This part, which it is unnecessary to enlarge upon, is compared, in certain Hindu writings, to a horse which helps a man to reach the end of his journey more quickly and easily, but without which he would still have been able to arrive. Rites and various methods point the way to metaphysical realization, but one could nevertheless ignore them and by unswervingly setting the mind and all powers of the being to the aim of this realization could finally attain the supreme goal; but if there are means which make the effort less laborious, why choose to neglect them? Is it confusing the contingent with the absolute to take into account the limitations of our human state, since it is from this state, itself contingent, that we are at present compelled to start in order to attain higher states, and finally the supreme and unconditioned state?

After considering the teachings common to all traditional doctrines we must now turn to the principal stages of metaphysical realization. The first is only preliminary and operates in the human domain and does not go beyond the limits of the individuality. It consists of an indefinite extension of this individuality of which the corporeal modality, which is all that is developed in the ordinary man, represents the smallest portion; it is from this corporeal modality that it is necessary to start by means borrowed from the sensible order, but which, however, must have repercussions in the other modalities of the human being. The phase in question is, in short, the realization or development of all the potentialities which are contained in the human individuality, and which, comprising, as they do, manifold extensions, reach out in diverse directions beyond the realm of the corporeal and sensible; and it is by these extensions that it is possible to establish communication with the other states.

This realization of the integral individuality is described by all traditions as the restoration of what is called the "primordial state" which is regarded as man's true estate and which moreover escapes some of the limitations characteristic of the ordinary state, notably that of the temporal condition. The person who attains this "primordial state" is still only a human individual and is without effective possession of any supra-individual states; he is nevertheless freed from time and the apparent succession of things is transformed for him into simultaneity; he consciously possesses a faculty which is unknown to the ordinary man and which one might call the "sense of eternity." This is of extreme importance, for he who is unable to leave the viewpoint of temporal succession and see everything in simultaneity is incapable of the least conception of the metaphysical order. The first thing to be done by those who wish to achieve true metaphysical understanding is to take up a position outside time, we say deliberately in "non-time," if such an expression does not seem too peculiar and unusual. This knowledge of the intemporal can, moreover, be achieved in some real measure, if incompletely, before having fully attained this "primordial state" which we are considering.

It might be asked perhaps: Why this appellation of "primordial state"? It is because all traditions, including that of the West (for the Bible says nothing different) are in agreement in teaching that this state was originally normal for humanity, whereas the present state is merely the result of a fall, the effect of a progressive materialization which has occurred in the course of the ages, and throughout the duration of a particular cycle. We do not believe in "evolution" in the sense that the moderns give the word. The so-called scientific hypotheses just mentioned in no way correspond to reality. It is not possible here to make more than bare allusion to the theory of cosmic cycles, which is particularly expounded in the Hindu doctrines; this would be going beyond our subject, for cosmology is not metaphysics even though the two things are closely related. It is no more than an application of metaphysics to the physical order, while the true natural laws are only the consequences, in a relative and contingent domain, of universal and necessary principles.

To revert to metaphysical realization: Its second phase corresponds to supra-individual but still conditioned states, though their conditions are quite different from those of the human state. Here, the world of man, previously mentioned, is completely and definitely exceeded. It must also be said that that which is exceeded is the world of forms in its widest meaning, comprising all possible individual states, for form is the common denominator of all these states; it is that which determines individuality as such. The being, which can no longer be called human, has henceforth left the "flow of forms," to use a Far-Eastern expression. There are, moreover, further distinctions to be made, for this phase can be subdivided. In reality it includes several stages, from the achievement of states which though informal still appertain to manifested existence, up to that degree of universality which is pure being.

Nevertheless, however exalted these states may be when compared with the human state, however remote they are from it, they are still only relative, and that is just as true of the highest of them, which corresponds to the principle of all manifestation. Their possession is only a transitory result, which should not be confused with the final goal of metaphysical realization; this end remains outside being and by comparison with it everything else is only a preparatory step. The highest objective is the absolutely unconditioned state, free from all limitation; for this reason it is completely inexpressible, and all that one can say of it must be conveyed in negative terms by divestment of the limits which determine and define all existence in its relativity. The attainment of this state is what the Hindu doctrine calls "Deliverance" when considered in connection with the Supreme Principle.

In this unconditioned state all other states of being find their place, but they are transformed and released from the special conditions which determined them as particular states. What remains is that which has a positive reality, since herein it is that all things have their own principle; the "delivered" being is truly in possession of the fullness of its own potentialities. The only things which have disappeared are the limiting conditions, which are negative, since they represent no more than a "privation" in the Aristotelian sense. Also, far from being a kind of annihilation, as some Westerners believe, this final state is, on the contrary, absolute plenitude, the supreme reality in the face of which all else remains illusion.

Let us add once more that every result, even partial, obtained by the being in the course of metaphysical realization are truly its own. This result constitutes a permanent acquisition for the being, of which nothing can deprive it; the work accomplished in this way, even if interrupted before it is completed, is achieved once and for all since it is beyond time. This is true even of merely theoretical knowledge, for all knowledge carries its benefit in itself, contrary to action, which is only a momentary modification of a being and is always separated from its various effects. These effects belong to the same domain and order of existence as that which has produced them. Action cannot have the effect of liberating from action, and its consequences cannot reach beyond the limits of individuality considered in its fullest possible extension. Action, whatever it may be, is not opposed to, and cannot banish, ignorance which is the root of all limitation; only knowledge can dispel ignorance as the light of the sun disperses darkness, and it is thus that the "Self," the immutable and eternal principle of all manifest and unmanifest states, appears in its supreme reality.

After this brief and very imperfect outline, which can only give the merest idea of metaphysical realization, it is absolutely essential to stress one point in order to avoid grave errors of interpretation; it is that all with which we are here concerned has no connection whatever with phenomena of any sort, however extraordinary. All phenomena are of the physical order; metaphysics is beyond the phenomenal, even if we use the word in its widest sense. It follows from this, amongst other inferences, that the states to which we are referring are in no way "psychological"; this must be specifically stated since strange confusions sometimes arise in this connection. By definition psychology can only be concerned with human states, and further, what it stands for today is only a very limited part of the potentialities of the individual, who includes far more than specialists in this science are able to imagine. The human individual is, at one and the same time, much more and much less than is ordinarily supposed in the West; he is greater by reason of his possibilities of indefinite extension beyond the corporeal modality, in short, of all that refers to what we have been studying; but he is also much less since, far from constituting a complete and sufficient being in himself, he is only an exterior manifestation, a fleeting appearance clothing the true being, which in no way affects the essence of the latter in its immutability.

It is necessary to insist on this point that the metaphysical domain lies entirely outside the phenomenal world, for the moderns hardly ever know or investigate anything other than phenomena; it is with these that they are almost exclusively concerned, as is demonstrated by the attention they have given to the experimental sciences. Their metaphysical ineptitude arises from the same tendency. Undoubtedly some phenomena may occur during the work for metaphysical realization, but in a quite accidental manner. They can also have unfortunate consequences, as things of this nature are only an obstacle for those who are tempted to attach importance to them. Those who are halted or turned aside by phenomena, and above all those who indulge in search for extraordinary "powers," have very little chance of pressing on to a realization beyond the point already arrived at before this deviation occurred.

This observation leads naturally to the rectification of some erroneous interpretations on the subject of the term "yoga." Has it not been claimed that what the Hindus mean by this word is the development of certain powers latent in the human being? What we are about to say will suffice to show that such a definition should be rejected. In reality the word "yoga" is the same as that which we have translated as literally as possible by the word "union" and which, correctly defined, thus means the supreme goal of metaphysical realization; the "yogi," in the strictest sense of the term, is solely the man who attains this end. However, it is true that in a wider sense the same terms, in some cases, may be applied to stages preparatory to "union" or even to simple preliminary means, as well as to the being who has reached states corresponding to those stages which these means are employed in order to attain. But how can it be supposed that a word primarily meaning "union" applies correctly and originally to breathing exercises or other things of that sort? These and other exercises, usually based on what we might call the science of rhythm, admittedly figure amongst the most usual means for the promoting of realization; but one must not mistake for the end that which amounts to no more than contingent and accidental aids, nor must one confuse the original meaning of a word with a secondary acceptation which is more or less distorted.

Referring to the original "yoga," and while declaring that it has always meant essentially the same thing, one must not forget to put a question of which we have as yet made no mention. What is the origin of these traditional metaphysical doctrines from which we have borrowed all our fundamental ideas? The answer is very simple, although it risks raising objections from those who would look at everything from an historical viewpoint: It is that there is no origin; by which we mean no human origin subjected to determination in time. In other words, the origin of tradition, if indeed the word origin has any applicability in such a case, is "non-human," as is metaphysics itself. Doctrines of this order have not appeared at any particular moment in the history of humanity; the allusion we have made to the "primordial state," and also what we have said of the intemporal nature of all that is metaphysical, enables one to grasp this point without too much difficulty, on condition that it be admitted, contrary to certain prejudices, that there are some things to which the historical point of view is not applicable. Metaphysical truth is eternal; even so, there have always existed beings who could truly and completely know. All that changes is only exterior forms and contingent means; and the change has nothing to do with what people today call "evolution," It is only a simple adaptation of such and such particular circumstances to special conditions of some given race or epoch. From this results the multiplicity of forms; but the basis of the doctrine is no more modified and affected than the essential unity and identity of the being is altered by the multiplicity of its states of manifestation.

Metaphysical knowledge, as well as the realization that will turn it into all that it truly ought to be, is thus possible everywhere and always, at least in principle and when regarded in a quasi-absolute sense; but in fact and in a relative sense, can it be said that this is equally possible in any sphere and without making the least allowance for contingencies? On this score we shall be much less positive, at least as far as realization is concerned; which is explained by the fact that in its beginning such a realization must take its support from the realm of contingencies. Conditions in the modern West are particularly unfavorable, so much so that such a work is almost impossible and can even be dangerous in the absence of any help from the environment and in conditions which can only impede or destroy the efforts of one who undertakes such a task. On the other hand, those civilizations which we call traditional are organized in such a way that one can find effectual aid, though this is not absolutely necessary, any more than anything else of an external kind; nevertheless without such help it is difficult to obtain effective results. Here is something which exceeds the strength of an isolated human individual, even if that individual possesses the requisite qualifications in other respects; also we do not want to encourage anyone, in present conditions, to embark thoughtlessly upon such an enterprise, and this brings us to our conclusion.

For us, the outstanding difference between the East and West (which means in this case the modern West), the only difference which is really essential (for all others are derivative), is on the one side the preservation of tradition with all that this implies, and on the other side the forgetting and loss of this same tradition; on one side the maintaining of metaphysical knowledge, on the other complete ignorance of all connected with this realm. Between civilizations which open to their elite the possibilities of which we have caught a glimpse and offer the most appropriate means for their effective realization (thus allowing of their full realization by some at least)—between those traditional civilizations and a civilization which has developed along purely material lines, what common measure can be found? And how, without being blinded by I know not what prejudices, dare one claim that material superiority compensates for intellectual inferiority? When we say intellectual, we mean by that the true intellectuality, that which is restricted by neither limitations of the human nor the natural order and which makes pure metaphysical knowledge possible in its absolute transcendence. It seems to me that only a moment's reflection on these questions leaves no doubt or hesitation as to the answer that should be given.

The material prosperity of the West is incontrovertible; nobody denies it, but it is hardly a cause for envy. Indeed one can go further; sooner or later this excessive material development threatens to destroy the West if it does not recover itself in time, and if it does not consider seriously a "return to the source," using an expression which is employed in certain Islamic esoteric schools. Today one hears from many quarters of the "defense of the West," but unfortunately it does not seem to be understood that it is against itself that the West needs to be defended, and that it is its own present tendencies which are the chief and most formidable of all the dangers which really threaten it. It would be as well to meditate deeply on this; one cannot urge this too strongly on all who are still capable of reflection. So it is with this that I will end my account; I have done my best to make it, if not fully comprehensible, at least suggestive of that Oriental intellectuality which no longer has any equivalent in the West. This has been a sketch, even if imperfect, of the true metaphysics, of that knowledge, which, according to the sacred works of India, is alone completely true, absolute, infinite, and supreme.

THE *VEDANTA* AND WESTERN TRADITION*

Ananda Coomaraswamy

> These are really the thoughts of all men in all ages and lands,
> they are not original with me.
> *Walt Whitman*

I

There have been teachers such as Orpheus, Hermes, Buddha, Lao-tzu, and Christ, the historicity of whose human existence is doubtful, and to whom there may be accorded the higher dignity of a mythical reality. Shankara, like Plotinus, Augustine, or Eckhart, was certainly a man among men, though we know comparatively little about his life. He was of south Indian Brahman birth, flourished in the first half of the ninth century A.D., and founded a monastic order which still survives. He became a *samnyasin*, or "truly poor man," at the age of eight, as the disciple of a certain Govinda and of Govinda's own teacher Gaudapada, the author of a treatise on the Upanisads in which their essential doctrine of the non-duality of the divine Being was set forth. Shankara journeyed to Benares and wrote the famous commentary on the *Brahma Sutra* there in his twelfth year; the commentaries on the Upanisads and *Bhagavad Gita* were written later. Most of the great sage's life was spent wandering about India, teaching and taking part in controversies. He is understood to have died between the ages of thirty and forty. Such wanderings and disputations as his have always been characteristically Indian institutions; in his days, as now, Sanskrit was the lingua franca of learned men, just as for centuries Latin was the lingua franca of Western countries, and free public debate was so generally recognized that halls erected for the accommodation of peripatetic teachers and disputants were at almost every court.

The traditional metaphysics with which the name of Shankara is connected is known either as the *Vedanta*, a term which occurs in

* Editor's Note: A Talk given for the Radcliffe College chapter of the Phi Beta Kappa Society, first published in *The American Scholar*, 8, 1939, and reprinted in *Coomaraswamy: Selected Papers, Vol. 2. Metaphysics*, ed. Roger Lipsey.

the Upanisads and means the "Vedas' ends," both as "latter part" and as "ultimate significance"; or as *Atmavidya*, the doctrine of the knowledge of the true "self" or "spiritual essence"; or as *Advaita*, "Non-duality," a term which, while it denies duality, makes no affirmations about the nature of unity and must not be taken to imply anything like our monisms or pantheisms. A gnosis (*jnana*) is taught in this metaphysics.

Shankara was not in any sense the founder, discoverer, or promulgator of a new religion or philosophy; his great work as an expositor consisted in a demonstration of the unity and consistency of Vedic doctrine and in an explanation of its apparent contradictions by a correlation of different formulations with the points of view implied in them. In particular, and exactly as in European Scholasticism, he distinguished between the two complementary approaches to God, which are those of the affirmative and negative theology. In the way of affirmation, or relative knowledge, qualities are predicated in the Supreme Identity by way of excellence, while in the way of negation all qualities are abstracted. The famous "No, no" of the Upanisads, which forms the basis of Shankara's method, as it did of the Buddha's, depends upon a recognition of the truth—expressed by Dante among many others—that there are things which are beyond the reach of discursive thought and which cannot be understood except by denying things of them.

Shankara's style is one of great originality and power as well as subtlety. I shall cite from his commentary on the *Bhagavad Gita* a passage that has the further advantage of introducing us at once to the central problem of the *Vedanta*—that of the discrimination of what is really, and not merely according to our way of thinking, "myself." "How is it," Shankara says, "that there are professors who like ordinary men maintain that 'I am so-and-so' and 'This is mine'? Listen: it is because their so-called learning consists in thinking of the body as their 'self.'" In the Commentary on the *Brahma Sutra* he enunciates in only four Sanskrit words what has remained in Indian metaphysics from first to last the consistent doctrine of the immanent Spirit within you as the only knower, agent, and transmigrant.

The metaphysical literature underlying Shankara's expositions consists essentially of the Four Vedas together with the Brahmanas and their Upanisads, all regarded as revealed, eternal, datable (as to their recension, in any case) before 500 B.C., together with the *Bhagavad Gita* and *Brahma Sutra* (datable before the beginning of the Christian era). Of these books, the Vedas are liturgical, the Brahmanas are explanatory of the ritual, and the Upanisads are devoted to the Brahma-doctrine or *Theologia Mystia*, which is taken for granted in the liturgy and ritual. The *Brahma Sutra* is a greatly condensed compendium of Upanisad doctrine, and the *Bhagavad Gita* is an exposition adapted to the understanding of those whose primary business has to do with the active rather than the contemplative life.

For many reasons, which I shall try to explain, it will be far more difficult to expound the *Vedanta* than it would be to expound the personal views of a modern "thinker," or even such a thinker as Plato or Aristotle. Neither the modern English vernacular nor modern philosophical or psychological jargon provides us with an adequate vocabulary, nor does modern education provide us with the ideological background which would be essential for easy communication. I shall have to make use of purely symbolic, abstract, and technical language, as if I were speaking in terms of higher mathematics; you may recall that Emile Mâle speaks of Christian symbolism as a "calculus." There is this advantage: the matter to be communicated and the symbols to be employed are no more peculiarly Indian than peculiarly Greek or Islamic, Egyptian or Christian.

Metaphysics, in general, resorts to visual symbols (crosses and circles, for example) and above all to the symbolism of light and of the sun—that which, as Dante says, "no object of sense in the whole world is more worthy to be made a type of God." But I shall also have to use such technical terms as essence and substance, potentiality and act, spiration and despiration, exemplary likeness, aeviternity, form and accident. Metempsychosis must be distinguished from transmigration and both from "reincarnation." We shall have to distinguish soul from spirit. Before we can know when, if ever, it is proper to render a given Sanskrit word by our word "soul" (*anima, psyche*), we must have known in what manifold senses the word "soul" has been employed in the European tradition; what kind of souls can be "saved"; what kind of soul Christ requires us to "hate" if we would be his disciples; what kind of soul Eckhart refers to when he says that the soul must "put itself to death." We must know what Philo means by the "soul of the soul"; and we must ask how we can think of animals as "soulless," notwithstanding that the word "animal" means quite literally "ensouled." We must distinguish essence from existence. And I may have to coin such a word as "nowever" to express the full and original meanings of such words as "suddenly," "immediately," and "presently."

The sacred literature of India is available to most of us only in translations made by scholars trained in linguistics rather than in metaphysics; and it has been expounded and explained—or as I should rather say, explained away—mainly by scholars provided with the assumptions of the naturalist and anthropologist, scholars whose intellectual capacities have been so much inhibited by their own powers of observation that they can no longer distinguish the reality from the appearance, the Supernal Sun of metaphysics from the physical sun of their own experience. Apart from these, Indian literature has either been studied and explained by Christian propagandists whose main concern has been to demonstrate the falsity and absurdity of the doctrines involved, or by theosophists by whom the doctrines have been caricatured with the best intentions and perhaps even worse results.

The educated man of today is, moreover, completely out of touch with those European modes of thought and those intellectual aspects of the Christian doctrine which are nearest those of the Vedic traditions. A knowledge of modern Christianity will be of little use because the fundamental sentimentality of our times has diminished what was once an intellectual doctrine to a mere morality that can hardly be distinguished from a pragmatic humanism. A European can hardly be said to be adequately prepared for the study of the *Vedanta* unless he has acquired some knowledge and understanding of at least Plato, Philo, Hermes, Plotinus, the Gospels (especially John), Dionysius, and finally Eckhart who, with the possible exception of Dante, can be regarded from an Indian point of view as the greatest of all Europeans.

The *Vedanta* is not a "philosophy" in the current sense of the word, but only as the word is used in the phrase *Philosophia Perennis*, and only if we have in mind the Hermetic "philosophy" or that "Wisdom" by whom Boethius was consoled. Modern philosophies are closed systems, employing the method of dialectics, and taking for granted that opposites are mutually exclusive. In modern philosophy things are either so or not so; in eternal philosophy this depends upon our point of view. Metaphysics is not a system, but a consistent doctrine; it is not merely concerned with conditioned and quantitative experience, but with universal possibility. It therefore considers possibilities that may be neither possibilities of manifestation nor in any sense formal, as well as ensembles of possibility that can be realized in a given world. The ultimate reality of metaphysics is a Supreme Identity in which the opposition of all contraries, even of being and not-being, is resolved;

its "worlds" and "gods" are levels of reference and symbolic entities which are neither places nor individuals but states of being realizable within you.

Philosophers have personal theories about the nature of the world; our "philosophical discipline" is primarily a study of the history of these opinions and of their historical connections. We encourage the budding philosopher to have opinions of his own on the chance that they may represent an improvement on previous theories. We do not envisage, as does the *Philosophia Perennis*, the possibility of knowing the Truth once and for all; still less do we set before us as our goal to become this truth.

The metaphysical "philosophy" is called "perennial" because of its eternity, universality, and immutability; it is Augustine's "Wisdom uncreate, the same now as it ever was and ever will be"; the religion which, as he also says, only came to be called "Christianity" after the coming of Christ. What was revealed in the beginning contains implicitly the whole truth; and so long as the tradition is transmitted without deviation, so long, in other words, as the chain of teachers and disciples remains unbroken, neither inconsistency nor error is possible. On the other hand, an understanding of the doctrine must be perpetually renewed; it is not a matter of words. That the doctrine has no history by no means excludes the possibility, or even the necessity, for a perpetual explicitation of its formulae, an adaptation of the rites originally practiced, and an application of its principles to the arts and sciences. The more humanity declines from its first self-sufficiency, the more the necessity for such an application arises. Of these explicitations and adaptations a history is possible. Thus a distinction is drawn between what was "heard" at the outset and what has been "remembered."

A deviation or heresy is only possible when the essential teaching has been in some respect misunderstood or perverted. To say, for example, that "I am a pantheist" is merely to confess that "I am not a metaphysician," just as to say that "two and two make five" would be to confess "I am not a mathematician." Within the tradition itself there cannot be any contradictory or mutually exclusive theories or dogmas. For example, what are called the "six systems of Indian philosophy" (a phrase in which only the words "six" and "Indian" are justified) are not mutually contradictory and exclusive theories. The so-called "systems" are no more or less orthodox than mathematics, chemistry, and botany which, though separate disciplines more or less scientific amongst themselves, are not anything but branches of one "science." India, indeed, makes use of the term "branches" to denote what the Indologist misunderstands to be "sects." It is precisely because there are no "sects" within the fold of Brahmanical orthodoxy that an intolerance in the European sense has been virtually unknown in Indian history—and for the same reason, it is just as easy for me to think in terms of the Hermetic philosophy as in terms of *Vedanta*. There must be "branches" because nothing can be known except in the mode of the knower; however strongly we may realize that all roads lead to one Sun, it is equally evident that each man must choose that road which starts from the point at which he finds himself at the moment of setting out. For the same reasons, Hinduism has never been a missionary faith. It may be true that the metaphysical tradition has been better and more fully preserved in India than in Europe. If so, it only means that the Christian can learn from the *Vedanta* how to understand his own "way" better.

The philosopher expects to prove his points. For the metaphysician it suffices to show that a supposedly false doctrine involves a contradiction of first principles. For example, a philosopher who argues for an immortality of the soul endeavors to discover proofs of the survival of personality; for the metaphysician it suffices to remember that "the first beginning must be the same as the last end"—from which it follows that a soul, understood to have been created in time, cannot but end in time. The metaphysician can no more be convinced by any so-called "proof of the survival of personality" than a physicist could be convinced of the possibility of a perpetual motion machine by any so-called proof. Furthermore, metaphysics deals for the most part with matters which cannot be publicly proved, but can only be demonstrated, i.e., made intelligible by analogy, and which even when verified in personal experience can only be stated in terms of symbol and myth. At the same time, faith is made relatively easy by the infallible logic of the texts themselves—which is their beauty and their attractive power. Let us remember the Christian definition of faith: "assent to a credible proposition." One must believe in order to understand, and understand in order to believe. These are not successive, however, but simultaneous acts of the mind. In other words, there can be no knowledge of anything to which the will refuses its consent, or love of anything that has not been known.

Metaphysics differs still further from philosophy in having a purely practical purpose. It is no more a pursuit of truth for truth's sake than are the related arts a pursuit of art for art's sake, or related conduct the pursuit of morality for the sake of morality. There is indeed a quest, but the seeker already knows, so far as this can be stated in words, what it is that he is in search of; the quest is achieved only when he himself has become the object of his search. Neither verbal knowledge nor a merely formal assent nor impeccable conduct is of any more than indispensable dispositive value—means to an end.

Taken in their materiality, as "literature," the texts and symbols are inevitably misunderstood by those who are not themselves in quest. Without exception, the metaphysical terms and symbols are the technical terms of the chase. They are never literary ornaments, and as Malinowski has so well said in another connection, "Technical language, in matters of practical pursuit, acquires its meaning only through personal participation in this type of pursuit." That is why, the Indian feels, the Vedantic texts have been only verbally and grammatically and never really understood by European scholars, whose methods of study are avowedly objective and noncommittal. The *Vedanta* can be known only to the extent that it has been lived. The Indian, therefore, cannot trust a teacher whose doctrine is not directly reflected in his very being. Here is something very far removed from the modern European concept of scholarship.

We must add, for the sake of those who entertain romantic notions of the "mysterious East," that the *Vedanta* has nothing to do with magic or with the exercise of occult powers. It is true that the efficacy of magical procedure and the actuality of occult powers are taken for granted in India. But the magic is regarded as an applied science of the basest kind; and while occult powers, such as that of operation "at a distance," are incidentally acquired in the course of contemplative practice, the use of them—unless under the most exceptional circumstances—is regarded as a dangerous deviation from the path.

Nor is the *Vedanta* a kind of psychology or Yoga a sort of therapeutics except quite accidentally. Physical and moral health are prerequisites to spiritual progress. A psychological analysis is employed only to break down our fond belief in the unity and immateriality of the "soul," and with a view to a better distinguishing of the spirit from what is not the spirit but only a temporary psycho-physical manifestation of one of the most limited of its modalities. Whoever, like Jung, insists upon translating the essentials of Indian or Chinese metaphysics into a psychology is merely distorting the meaning of the texts. Modern psychology has, from an Indian point of view, about the same values that attach to spiritualism and magic and other "superstitions." Finally, I must point out that the metaphysics, the *Vedanta*, is not a form of mysticism, except in the sense that with Dionysius we can speak of a *Theologia Mystica*. What is ordinarily meant by "mysticism" involves a passive receptivity—"we must be able to let things happen in the psyche" is Jung's way of putting it (and in this statement he proclaims himself a "mystic"). But metaphysics repudiates the psyche altogether. The words of Christ, that "No man can be my disciple who hateth not his own soul," have been voiced again and again by every Indian guru; and so far from involving passivity, contemplative practice involves an activity that is commonly compared to the blazing of a fire at a temperature so high as to show neither flickering nor smoke. The pilgrim is called a "toiler," and the characteristic refrain of the pilgrim song is "keep on going, keep on going." The "Way" of the Vedantist is above all an activity.

II

The *Vedanta* takes for granted an omniscience independent of any source of knowledge external to itself, and a beatitude independent of any external source of pleasure. In saying "That art thou," the *Vedanta* affirms that man is possessed of, and is himself, "that one thing which when it is known, all things are known" and "for the sake of which alone all things are dear." It affirms that man is unaware of this hidden treasure within himself because he has inherited an ignorance that inheres in the very nature of the psycho-physical vehicle which he mistakenly identifies with himself. The purpose of all teaching is to dissipate this ignorance; when the darkness has been pierced nothing remains but the Gnosis of the Light. The technique of education is, therefore, always formally destructive and iconoclastic; it is not the conveyance of information but the education of a latent knowledge.

The "great dictum" of the Upanisads is, "That art thou." "That" is here, of course, *Atman* or Spirit, *Sanctus Spiritus*, Greek *pneuma*, Arabic *ruh*, Hebrew *ruah*, Egyptian *Amon*, Chinese *ch'i*; *Atman* is spiritual essence, impartite, whether transcendent or immanent; and however many and various the directions to which it may extend or from which it may withdraw, it is unmoved mover in both intransitive and transitive senses. It lends itself to all modalities of being but never itself becomes anyone or anything. That than which all else is a vexation—That art thou. "That," in other words, is the *Brahman*, or God in the general sense of Logos or Being, considered as the universal source of all Being—expanding, manifesting, and productive, font of all things, all of which are "in" him as the finite in the infinite, though not a "part" of him, since the infinite has no parts.

For the most part, I shall use the word *Atman* hereafter. While this *Atman*, as that which blows and enlightens, is primarily "Spirit," because it is this divine Eros that is the quickening essence in all things and thus their real being, the word *Atman* is also used reflexively to mean "self"—either "oneself" in whatever sense, however gross, the notion may be entertained, or with reference to the spiritual self or person (which is the only knowing subject and essence of all things, and must be distinguished from the affected and contingent "I" that is a compound of the body and of all that we mean by "soul" when we speak of a "psychology"). Two very different "selves" are thus involved, and it has been the custom of translators, accordingly, to render *Atman* as "self," printed either with a small or with a capital s according to the context. The same distinction is drawn, for example, by St. Bernard between what is my "property" (*proprium*) and what is my very being (*esse*). An alternative Indian formulation distinguishes the "knower of the field"—viz. the Spirit as the only knowing subject in all things and the same in all—from the "field," or body-and-soul as defined above (taken together with the pastures of the senses and embracing therefore all things that can be considered objectively). The *Atman* or *Brahman* itself cannot be thus considered: "How couldst thou know the knower of knowing?"—or in other words, how can the first cause of all things be one of them?

The *Atman* is impartite, but it is apparently divided and identified into variety by the differing forms of its vehicles, mouse or man, just as space within a jar is apparently signate and distinguishable from space without it. In this sense it can be said that "he is one as he is in himself but many as he is in his children," and that "participating himself, he fills these worlds." But this is only in the sense that light fills space while it remains itself without discontinuity; the distinction of things from one another thus depending not on differences in the light but on differences in reflecting power. When the jar is shattered, when the vessel of life is unmade, we realize that what was apparently delimited had no boundaries and that "life" was a meaning not to be confused with "living." To say that the *Atman* is thus at once participated and impartible, "undivided amongst divided things," without local position and at the same time everywhere, is another way of stating what we are more familiar with as the doctrine of Total Presence.

At the same time, every one of these apparent definitions of the Spirit represents the actuality in time of one of its indefinitely numerous possibilities of formal manifestation. The existence of the apparition begins at birth and ends at death; it can never be repeated. Nothing of Shankara survives but a bequest. Therefore though we can speak of him as still a living power in the world, the man has become a memory. On the other hand, for the gnostic Spirit, the Knower of the field, the Knower of all births, there can never at any time cease to be an immediate knowledge of each and every one of its modalities, a knowledge without before or after (relative to the appearance or disappearance of Shankara from the field of our experience). It follows that where knowledge and being, nature and essence are one and the same, Shankara's being has no beginning and can never cease. In other words, there is a sense in which we can properly speak of "my spirit" and "my person" as well as of "the Spirit" and "the Person," notwithstanding that Spirit and Person are a perfectly simple substance without composition. I shall return to the meaning of "immortality" later, but for the present I want to use what has just been said to explain what was meant by a nonsectarian distinction of points of view. For, whereas the Western student of "philosophy" thinks of *Samkhya* and *Vedanta* as two incompatible "systems," because the former is concerned with the liberation of a plurality of Persons and the latter with the liberty of an inconnumerable Person, no such antinomy is apparent to the Hindu. This can be explained by pointing out that in the Christian texts, "Ye are all one in Christ Jesus" and "Whoever is joined unto the Lord is one spirit," the plurals "ye" and "whoever" represent the *Samkhya* and the singular "one" the *Vedanta* point of view.

The validity of our consciousness of being, apart from any question of being So-and-so by name or by registrable characters, is accordingly taken for granted. This must not be confused with the argument, "Cogito ergo sum." That "I" feel or "I" think is no proof that "I" am; for we can say with the Vedantist and Buddhist that this is merely a conceit, that "feelings are felt" and "thoughts are thought," and that all this is a part of the "field" of which the spirit is the surveyor, just as we look at a picture which is in one sense a part of us though we are not in any sense a part of it. The question is posed accordingly: "Who art thou?" "What is that self to which we should resort?" We recognize that "self" can have more than one meaning when we speak of an "internal conflict"; when we say that "the spirit is willing but the flesh is weak"; or when we say, with the *Bhagavad Gita*, that "the Spirit is at war with whatever is not the Spirit."

Am "I" the spirit or the flesh? (We must always remember that in metaphysics the "flesh" includes all the aesthetic and recognitive faculties of the "soul.") We may be asked to consider our reflection in a mirror, and may understand that there we see "ourself"; if we are somewhat less naive, we may be asked to consider the image of the psyche as reflected in the mirror of the mind and may understand that this is what "I" am; or if still better advised, we may come to understand that we are none of these things—that they exist because we are, rather than that we exist inasmuch as they are. The *Vedanta* affirms that "I" in my essence am as little, or only as much, affected by all these things as an author-playwright is affected by the sight of what is suffered or enjoyed by those who move on the stage—the stage, in this case, of "life" (in other words, the "field" or "pasture" as distinguished from its aquiline surveyor, the Universal Man). The whole problem of man's last end, liberation, beatitude, or deification is accordingly one of finding "oneself" no longer in "this man" but in the Universal Man, the *forma humanitatis*, who is independent of all orders of time and has neither beginning nor end.

Conceive that the "field" is the round or circus of the world, that the throne of the Spectator, the Universal Man, is central and elevated, and that his aquiline glance at all times embraces the whole of the field (equally before and after the enactment of any particular event) in such a manner that from his point of view all events are always going on. We are to transfer our consciousness of being, from our position in the field where the games are going on, to the pavilion in which the Spectator, on whom the whole performance depends, is seated at ease.

Conceive that the right lines of vision by which the Spectator is linked to each separated performer, and along which each performer might look upward (inward) to the Spectator if only his powers of vision sufficed, are lines of force, or the strings by which the puppet-master moves the puppets for himself (who is the whole audience). Each of the performing puppets is convinced of its own independent existence and of itself as one amongst others, which it sees in its own immediate environment and which it distinguishes by name, appearance, and behavior. The Spectator does not, and cannot, see the performers as they see themselves, imperfectly, but he knows the being of each one of them as it really is—that is to say, not merely as effective in a given local position, but simultaneously at every point along the line of visual force by which the puppet is connected with himself, and primarily at that point at which all lines converge and where the being of all things coincides with being in itself. There the being of the puppet subsists as an eternal reason in the eternal intellect—otherwise called the Supernal Sun, the Light of lights, Spirit and Truth.

Suppose now that the Spectator goes to sleep: when he closes his eyes the universe disappears, to reappear only when he opens them again. The opening of eyes ("Let there be light") is called in religion the act of creation, but in metaphysics it is called manifestation, utterance, or spiration (to shine, to utter, and to blow being one and the same thing *in divinis*); the closing of eyes is called in religion the "end of the world," but in metaphysics it is called concealment, silence, or despiration. For us, then, there is an alternation or evolution and involution. But for the central Spectator there is no succession of events. He is always awake and always asleep; unlike the sailor who sometimes sits and thinks and sometimes does not think, our Spectator sits and thinks, and does not think, nowever.

A picture has been drawn of the cosmos and its overseeing "Eye." I have only omitted to say that the field is divided by concentric fences which may conveniently, although not necessarily, be thought of as twenty-one in number. The Spectator is thus at the twenty-first remove from the outermost fence by which our present environment is defined. Each player's or groundling's performance is confined to the possibilities that are represented by the space between two fences. There he is born and there he dies. Let us consider this born being, So-and-so, as he is in himself and as he believes himself to be—"an animal, reasoning and mortal; that I know, and that I confess myself to be," as Boethius expresses it. So-and-so does not conceive that he can move to and fro in time as he will, but knows that he is getting older every day, whether he likes it or not. On the other hand, he does conceive that in some other respects he can do what he likes, so far as this is not prevented by his environment—for example, by a stone wall, or a policeman, or contemporary mores. He does not realize that this environment of which he is a part, and from which he cannot except himself, is a causally determined environment; that it does what it does because of what has been done. He does not realize that he is what he is and does what he does because others before him have been what they were and have done what they did, and all this without any conceivable beginning. He is quite literally a creature of circumstances, an automaton, whose behavior could have been foreseen and wholly explained by an adequate knowledge of past causes, now represented by the nature of things—his own nature included. This is the well-known doctrine of *karma*, a doctrine of inherent fatality, which is stated as follows by the *Bhagavad Gita*, XVIII.20, "Bound by the working (*karma*) of a nature that is born in thee and is thine own, even that which thou desirest not to do thou doest willy-nilly." So-and-so is nothing but one link in a causal chain of which we cannot imagine a beginning or an end. There is nothing here that the most pronounced determinist can disagree with. The metaphysician—who is not, like the determinist, a "nothing-morist" (*nastika*)—merely points out at this stage that only the working of life, the manner of its perpetuation, can thus be causally explained; that the existence of a chain of causes presumes the logically prior possibility of this existence—in other words, presumes a first cause which cannot be thought of as one amongst other mediate causes, whether in place or time.

To return to our automaton, let us consider what takes place at its death. The composite being is unmade into the cosmos; there is nothing whatever that can survive as a consciousness of being So-and-so. The elements of the psycho-physical entity are broken up and handed on to others as a bequest. This is, indeed, a process that has been going on throughout our So-and-so's life, and one that can be most clearly followed in propagation, repeatedly described in the Indian tradition as the "rebirth of the father in and as the son." So-and-so lives in his direct and indirect descendants. This is the so-called Indian doctrine of "reincarnation"; it is the same as the Greek doctrine of metasomatosis and metempsychosis; it is the Christian doctrine of our preexistence in Adam "according to bodily substance and seminal virtue"; and it is the modern doctrine of the "recurrence of ancestral characters." Only the fact of such a transmission of psycho-physical characters can make intelligible what is called in religion our inheritance of original sin, in metaphysics our inheritance of ignorance, and by the philosopher our congenital capacity for knowing in terms of subject and object. It is only when we are convinced that nothing happens by chance that the idea of a Providence becomes intelligible.

Need I say that this is not a doctrine of reincarnation? Need I say that no doctrine of reincarnation, according to which the very being and person of a man who has once lived on earth and is now deceased will be reborn of another terrestrial mother, has ever been taught in India, even in Buddhism—or for that matter in the Neoplatonic or any other orthodox tradition? As definitely in the Brahmanas as in the Old Testament, it is stated that those who have once departed from this world have departed forever, and are not to be seen again amongst the living. From the Indian as from the Platonic point of view, all change is a dying. We die and are reborn daily and hourly, and death "when the time comes" is only a special case. I do not say that a belief in reincarnation has never been entertained in India. I do say that such a belief can only have resulted from a popular misinterpretation of the symbolic language of the texts; that the belief of modern scholars and theosophists is the result of an equally naive and uninformed interpretation of texts. If you ask how such a mistake could have arisen I shall ask you to consider the following statements of Saints Augustine and Thomas Aquinas: that we were in Adam "according to bodily substance and seminal virtue"; "the human body preexisted in the previous works in their causal virtues"; "God does not govern the world directly, but also by means of mediate causes, and were this not so, the world would have been deprived of the perfection of causality"; "As a mother is pregnant with the unborn offspring, so the world itself is pregnant with the causes of unborn things"; "Fate lies in the created causes themselves." If these had been texts extracted from the Upanisads or Buddhism, would you not have seen in them not merely what is really there, the doctrine of *karma*, but also a doctrine of "reincarnation"?

By "reincarnation" we mean a rebirth here of the very being and person of the deceased. We affirm that this is an impossibility, for good and sufficient metaphysical reasons. The main consideration is this: that inasmuch as the cosmos embraces an indefinite range of possibilities, all of which must be realized in an equally indefinite duration, the present universe will have run its course when all its potentialities have been reduced to act—just as each human life has run its course when all its possibilities have been exhausted. The end of an aeviternity will have been reached without any room for any repetition of events or any recurrence of past conditions. Temporal succession implies a succession of different things. History repeats itself in types, but cannot repeat itself in any particular. We can speak of a "migration" of "genes" and call this a rebirth of types, but this reincarnation of So-and-so's character must be distinguished from the "transmigration" of So-and-so's veritable person.

Such are the life and death of the reasoning and mortal animal So-and-so. But when Boethius confesses that he is just this animal, Wisdom replies that this man, So-and-so, has forgotten who he is. It is at this point that we part company with the "nothing-morist," or "materialist" and "sentimentalist" (I bracket these two words because "matter" is what is "sensed"). Bear in mind the Christian definition of man as "body, soul, and spirit." The *Vedanta* asserts that the only veritable being of the man is spiritual, and that this being of his is not "in" So-and-so or in any "part" of him but is only reflected in him. It asserts, in other words, that this being is not in the plane of or in any way limited by So-and-so's field, but extends from this field to its center, regardless of the fences that it penetrates. What takes place at death, then, over and above the unmaking of So-and-so, is a withdrawal of the spirit from the phenomenal vehicle of which it had been the "life." We speak, accordingly, with strictest accuracy when we refer to death as a "giving up of the ghost" or say that So-and-so "expires." I need, I feel sure, remind you only in parenthesis that this "ghost" is not a spirit in the Spiritualist's sense, not a "surviving personality," but a purely intellectual principle such as ideas are made of; "ghost" is "spirit" in the sense that the Holy Ghost is *Sanctus Spiritus.* So then, at death, the dust returns to dust and the spirit to its source.

It follows that the death of So-and-so involves two possibilities, which are approximately those implied by the familiar expressions "saved" or "lost." Either So-and-so's consciousness of being has been self-centered and must perish with himself, or it has been centered in the spirit and departs with it. It is the spirit, as the Vedantic texts express it, that "remains over" when body and soul are unmade. We begin to see now what is meant by the great commandment, "Know thyself." Supposing that our consciousness of being has been centered in the spirit, we can say that the more completely we have already "become what we are," or "awakened," before the dissolution of the body, the nearer to the center of the field will be our next appearance or "rebirth." Our consciousness of being goes nowhere at death where it is not already.

Later on we shall consider the case of one whose consciousness of being has already awakened beyond the last of our twenty-one fences or levels of reference and for whom there remains only a twenty-second passage. For the present let us consider only the first step. If we have taken this step before we die—if we have been to some degree living "in the spirit" and not merely as reasoning animals—we shall, when the body and soul are unmade into the cosmos, have crossed over the first of the fences or circumferences that lie between ourselves and the central Spectator of all things, the Supernal Sun, Spirit and Truth. We shall have come into being in a new environment where, for example, there may still be a duration but not in our present sense a passage of time. We shall not have taken with us any of the psycho-physical apparatus in which a sensitive memory could inhere. Only the "intellectual virtues" survive. This is not the survival of a "personality" (that was a property bequeathed when we departed); it is the continued being of the very person of So-and-so, no longer encumbered by the grossest of So-and-so's former definitions. We shall have crossed over without interruption of consciousness of being.

In this way, by a succession of deaths and rebirths, all of the fences may be crossed. The pathway that we follow will be that of the spiritual ray or radius that links us with the central Sun. It is the only bridge that spans the river of life dividing the hither from the farther shore. The word "bridge" is used advisedly, for this is the "causeway sharper than a razor's edge," the Cinvat bridge of the Avesta, the "brig of dread," familiar to the folklorist, which none but a solar hero can pass; it is a far-flung bridge of light and consubstantial with its source. The Veda expresses it "Himself the Bridge"—a description corresponding to the Christian "I am the Way." You will have divined already that the passage of this bridge constitutes, by stages that are defined by its points of intersection with our twenty-one circumferences, what is properly called a transmigration or progressive regeneration. Every step of this way has been marked by a death to a former "self" and a consequent and immediate "rebirth" as "another man." I must interpolate here that this exposition has inevitably been oversimplified. Two directions of motion, one circumferential and determinate, the other centripetal and free, have been distinguished; but I have not made it clear that their resultant can be properly indicated only by a spiral.

But the time has come to break down the spatial and temporal materialism of our picture of the cosmos and of man's pilgrimage from its circumference to its center and heart. All of the states of being, all of the So-and-sos that we have thought of as coming into being on superimposed levels of reference, are within you, awaiting recognition: all of the deaths and rebirths involved are supernatural—that is, not "against Nature" but extrinsic to the particular possibilities of the given state of being from which the transmigration is thought of as taking place.

Nor is any time element involved. Rather, since temporal vicissitudes play no part in the life of the spirit, the journey can be made in part or in its entirety, whether before the event of natural death, at death, or thereafter. The Spectator's pavilion is the Kingdom of Heaven that is within you, viz. in the "heart" (in all Oriental and ancient traditions not only the seat of the will but of the pure intellect, the place where the marriage of Heaven and Earth is consummated); it is there only that the Spectator can himself be seen by the contemplative—whose glance is inverted, and who thus retraces the path of the Ray that links the eye without to the Eye within, the breath of life with the Gale of the Spirit.

We can now, perhaps, better understand all that is meant by the poignant words of the Vedic requiem, "The Sun receive thine eye, the Gale thy spirit" and can recognize their equivalent in "Into thy hands I commend my spirit," or in Eckhart's "Eye wherewith I see God, that is the same eye wherewith God sees in me; my eye and God's eye, that is one eye and one vision and one knowing and one love," or St. Paul's "shall be one spirit." The traditional texts are emphatic. We find, for example, in the Upanisads the statement that whoever worships, thinking of the deity as other than himself, is little better than an animal. This attitude is reflected in the proverbial saying, "To worship God you must have become God"—which is also the meaning of the words, to "worship in spirit and in truth." We are brought back to the great saying, "That art thou," and have now a better idea, though a far from perfect understanding (because the last step remains to be taken), of what "That" may be. We can now see how traditional doctrines (distinguishing the outer from the inner, the worldly from the other-worldly man, the automaton from the immortal spirit), while they admit and even insist upon the fact that So-and-so is nothing but a link in an endless causal chain, can nevertheless affirm that the chains can be broken and death defeated without respect to time: that this may happen, therefore, as well here and now as at the moment of departure or after death.

We have not even yet, however, reached what is from the point of view of metaphysics defined as man's last end. In speaking of an end of the road, we have so far thought only of a crossing of all the twenty-one barriers and of a final vision of the Supernal Sun, the Truth itself; of reaching the Spectator's very pavilion; of being in heaven face to face with the manifested Eye. This is, in fact, the conception of man's last end as envisaged by religion. It is an aeviternal beatitude reached at the "Top of the Tree," at the "Summit of contingent being"; it is a salvation from all the temporal vicissitudes of the field that has been left behind us. But it is a heaven in which each one of the saved is still one amongst others, and other than the Sun of Men and Light of lights himself (these are Vedic as well as Christian expressions); a heaven that, like the Greek Elysium, is apart from time but not without duration; a resting place but not a final home (as it was not our ultimate source, which was in the nonbeing of the Godhead). It remains for us to pass through the Sun and reach the Empyrean "home" of the Father. "No man cometh to the Father save *through* me." We have passed through the opened doorways of initiation and contemplation; we have moved, through a process of a progressive self-naughting, from the outermost to the innermost court of our being, and can see no way by which to continue—although we know that behind this image of the Truth, by which we have been enlightened, there is a somewhat that is not in any likeness, and although we know that behind this face of God that shines upon the world there is another and more awful side of him that is not man-regarding but altogether self-intent—an aspect that neither knows nor loves anything whatever external to itself. It is our own conception of Truth and Goodness that prevents our seeing Him who is neither good nor true in any sense of ours. The only way on lies directly *through* all that we had thought we had begun to understand: if we are to find our way in, the image of "ourselves" that we still entertain—in however exalted a manner—and that of the Truth and Goodness that we have "imagined" *per excellentiam*, must be shattered by one and the same blow. "It is more necessary that the soul lose God than that she lose creatures . . . the soul honors God most in being quit of God . . . it remains for her to be somewhat that he is not . . . to die to all the activity denoted by the divine nature if she is to enter the divine nature where God is altogether idle . . . she forfeits her very self, and going her own way, seeks God no more" (Eckhart). In other words, we must be one with the Spectator, both when his eyes are open and when they are shut. If we are not, what will become of us when he sleeps? All that we have learned through the affirmative theology must be complemented and fulfilled by an Unknowing, the *Docta Ignorantia* of Christian theologians, Eckhart's *Agnosia*. It is for this reason that such men as Shankara and Dionysius have so strongly insisted upon the *via remotionis*, and not because a positive concept of Truth or Goodness was any less dear to them than it could be to us. Shankara's personal practice, indeed, is said to have been devotional—even while he prayed for pardon because he had worshipped God by name, who has no name. For such as these there was literally nothing dear that they were not ready to leave.

Let us enunciate the Christian doctrine first in order the better to understand the Indian. The words of Christ are these: that "I am the door; by me if any man enter in, he shall be saved, and shall pass in and out." It is not enough to have reached the door; we must be admitted. But there is a price of admission. "He that would save his soul, let him lose it." Of man's two selves, the two *Atmans* of our Indian texts, the self that was known by name as So-and-so must have put itself to death if the other is to be freed of all encumbrances—is to be "free as the Godhead in its nonexistence."

In the Vedantic texts it is likewise the Sun of men and Light of lights that is called the doorway of the worlds and the keeper of the gate. Whoever has come thus far is put to the test. He is told in the first place that he may enter according to the balance of good or evil he may have done. If he understands he will answer, "Thou canst not ask me that; thou knowest that whatever 'I' may have done was not of 'my' doing, but of thine." This is the Truth; and it is beyond the power of the Guardian of the Gate, who is himself the Truth, to deny himself. Or he may be asked the question, "Who art thou?" If he answers by his own or by a family name he is literally dragged away by the factors of time; but if he answers, "I am the Light, thyself, and come to thee as such," the Keeper responds with the words of welcome, "Who thou art, that am I; and who I am, thou art; come in." It should be clear, indeed, that there can be no return to God of anyone who still is anyone, for as our texts express it, "He has not come from anywhere or become anyone."

In the same way, Eckhart, basing his words on the logos, "If any man hate not father and mother, . . . yea and his own soul also, he cannot be my disciple," says that "so long as thou knowest who thy father and thy mother have been in time, thou art not dead with the real death"; and in the same way, Rumi, Eckhart's peer in Islam, attributes to the Keeper of the Gate the words, "Whoever enters saying 'I am so and so,' I smite in the face." We cannot, in fact, offer any better definition of the Vedic scriptures than St. Paul's "The word of God is quick and powerful, and sharper than any two-edged sword, extending even unto the sundering of soul from spirit": "Quid est ergo, quod debet homo inquirere in hac vita? Hoc est ut sciat ipsum." "Si ignoras te, egredere!"

The last and most difficult problem arises when we ask: what is the state of the being that has thus been freed from itself and has returned to its source? It is more than obvious that a psychological explanation is out of the question. It is, in fact, just at this point that we can best confess with our texts, "He who is most sure that he understands, most assuredly misunderstands." What can be said of the *Brahman*—that "He is, by that alone can He be apprehended"—can as well be said of whoever has become the *Brahman*. It cannot be said *what* this is, because it is not any "what." A being who is "freed in this life" (Rumi's "dead man walking") is "in the world, but not of it."

We can, nevertheless, approach the problem through a consideration of the terms in which the Perfected are spoken of. They are called either Rays of the Sun, or Blasts of the Spirit, or Movers-at-Will. It is also said that they are fitted for embodiment in the manifested worlds: that is to say, fitted to participate in the life of the Spirit, whether it moves or remains at rest. It is a Spirit which bloweth as it will. All of these expressions correspond to Christ's "shall pass in and out, and shall find pasture." Or we can compare it with the pawn in a game of chess. When the pawn has crossed over from the hither to the farther side it is transformed. It becomes a minister and is called a mover-at-will, even in the vernacular. Dead to its former self, it is no longer confined to particular motions or positions, but can go in and out, at will, from the place where its transformation was effected. And this freedom to move at will is another aspect of the state of the Perfected, but a thing beyond the conception of those who are still mere pawns. It may be observed, too, that the erstwhile pawn, ever in danger of an inevitable death on its journey across the board, is at liberty after its transformation either to sacrifice itself or to escape from danger. In strictly Indian terms, its former motion was a crossing, its regenerate motion a descent.

The question of "annihilation," so solemnly discussed by Western scholars, does not arise. The word has no meaning in metaphysics, which knows only of the non-duality of permutation and sameness, multiplicity and unity. Whatever has been an eternal reason or idea or name of an individual manifestation can never cease to be such; the content of eternity cannot be changed. Therefore, as the *Bhagavad Gita* expresses it, "Never have I not been, and never hast thou not been."

The relation, in identity, of the "That" and the "thou" in the logos "That art thou" is stated in the *Vedanta* either by such designations as

"Ray of the Sun" (implying filiation), or in the formula *bhedabheda* (of which the literal meaning is "distinction without difference"). The relation is expressed by the simile of lovers, so closely embraced that there is no longer any consciousness of "a within or a without," and by the corresponding Vaishnava equation, "each is both." It can be seen also in Plato's conception of the unification of the inner and the outer man; in the Christian doctrine of membership in the mystical body of Christ; in St. Paul's "whoever is joined unto the Lord is one spirit"; and in Eckhart's admirable formula "fused but not confused."

I have endeavored to make it clear that Shankara's so-called "philosophy" is not an "enquiry" but an "explicitation"; that ultimate Truth is not, for the Vedantist, or for any traditionalist, a something that remains to be discovered but a something that remains to be understood by Everyman, who must do the work for himself. I have accordingly tried to explain just what it was that Shankara understood in such texts as *Atharva Veda* X.8.44: "Without any want, contemplative, immortal, self-originated, sufficed with a quintessence, lacking in naught whatever: he who knoweth that constant, ageless, and ever-youthful Spirit, knoweth indeed him-Self, and feareth not to die."

A WISH FOR HARMONY*

His Holiness the Dalai Lama

Spiritual brothers and sisters, it is a great joy and privilege for me to have the opportunity to participate in this dialogue and to open the John Main Seminar entitled "The Good Heart." I would like to express my deep appreciation to all those who have helped to organize this event.

I am grateful for the warm words of welcome from the Lady Mayor, and I am very encouraged by her reference to the harmony and understanding that exists among the various communities and religious traditions in this borough, which she described as multicultural, multiethnic, and multireligious. I would like to express my thanks for that.

I met the late Father John Main many years ago in Canada and was impressed to meet a person in the Christian tradition who emphasized meditation as a part of spiritual practice. Today, at the beginning of this Seminar, I think it is very important for us to remember him.

I am also happy to see so many familiar faces and to have the opportunity to meet new and old friends here.

Despite many material advances on our planet, humanity faces many, many problems, some of which are actually of our own creation. And to a large extent it is our mental attitude—our outlook on life and the world—that is the key factor for the future—the future of humanity, the future of the world, and the future of the environment. Many things depend on our mental attitude, both in the personal and public spheres. Whether we are happy in our individual or family life is, in a large part, up to us. Of course, material conditions are an important factor for happiness and a good life, but one's mental attitude is of equal or greater importance.

As we approach the twenty-first century, religious traditions are as relevant as ever. Yet, as in the past, conflicts and crises arise in the name of different religious traditions. This is very, very unfortunate. We must make every effort to overcome this situation. In my own experience, I

* Editor's Note: A Talk for the John Main Seminar, London, 1994.

have found that the most effective method to overcome these conflicts is close contact and an exchange among those of various beliefs, not only on an intellectual level, but in deeper spiritual experiences. This is a powerful method to develop mutual understanding and respect. Through this interchange, a strong foundation of genuine harmony can be established.

So I am always extremely happy to participate in religious dialogue. And I am particularly happy to spend these few days talking with you and practicing my broken English! When I spend a few weeks on retreat in Dharamsala, my residence in India, I find that my broken English becomes even poorer, so these days of exchange will give me a much-needed opportunity to practice.

Since it is my belief that harmony among different religious traditions is extremely important, extremely necessary, I would like to suggest a few ideas on ways it can be promoted. First, I suggest we encourage meetings among scholars from different religious backgrounds to discuss differences and similarities in their traditions, in order to promote empathy and to improve our knowledge about one another. Secondly, I suggest that we encourage meetings between people from different religious traditions who have had some deeper spiritual experiences. They need not be scholars, but instead genuine practitioners who come together and share insights as a result of religious practice. According to my own experience, this is a powerful and effective means of enlightening each other in a more profound and direct way.

Some of you may have already heard me mention that on a visit to the great monastery at Montserrat in Spain, I met a Benedictine monk there. He came especially to see me—and his English was much poorer than mine, so I felt more courage to speak to him. After lunch, we spent some time alone, face to face, and I was informed that this monk had spent a few years in the mountains just behind the monastery. I asked him what kind of contemplation he had practiced during those years of solitude. His answer was simple: "Love, love, love." How wonderful! I suppose that sometimes he also slept. But during all those years he meditated simply on love. And he was not meditating on just the word. When I looked into his eyes, I saw evidence of profound spirituality and love—as I had during my meetings with Thomas Merton.

These two encounters have helped me develop a genuine reverence for the Christian tradition and its capacity to create people of such goodness. I believe the purpose of all the major religious traditions is not to construct big temples on the outside, but to create temples of goodness and compassion *inside*, in our hearts. Every major religion has the potential to create this. The greater our awareness is regarding the value and effectiveness of other religious traditions, then the deeper will be our respect and reverence toward other religions. This is the proper way for us to promote genuine compassion and a spirit of harmony among the religions of the world.

In addition to encounters among scholars and experienced practitioners, it is also important, particularly in the eyes of the public, that leaders of the various religious traditions occasionally come together to meet and pray, as in the important meeting at Assisi in 1986. This is a third simple yet effective way to promote tolerance and understanding.

A fourth means of working toward harmony among the world's religions is for people of different religious traditions to go on pilgrimages together to visit one another's holy places. A few years ago, I started doing this practice myself in India. Since then, I have had the opportunity to travel as a pilgrim to Lourdes, the holy place in France, and to Jerusalem. In these places, I prayed with the followers of the various religions, sometimes in silent meditation. And in this prayer and meditation I felt a genuine spiritual experience. I hope this will set an example, serve as a sort of precedent, so that in the future it will be regarded as quite normal for people to join together in pilgrimages to holy sites and share the experience of their different religious backgrounds.

Finally, I would like to come back to the subject of meditation and to my Christian brothers and sisters who practice meditation in their daily lives. I believe this practice is extremely important. Traditionally in India, there is *samadhi* meditation, "stilling the mind," which is common to all the Indian religions, including Hinduism, Buddhism, and Jainism. And in many of these traditions, certain types of *vipasyana*, "analytical meditation," are common as well. We might ask why *samadhi*, "stilling the mind," is so important. Because *samadhi*, or focusing meditation, is the means to mobilize your mind, to channel your mental energy. *Samadhi* is considered to be an essential part of spiritual practice in *all* the major religious traditions of India because it provides the possibility to channel all one's mental energy and the ability to direct the mind to a particular object in a single-pointed way.

It is my belief that if prayer, meditation, and contemplation—which is more discursive and analytic—are combined in daily practice, the effect on the practitioner's mind and heart will be all the greater. One of the major aims and purposes of religious practice for the individual is an inner transformation from an undisciplined, untamed, unfocused state of mind toward one that is disciplined, tamed, and balanced. A person who has perfected the faculty of single-pointedness will definitely have a greater ability to attain this objective. When meditation becomes an important part of your spiritual life, you are able to bring about this inner transformation in a more effective way.

Once this transformation has been achieved, then in following your own spiritual tradition, you will discover that a kind of natural humility will arise in you, allowing you to communicate better with people from other religious traditions and cultural backgrounds. You are in a better position to appreciate the value and preciousness of other traditions because you have seen this value from within your own tradition. People often experience feelings of exclusivity in their religious beliefs—a feeling that one's own path is the only true path—which can create a sense of apprehension about connecting with others of different faiths. I believe the best way to counter that force is to experience the value of one's own path through a meditative life, which will enable one to see the value and preciousness of other traditions.

In order to develop a genuine spirit of harmony from a sound foundation of knowledge, I believe it is very important to know the fundamental differences between religious traditions. And it is possible to understand the fundamental differences, but at the same time recognize the value and potential of each religious tradition. In this way, a person may develop a balanced and harmonious perception. Some people believe that the most reasonable way to attain harmony and solve problems relating to religious intolerance is to establish one universal religion for everyone. However, I have always felt that we should have different religious traditions because human beings possess so many different mental dispositions: one religion simply cannot satisfy the needs of such a variety of people. If we try to unify the faiths of the world into one religion, we will also lose many of the qualities and richnesses of each particular tradition. Therefore, I feel it is better, in spite of the many quarrels in the name of religion, to maintain a variety of religious traditions. Unfortunately, while a diversity of religious traditions is more suited to serve the needs of the diverse mental dispositions among humanity, this diversity naturally possesses the potential for conflict and disagreement as well. Consequently, people of every religious tradition must make an extra effort to try to transcend intolerance and misunderstanding and seek harmony.

These are a few points that I thought would be useful at the beginning of the Seminar. Now I am looking forward to the challenge of exploring texts and ideas that are not familiar to me. You've given me a heavy responsibility, and I will try my best to fulfill your wishes. I really feel it a great honor and privilege to be asked to comment on selected passages of the Holy Scripture—a scripture I must admit I am not very familiar with. I must also admit that this is the first time I have tried to do such a thing. Whether it will be a success or failure, I don't know! But in any case, I will try my best. Now I'll chant a few verses of auspiciousness and then we will meditate.

[The modesty, like his smile, was genuine. When the audience laughed, the laughter seemed partly out of surprise at the lack of self-importance in the man and also a gesture of friendly encouragement. It was the beginning of a rapport that, in the next few days, would lead to a climax of shared feeling and thought in an atmosphere of respect and love.

The lights in the hall were turned out, and in the soft light coming only through the windows, the audience collected itself as His Holiness closed his eyes and intoned an ancient Tibetan prayer:]

Replete with excellence like a mountain of gold,
The triple worlds' saviors, freed from the three taints,
Are the buddhas, their eyes like lotuses in bloom;
They are the world's first auspicious blessing.

The teachings they imparted are sublime and steadfast,
Famed in the triple worlds, honored by gods and humans alike.
That holy teaching grants peace to all sentient beings;
This is the world's second auspicious blessing.

The sacred community, rich with learning, is honored
By humans, gods, and demi-gods.
That supreme community is modest, yet the site of glory;
This is the world's third auspicious blessing.

A Wish for Harmony

The Teacher has come into our world;
The teaching shines like the sun's rays;
The teaching masters, like siblings, are in concord;
Let there thus be auspicious blessings for the teachings
to remain for long.

Song: "All shall be well. All shall be well. And all manner of things shall be well."

ANTI-THEOLOGY AND THE RIDDLES OF ALCYONE*

Whitall Perry

Some readers of this journal may have come upon the writings of Alan Watts and wondered why he apparently aligned his outlook for a time with the work of Schuon, Guénon, Coomaraswamy—only to draw away again. The answer is simple: a speculative intelligence brought him hither, and a spiritual unintelligence removed him thither—thither being in modern parlance the "anti-guru" mode of intellection for which Krishnamurti can be considered a leading exponent. Watts, an Anglican-trained theologian who has dipped into Oriental metaphysics, sets forth the pattern of this transition in *Beyond Theology: The Art of Godmanship*,[1] a crazy pastiche of esoteric insights and false deductions, yet typically symptomatic of the ills to which so much of the pseudo-spiritual flesh of our times is heir.

He tells us he broke away from the *philosophia perennis* outlook because "there is not a scrap of evidence that the Christian hierarchy was ever aware of itself as one among several lines of transmission for a universal tradition," whereas "the so-called 'traditionalist school' . . . regards every orthodox spiritual tradition as a more-or-less deliberate adaptation of the *philosophia perennis* to the needs of different cultures." The truth is, exclusivity is not the prerogative of Christianity: there never has been a religion East or West that did not require what Watts calls "an all-or-nothing commitment," and certainly none of the above-named proponents of the perennial wisdom ever claimed otherwise. It is quite another matter that a few sages in all traditions have recognized the same transcendent unity underlying divergent forms—Sri Ramakrishna, for example, where he says that "It is one and the same Avatara that, having plunged into the ocean of life, rises up in one place and is known as Krishna, and diving down again rises in another place and is known as Christ," or Nicholas of Cusa (whom Watts would appropriate to his ends) when he says "Hence

* Editor's Note: Originally appeared in *Studies in Comparative Religion*, 6:3, 1972.

[1] Cleveland and New York: Meridian Books, The World Publishing Company, 1968.

there is a single religion and a single creed for all beings endowed with understanding, and this religion is presupposed behind all the diversity of rites."

The author of *Beyond Theology* assumes a stance which he begs the reader not to mistake for blasphemy, or even "the Devil himself," but to accept simply as the role of "Jester" at the Court of Heaven presiding as it were over a masque being played out between *Atman* and the human ego. Watts, however, is no Omar Khayyam: to qualify for the Fool at Court, one has both to know the palace rules and who holds command, whereas our Jester knows neither—a diplomatic gaffe compounded by his total cynicism as to the possibility of there being any Court or King at all. "Seriously, is it plausible to conceive our universe as something run on the lines of Egyptian, Persian, and Byzantine monarchies, with their thrones and judgments, their dungeons, torture chambers, and scaffolds? To say that the traditional Christian imagery of God as the heavenly King is to be understood as myth rather than fact . . . is only to say that the general climate of twentieth-century knowledge and thought has made it [the existence of such a being] thoroughly implausible and slightly comic. And so long as we are exhorted in church services to address ourselves (for example) 'with a pure heart and a humble voice unto the throne of the heavenly grace,' the very idea of God will be contaminated with this now ridiculous image. It is simply unimaginable that the universe of modern astronomy and physics, biology and chemistry, should be the creation of any such pompous potentate; our world is much too astonishing for any explanation of that kind to be meaningful. . . . To sophisticated theologians it may seem somewhat naive . . . to whip such a dead horse." Watts can think he has learned something from the Hindus about Immanence, but anything to do with Transcendence is beyond his grasp, being as he is in complete ignorance concerning metaphysical principles and by consequence the theory of emanations descending from the noumenal to the phenomenal world. For him the doctrine of the archetypes is a dead letter; yet it is this doctrine that enables Hermes, for example, to say that earthly kings "hold their sovereignty after His likeness," that is, "the supreme King of the universe."

God can as well lack majesty ("Highness") as a mountain can lack height.

As for the palace rules, the author of this manual on "Godmanship" could not care less, but the fact is that religion being by definition profoundly aristocratic, its language will necessarily be characterized by dignity and nobility. Watts is a skilful writer who knows perfectly well how to turn a phrase, and he has chosen to punctuate his points with consummate vulgarity. Indeed, the author leaves the reader with the impression that he has been traumatized by a frightful Anglican public-school syndrome. "Raised in this atmosphere, children never cease to feel that this is a world in which they do not really belong. Thus educated, men go through life on tiptoe, ever fearing to offend the mysterious Authority behind things, and the claim to be one Self with the eternal Ground of the world is felt to be the ultimate impertinence and effrontery. Christianity does not have to remain in this nursery and boarding school atmosphere. The ultimate identity of man with God is not identity with this Commander-in-Chief of the universe."

All this notwithstanding, Watts manifests a genuine appreciation of spiritual forms, such as the Latin Mass, Gregorian chant, the *Philokalia*, and "cathedrals, abbeys, priories, parish churches, and oratories in the enchanted stone of Romanesque (Norman) and Gothic masons." And no one could surpass his strictures on the Protestant establishment: "The insides of most Protestant churches resemble court-houses or town halls, and the focal point of their services is a serious exhortation from a man in a black gown. No golden lights, no bells, incense, and candles. No mystery upon an altar or behind an iconostasis. But people brought up in this atmosphere seem to love it. It feels warm and folksy, and leads, on the one hand, to hospitals, prison reform, and votes for all, and, on the other, to sheer genius for drabness, plain cooking ungraced with wine, and constipation of the bright emotions—all of which are considered virtues. If I try to set aside the innate prejudices which I feel against this religion, I begin to marvel at the depth of its commitment to earnestness and ugliness. For there is a point at which certain types of ugliness become fascinating, where one feels drawn to going over them again and again, much as the tongue keeps fondling a hole in a tooth. I begin to realize that those incredibly plain people, with their almost unique lack of color, may after all be one of the most astonishing reaches of the divine *maya*—the Dancer of the world as far out from himself as he can get, dancing not-dancing."

Yet with all this, Watts has no sense of the sacred: "Every Easter Sunday should be celebrated with a solemn and reverent burning of the Holy Scriptures, for the whole meaning of the resurrection and ascension of Christ into heaven ('which is within you') is that Godmanhood is to be discovered here and now inwardly, not in the letter of the Bible." And again: "Is it really of any great interest to ask whether Jesus was literally and historically born of a virgin and resurrected physically after his death? This kind of emphasis makes him a human freak, like a two-headed baby." With how many heads was that similitude coined?

The central argument of the book, based on a misconstruction of the Hindu teachings on *lila* and *maya*, is that no meaningful solution to the ills of existence is ever going to be achieved in Christian theological terms of an Absolute Potentate lording it (in the vein of the author) over a creature arbitrarily produced *ex nihilo*, then banished by the Fall, and ever after sadistically condemned—out of "loving chastisement"—to a moral rectitude in view of Redemption that by human definition is never achievable—until man goes *beyond theology* in a game of "Godmanship" where he discovers the delightful joke that he has really all along been the Divine Self (*Atman*) disguised (*maya*) as the ego in an "eternal dance of hide-and-seek" (*lila*). The tables are now turned: what was formerly thought to be outside or above ourselves is all at once seen to be within our very most center; "we" in reality are only so many variants of the one "I" whose "sport" is to scare "Himself" senseless with the most frightful nightmares He can invent about "otherness," until when the universe is rent with shrieks of horror, the "Divine Jokester" calls the whole thing off by awakening with laughter that turns the agony into the ecstasy which all along it really was in disguise.[2] The point is, "as soon as you realize that you *are* the Center, you have no further need to see it, to try to make it an object or an experience. This is why the mystics call the highest knowledge unknowing.... When the material world is no longer asked to provide the eternal home it is suddenly and amazingly transfigured. Its impermanence becomes a dance instead of a mockery. . . . It is likewise the body resurrected and the Paradise Garden. For death and the Last Day are when our conventional identity comes to the end of its tether and we 'give up the ghost' of the isolated ego." By thus reducing eschatology to its proper perspective, we are delivered on the one hand from "the tedium of immortality" and "the monstrous notion of a physical universe containing the risen bodies of all our friends and relations permanently pickled in Spirit," and on the other from "the Church's disagreeable insistence on the reality of the totally malignant spirit of cosmic evil, [and] on everlasting damnation." Seen

[2] A theme already developed in Gerald Heard's *Pain, Sex, and Time.*

within this new framework, "the Christian mythos has the possibility of blossoming into the most joyously exuberant, swinging, colorful, and liberated religion there ever was. Heaven need not wait for the grave." We have more than an echo here of the Rev. Harvey Cox's carnival-spirit religion. For Watts, the pure materialist "is either a slob or a bore," while the pure mystic "is more of a Euclidean proposition than a human being." But the author, like R. C. Zaehner, believes the moment has arrived for "a really thoroughgoing spiritual materialism . . . a true marriage of Heaven and Earth"; and in this sense Karl Barth's term "theology of crisis" points up the providential nature of the thorny aspects of Christianity, as being "the writhings which precede revelation; they are like the pangs of a woman in labor, but here in labor for the birth of a new kind of consciousness and a new apprehension of man's identity."

And now Watts draws us into his confidence: "In writing this book, I am to some extent letting the cat out of the bag by publishing things which should be communicated in secret. . . . The esoteric is . . . what we communicate with winks rather than words. . . . But the very fact that sexual love and overt sexual imagery is the principal Christian taboo points directly to what must be, in fact, the *mysterium tremendum*, the inner and esoteric core of the religion. . . . The Church reeks of sexuality because it is the one thing intentionally and obviously absent, the one thing definitely concealed, and thus the one thing really important." His argument runs that prudery is all part of the cosmic play intentionally cultivated to intensify sexual pleasure, whereas a libertine indulgence would glut the joy. Repressed sexuality is even seen as being at the core of the Inquisition. By joining in this cosmic game of "lust/guilt, prudery/prurience," man is participating in "the eternal oscillation of in/out, lost/found, and yes/no. And this oscillation is also the *vac*, the primordial sound or word, AUM, whereby all things are brought into manifestation, and thus the equivalent of the Word in Christianity." Hence, "if Christianity really means what it says about the union of the Word and the Flesh, the resolution of the problem must be the divinization of sexuality."

One has to insert a parenthesis here and ask where the author relates his own intelligence to the teachings of Christ. "Poor Jesus! If he had known how great an authority was to be projected upon him, he would never have said a word. His literary image in the Gospels has . . . become far more of an idol than anything graven . . . so that today the most genuinely reverent act of worship is to destroy that image. In his own words, 'It is expedient for you that I go away, for if I go not away, the Paraclete (the Holy Spirit) cannot come unto you.' . . . To insist on the historicity of the Christian myth is to remove Christ to the sterile distance of an archaeological curiosity."

After this sobering *mise au point*, we can return to the more serious business of "Godmanship," or what the author calls "making 'celestial whoopee.' . . . The Indian image of the universe as a manifestation or emanation of the divine is such a simple and plausible game-form. . . . It permits gut-shaking seriousness up to the very last micro-second□to the bullet in the brain, or to the twist of some demon's red-hot trident in the tenderest vitals of a hypocrite in hell, so that just beyond the point when everything reaches final and perfect evil, the scream turns suddenly into the ringing voice that says, 'I am Alpha and Omega, the Beginning and the End!'" Thus is the "sadism" of Christian theology "transfigured" into the more comprehensive "masochism" of Oriental doctrines.

It is likewise the encounter of the "I" with the "Eye." In the chapter "Who *Is* Who?," Watts describes this union: "If only I had the rubber necks of the people in the hymn who aspire

> Prostrate before thy Throne to lie
> And gaze and gaze on thee!

"At the same instant I become aware of those Eyes watching me right through the back of my head—Eyes that bore implacably into the most tender and disreputable centers of my soul . . . until everything is just one Eye. And because there is no brow, no face, I cannot tell what expression that Eye has. It just looks, and I can't stand it. I start running, running in blind panic down the corridors of the temple; but every way I turn I am running straight into that Eye. I drop to the floor, curl up, shut my eyes, and cover my head. Yet the Eye comes at me from deep inside me—vaster than ever, filling all thinkable space.

"There is nowhere—nowhere at all—left to go. . . . The only shred of myself that I can find is just the terror, the running away from that Eye. . . . There is nowhere for terror to go, no one to answer the screams, no darkness to cover me, no place to bury the body. And, just then, I am the Eye. For 'the eye with which I see God,' said Eckhart, 'is the same eye with which God sees me.'"

It only remains now to find out how we, too, can share in this oneness. The secret comes through not desiring it. "The final meaning of negative theology, of knowing God by unknowing, of the abandonment of idols both sensible and conceptual, is that ultimate faith is not in or upon anything at all. It is complete letting go." For the technique of mastering this "negative theology"—a misnomer of "anti-theology"—Watts on the final page of his book turns the reader over to Krishnamurti.

Inspired by certain Messianic speculations of Madame Blavatsky, two of her disciples in the Theosophical Society, the Rev. C. W. Leadbeater and Annie Besant (a "reincarnation" of Giordano Bruno, and prior to that, Hypatia), undertook to expedite the coming of the future Maitreya Buddha by themselves fixing on a vessel of election for the purpose. Thus within the first decade of our century a young Hindu, J. Krishnamurti, predestined through thirty previous "incarnations" and an "Initiate" of the "Great White Lodge" somewhere in Tibet, was recognized as the providential vehicle to incorporate the Second Advent; he was accordingly invested at Adyar, India, with the name Alcyone, made head of an Order ("Star in the East"), and sent to Oxford to complete the polishing necessary for the mission.

He repudiated the whole comedy in 1929, dissolving the Order, rejecting Theosophy as just another "system," and renouncing all claims to be a World Teacher. His sobriquet has been kept in this article, however, since even if he left the Theosophists, he has retained the "*samskaras*" (members of the Society still revere him) and done nothing to dispel the illusion that he has a crucial message for mankind about the possibility of an inner transformation of individuality with its consequent outward transformation of society. Give what explanation one will—his charisma, the social unrest and personal insecurity of his audience, the flattery of an "anti-doctrine" that disowns orthodoxies and commitments—Krishnamurti has attracted masses for some half a century who buy his books, sit spellbound at his lectures, follow his seminars at Saanen, Switzerland, and now send their children to his Educational Center at Brockwood Park in Hampshire. A glance at the dialogues reproduced in any of his numerous books betrays a bourgeois banality camouflaged solely by a smoke screen of sophistries and by what Marco Pallis calls "the rather repellent sophistication of his mode of expression."

As a prerequisite for understanding his "method," Krishnamurti says it is essential that we discard all our previous thought reflexes and conditionings. The first notion to get rid of, then, is that this work has anything whatever to do with religion—with religion orthodox, revealed, or in any way consecrated—unless the word is to lose all meaning. This is given on his own authority (although he says "there is no authority whatsoever") throughout his teachings which hold the revelations and practices of the world faiths in contempt: "Thought has cleverly said that there is a permanent, eternal self in yourself. . . . Thought has created the idea of an eternal self—the soul, the Atman—in order to find safety, hope."[3] To follow him means not belonging "to any particular dogma, religion, church, and all that immature nonsense."[4] "A devout Catholic, practicing his belief day after day, will experience the figure of Christ in his vision or dreams. That only strengthens his conditioning, therefore such a person is not free to observe; he remains a little bourgeois, caught in his own particular belief, his own particular dogma, inviting the world to enter his cage"[5] "So one depends inwardly more and more on something—a drug, a Master, a guru, a belief—and so there is more dependence and more resistance and more fear."[6] We read further on that the mind has everlastingly sought "the immortal and the timeless," which can only be attained in that freedom which comes from going beyond mind: "Because I have no principle—which is a conclusion—I have no ideology and there is freedom." Mind is the result of conditioning, he tells us elsewhere in the same book. "When we are violent and angry, that violence is part of the animal. We have evolved from the higher apes, we have got that violence in us. Aren't you the result of yesterday? . . . The whole Asiatic world believes that there is a soul, that there is the Atman. You can be conditioned to believe anything."[7]

Again, "there are innumerable gurus all over the world . . . who practice various systems of meditation. . . . A system implies not only the authority of the one who has achieved and who says, 'I know,' but it also means to practice, day after day, in the hope of achieving some

[3] *Talks and Dialogues Saanen 1967*, Netherlands: Servire, 1969.

[4] Ibid.

[5] *Talks and Discussions at Brockwood Park 1969*, Servire/Wassenaar, 1970.

[6] Ibid.

[7] It is fantastic that one Asiatic alone should think he has escaped this "conditioning." Thus are his arguments rendered nugatory, following the dictum of Aristotle (*Metaphysics* XI.8.30): "A science of the accidental is not even possible . . . for all science is of that which is always or for the most part, but the accidental is in neither of these classes."

particular result. . . . If I practice something daily . . . my mind becomes more and more dulled as it gets caught in the habit of a routine. So one has to reject all systems because they are unintelligent."[8]

How, then are we to get beyond mind? By cultivating awareness: "An essential part of meditation is this understanding of the difference between concentration and attention. Concentration demands effort; awareness or attention does not. . . . Where there is concentration there is exclusion and resistance; and where there is resistance there is conflict and the way of duality. I think that is fairly clear?"[9] What is clear is that the speaker does not know the etymology of the word he is attacking, for it means a con-centering or "synthesis" (*samadhi*) of our powers, an inclusive faculty transcending and resolving dualities, and exclusive uniquely of distractions, of the conventional mind activity which the speaker himself maintains must be stilled.

But since Krishnamurti claims not to be a teacher, what is the sound all about? He claims that a teaching received "is already a secondhand thing"; therefore who is beguiling whom? Is he the dupe of his audience, or vice versa? The answer is: both—it is only through their mutual ignorance that the comedy is perpetuated; while criticizing the thought of his questioners for "chasing its tail," he is doing nothing other himself. To use another metaphor, he saws the branch on which he sits; for in default of a common denominator or minimal cognitive adequation between agent and recipient, no communication is possible, and ideas are voided in a flux of empty utterances.

Furthermore, either his "message" is timeless, in which case it is madness to believe Krishnamurti the first to promulgate it, or it is not, in which case it is a passing fad without interest. The man is in fact a victim of the very thought conditioning he would reject, being a product of the Brahmanic heritage from which he has deviated. The violence of his reaction against religion is a manifestation even of exactly the sort of antagonism, resistance, opposition, and conflict which he pretends to be rejecting. Moreover, every spiritual anomaly is nothing but the distortion of truth. With Watts it is a perversion of negative theology and a confusion between the ego and the Self. Krishnamurti's aberration is the same thing in a more "Hindu" mode, a distortion of the *via negativa* (*neti, neti*) of Advaita Vedanta. If he were a caste

[8] Ibid.

[9] Ibid.

Hindu practicing the *sadhanas* and *dharmasastra*, he could have an ashram and pursue the Shankaran method of "non-identification of the self with the non-Self." For it is perfectly true that the map is not the country it portrays, that spiritual attainment can only be had through a reversal of values, a rupture with habit, a spontaneous immediacy that cannot be "communicated," and hence a "leap into the dark." But these are things that every spiritual master knows.

Let us, however, envisage the manner in which Krishnamurti himself might answer these charges. For this we can now hold an *imaginary* forum where his questioners bait him with some of the objections just put forth:

Question: Some people say you are sawing the branch you sit on.
ANSWER: Who is sitting on the branch? Is thought sitting on that branch? Because if so, then it is good, because that is precisely what we want, namely, to saw thought off from its own habit-formed foundations. If thought ceases to see the duality between itself and the branch, then who is there to stay on the branch or fall off? If on the other hand thought remains conditioned to the idea of sawing at something in order to obtain a result, then when the branch comes down the situation creating the complex is dissolved and so in either case release is obtained.

Question: Sir, spiritual teachers claim that the Truth is always one and the same, being beyond all relativity and change. If therefore, we admit that the founders of all the great religions of the world were adequate vehicles of the Truth, what is it you have to tell us that they did not already teach? According to this view, if what you say is true, then it has always been true; and if it is something that has only been discovered now, then it belongs to the realm of relativity and thus has no value.
ANSWER: I like this question. It is a good question, because it betrays all the errors with which thought is plagued. Did Jesus create a system? Did Krishna, or Buddha? Jesus said, "the wind bloweth where it listeth." What system do we find here? Krishna says in the *Gita:* "Giving up all Dharmas, come unto Me alone for refuge." And the Buddha, what did he say? Do you know the Flower Sermon, sir? He held up a flower. That was all!

One understands something before the thought enters. But we are prejudiced with the human habit to formulate and separate into systems, and so we have Hinduism and Christianity, Capitalism and Communism, Catholics versus Protestants. And then we have religious wars, political wars; people want peace and their very desire for it breeds conflict. In our striving we become neurotic. I have a neurosis. I want love, and then there is a sexual desire—not the sex, but the habit bred by thought that without the desire I cannot find satisfaction. And so I pursue my desire, and this brings jealousy, the fear of being betrayed, the idea I have of how I should be loved, and not obtaining it. And what then, sir, happens to love, to living in pure creative energy? Is it not uselessly dissipated because I am neurotic? And so you ask if this possibility for energy is something that has only been discovered now, and I answer that it has always been there, otherwise of course it is not true. But these things are not conjectures, and the proof is that you can see for yourself that there is neurosis and conflict in the world; it is not I who invented them. And there is always the wish to end the conflict and live in peace, which shows that something stands in the way of happiness. And is this thing not time? And what creates time? Time is the creation of thought, brought about by planning and organizing and systematizing what should be spontaneous. And so we are kept in duality, and kept from gaining access to spontaneous energy outside of time. Therefore, sir, if you ask if these ideas are new, I answer that new and old can have no meaning outside of time, and so if we can get rid of time, then the problem is solved of itself and the question has no more meaning.[10]

Question: I am not satisfied that this answers the point that was raised. You appear to evade the issue by constantly shifting your reasoning and . . .
ANSWER: Madam, please do not go further; I want all of you to stop on these words; consider carefully the trap we are getting into! Does this not illustrate just that conditioning which reason has built into all of us through centuries of automatic prejudice against change? You have the opportunity to profit from what you call shifting reasoning only if you can cultivate the awareness necessary to accept change with a quiet mind and then . . .

Question: Sir, I throw in the sponge.
ANSWER: Oh, I beg you not to do that, for you are thereby only creating a new conflict, a series of tensions; you are simply reinforcing

[10] In case this is confusing the reader, let him know that error is also "timeless"—in the way that hell is.

your sense of separativity and fragmentation, thus obliging us to start the whole discussion over again from where we just left off.

People like Heard, Huxley, Watts, Zaehner, Krishnamurti, Teilhard de Chardin, Aurobindo, Gopi Krishna and so forth are only the tip of the iceberg, but whatever their point of departure and particular persuasion, they are all in one way or another spokesmen for a New Religion (Watts even has a name for it, the "Church of All Fools") and have in common these salient characteristics: *a patent individualism, a scientific and moralistic humanism, evolutionism, a relativistic "intuitionism," inability to grasp metaphysical and cosmological principles and the realities of the Universal domain, a mockery (latent or overt) of the sacred, a prodigious dearth of spiritual imagination, no eschatological understanding, a pseudo-mysticism in the form of a "cosmic consciousness."*

A patent individualism: As just one example, both Watts and Krishnamurti say that the illusive separativity between the ego and *Atman* is engendered by the very feeling one has of separativity. How then can we get rid of this feeling? By dropping even the desire to get rid of it ("holy cunning")! For the life of the ego is perpetuated in a self-conscious dualism forever oscillating between yes and no, pleasure and pain, hope and deception, desire and frustration. Watts gives by way of illustration the dilemma of wanting to be humble, and being proud of one's humility, and proud of seeing through one's pride in one's humility, ad infinitum; or again, the predicament of the religious praying for the grace to have pure love of God, and being tormented by the secret apprehension that self-will lurks in the shadow of this effort at selflessness. Admittedly the ego as such has no means of transcending individuality, but that is not the problem; and the pre-occupation of the authors in question with artificial stalemates of this kind actually betrays a dualism on their part that is irresolvable thanks purely to their "closed system" of egocentric subjectivity—the forfeit of their individualism. In reality the soul is more than just the ego, as appears in the Gospel passage: "Lord, I believe; help thou mine unbelief"; there is also its immortal, transpersonal center (*duo sunt in homine*) whose natural abode is the supernal world; and a contemplative on the spiritual path is centered in the sacraments—of non-human origin—so that the workings of the ego are peripheral and already in some way external or foreign to himself—a commotion removed to the outer horizon for which he can only feel detachment or holy disdain (*contemptus mundi*).

A scientific and moralistic humanism: The New Religion school unequivocally advocates a materialistic faith with man at the center, a faith wedded to technology for the betterment of the human race. In its view, science—the product of discursive reasoning born of that "fuller consciousness" which is at once the fruit and ransom of the "Fall"—has outstripped dualistic reasoning's ability to keep pace; and the remedy for this lies in some sort of "yoga" capable of healing on a higher plane the present scission between the rational but divisive ego and the cosmic All, thus endowing man with the "vision" to exploit technology for purely philanthropic ends.

Evolutionism: Progress is for these anti-dogmatists notwithstanding an uncontested dogma. As indicated just above, they conceive the human race prior to the "Fall" composed of sub-rational creatures enjoying through their faculty of instinct an "existential" identity with the cosmos (Teilhard's "collective co-consciousness"); the "Fall"—quotation marks are used because for these people it is really an evolutional advance—is a picturesque fable to describe the conscious accession of free will and reason, although these evolutionists are pleased to exploit the theological term, since effectively there is in the ego's emergence a "descent" into discursive, analytical thought ("the knowledge of good and evil"), and a certain taint of "sin": self-will perforce begets pride. "Redemption" (at-one-ment) must accordingly be construed as the next evolutional breakthrough to be achieved when the social tensions of the present day have reached their ultimate crisis point (*kairos*), thus exploding into the birth of the superman, the apocatastatic Parousia, at one again with the cosmos—and all his gadgetry along to boot. What traditional doctrines without exception teach is exactly the inverse: namely, that prelapsarian humanity lived in unity by the light of the Intellect (which can only be called "instinct" at the risk of admitting that apes likewise were created "in the image of God"), that the Fall came from the veiling of this Intellect through various causes, and that macrocosmic salvation is tantamount to the unveiling once more of this Intellect through the reversal of these causes, and the restoration of salvageable mankind to its pristine state.

A relativistic "intuitionism": This is characterized by thought which is "floating," sentimental, and vague—albeit clever, or even "scintillating." Reason here is "dynamic" and subjective, and thus prone to attribute purely psychological motives to even the greatest manifestations of spirituality and wisdom; it scorns intellectual, contemplative, and "static" objectivity as being pharisaism or "retreatism," while leaning uncritically at the same time towards parapsychology, the phenomenal, and other prolongations of extra-sensory exoticism.

Inability to grasp principles: Watts believes the idea of God can only become intelligible and central when we transpose concepts of *height* into terms of *depth*, or the Ground of all existence. If he understood the hierarchy of the states of being, "descending" or "exteriorizing" from the Universal to the individual order, questions of spatial orientation would be a matter of terminology; but as precisely he conceives of "up" and "down" in a purely individual, quasi-physical sense, to relegate Heaven to the Abyss is not just a figure of speech. Admittedly an abstract Ground may flatter the sophistications of intelligence in a way that a Personal God "on high" does not; however, there still remains the metacosm, and the macrocosm with its essences, exemplars, principalities, and archetypes, and the relationship of the microcosm to all this; in fact, when it comes to how the visible world is produced from the invisible, these authors are singularly silent. Their data seems limited to what science has to teach about pure energy being the substratum of phenomenal existence, with the reservation that this force or "vibration" is considered by them to be endowed with some kind of "intelligence."

Mockery of the sacred: That may seem a strong word, but the attitude *de facto* of these New Religion partisans amounts to this; totally foreign to their "fixation" on change and becoming is a world view based on the finality of an Absolute, unchanging Principle, Eternal, Infinite, always the same unto Itself, and which in differing modalities—of non-human, timeless origin—reveals Itself through Avataric descents, sacred scripture, and by extension the divine aspirations of saints and sages. When belief in infallibility no longer prevails, the certitude in unshakable authority crumbles, —Krishna, Buddha, Christ, Muhammad, Lao-tse are relegated to the fallible, individual plane, and everyone is henceforth on his own, making impertinence well-nigh irresistible.

A prodigious dearth of spiritual imagination: This follows of itself from what precedes. For a few very bright gentlemen of our century, university-trained in Western culture, to speak as though they have discovered spiritual truths of which the entire humanity of the world has hitherto been in ignorance,—that untold millions of Hindus, Buddhists, Taoists, Confucianists, Shintoists, Jews, Christians, Muslims, plus countless other ethnic groups have all shared in common the same errors concerning a Personal God, an afterlife, the immortality of the soul, the necessity of rites, and so on—and for these personages to hold forth as though there had never been Solomon, Shankara, Plato, Ibn Arabi, Eckhart, Nagarjuna, Chuang-tse, and the rest—for such a phenomenon to be possible surely the politest explanation one can give is lack of imagination.

No eschatological understanding: The expression in the first paragraph of this article, "dipped into," is used advisedly, as anything deeper than a dilettantish approach would force the minimal recognition that Oriental doctrines are no more accommodating than Christianity: all religions basically agree in their eschatologies, in their moral injunctions and stress on virtues relative to man's ultimate ends, in their promises and warnings of future rewards and punishments pertaining to beatitudes and immensities for which the present world is but the threshold. To the New Religion school, however, all this is a closed book.

"Cosmic consciousness": There is the conviction here that man has potential access to vastly extended realms of consciousness underlying his habitual perceptions, and that the mystics—whatever their exaggerations and excesses and supernatural embroidering, and despite the clumsiness of their presumed trial and error ascesis, plus the portion that can be written off as pure hysteria—do in fact have the not unappreciable merit of being forerunners in this direction by pointing to some common ground of awareness or reality that exists beyond any reasonable doubt. The awaited consciousness of the future is "cosmic" in that it will reunite the ego—stranded since the "Fall"—with the common Ground of all existence; and this, in the words of Watts, "is the mighty self-abandonment which gives birth to the stars."

Provided, that is, the stars have yet to be born. . . .

This essay can best be terminated with the following clarification by Frithjof Schuon: "All these movements are characterized by the detachment they affect in respect to pure doctrine, the incorruptibility of which they hate; for them this purity is 'dogmatism': they fail to understand that the Truth does not deny forms from without, but transcends them from within."

"Orthodoxy contains and guarantees infinitely precious values which man could never draw from himself."[11]

[11] *Spiritual Perspectives and Human Facts*, chap. IV., Perennial Books Limited, Pates Manor, Bedfont, Middlesex, 1987.

II

IN THE TRACKS OF EASTERN WISDOM

I know him, that great Purusha
Of the color of the sun,
Beyond all darkness.
He who has known him
Goes beyond death.
There is no other way.

Svetasvatara Upanishad

THE TIBETAN TRADITION*
Its Presiding Idea

Marco Pallis

Some years ago, when writing my book *Peaks and Lamas*, I set myself the task of describing, stage by stage, those wanderings along the Himalayan borderland which had led me to the discovery of that form of spirituality that has its home on the snowy tableland of Tibet. It goes without saying, however, that the picture presented at that time remained incomplete in many ways; anything like a detailed analysis of the various strands that together go to weave the web of Tibetan life could only be undertaken by one who had first gained access to Tibet proper, where the civilization in question could be studied under its most typical as well as its most vigorous form; but it was not until 1947 that the necessary authorization to enter the country was granted. Nevertheless, enough had been learned up to date to allow of a number of generalizations affecting the whole Tibetan world, since it is plainly evident that through its far-flung territories a certain type of human existence is recognizable, owing both its essential unity and its outward form to the influence of the selfsame tradition, having done so, moreover, for many centuries. One has but to compare the account contained in the biography of the poet-saint Mila Repa with what is to be seen today to become convinced of the extraordinary unity, as well as vitality, of Tibetan institutions. Apart from such changes as must come, almost imperceptibly, with the mere passage of time, the ways in which people think, act, and speak and the standards by which they judge men and things do not appear to have altered in any very fundamental way since those early days, and the life of Mila Repa still provides the best-drawn picture of Tibetan life that exists, besides offering a most vivid commentary on that doctrine which, above all else, has given to that life both shape and direction.

The last remark calls for some additional comment, since it contains an allusion to a question of very wide import, one that is of

* Editor's Note: Chapter 9 of *The Way and the Mountain.*

general applicability to all traditional civilizations and not merely to Tibet—namely, the question of what is the principle of discrimination between one form of the Perennial Wisdom and another, causing them to be externally distinct as well as consistent internally; for without the operation of some such principle there would be no excuse for a formal discontinuity as between the several traditions, serving as they all do as ways of approach to the imperishable Knowledge, from which every thought of distinction is manifestly to be excluded, whether of form or otherwise.

The fact is that every civilization that can be called authentic is endowed with a principle of unity peculiar to itself, which is reflected, in varying degrees, in all the institutions of the civilization in question. By a principle of unity is meant a predominant idea, corresponding to a given aspect of the truth, which has been recipient of particular emphasis and for the expressing of which, if one may so put it, that civilization shows a peculiar "genius." Emphasis on an aspect must, however, have its price: that is to say, the highlight of attention cannot be focused on one aspect of reality without producing its compensating shadows, affecting other aspects. Each separate formal embodiment of the traditional wisdom, therefore, corresponds, as it were, to a difference of intellectual perspective; and the key to the understanding of whatever is explicit or implicit in any given form resides in a thorough assimilation of the dominant idea running through that form—in other words, of its principle of unity.

In seeking to determine which is the principle of unity animating the Tibetan civilization one must beware of being satisfied with an easy answer, such as saying that this principle is no other than the Buddhist doctrine itself; for though this statement is correct as far as it goes, it lacks precision, failing as it does to indicate which one, out of a whole body of ideas comprised within the one doctrinal plan, has been recipient of that greater emphasis required for the molding of an entire traditional structure according to a particular form, and, as it were, in its image. Though one knows that Buddhism, by imposing certain fundamental ideas, has become the rule of life over very wide areas extending from Ceylon to Japan and that this has produced a certain community of outlook among all the peoples that have come within the Buddhist orbit, one cannot fail to recognize that in this general whole certain clearly distinguishable forms of civilization are to be found, the intellectual frontiers of which are not primarily determined by the Buddhist influence. The common presence of Buddhism does not, for instance, warrant one's placing the Chinese and Tibetan civilizations under one heading, even though they are next-door neighbors; and if Buddhism is admittedly a factor affecting both, this fact has been insufficient to produce any very marked likeness in their respective points of view, let alone identity.

The chief difference between them lies in the fact that whereas in Tibet the Buddhist tradition is everything, having completely replaced its Bon-po predecessor, in China Buddhism was something in the nature of a graft, admittedly a most timely and successful one, upon a civilization of which the pattern, in all essentials, had already been set before the importation of the foreign influence. Since nothing in the existing Chinese form was found to be actually incompatible with the Buddhist point of view, the latest arrival from India found no difficulty in taking its place in the traditional life of the Far East on equal terms with its two other great constituents, namely Taoism, representative of an intellectuality so refined as to be adapted for the use of an exceptionally qualified elite only, and Confucianism. This latter is not, as is commonly supposed, a separate creation, still less a "religion," but corresponds to that side of the Chinese tradition in which all without exception are able to participate, concerning itself as it does with social institutions and human relationships in general—the latter being given expression especially through its characteristic concepts of the race, the family, and the family ancestors. It might also be mentioned, in passing, that in the course of time Buddhism and Taoism engaged in many intellectual exchanges, some of which gave rise to that school, so rich in spiritual initiative, that is commonly known in the West under its Japanese name of Zen.

Similar considerations apply equally well in India during the centuries when Hinduism and Buddhism co-existed there as separate currents of tradition: both continued to belong to the same civilization, the characteristic forms of which had been laid down at a time long anterior to the specific formulation of the Buddhist teachings. In any case, both in virtue of its origin and by the nature of its thought, Buddhism remains an Indian doctrine, having derived most of its basic conceptions, if not all, from the common root-stock of the Indian metaphysic. It is not on that score that Buddhism can be called original; nor, indeed, does it put forward any such claim, since the Buddha Himself was always at pains to repudiate, as a monstrous heresy, any suggestion that he had come to teach something new in the matter of doctrine; it is only modern Western writers, themselves imbued with humanistic prejudices, who have been determined at all costs to discover in Buddhism a radical innovation amounting to a revolt against the traditional spirit, and in the Buddha an early revolutionary working on Protestant lines.

Where Buddhism was highly original, however, was in respect of its methods, affecting both the way of expounding the ever-abiding principles and the forms of spiritual discipline that went with their knowledge. Indeed, but for a large measure of originality in the manner of restating the eternal truths, the Buddhist apostles would have been unable to carry out their appointed task of adapting the Indian metaphysic so as to render it eventually assimilable by non-Indian peoples, especially by the Yellow races, whose mentality was so very different from that of the Indians.

The Tibetan branch was one of the latest offshoots from the main stem of Buddhism, having only come into being during the seventh and eighth centuries after Christ, chiefly through the work of Indian monks from Bengal and Kashmir. While accepting all the basic ideas taught by the Buddha, which it continued to share with all the other peoples of similar spiritual allegiance, Tibet early developed certain clearly marked features of its own, to the point of giving rise to a distinct form of civilization, comparable, on every count, with the other principal traditional forms of the world. This is possibly due in part to the incorporation of such features of the previous Bon-po tradition as could usefully be readapted; it seems unlikely, however, that any element specific to a form actually in process of replacement by another form would retain sufficient intrinsic vitality to provide a whole civilization with its principle of unity, in the sense given to that term at the beginning of this chapter—that is to say, with an idea both distinct and powerful enough to create and nourish its own forms, conferring on them the means for perpetuating their own character through long ages and of impressing it firmly and unmistakably upon the face of things and upon the thoughts of men.

In fact, the idea that enjoys pride of place in the Tibetan tradition is one that figures in the Buddhist doctrine as originally introduced from India. This presiding idea, coloring the outlook of sage and simple peasant alike (as we were repeatedly enabled to observe during our journeys), is the conception of Bodhisattvahood, the state of the fully awakened being who, though under no further constraint by that Law of Causality which he has transcended, yet freely continues to espouse the vicissitudes of the Round of Existence in virtue of his Self-identification with all the creatures still involved in egocentric delusion and consequent suffering. Such an attitude must not, however, be confused with a kind of sentimental "altruism" in the social sense; indeed a moment's reflection will show that one who has finally been set free from the false notion of a permanent "I," personally experiencable, is at the same time automatically rid of its correlative notion of "other." The *Bodhisattva* behaves as he does precisely because, for him, any kind of conceptual polarization is inoperative, because, to his singleness of eye, all contrasted pairs such as the Round of Existence and *Nirvana*, Bondage and Deliverance, Body-Mind and Spirit, together with all the subsidiary oppositions born of such contrasts, are alike cancelled in the unity—or, as the Tibetans would say, in the "two-lessness"—of That which he himself realizes as the All-Principle (Tibetan *Kun-ji*), eternal Cause and ground of all phenomenal existence.

The Bodhisattva's compassion, or what in human language is described as such, translates into individually intelligible terms the universal "non-altruity" of his point of view; even while in *Nirvana* he experiences the world, according to that measure of reality which belongs to it—and one must not forget that suffering, in the deepest sense of the word, is inseparable from the very fact of becoming, which cannot in any sense be experienced without it. Likewise, even when dwelling in the midst of a changeful world, he does not cease to know the changeless bliss of *Nirvana*, and if to us the two experiences seem distinct and mutually exclusive, they are not so to the possessor of true insight, because such a one never feels tempted to abstract one or other of them from the unity of their common and transcendent principle, so that, from his point of view, they are not even conceivable apart. Thus the *Bodhisattva*, through a perfect realization of his own essential identity with all beings, thereby suffers with them and for them, as the eternal victim self-immolated upon the altar of their existence; but even in that suffering itself he perceives the joy unspeakable—both the light and its inseparable shadows alike yield up their closest-guarded secret under the scrutiny of his incorruptible impartiality.[1]

[1] A parallel, though one very different in its formal expression, can be established by reference to Christian theology, in that it can be said that the ultimate goal of the Christian life consists in giving complete effect to the Doctrine of the Two Natures, central theme of the Christian tradition as such, whereby Jesus, the Man of Sorrows, and the Glorified Christ eternally seated at the right hand of Power are simultaneously realized as one and not two; or, in other words, the Christ who suffered crucifixion

The status of a *Bodhisattva* has been defined (though, strictly speaking, the very word "definition," implying as it does the idea of limitation, is here inapplicable) as that of one who realizes Wisdom as Knowledge of the Void, and Method as Universal Compassion; the first-named representing the purely transcendent aspect of his realization, while the second implies an unblurred recognition of the Face of Divinity even through the veil of separativity as constituted by the worlds—in other words, a not merely theoretical but an effective awareness that the transcendent aspect of Truth is not other than the immanent and vice versa. Thus, if the being is first called upon to seek "deliverance" from form and its restrictions in order to become awake to that reality which dwells "beyond names and forms," yet, in the deepest sense of all, it can be said, following the *Lankavatara Sutra*, that there is really nothing to be acquired, nothing to be delivered from, no Way, no Goal, no Round, no *Nirvana*, nor indeed anything needing to be done or undone. However, lest this kind of paradoxical statement, so common in the Mahayanist writings, should be unconsciously twisted into an excuse for taking up a "quietist" position, it is well to remember that the knowledge in question itself implies the most intensely "active" attitude conceivable, a concentration so impenetrable that it is a matter of indifference to its possessor whether he happens to find himself in the most secluded of mountain retreats or engaged on exemplary and redemptive work among the crowded habitations of men, or else in one of the heavens—or the hells. His is not a solitude that depends on any special conditions of place or time, true solitude being indeed but another name for that Voidness which is also the Fullness, a first-fruit of that self-naughting which is also Self-knowing.

Three levels are broadly distinguishable in respect of the comprehension of the Real: first, things may be regarded from the point of view of Ignorance, which is that of the ordinary man, concerned as he is with appearances and with his own reactions to them. It is he, the "common man," held up to flattery in our day as if he were a very pattern of humanity, who is the pathetic dreamer, the incorrigible

temporally upon the tree at Calvary and upon the cross of His own incarnation as a finite being, and indeed cosmically upon the very fact of Creation itself, and that Word of God by whom all things were made, though they respectively suggest notions of suffering and blissfulness that to the eye of ignorance seem mutually exclusive or, at best, successively realizable, are essentially inseparable conceptions neither of which can be fully realized in isolation from the other.

sentimentalist, the romantic, in contrast to the spiritual man, now at a discount, who is the only true realist, the "practical man" in the widest sense of the word. From an ignorant or "profane" point of view things are considered under the aspect of separativity only, and treated as if they were self-contained entities, that is to say, as if each of them were "carrying within itself its own sufficient cause." Under such circumstances the manifested world appears in the guise of an unresolvable multiplicity, in which the individualization and consequently the opposition of persons or things (through their mutual limitation and inescapable competition) is raised to the highest possible power, thus spelling insecurity and suffering for all concerned: such being, moreover, the inevitable fruit of dualism, of participation in the Tree of Knowledge of Good and Evil.

Secondly, there is the view that comes with an awakening perception of the fallacy underlying the world and its formal appearances. In that case the disillusioned being seeks deliverance in the formlessness of the Unmanifest, where all things subsist unchanged and unchangeable within the bosom of their parent cause, in a state that might be described as one of permanent actuality, whence their coming out to be manifested in one of the worlds can only partake of the nature of an illusion; that is to say, their existence pertains to a lesser order of reality that masks, by the various phenomena it gives rise to, its own lack of true selfhood.[2] This point of view corresponds with the attainment of a *Nirvana* still able to be regarded as one of the twin terms of an opposition, the other term being that state of Ignorance mentioned previously, whereby beings remain imprisoned in the Round and subject to change and suffering. Those who attain such a state of knowledge are usually referred to, in the Mahayanist books, under the name of *Pratyeka* Buddhas (the Tibetan equivalent means "Self-Buddhas"), with whom are also coupled those whom the

[2] One must remind the reader that current loose speaking has practically converted the word "illusion" into a synonym of "unreal"; and this in turn has given rise to frequent misunderstandings on the subject of the Buddhist teachings about the illusory nature of the world and its contents. Nothing can ever be opposable to reality; something that is truly unreal cannot enjoy any kind of existence, not even in imagination; whereas an illusion is something that more or less makes game of the senses of an observer by seeming to possess a character other than its own; typically by appearing more self-sufficient than it really is.

Tibetans call "hearers" (in Sanskrit known as *Sravakas*) and who are supposed, though somewhat unfairly, to represent the devotees of the rival Hinayanist school, that to which the southern Buddhists, those of Ceylon and Burma, belong. These two types have provided a favorite target for criticism on the part of all the Mahayanist writers, whose mention of them has come to constitute a kind of refrain, a matter of "method," probably, rather than one to be taken as referring to actual facts. Thus it is said that the *Sravakas* and *Pratyeka* Buddhas rest content with deliverance as far as they themselves are concerned (hence the name "Self-Buddhas"), but fail to include in their point of view all their fellow beings still condemned to struggle in the whirlpool of the Round; in other words, they succeed in breaking loose from the world and its illusion, but they are unable to reintegrate it positively, stopping short, as they do, at negation. For such as they, therefore, *Nirvana*, Deliverance, though undoubtedly attained in one sense, yet remains essentially as the Non-Round; just as the Round itself continues to be similarly regarded as Non-*Nirvana*, without any means being found of reducing the contrasted experiences to unity. Thus the withdrawal of attention from the world as such, which marks a legitimate and indeed a necessary stage in the process of enlightenment, if it should ever be taken for a final term, can land one in an intellectual blind alley, bringing about a kind of lofty self-imprisonment, a withdrawal into a blissful supra-consciousness which yet implies privation of the one essential thing, since it stops short of the supreme non-duality.

Thirdly and lastly, there is the point of view (if one can still describe as such what is really a total synthesis embracing all possible points of view) of Bodhisattvahood, whereby the essential non-duality of the Round, represented by Form, and of *Nirvana*, represented by Voidness, is clearly perceived as Knowledge compared to which, as a typical Mahayanist writer would probably have added, "all the virtues and achievements of countless millions of *Pratyeka* Buddhas and *Sravakas* during successive aeons are nothing worth." This supreme realization, goal of the spiritual life, goes under the name of the *Prajna Paramita* or Wisdom Transcendent (the Tibetans actually give it as "the transcending of Wisdom"); and a *Bodhisattva* is one who has succeeded in realizing this doctrine effectively, so that it can be said that possession of the *Prajna Paramita* constitutes the characteristic *note* by which the *Bodhisattva* is to be known.[3]

Once having realized it, and from the very fact of having done so, the *Bodhisattva*, though no longer involved in Existence under any law of necessity, freely decides—so the saying goes—"to remain in the Round as long as a single blade of grass shall remain undelivered from suffering," so that one and all may pass together through *Nirvana*'s gates as the single, recollected non-duality they already are in essence. Needless to say, however, the sentimentalism of the masses, even in Tibet, does not spare this doctrine altogether, for even there people will persist in reading into its symbolism some kind of moral lesson, according to which the *Bodhisattva*, in contrast to the selfish *Pratyeka* Buddhas, "refuses *Nirvana*," out of compassion for the beings (ourselves!) undergoing the painful experiences of the Round of Existence. Rightly interpreted, even such a colored picture is not entirely devoid of sense; its underlying implications are fairly clear, but naturally the tendency of simple minds is to take each detail separately and literally, thus sacrificing the unity of the idea in favor of some version more in accord with their own individualistic bias.

There is, however, one difficulty of interpretation which does actually arise from the fact that, according to the usual convention, Bodhisattvahood denotes a state penultimate to the attainment of Buddhahood and not the supreme realization itself. Thus it is said that the *Bodhisattva* "takes possession" of the final revelation that makes of him a Buddha, and similarly the Buddha is spoken of as having been "still a *Bodhisattva*" at such and such a time. In face of what has been said above it may well be asked how a *Bodhisattva* can be regarded as inferior in status to a Buddha, seeing that Bodhisattvahood, as we have already seen, corresponds by definition to the state of one who not only has realized the Void, in a transcendent sense, but also has realized it in the World itself, in an immanent sense, this double realization (as we are still forced to describe it) being for him not two-fold but one and only. It is evident that the attainment of this, the supreme unitive Knowledge, is in fact that which constitutes *Nirvana* or Buddhahood,

[3] There is a famous formula that expresses this doctrine as concisely as possible; it is taken from the *sutra* bearing the same title of *Prajna Paramita* and runs as follows: "Form (it is) void: The Void Itself (is) form."

By these words the Supreme Identity is given expression, hence this sentence may be regarded as an epitome of all Knowledge. In Tibetan, the fact that a separate word "is" does not enter into the composition of this formula greatly adds to its doctrinal power.

so that it is difficult to see how Bodhisattvahood can be referred to as a penultimate state at all—yet the very existence of the two separate terms must be intended to correspond to some reality in spite of an apparent redundancy affecting their use in certain contexts.

The explanation appears to lie in a variable use of the name *Bodhisattva* itself. In the first place it can be used more loosely, in order to denote the all-but-perfected saint, on the threshold of Buddhahood, or even any unusually saintly person—I was once told, for instance, that "we will find you 'a *Bodhisattva*' to be your teacher." In the second place it can be used in reference to one who is identical with Buddha by right of Knowledge, but who, in the exercise of his work of salvation for the benefit of creatures, *recapitulates* the stages of the Way for *exemplary reasons*, as a "shower of the Way."[4] In that sense he redescends into the Round rather than remains in it, though the latter impression may be produced on the minds of beings, prone to deception by passing appearances. One then has to do with an *Avatara* (to use the well-known Sanskrit term); that is to say, with a specific descent of the Principle into Manifestation, a descent—to quote the words of Ananda Coomaraswamy—of the Light of Lights, as *a* light but not as another Light. As we have just pointed out, such a descent implies the assumption of a limit—in other words, of an individual form, or of something analogous if the descent were to take place into a world other than our own, defined, as it would then be, by another set of conditions; but such a self-limiting need not shock us, since the realization of the *Prajna Paramita*, of the essential non-duality of the Void and Form, obviously carries with it the power of assuming any and every form at will, as well as no form. Thus it is written of him who is established in this Knowledge that "there will be no end of my *Avatara*s, who will appear in inconceivable millions of numbers and shapes, and who will adopt various methods suitable for the control of every kind of being."

At this point it may be advisable to guard against a possible misunderstanding as being one likely to arise in consequence of certain prevailing tendencies of present-day thought. That such might well be the case is evidenced by the following question that was recently put to me by a friend who asked whether, according to the precedent of the *Bodhisattva*'s non-withdrawal from the Round of Existence, one

[4] This title is one that is habitually bestowed on the Buddha Himself.

was not justified in regarding as fundamentally sound the attitude of the man who says that he is prepared to make the best of the world as he finds it, enjoying life as far as he can, without troubling his head overmuch with thoughts of the beyond and the hereafter; was this not an indication of a more realistic outlook, it was asked, than the "other-worldliness" of the typically religious view of life?

At a first examination it might indeed appear that those who argue thus are not entirely at fault. Nevertheless, there is a fallacy lurking behind the question so put, even without taking into account the mixture of motives behind it, motives that are bound up with a hankering, on the part of the modern world, after a belief that the fruits of spirituality can be enjoyed without renouncing certain cherished habits and prejudices of an egocentric nature; while there also enters in sometimes a not entirely ununderstandable feeling of sympathy for the good-natured tolerance of the man who is prepared to live and let live, as contrasted with the narrow exclusiveness that so frequently mars the purity of an otherwise sincere religious outlook.

The real defect in the argument, however, is of quite a different order from these superficial matters of feeling, residing as it does in a false assimilation made on the strength of a purely specious likeness between the attitude of the amiable, easy-going, and common-sense person already mentioned and that of the *Bodhisattva*, with his realization of universal non-duality. The two cases differ fundamentally for the simple reason that in the first instance the world is accepted *passively*—that is to say, is taken at its face value, under the aspect of separativity extending to everything within it, without any serious attempt being made to reduce things to unity through the knowledge of a principle superior to their multiplicity and distinction. The phenomenal reality of the world is thus treated as if it were valid in its own right; in other words, it is considered from the point of view of Ignorance, and this is as true in the case of a man who tries to make the best of things as of a confirmed pessimist. At most one has to do with a more amiable brand of profanity, as compared with what is obviously a more disagreeable one.

Such a view of things does in fact start off by ignoring what is a prime condition for any aspirant towards Bodhisattvahood; namely, an understanding of the essentially impermanent character of the world and its contents, not merely in a theoretical sense, as when one studies a doctrine through books, nor in an "ideal" sense, through developing a kind of vague sympathy for that same doctrine, but effectively, so that the knowledge in question may take root in one's very being, causing the self-sufficiency of separate objects to lose all its fascination for the mind; for only when attention has been thus withdrawn from whatever is fragmentary and perishable will it be possible to become poised in "one-pointed" contemplation of That which alone possesses the true nature of Selfhood, "being unto Itself its own sufficient Cause."

One of the author's early teachers, the monk-painter Gyalthsan of Phiyang in Ladak, repeatedly said that without an effective grasp of the Doctrine of Impermanence all further progress in the Way was an impossibility; in this negating of all that is in itself negative (because regarded in abstraction from its principle) is to be found the clue to the mystery. It can thus be readily understood that if the *Bodhisattva* is free to remain in the world for the sake of the creatures still subject to the delusion of separativity, he does so with his eyes open. Where they see "other" things all around them, things that seem to them only too solid and substantial, he only perceives their voidness, or in other words their lack of genuine Self-nature. Multiple forms that, to the creature, appear opaque and self-contained have become for him of such perfect transparency as to reveal, or to veil no longer, the supreme Suchness, devoid as it is of all particularization, restriction, relativity, distinction, and the like. Nay, more, to his singleness of eye, the negative Voidness of worldly objects and the positive Voidness that translates a freedom from form and all other limiting conditions are but one Voidness unqualified, coinciding, as they do, in that ultimate Reality concerning which all one dares to say is "Not this, not this."

Whereas the profane man, the "ordinary person," is in the Round by compulsion of mediate causes, "under the law" as St. Paul would have said, the *Bodhisattva* is there but "in sport," that is to say freely, in virtue of his identification with that which being alone absolutely unlimited is also alone absolutely free. Where the former submits to the world and its ways, with or without a semblance of willingness, but in any case in passive mode, the latter may be said to reintegrate the world in active mode; while somewhere midway between these two positions can be placed the *Pratyeka* Buddha (with whom the common run of religious-minded persons might be associated, since their picture of a personal salvation is in many ways comparable with his, though on a more restricted plane), of whom it can be said that he has effectively rejected the bonds of worldly existence (by realizing its impermanence), but has stopped short of reintegrating it. In his case it is rather *Nirvana* that is accepted in passive mode, as against the *Bodhisattva*'s realization, which is active through and through to the point of melting away every factor of opposition in the ultimate crucible of non-dual knowledge. Thus, for him, the realization of the impermanence of the world and the eventual reintegration of that world hang together: the first, leading to Knowledge of the universal voidness, corresponds to Wisdom, and the second, symbolized by the *Bodhisattva*'s Compassion, corresponds to Method, this twofold realization being, as already mentioned, the "note" by which true Bodhisattvahood can be recognized. This disposes of any claims made on behalf of the man who attempts to integrate either himself or the world without at the same time fathoming their impermanence in more than just the superficial sense of a theoretical admission that everything must some day have an end. It was important to clear up this point before returning to the consideration of the *Bodhisattva* as he appears from the standpoint of humanity—that is to say, under the inevitable fragmentation into aspects that goes with any view short of his own all-embracing comprehension. From the point of view of individual beings, that aspect of his realization which strikes them most vividly is his Compassion, the fundamental character of which has, I hope, been made somewhat clearer as a result of the foregoing rather long-drawn out theoretical explanations.

It must be repeated that this "Cosmic Charity" (to borrow an expressive term belonging to the Islamic doctrine) is something essentially different from the ordinary human feelings of pity, hopelessly tangled, as they usually are, with self-pity; though it would also be true to say that whatever is genuine in human pity is a reflection, at the individual level, of the limitless compassion flowing out of the *Bodhisattva*'s heart, for which reason even that feeling is able to be taken for an adequate symbol of its universal prototype. It is also good to remember that perfect charity is not a quality opposable to justice, to order, or harmony in the widest sense, since its realization is an impossibility in default of an equally perfect impartiality or "non-attachment." Towards the suffering beings in the Round, continually drugged with the three poisons of Ignorance, Anger, and Desire-Attachment, the *Bodhisattva*, like the good physician that he is, will exercise his merciful office not with a view to a mere assuaging of symptoms that will leave the more deep-seated causes of the disease untouched; but in the manner most conducive to his patient's real recovery he will be prepared to employ every kind of "skilful means," which may at times partake of the severest character, and he will show himself under every appropriate aspect, from the gentlest to the most appalling, nor will he stop short at any ministration however pleasant or however rigorous until, as the saying goes, "the last blade of grass shall have attained Deliverance."

This lesson is clearly brought out in the iconographical representations of the various *Bodhisattvas* such as are displayed on the walls of every temple, for they are made to appear not merely under their benign or attractive forms but also in a guise grim and fearsome to behold. Even the All-Merciful Chenrezig himself, the supreme protector of Tibet and explicit type of a Buddha's mercy, displays awe-inspiring forms for the sake of sinners and their conversion. Similarly, the *Bodhisattva* of Wisdom, *Jampal*, can also appear as *Dorje-Jigched*, the Ever-subsisting Maker of Fear, chosen to be the chief tutelary of the Yellow-Hatted Order, this aspect being depicted as a most terrible apparition, many-headed and provided with countless limbs, clasped in the arms of his equally bloodthirsty Consort-Energy and dancing ecstatically upon the prostrate bodies of men and animals, whose ignorance makes them his victims. Those who are able to penetrate into the symbolism of this redoubtable double of the All-Wise One will also know that his dance is no other than the Round of Existence itself and his kingdom the very process of Becoming. If the presence of an individual form, with the restrictions that this implies, spells a proportionate measure of suffering for the being concerned, that suffering (which must of course be interpreted in the widest possible sense of the word) can itself be considered under either of the two complementary aspects of justice and mercy: under the first, because privation, such as is implied by the existence of a limit of any kind, produces suffering of its own accord, because, fundamentally, the suffering *is* the privation and not something added to it by way of retributive sanction or otherwise—though at a certain level of realization the latter symbolism is both theoretically legitimate as well as useful practically when considered from the point of view of the being's own spiritual development; under the second, because suffering, in so far as it leads men into self-questioning, is able to become a pointer towards the spiritual path, being thus indeed counted as the first of the Four Truths that together constitute the Buddha's call to a radical change of heart, to that *metanoesis* which is so inadequately rendered by the word "repentance" with its implicitly sentimental notion of regret. Viewed under such an aspect, therefore, suffering must be regarded first and foremost as part of the mechanism of a merciful providence, but for which there would be small hope of deliverance for anyone. It is not a question of trying to explain away the facts of suffering "optimistically" by resorting to the use of a euphemistic phraseology, but of showing the place that it occupies in relation to the aspect of divine Clemency, as well as its more obvious connection with the complementary aspect of Rigor.

The above considerations also have some bearing on a point that has often worried European students of Eastern doctrines, who fail to understand how Desire, whether admitted to play the leading part in the Round of Existence ascribed to it by Buddhism or not, can ever come to be extinguished in a being; since it is evident that it cannot be restrained by sheer will-power such as can only stop short at dealing with the action prompted by this or that desire, either by way of impulsion or repression, whereas the desire itself will have arisen, in the first place, out of the substratum of the being's unconsciousness where the will is inoperative; this, quite apart from the fact that the nature of Will itself is too closely related to that of Desire pure and simple to provide an entirely adequate instrument for its control. For the average Western mind, with its habit of concentrating all its attention on problems of moral casuistry—that is to say, on questions concerning the right or wrong use of will-power in respect of actions—the Buddha's teaching on the subject of desire and its cessation is apt to prove extremely puzzling.

Yet this side of the doctrine is not so abstruse as to defy at least a theoretical grasp of the principles underlying it. What is usually missed in the argument is the fact that, just as in the case of suffering, unsatisfied desire, though in one sense an evil in that it interposes a distraction between the being and its realization of unity, is also just (therefore a good) in so far as it genuinely registers a lack of something—the pertinent question is a lack of what? In fact all our separate desires are proportioned exactly to the measure of our privation of the One Essential, and if we treat different things as successively desirable or the reverse, this habit arises from a failure to understand that nothing whatsoever can be called desirable excepting only *The Desirable*, whence it is easy to see that the extinction of all desire and its fulfillment hang together, in exactly the same sense as death to self (the "self-denial" of the Gospels) and birth to Self spell one and the same thing. Our alternate loves and hates, from the most trivial to the most noble or ignoble are, one and all, an unconscious tribute laid by Ignorance at the feet of Knowledge, so that, in that sense, they once again are as much an expression of the Divine Mercy (because their attendant suffering is the factor that continually impels a being to seek a way of liberation) as they are an expression of the Divine Rigor through the privation registered by their very presence, which constitutes its own automatically operative sanction.

Let us return, however, to the consideration of the symbolism behind the great variety of forms described in the Tantric books or otherwise occurring in works of art of Tantric inspiration, a symbolism that, moreover, provides a most important *technical* resource for the practice of the various spiritual disciplines attached to the Tantric doctrines, both Hindu and Buddhist. Thus one is led to see that the kindlier aspects can, when necessary, be made to function as their own apparent opposites, by which means both the complementarism and the interpenetration of the aspects of mercy and severity are vividly brought out, only to be succeeded by the coincidence of those same two aspects in a "two-less" identity that dissolves all the force of their opposition. Again and again the symbolical relationships are reversed in an unending play of antithesis and identification, as beatific forms give way to fierce ones, the most repellent features of which are, however, in their turn found to symbolize characteristic attributes of the benign aspect and so on; until in the end, by dint of alternate manifestation, interchange, and dissolution of forms, Form itself loses its restrictive power over the mind of the devotee, leaving him henceforth free to contemplate through the eye of true Intelligence the non-duality of That which is to be known by those who find the way to carry their solitude ever with them, even in the world. So is one brought back once again to the *Bodhisattva*'s knowledge, whereby the immanent is seen to be ultimately indistinguishable from the transcendent, the phenomenal from the real, the world of forms from the Void Itself. In all this there is never a question of any "monistic" or "pantheistic" confusion—one is bound to mention this point in view of repeated attempts to foist these purely Western notions, not very old at that, upon Oriental thought, from a variety of motives—but of the realization of a unity which is called "two-less" from the very fact that in it all things are essentially "fused but not confused," to quote a phrase of Meister Eckhart.

This two-less Knowledge, possession of which constitutes the Sage, is as the warp to the entire weft of Tibetan tradition. One encounters it at every turn, now more explicit, now at once veiled and revealed by symbols, now faintly echoed in the thoughts and words of quite simple people, like a theme that unfolds itself in continual self-pursuit through an endless series of episodes and modulations, a fugue that will not modulate into its final close "so long as one insect or one blade of grass remains undelivered from the Round." The *Bodhisattva* provides the specific type of the spiritual life in Tibet, and it is in such terms that the idea of "sanctity" is always interpreted in all the lands where the lamaic tradition holds sway.

Space does not allow of anything like a comprehensive survey of the manifold applications to which the conception of Bodhisattvahood has given rise in all orders; nor would such an attempt work out profitably for the reader, since it could only result in leaving the essential idea snowed under a mass of indigestible, if separately interesting, detail; the important thing to grasp, however, is that it is this doctrine that gives its form to the idea of spirituality as conceived in all the Tibetan world, especially under its two principal aspects of Compassion and Skilful Means. Sufficient has been said concerning what the former is or is not for little room to be left for misunderstanding as to the nature of this characteristic trait of the *Bodhisattva;* while in regard to the latter one can only point out the fact that the saint, in Tibet, is regarded first and foremost as one endowed with "skill," as it were an "artist in spirituality," and only secondarily under the aspect of individual goodness. Here one sees a certain difference of point of view, as between the Buddhist and the ordinary Christian picture of sainthood, bound up with the degrees of emphasis respectively given to ethical and intellectual values. Not that one wishes to suggest the existence of a fundamental incompatibility between the two conceptions; all that need be pointed out is that in the Buddhist tradition the practice of those portions of "the Eightfold Path" that relate to action and moral behavior in general, though considered indispensable just as in the case of the sister tradition, are on the whole taken for granted when speaking of the saints, the chief attention in their case being drawn to the purely intellectual virtue of Perfect Contemplation, which forms the climax of the eightfold catalogue; whereas in the case of Christianity, though its teaching on the supremacy of Contemplation over Action does not differ in principle from that of the Oriental traditions, there has been a certain tendency, much increased in modern times through the intrusion of "humanism" (itself an anti-Christian movement), to overstress individual and especially social considerations. Moreover, abuses apart, such a tendency always goes to a certain extent with the "religious" as compared with the purely metaphysical point of view, influencing not only popular conceptions but also many perfectly orthodox formulations of the doctrine itself.

Two examples will have to suffice as illustrations of the workings of the *Bodhisattva* idea in the spiritual life of the Tibetans. The one applies to the people at large, though admittedly at many different degrees of comprehension; the other to those who have proceeded a considerable way in the direction of realization, or at least whose aspirations and efforts are definitely set in that direction. The first example is taken from the widespread practice of invocation, usually on a rosary, of the *Mani* formula [*Om Mani Padme Hum*], which itself embodies a traditional communication the origin of which goes back to the *Bodhisattva* Chenrezig, the Patron of Tibet, for whose influence the person of the Dalai Lama himself serves as a focus.

When a person is about to begin saying his rosary he often preludes his reciting of the actual formula by a short dedicatory verse in honor of Chenrezig, its originator, addressed to him under his alternative name of the All-Compassionate. After this follows the repetition of the *Mani*, for a longer or shorter time, with more or less concentration as the case may be. When these devotions are finished, the invoking person (who incidentally will have been the recipient of an initiation authorizing him to use this particular mantric support) concludes with another short verse, the gist of which is as follows: "By the merit of this (invocation) to (my) self having accrued (i.e. by my having realized) the power of Chenrezig, may beings without a single exception be established in the land of the Norm (that is to say, may they attain the supreme realization)." However attentively or carelessly these thoughts may be uttered, they contain an explicit as well as implicit reference to the "*Bodhisattva*'s vow" not to enter *Nirvana* before all beings have been delivered from the Round and its suffering; the important thing to note in the present instance is that this formula postulates a point of view that does not stop short at a personal deliverance, like that for which the *Pratyeka* Buddhas are constantly being reproached, since is goes as far as actually to envisage a redescent into the world with a view to its eventual reintegration in the divine Non-Duality. That it should be possible for a conception of this order to be attached to a spiritual practice as popular as the *Mani* has become in Tibet is extremely significant.

Naturally too much must not be read into the above statement; the fact is that Tibetans, like other people, do often dream of spending more or less prolonged periods of carefree enjoyment in other and happier worlds, such as the Western Paradise presided over by Chenrezig and his teacher the Buddha Amitabha. The simple-minded likewise indulge in visions of a happy rebirth in a literal sense here on earth, forgetful as they are of the oft-quoted phrase declaring "the individual(ity) to be perishable, and devoid of true self(hood)"; yet the fact remains that even in the case of a method so generally practiced the expressed intention goes far beyond the individual order, and indeed to the point of embracing the totality of beings and worlds in a single universal synthesis in which individual distinctions find no place; so that it can justly be claimed that the *metaphysical horizon* against which the invocation is to be carried out is literally limitless by its own showing and that no concession of principle has actually been made by way of encouraging self-interest of a limiting kind.

All that now remains is to speak of those who occupy the other end of the intellectual scale from the many simple people who, in comparative unconsciousness, give utterance to the *Bodhisattva*'s awe-inspiring vow as they finish telling the beads of their rosaries: we are thinking of those persons (and they are by no means rare in Tibet) who have felt the call to self-dedication in the spiritual life so imperatively as to be unable to divide their energies any further, as between the pursuit of the supreme knowledge and ordinary private interests of whatever order. These people commonly go under the name of *naldjorpa*s meaning "obtainers of tranquility," because they have cut themselves free of the multi-directional pulls of a life lived more or less profanely, leaving themselves in a state of "one-pointed" contemplation that no distraction coming from outside is henceforward able to disturb. This uncompromising expression of the urge towards spiritual wholeness will provide us with our second example, which can, however, only be described in the most general terms, since one who has not himself realized, in a high degree, the descent of the *Bodhisattva* into his own heart is unfitted to offer any really profound comment on the subject; and the same applies to his hearers, who unless they are able, by resorting to the appropriate means, to approach a similar realization, will be equally incapable of understanding the deeper significance of the doctrine offered to them. All that one can be concerned with here is not so much the nature of the *naldjorpa* experience in itself—about which one is not in a position to pronounce—as the part which that experience, whatever may be its nature, plays in the Tibetan tradition as a whole and what kind of influence it represents in regard to giving its specific form to the idea of sainthood lived according to the *Bodhisattva* pattern.

One reservation must be made, however; not everyone loosely described as a *naldjorpa* is so effectively, and due allowance must be made for some who, though possibly qualified to embrace the life of spiritual abandonment, have for one reason or another strayed from the strait and narrow path, whether by yielding to the lure of unusual psychic and physical powers (such as often develop incidentally as a result of following certain disciplines) or from any other cause equally irrelevant.[5] These people, though they may continue to style themselves *naldjorpas* and be accepted as such, have really arrived at an intellectual dead-end, or even worse in some cases. Nevertheless the real thing not only exists, but it is that element which, above all, lends color to the whole spiritual life in Tibet, constituting, as it were, the *axis* in relation to which all else must be situated and ultimately judged.

The genuine *naldjorpa*, in principle as in practice, stands outside the pale of society, so much so that if he has been a monk he usually casts off the monastic habit (and the rule it represents) as a sign that he has cut adrift from all that goes with organized existence, letting "the wind that bloweth where it listeth" carry him in whatever direction it will. Often he is to be discovered among the hermits dwelling on the edge of the great glaciers, or else wandering along one of the many tracks that lead hither and thither across the plateau, and even sometimes, as in the case of the late Abbot of Lachhen for instance, staying quietly not far from human dwellings, in fairly close touch with social life though no longer involved in it. Or again, if he be so minded, there is nothing to prevent him from seemingly participating in outward activities—activities which other men may interpret as they please, but which, for him, will ever remain an expression of his own untroubled solitude of spirit.

[5] Professed spiritual seekers of European origin seem especially prone to develop an unhealthy interest in extraordinary phenomena of all kinds, and that despite the calculated warnings of so many of the great teachers of both East and West. An innate curiosity as well as an experimentalism that is constantly being stimulated by modern "scientific" training and propaganda is largely responsible for this tendency, which is only too apt to turn into an insatiable craving, as a result of which the person concerned, when he does not suffer serious psychological perversion, at least becomes fatally imprisoned in the world of appearances and in an egocentric enjoyment of marvels, real or supposed.

Most, if not all, of these contemplatives are initiates of some particular spiritual line of which a number exist, each having certain methods peculiar to itself such as will entail the presence of special qualifications in those who aspire to practice them. Through an unbroken traditional succession from Master to pupil, each such line may be said to constitute a separate current of spiritual influence, a channel that after issuing from the same parent stream will by and by go to lose itself, with all the others, in the uncharted ocean, large as the *Bodhisattva*'s compassion, which is called Knowledge of the Voidness.

One misconception must be avoided, however, since it is likely to arise with certain habits of mind and since it also makes a peculiarly subtle appeal: the *Bodhisattva*'s vow must never be taken to imply that the saving of mankind, or even of all creation, should become *an end in itself* for the apprentice in spirituality. Nothing short of the naked Truth, shorn of all contingencies and restrictions, merits to be called Desirable, its pursuit alone can be called Activity unqualified; only one who has been stripped of his attachments to everything except the Truth without a rival or associate can hope to attain that Truth. Having attained it, he does, in fact, become qualified to save the world, but should he at any stage yield to the supremely diabolical temptation (the one offered by Satan to Christ upon the high mountain) of making the world's salvation into his overriding aim, then he must pay the price of his altruistic idolatry and remain irremediably chained to the world and its otherness. A hair separates the two positions, and one can only recall in this connection the remark quoted earlier to the effect that saving the world is the *Bodhisattva*'s sport. The danger of which we have been speaking represents the ultimate temptation of the saint, being both the hardest to detect and the most fatal if yielded to. This warning is, moreover, operative not only at the highest level but even at inferior levels too; to causes of this order must be ascribed the non-success that in so large a measure attends the well-meaning and often strenuous efforts of humanitarian-minded people the world over, for it is their very obsession with the cause of "others" that spells eventual defeat, in spite of their own obvious sincerity.

Tibetans, on the other hand, even the comparatively ignorant among them, seem to have retained some grasp of the principle at work; they look upon the *naldjorpas* as being first and foremost protectors of humanity, without whose "actionless activity" the ship of mankind would irremediably founder. Unentangled, as they are, in either duties or rights, whether of the family or the state or of a professional kind, it is their very impartiality towards worldly affairs that constitutes their power, one in which other men who are still, to a greater or lesser extent, "involved" in various ties of an individual and social kind can also participate, if indirectly. For this reason, it would appear not so much wicked as *suicidal* if society were, on any plea, to try to place restrictions in the way of those who wish to join the ranks of this spiritual elite, even while frankly admitting that those ranks will contain a certain proportion of self-deceived persons and even some who might be tempted to make capital out of the reverence in which they are held by the people at large.

Moreover, no one would ever think of impertinently questioning the motives or methods of anyone so engaged. Every Tibetan understands that sainthood, at any degree of realization, will imply a different set of values from those that govern the judgment of the ordinary man: what the latter regards as important and obvious will often, to the spiritually minded, seem trivial and, in any case, highly contestable. Indeed, the last statement itself betrays an inaccuracy: for one who *knows*, by the direct insight born of realization, the kind of questions that trouble the ignorant do not even arise, nor do they enter into the realm of choice or discussion. True intelligence flies straight to the mark; it requires no tortuous marshalling of pros and cons to bolster up its conclusions. Nothing would seem more illogical to the Tibetan mind than to expect the same kind of judgment from a Knower, even from one who is so to a qualified extent only, and an ignoramus, which, in the deepest sense, is the state of the majority of mankind, including most of those whom the world looks on as learned or strong or efficient; for it is they, and those who admire and follow them, who truly are the unpractical visionaries, as compared with the *naldjorpa*, who is the unshakable realist because like Mary in the Gospel he "hath chosen that good part."

It must not be thought that this recognition of the freedom to be earned through following the spiritual path will imply any kind of antinomianism, though some may have been tempted to think so. A realization that places one in a state of complete harmony with the source of all law can absolve one from its manifold applications but cannot oppose one to it in principle; moreover it is knowledge that provides a valid sanction for all applications on the legal plane (one is referring to law in the very widest sense of the word), and not vice versa. At the very highest level, therefore, the realization that "His service is perfect freedom," from being merely theoretical becomes effective, and one who attains this state can rightly claim that he is no longer "under the law," but is, as the Hindus would say, henceforth "beyond caste."

The foregoing observation, however, gives rise to another, no less important in its way, since it affects those people—and they are not a few—who have come to yearn for a life of non-attachment, but who think that they will attain it by a premature and purely external casting-off of the bonds of form, whether religious or other. This state of mind on the part of the would-be "mystic"[6] is frequently evidenced by the habit of ceaselessly tilting at "orthodoxy," professedly in the name of "the spirit" as against "the letter," and by an instinctive fear and suspicion of whatever pertains to the formal order in general. Into this attitude of mind many different elements have entered—individualism, sentimentalism, and humanistic influences generally. What these people miss is the fact that there are two ways of being outside form, the one supra-formal, because form has been transcended, the other infra-formal, because its possibilities as a "support" of realization at a certain level have been neglected. The one gives access to the formless Truth, seat of freedom and universality, the other represents the most abysmal kind of ignorance, compared with which the formal attachments affecting even the most narrow-minded person must be looked upon as a state of comparative liberty. Form, to be transcended, must first of all be realized and thus integrated; it is impossible to *skip* the experience of form, and the wish to do so, in the name of personal liberty, merely betrays a futile kind of self-conceit. This temptation is especially strong among Western advocates of a return to spiritual values at the present moment, by reason of the individualistic turn of their minds, fostered in the course of their education. On this whole subject of form a great confusion of thought has occurred, which has not spared even those who appear, in other respects, to be highly gifted. What so many people refuse to face is the fact that in a time of intellectual confusion, form, "the letter," provides almost the last thread connecting fallen man with the sources of his spirituality, so that it would be almost true to say that today it matters more to

[6] It should be noted that any thoughtless use of the term "mystic" and its derivatives has here been carefully avoided. Whatever meaning this word may originally have borne, later and, more especially, recent usage has so confused the issue as to make it difficult of application outside the sphere where it belongs historically, namely that of Christian theology coupled with certain modes of realization attached to the same.

observe forms correctly than to be "good"—a hard saying, perhaps, and a paradox, but one worth pondering over.

In a country like Tibet—or indeed anywhere in the wide world where the continuity of tradition has hitherto remained substantially unbroken—an intending *naldjorpa* will necessarily set out on his journey from a point situated somewhere in a traditional whole all the constituent forms of which will themselves already have been molded or *informed* under the influence of the selfsame idea that he is in process of realizing integrally and beyond every limitation of form. For this is in fact what tradition means—it is time people were reminded of it—namely, an effective communication of principles of more-than-human origin, whether indirectly and at several removes, through use of forms that will have arisen by applying those principles to contingent needs, or else immediately, after an "exhausting" of whatever makes for formal restriction of any kind, including the human individuality itself.

Thus the true *naldjorpa* (after whom the aspirant is similarly named only in anticipation and, as it were, by courtesy) is both he who realizes fully and effectively what others at best learn only partially through the various theoretical formulations of the doctrine as well as through their own participation in the traditional institutions generally, and also he who, through a similar realization, himself becomes at one with the eternal fountainhead of tradition; for him his approach to the goal is rather in the nature of a homecoming, a recollection, than a fresh acquisition in the spiritual field; while, on its side, the tradition, as revealed through the line of realized sages and their successors, is but a redescent, spontaneously undertaken, into that same world of men whence the *naldjorpa* had originally started out on his way, in the days of his comparative ignorance. The intimate interconnection between the two functions is not difficult to perceive.

Nor is it difficult to recognize the prototype of which this picture is a tracing: the twofold course of outgoing and return, which true insight knows as "not-two," the laborious ascent towards the highest eminences of awareness and the "compassionate" redescent into the valley, is not all this but another version of the oft-told tale of Bodhisattvahood presently renewed, whereby it is also made plain that Tradition is itself an aspect of that providential redescent into the Round, one of the "skilful means" wherewith the *Bodhisattva* "playfully" works for creatures? A traditionless existence, whether for a single individual or a whole group, is one in which the presence of the

Bodhisattva passes unnoticed, in which the *naldjorpa* is without honor, in which mankind, refusing to listen to any talk of self-abandonment, is abandoned to its own devices, as the very name of "humanism" so plainly confesses. This is the first of the lessons to be learned by a sojourn in the places where tradition still prevails, where it has not yet been entirely forgotten that without the guidance, both direct and indirect, of those who have themselves taken possession of the summit, thus qualifying themselves, if need be, for a retracing of the way for the benefit of all the creatures whom "otherhood" still holds under its spell, the supreme peak will remain for ever unclimable.

One can but repeat it: a personal reintegration in an authentically traditional form, as well as a "normal" participation in its attendant institutions, is an indispensable prelude to any adventure into the path of non-formal knowledge; by this means the individuality is conditioned, "tamed" as the Tibetans would say, in preparation for the supreme task that lies ahead. To those aspirants after the spiritual life who, in a purely negative sense at least, have come to reject the modern world and its profanity, but who, as far as any positive action is concerned, waver on the threshold perplexed by doubts as to the next step to be taken—to such as these the only advice that can be offered is the traditional one: namely, that they should first put themselves to rights as regards the formal order (wherein they are situated in virtue of the fact of being individuals at all) by regular adherence to a tradition; after which they should make use to the fullest extent of "the means of Grace" provided within the framework of that tradition, all the while testing their own success or otherwise by reference to its theory—that is, to its canonical formulations. Lastly, if and when a call to the beyond becomes irresistible, they should place themselves under the guidance of a spiritual master, the *guru* or "Root Lama" who is destined to introduce them into the path followed through the ages by the blessed company of the "thus-gone" (*Tathagatas*)—call them Buddhas, Yogis, Sufis, or what you will.

But one must beware of unauthorized teachers and bogus initiations; for the modern world has produced a heavy crop of self-appointed guides, mostly men who toy with the equivocal term "mysticism"; here again traditional "orthodoxy" is about the only available touchstone and safeguard, a case of form acting as a protective envelope for the formless, by lending to it its body. But protection always will be purchased at the price of restriction—this rule holds good in all orders, the social order included—hence the danger of "idolatry," which precisely consists in ascribing to any form in itself the unqualified character that belongs alone to the integral and formless Truth. Anywhere short of the goal, the way of realization will imply a certain polar balance between these two conceptions, the provisional and "symbolical" validity of forms and the untrammeled freedom of voidness. The Way has been fittingly called "narrow" and compared to walking along a razor's edge: by describing His tradition as the Middle Way the Buddha was expressing a similar idea. Bodhisattvahood is the virtue of being freed from both horns of the perennial dilemma, Form *versus* Void, by realizing them alike in their common and essential twolessness. Likewise the *Bodhisattva*'s compassionate mission for the sake of dwellers in the land of Becoming is itself the free expression of that same non-dual Knowledge that is, for him, the source of his redemptive power as well as his own intrinsic qualification.

TAOISM*

Huston Smith

No civilization is monochrome. In China the classical tones of Confucianism have been balanced not only by the spiritual shades of Buddhism but also by the romantic hues of Taoism.

The Old Master

According to tradition Taoism (pronounced Dowism) originated with a man named Lao Tzu, said to have been born about 604 B.C. He is a shadowy figure. We know nothing for certain about him and scholars wonder if there ever was such a man. We do not even know his name, for Lao Tzu—which can be translated "the Old Boy," "the Old Fellow," or "the Grand Old Master"—is obviously a title of endearment and respect. All we really have is a mosaic of legends. Some of these are fantastic; that he was conceived by a shooting star, carried in his mother's womb for eighty-two years, and born already a wise old man with white hair. Other parts of the story do not tax our credulity: that he kept the archives in his native western state, and that around this occupation he wove a simple and unassertive life. Inferences concerning his personality derive almost entirely from a single slim volume that is attributed to him. From this some conclude that he was probably a solitary recluse who was absorbed in occult meditations; others picture him as down to earth—a genial neighbor with a lively sense of humor.

The only purportedly contemporary portrait, reported by China's first historian, Ssu-ma Ch'ien, speaks only of the enigmatic impression he left—the sense that he possessed depths of understanding that defied ready comprehension. According to this account Confucius, intrigued by what he had heard of Lao Tzu, once visited him. His description suggests that the strange man baffled him while leaving him respectful. "I know a bird can fly; I know a fish can swim; I know animals can run. Creatures that run can be caught in nets; those that swim can be

* Editor's Note: Chapter 5 of *The World's Religions.*

caught in wicker traps; those that fly can be hit by arrows. But the dragon is beyond my knowledge; it ascends into heaven on the clouds and the wind. Today I have seen Lao Tzu, and he is like the dragon!"

The traditional portrait concludes with the report that Lao Tzu, saddened by his people's disinclination to cultivate the natural goodness he advocated and seeking greater personal solitude for his closing years, climbed on a water buffalo and rode westward toward what is now Tibet. At the Hankao Pass a gatekeeper, sensing the unusual character of the truant, tried to persuade him to turn back. Failing this, he asked if the "Old Boy" would not at least leave a record of his beliefs to the civilization he was abandoning. This Lao Tzu consented to do. He retired for three days and returned with a slim volume of five thousand characters titled *Tao Te Ching*, or *The Way and Its Power*. A testament to humanity's at-home-ness in the universe, it can be read in half an hour or a lifetime, and remains to this day the basic text of Taoist thought.

What a curious portrait this is for the supposed founder of a religion. The Old Boy didn't preach. He didn't organize or promote. He wrote a few pages on request, rode off on a water buffalo, and that was it as far as he was concerned. How unlike the Buddha, who trudged the dusty roads of India for forty-five years to make his point. How unlike Confucius, who pestered dukes and princes, trying to gain an administrative foothold (or at least a hearing) for his ideas. Here was a man so little concerned with the success of his surmises, to say nothing of fame and fortune, that he didn't even stay around to answer questions. And yet, whether the story of his life is fact or fiction, it is so true to Taoist attitudes that it will remain a part of Taoism forever. Emperors would claim this shadowy figure as their ancestor, and even scholars—though they do not see the *Tao Te Ching* as having been written by a single hand and do not think it attained the form in which we have it until the second half of the third century B.C.—concede that its ideas cohere to the point where we must posit the existence of *someone* under whose influence the book took shape, and have no objection to our calling him Lao Tzu.

The Three Meanings of Tao

On opening Taoism's bible, the *Tao Te Ching*, we sense at once that everything revolves around the pivotal concept of *Tao* itself. Literally, this word means path, or way. There are three senses, however, in which this "way" can be understood.

First, *Tao* is the *way of ultimate reality*. This *Tao* cannot be perceived or even clearly conceived, for it is too vast for human rationality to fathom. The *Tao Te Ching* announces in its opening line that words are not equal to it: "The *Tao* that can be spoken is not the true *Tao*." Nevertheless, this ineffable and transcendent *Tao* is the ground of all that follows. Above all, behind all, beneath all is the Womb from which all life springs and to which it returns. Awed by the thought of it, the author/editor of the *Tao Te Ching* bursts recurrently into praise, for this primal *Tao* confronts him with life's basic mystery, the mystery of all mysteries. "How clear it is! How quiet it is! It must be something eternally existing!" "Of all great things, surely *Tao* is the greatest." But its ineffability cannot be denied, so we are taunted, time and again, by Taoism's teasing epigram: "Those who know don't say. Those who say don't know."[1]

Though *Tao* is ultimately transcendent, it is also immanent. In this secondary sense it is the *way of the universe*, the norm, the rhythm, the driving power in all nature, the ordering principle behind all life. Behind, but also in the midst of all life, for when *Tao* enters this second mode it "assumes flesh" and informs all things. It "adapts its vivid essence, clarifies its manifold fullness, subdues its resplendent luster, and assumes the likeness of dust." Basically spirit rather than matter, it cannot be exhausted; the more it is drawn upon, the more it flows, for it is "that fountain ever on," as Plotinus said of his counterpart to the *Tao*, his One. There are about it marks of inevitability, for when autumn comes "no leaf is spared because of its beauty, no flower because of its fragrance." Yet, ultimately, it is benign. Graceful instead of abrupt, flowing rather than hesitant, it is infinitely generous. Giving life to all things, it may be called "the Mother of the World." As nature's agent *Tao* in this second form resembles Bergson's *elan vital*, as nature's orderer, it resembles the *lex aeterna* of the Classical West, the eternal law that structures the world. Charles Darwin's colleague, George Romanes, could have been speaking of it when he referred to "the integrating principle of the whole—the Spirit, as it were, of the universe—instinct without contrivance, which flows with purpose."

In its third sense *Tao* refers to *the way of human life* when it meshes with the *Tao* of the universe as just described. Most of what follows in this chapter will detail what the Taoists propose that this way of life

[1] *Tao Te Ching*, chapter 56.

should be. First, however, it is necessary to point out that there have been in China not one but three Taoisms.

Three Approaches to Power and the Taoisms That Follow

Tao Te Ching, the title of Taoism's basic text, has been translated *The Way and Its Power.* We have seen that the first of these substantive terms, the Way, can be taken in three senses. Now we must add that this is also true of the second substantive term, power. Corresponding to the three ways *te* or power can be approached, there have arisen in China three species of Taoism so dissimilar that initially they seem to have no more in common than homonyms, like blew/blue or sun/son, that sound alike but have different meanings. We shall find that this is not the case, but first the three species must be distinguished. Two have standard designations, Philosophical Taoism and Religious Taoism respectively; and because many more people were involved with Religious Taoism it is often called Popular Taoism as well. The third school (which will come second in our order of presentation) is too heterogeneous to have acquired a single title. Its population constitutes an identifiable cluster, however, by virtue of sharing a common objective. All were engaged in vitalizing programs that were intended to facilitate *Tao*'s power, its *te*, as it flows through human beings.

Efficient Power: Philosophical Taoism

Unlike Religious Taoism, which became a full-fledged church, Philosophical Taoism and the "vitalizing Taoisms," as we shall clumsily refer to the second group, remain relatively unorganized. Philosophical Taoism is reflective and the vitalizing programs active, but no more than the Transcendentalist movement in New England or contemporary physical fitness programs are they formally institutionalized.

They share a second similarity in that both are self-help programs. Teachers are involved, but they are better thought of as coaches who train their students—guiding them in what they should understand, in the case of Philosophical Taoism, and in what they should do in the vitalizing regimens. In decided contrast to Religious Taoists, those in these first two camps work primarily on themselves.

The differences between them have to do with their respective stances toward the power of the *Tao* on which life feeds. To put the difference pointedly, Philosophical Taoists try to conserve their *te* by expending it efficiently, whereas "vitality" Taoists work to increase its available supply.

Because Philosophical Taoism is essentially an attitude toward life, it is the most "exportable" Taoism of the three, the one that has the most to say to the world at large, and as such will receive the longest treatment—not until the second half of this chapter, however. Here we shall only identify it to place it in its logical position before proceeding with its two sister Taoisms.

Called School Taoism in China, Philosophical Taoism is associated with the names of Lao Tzu, Chuang Tzu, and the *Tao Te Ching*. We can connect it with power by remembering that philosophy seeks knowledge and, as Bacon told the world pointedly, "knowledge is power"; to know how to repair a car is to have power over it. Obviously, the Taoists' eyes were not on machines; it was life that they wanted to repair. Knowledge that empowers life we call wisdom; and to live wisely, the Taoist philosophers argued, is to live in a way that conserves life's vitality by not expending it in useless, draining ways, the chief of which are friction and conflict. We shall examine Lao Tzu and Chuang Tzu's prescriptions for avoiding such dissipations in the second half of this chapter, but we can anticipate a single point here. Their recommendations revolve around the concept of *wu wei*, a phrase that translates literally as inaction but in Taoism means pure effectiveness. Action in the mode of *wu wei* is action in which friction—in interpersonal relationships, in intra-psychic conflict, and in relation to nature—is reduced to the minimum. We turn now to the vitality cults as our second species of Taoism.

Augmented Power: Taoist Hygiene and Yoga

Taoist "adepts"—as we shall call the practitioners of this second kind of Taoism because all were engaged in training programs of some sort, many of them demanding—were not willing to settle for the philosophers' goal of managing their allotments of the *Tao* efficiently. They wanted to go beyond conserving to increasing the quota of the Tao they had to work with. In accounting terms we can say that if Philosophical Taoists worked at increasing net profits by cutting costs (reducing needless energy expenditures), Taoist adepts wanted to increase gross income.

The word *ch'i* cries out to be recognized as the rightful entry to this second school, for though it literally means breath, it actually means vital energy. The Taoists used it to refer to the power of the *Tao* that they experienced coursing through them—or not coursing because it was blocked—and their main object was to further its flow. *Ch'i* fascinated these Taoists. Blake registered their feelings precisely when he exclaimed, "Energy is delight," for energy is the life force and the Taoists loved life. To be alive is good; to be more alive is better; to be always alive is best, hence the Taoist immortality cults. To accomplish their end of maximizing *ch'i*, these Taoists worked with three things: matter, movement, and their minds.

Respecting *matter*, they tried eating things—virtually everything, it would seem—to see if *ch'i* could be augmented nutritionally. In the course of this experimentation, they developed a remarkable pharmacopia of medicinal herbs,[2] but in a way this was incidental. What they really wanted was not cure but increase—increase and extension of the life force, the ultimate guarantor of which would be the much-sought elixir of life that would insure physical immortality.[3] Sexual experiments were also performed. In one such experiment men hypothesized that if they retained their semen during intercourse by pressing the ball of the thumb against the base of the penis at the moment of ejaculation, thereby diverting the semen into their own bodies,[4] they would absorb the *yin* of their female partners without dissipating their own *yang* energy. Breathing exercises were also developed. Working with air, the subtlest form of matter, they sought to draw *ch'i* from the atmosphere.

These efforts to extract *ch'i* from matter in its solid, liquid, and gaseous forms were supplemented by programs of bodily *movement* such as *t'ai chi chuan,* which gathers calisthenics, dance, meditation, *yin/yang* philosophy, and martial art into a synthesis that in this case was designed to draw *ch'i* from the cosmos and dislodge blocks to its internal flow. This last was the object of acupuncture as well.

[2] "Any list of the drugs used by the ancient Chinese doctors, for many of which there is ample historical if not laboratory evidence of efficacy, leaves the entire Western world of medicine open to accusations of negligence and haughtiness" (Richard Selzer, *Mortal Lessons: Notes on the Art of Surgery* [New York: Simon & Schuster, 1987], p. 116).

[3] Immortality had both crude and subtle readings in Taoism. Michael Saso writes that "a Taoist is by definition a man who seeks immortality in the present life," but he goes on to add that for many this immortality "is not so much a longevity whereby man does not die but a state wherein he does not descend to the punishments of a fiery underworld after death" (*Taoism and the Rite of Cosmic Renewal* [Pullman: Washington State University Press, 1989], p. 3).

[4] In actuality the semen then entered the bladder, where it was expelled with the urine, but the Chinese did not know this.

Finally, turning to the *mind* itself, contemplatives, many of them hermits, developed Taoist meditation. This practice involved shutting out distractions and emptying the mind to the point where the power of the *Tao* might bypass bodily filters and enter the self directly.

This third way of increasing *ch'i* is more abstract than the others, so more needs to be said about it. The quickest gateway to understanding meditational Taoism is via Hindu *raja yoga*, the way to God through psychophysical exercises. Whether or not China borrowed from India on this score, the physical postures and concentration techniques of Taoist meditation are so reminiscent of *raja yoga* that sinologists import the Sanskrit term and call it Taoist *yoga*. Still, the Chinese gave their *yoga* a distinctive twist. Their ubiquitous social concern led them to press the possibility that the *ch'i* that *yogis* accumulated through meditation could be transmitted psychically to the community to enhance its vitality and harmonize its affairs. Side by side with the Confucianists, who were working on the socializing *te* of moral example and ritualized etiquette, Taoist *yogis* sought to harness the *Tao* directly, drawing it first into their own heart-minds and then beaming it to others. *Yogis* who managed this feat would for the most part be unnoticed, but their life-giving enterprise did more for the community than the works of other benefactors.

We border on Philosophical Taoism here because animating this yogic Taoism was a dawning fascination in China with the inner as opposed to the outer self. Children do not separate these two sides of their being, and neither did early peoples. Yogic or meditational Taoism arose as the advancing self-consciousness of the Chinese brought subjective experience to full view. Novel, momentous, exciting, this world of the inner self invited exploration. So enthralling did it appear to its early explorers that matter suffered by comparison; it was mere shell and accretion. Still, the inner world housed a problem. Successive deposits of worry and distraction so silted the soul that their deposits had to be removed until "the self as it was meant to be" could surface. Pure consciousness would then appear, and the individual would see not merely "things perceived" but "that by which we perceive."

To arrive at this inwardness it was necessary to reverse all self-seeking and cultivate perfect cleanliness of thought and body. Pure spirit can be known only in a life that is "garnished and swept." Only where all is clean will it reveal itself; therefore "put self aside." Perturbing emotions must likewise be quelled. Ruffling the surface of the mind, they prevent introspection from seeing past them to the springs of consciousness beneath. (The proximity to Philosophical Taoism is becoming strong.) Desire and revulsion, grief and joy, delight and annoyance—each must subside if the mind is to return to its original purity, for in the end only peace and stillness are good for it. Let anxiety be dispelled and harmony between the mind and its cosmic source will come unsought.

> It is close at hand, stands indeed at our very side; yet is intangible, a thing that by reaching for cannot be got. Remote it seems as the furthest limit of the Infinite. Yet it is not far off, every day we use its power. For the Way of the Vital Spirit fills our whole frames, yet man cannot keep track of it. It goes, yet has not departed. It comes, yet is not here. It is muted, makes no note that can be heard, yet of a sudden we find that it is there in the mind. It is dim and dark, showing no outward form, yet in a great stream it flowed into us at our birth.[5]

Selflessness, cleanliness, and emotional calm are the preliminaries to arriving at full self-knowledge, but they must be climaxed by deep meditation. "Bide in silence, and the radiance of the spirit shall come in and make its home." For this to happen all outward impressions must be stilled and the senses withdrawn to a completely interior point of focus. Postures paralleling the Indian *asana*s were recommended, and the breath must be similarly controlled; it must be as soft and light as that of an infant, or even an embryo in the womb. The result will be a condition of alert waiting known as "sitting with a blank mind."

And when the realization arrives, what then? With it come truth, joy, and power. The climactic insight of meditational Taoism came with the impact of finality, everything at last having fallen into place. The condition could not be described as merely pleasurable. The direct perception of the source of one's awareness as "serene and immovable, like a monarch on a throne," brought joy unlike any hitherto known. The social utility of the condition, however, lay in the extraordinary power it provided over people and things, a power in fact which "could shift Heaven and Earth." "To the mind that is still, the whole universe surrenders." We have spoken of India in connection with this psychic power, but St. John of the Cross offers an identical promise: "Without labor you shall subject the peoples, and things shall be subject to you."

[5] Quoted by Arthur Waley, *The Way and Its Power*, 1934, reprint (London: Allen & Unwin, 1958), pp. 48-49.

Without lifting a finger overtly, a ruler who was adept in "stillness" could order a whole people with his mystical-moral power. A ruler who is desireless himself and has this much psychic power automatically turns his subjects from their unruly desires. He rules without even being known to rule.

> The sage relies on actionless activity;
> Puts himself in the background; but is always to the fore.
> Remains outside; but is always there.
> Is it not just because he does not strive for any personal end
> That all his personal ends are fulfilled?[6]

The Taoist *yogis* recognized that they could not hope for much understanding from the masses, and they made no attempt to publicize their position. When they did write their words tended to be veiled and cryptic, open to one interpretation by initiates and another by the general public. Part of the reason they wrote this way doubtless stemmed from their sensitivity to the lampooning that mysticism attracts from the uncongenial. We find even Chuang Tzu burlesquing their breathing exercises, reporting that these people "expel the used air with great energy and inhale the fresh air. Like bears, they climb trees in order to breathe with greater ease." Mencius joined in the fun. He likened those who sought psychic short-cuts to social harmony to impatient farmers who tug gently on their crops each night to speed their growth. Despite such satire Taoist *yoga* had an appreciable core of practitioners. Some sinologists consider it the basic perspective from which the *Tao Te Ching* was written. If this is true it is a testament to the veiled language of the book, for it is usually read in the philosophical way we shall come to. Before we turn to that way, however, we must introduce the third major branch of Taoism, which is religious.

Vicarious Power: Religious Taoism

Philosophical Taoism sought to manage life's normal quotient of the *Tao* efficiently, and energizing Taoism sought to boost its base supply, but something was lacking. Reflection and health programs take time, and the average Chinese lacked that commodity. Yet they too needed help; there were epidemics to be checked, marauding ghosts

[6] *Tao Te Ching*, chapters 2 and 7, Arthur Waley's translation.

to be reckoned with, and rains to be induced or stopped as occasions demanded. Taoists responded to such problems. The measures they devised paralleled many of the doings of freelance soothsayers, psychics, shamans, and faith healers who came by their powers naturally and constituted the unchanging landscape of Chinese folk religion. Religious Taoism institutionalized such activities. Influenced by Buddhism, which entered China around the time of Christ, the Taoist church—in Chinese the *Tao Chiao*, "Church Taoism" or "Taoist Teachings" took shape in the second century A.D. It was anchored in a pantheon whose three originating deities included Lao Tzu. From these divinities sacred texts derived, which (by virtue of their divinely revealed origin) were accepted as true without reservation. The line of "papal" succession in the Taoist church continues down to the present in Taiwan.

Popular, Religious Taoism is a murky affair. Much of it looks—from the outside, we must always keep in mind—like crude superstition; but we must remember that we have little idea what energy is, how it proceeds, or the means by which (and extent to which) it can be augmented. We do know that faith healing can import or release energies, as does faith itself, including faith in oneself. Placebos likewise have effects. When we add to these the energies that magnetic personalities, rabble-rousers, and even pep rallies can generate, to say nothing of mysterious reserves that hypnotists tap into, concerning which we haven't an explanatory clue—if all this is borne in mind, it may temper our superciliousness and allow us to give Religious Taoism a fair hearing. In any case its intent is clear. "The Taoist priesthood made cosmic life-power available for ordinary villagers."[7]

The texts of this school are crammed with descriptions of rituals that, if exactly performed, have magical effects, and the word *magic* here holds the key to sacerdotal, specifically religious, Taoism. The word must be freed, however, from the conventional meaning that has encrusted it. In its modern meaning, magic is trickery; it refers to performers who deceive audiences in ways that create the illusion that preternatural powers are at work. Traditionally, by contrast, magic was highly regarded. Jacob Boehme went so far as to assert that "magic is the best theology, for in it true faith is grounded. He is a fool that reviles it, for he knows it not and is more a juggler than a theologian

[7] Daniel Overmyer, *Religions of China* (New York: Harper & Row, 1986), p. 39.

of understanding." Traditionally, magic was understood as the means by which higher, occult powers are tapped for use in the visible world. Proceeding on the assumption that higher powers exist—the subtle rules the dense; energy rules matter, consciousness rules energy, and superconsciousness rules consciousness—magic made these powers available. When a hypnotist tells a subject that when his shoulder is touched his body will become rigid, and that happens—assistants can then place the subject's feet on one chair and his head on another without his body slumping—we come close to magic in the traditional sense, for the hypnotist calls into play powers that are not only astonishing but mysterious. Still, hypnotism falls short of magic in that the hypnotist is neither in an exceptional state of consciousness nor belongs to a sacerdotal order that is believed to be divinely empowered. For a genuine instance of magic in its traditional sense, we must turn to something like Peter's healing of Aeneas as reported in Acts 9:32-34.

> Now as Peter went here and there among all the believers, he came down also to the saints living in Lydia. There he found a man named Aeneas, who had been bedridden for eight years, for he was paralyzed. Peter said to him, "Aeneas, Jesus Christ heals you; get up and make your bed!" And immediately he got up.

Note that this was not a miracle. It would have been a miracle if Christ had empowered the paralytic Aeneas to climb out of bed without Peter's help, effecting thereby an instance of what clinicians refer to as spontaneous remission. As it was, Peter had a role in the cure, a necessary role we may assume, and we are confronted with magic; sacred magic, as it happens, for if a demon had been invoked for malevolent purposes, sorcery would have been at work.

It was under the rubric of magic as thus traditionally conceived that the Taoist church—dividing the territory with freelance wizards, exorcists, and shamans—devised ways to harness higher powers for humane ends.

The Mingling of the Powers

Philosophical Taoism, vitalizing programs for increasing one's individual *ch'i*, and the Taoist church: the three branches of Taoism, which at first seemed to have little in common, now show their family resemblances. All have the same concern—how to maximize the *Tao*'s animating *te*—and the specifics of their concerns fall on a continuum. The continuum begins with interest in how life's normal allotment of *ch'i* can be deployed to best effect (Philosophical Taoism). From there it moves on to ask if that normal quotient can be increased (Taoist vitalizing programs). Finally, it asks if cosmic energies can be gathered, as if by a burning glass, to be deployed vicariously for the welfare of people who need help (popular or Religious Taoism).

The danger in this arrangement is that in the interest of clarity the lines between the three divisions have been drawn too sharply. No solid walls separate them; the three are better regarded as currents in a common river. Throughout history each has interacted with the other two, right down to Taoism in Hong Kong and Taiwan today. John Blofeld, who lived in China for the twenty years preceding the Communist revolution, reported that he had never met a Taoist who was not involved to some degree with all three schools.

We can summarize. To *be* something, to *know* something, and *to be capable of* something is to rise above the superficial. A life has substance to the degree that it incorporates the profundity of mysticism (Taoist *yoga*), the direct wisdom of gnosis (Philosophical Taoism), and the productive power of magic (Religious Taoism). Where these three things come together there is a "school," and in China the school this chapter describes is Taoism. It is now time to return to Philosophical Taoism and give it its due hearing.

Creative Quietude

The object of Philosophical Taoism is to align one's daily life to the *Tao*, to ride its boundless tide and delight in its flow. The basic way to do this, we earlier noted, is to perfect a life of *wu wei*. We have seen that *wu wei* should not be translated as do-nothingness or inaction, for those words suggest a vacant attitude of idleness or abstention. Better renderings are pure effectiveness and creative quietude.

Creative quietude combines within a single individual two seemingly incompatible conditions—supreme activity and supreme relaxation. These seeming incompatibles can coexist because human beings are not self-enclosed entities. They ride an unbounded sea of *Tao* that sustains them, as we would say, through their subliminal minds. One way to create is through following the calculated directives of the conscious mind. The results of this mode of action, however, are seldom impressive; they tend to smack more of sorting and arranging than of inspiration. Genuine creation, as every artist knows, comes when the more abundant resources of the subliminal self are somehow tapped. But for this to happen a certain dissociation from the surface self is needed. The conscious mind must relax, stop standing in its own light, let go. Only so is it possible to break through the law of reversed effort in which the more we try the more our efforts boomerang.

Wu wei is the supreme action, the precious suppleness, simplicity, and freedom that flows from us, or rather through us, when our private egos and conscious efforts yield to a power not their own. In a way it is virtue approached from a direction diametrically opposite to that of Confucius. Confucius turned every effort to building a pattern of ideal responses that might be consciously imitated. Taoism's approach is the opposite—to get the foundations of the self in tune with *Tao* and let behavior flow spontaneously. Action follows being; new action will follow new being, wiser being, stronger being. The *Tao Te Ching* puts this point without wasting a word. "The way to do," it says, "is to be."

How are we to describe the action that flows from a life that is grounded directly in *Tao*? Nurtured by a force that is infinitely subtle, infinitely intricate, it is a consummate gracefulness born from an abundant vitality that has no need for abruptness or violence. One simply lets the *Tao* flow in and flow out again until all life becomes a dance in which there is neither feverishness nor imbalance. *Wu wei* is life lived above tension:

> Keep stretching a bow
> You repent of the pull,
> A whetted saw
> Grows thin and dull. (ch. 9)[8]

Far from inaction, however, it is the embodiment of suppleness, simplicity, and freedom—a kind of pure effectiveness in which no motion is wasted on bickering or outward show.

> One may move so well that a footprint never shows,
> Speak so well that the tongue never slips,
> Reckon so well that no counter is needed. (ch. 27)

[8] Unless otherwise specified, quotations in this section and the next are from the *Tao Te Ching*. Those from chapters 8, 15, 24, 31, and 78 are from Stephen Mitchell's renderings in his *Tao Te Ching* (New York: Harper & Row, 1988); those from chapters 9, 12, 17, 23, 27, 29, and 30 are from Witter Bynner's *The Way of Life According to Laotzu*, 1944, reprint (New York: Putnam, 1986).

Effectiveness of this order obviously requires an extraordinary skill, a point conveyed in the Taoist story of the fisherman who was able to land enormous fish with a thread because it was so delicately made that it had no weakest point at which to break. But Taoist skill is seldom noticed, for viewed externally *wu wei*—never forcing, never under strain—seems quite effortless. The secret here lies in the way it seeks out the empty spaces in life and nature and moves through these. Chuang Tzu, the greatest popularizer of Philosophical Taoism, makes this point with his story of Prince Wen Hui's cook whose cleaver seemed never to lose its edge. When he cut up an ox, out went a hand, down went a shoulder. He planted a foot, he pressed with a knee, and the ox fell apart with a whisper. The bright cleaver murmured like a gentle wind. Rhythm! Timing! Like a sacred dance. Like "The Mulberry Grove," like ancient harmonies! Pressed for his secret, the cook replied: "There are spaces in the joints; the blade is thin and keen. When this thinness finds that space, there is all the room you need! It goes like a breeze! Hence I have this cleaver nineteen years as if newly sharpened!"[9]

The natural phenomenon that the Taoists saw as bearing the closest resemblance to *Tao* was water. They were struck by the way it would support objects and carry them effortlessly on its tide. The Chinese characters for swimmer, deciphered, mean literally "one who knows the nature of water." Similarly, one who understands the basic life force knows that it will sustain one if one stops thrashing and flailing and trusts oneself to its support.

> Do you have the patience to wait
> till your mud settles and the water is clear?
> Can you remain unmoving
> till the right action arises by itself? (ch. 15)

Water, then, was the closest parallel to the *Tao* in the natural world. But it was also the prototype of *wu wei*. They noticed the way water adapts itself to its surroundings and seeks out the lowest places. So too,

> The supreme good is like water,
> which nourishes all things without trying to.

[9] Adapted from Thomas Merton's translation in his *The Way of Chuang Tzu* (New York: New Directions, 1965), pp. 45-47.

It is content with the low places that people disdain.
Thus it is like the *Tao*. (ch. 8)

Yet despite its accommodation, water holds a power unknown to hard and brittle things. In a stream it follows the stones' sharp edges, only to turn them into pebbles, rounded to conform to its streamlined flow. It works its way past frontiers and under dividing walls. Its gentle current melts rocks and carries away the proud hills we call eternal.

Nothing in the world
is as soft and yielding as water.
Yet for dissolving the hard and inflexible,
nothing can surpass it.
The soft overcomes the hard;
the gentle overcomes the rigid.
Everyone knows this is true,
but few can put it into practice. (ch. 78)

Infinitely supple, yet incomparably strong—these virtues of water are precisely those of *wu wei* as well. The person who embodies this condition, says the *Tao Te Ching*, "works without working." Such a one acts without strain, persuades without argument, is eloquent without flourish, and achieves results without violence, coercion, or pressure. Though the agent may be scarcely noticed, his or her influence is in fact decisive.

A leader is best
When people barely know that he exists.
Of a good leader, who talks little,
When his work is done, his aim fulfilled,
They will say, "We did this ourselves." (ch. 17)

A final characteristic of water that makes it an appropriate analogue to *wu wei* is the clarity it attains through being still. "Muddy water let stand," says the *Tao Te Ching*, "will clear." If you want to study the stars after being in a brightly lit room, you must wait twenty minutes for your eyes to dilate for their new assignment. There must be similar periods of waiting if the focal length of the mind is to readjust, withdrawing from the world's glare to the internal recesses of the soul.

The five colors can blind,
The five tones deafen,

> The five tastes cloy.
> The race, the hunt, can drive men mad
> And their booty leave them no peace.
> Therefore a sensible man
> Prefers the inner to the outer eye. (ch. 12)

Clarity can come to the inner eye, however, only insofar as life attains a quiet that equals that of a deep and silent pool.

Other Taoist Values

Still following the analogy of water, the Taoists rejected all forms of self-assertiveness and competition. The world is full of people who are determined to be somebody or give trouble. They want to get ahead, to stand out. Taoism has little use for such ambitions. "The ax falls first on the tallest tree."

> He who stands on tiptoe
> Doesn't stand firm.
> He who rushes ahead
> Doesn't go far.
> He who tries to shine
> dims his own light. (ch. 24)

Their almost reverential attitude toward humility led the Taoists to honor hunchbacks and cripples because of the way they typified meekness and self-effacement. They were fond of pointing out that the value of cups, windows, and doorways lies in the parts of them that are not there. "Selfless as melting ice" is one of their descriptive figures. The Taoists' refusal to clamber for position sprang from a profound disinterest in the things the world prizes. The point comes out in the story of Chuang Tzu's visit to the minister of a neighboring state. Someone told the minister that Chuang Tzu was coming in the hope of replacing him. The minister was alarmed. But when Chuang Tzu heard of the rumor he said to the minister:

> In the South there is a bird. It is called *yuan-ch'u*. Have you heard of it? This *yuan-ch'u* starts from the southern ocean and flies to the northern ocean. During its whole journey it perches on no tree save the sacred Wo-tung, eats no fruit save that of the Persian Lilac, drinks only at the Magic Well. It happened that an owl that had got hold of the rotting carcass of a rat looked up as this bird flew by, and terrified lest the *yuan-ch'u* should stop and snatch at the succulent morsel, it

> screamed, "Shoo! Shoo!" And now I am told that you are trying to "shoo" me off from this precious Ministry of yours.[10]

So it is with most of the world's prides. They are not the true values they are thought to be. What is the point of competition or assertiveness? The *Tao* seems to get along very well without them.

> Nature does not have to insist,
> Can blow for only half a morning,
> Rain for only half a day. (ch. 23)

People should avoid being strident and aggressive not only toward other people but also toward nature. On the whole, the modern Western attitude has been to regard nature as an antagonist, an object to be squared off against, dominated, controlled, conquered. Taoism's attitude is the opposite of this. There is a profound naturalism in Taoist thought, but it is the naturalism of a Rousseau, a Wordsworth, a Thoreau, not that of a Galileo or Bacon.

> Those who would take over the earth
> And shape it to their will
> Never, I notice, succeed.
> The earth is like a vessel so sacred
> That at the mere approach of the profane
> It is marred
> And when they reach out their fingers it is gone. (ch. 29)

Nature is to be befriended. When the British scaled earth's highest peak, the exploit was widely hailed as "the conquest of Everest." D. T. Suzuki remarked: "We orientals would have spoken of befriending Everest." The Japanese team that scaled Anapurna, the second highest peak, climbed to within fifty feet of the summit and deliberately stopped, provoking a Western mountaineer to exclaim in disbelief, "That's class!" Taoism seeks attunement with nature, not dominance. Its approach is ecological, a characteristic that led Joseph Needham to point out that despite China's backwardness in scientific theory she early developed "an organic philosophy of nature closely resembling that which modern science has been forced to adopt after

[10] Burton Watson (tr.), *Chuang Tzu: The Basic Writings* (New York: Columbia University Press, 1964), pp. 109-10.

three centuries of mechanical materialism." The ecological approach of Taoism has inspired many Western architects, most notably Frank Lloyd Wright. Taoist temples do not stand out from their surroundings. They nestle against the hills, back under the trees, blending in with the environment. At best, human beings do likewise. Their highest achievement is to identify themselves with the *Tao* and let it work its magic through them.

This Taoist approach to nature deeply affected Chinese art. It is no accident that the greatest periods of Chinese art have coincided with upsurges of Taoist influence. Before assuming brush and silk, painters would go out to nature and lose themselves in it, to become, say, the bamboo that they would paint. They would sit for half a day or fourteen years before making a stroke. The Chinese word for landscape painting is composed of the radicals for mountain and water, one of which suggests vastness and solitude, the other pliability, endurance, and continuous movement. The human part in the vastness is small, so we have to look closely for human beings in the paintings if we find them at all. Usually, they are climbing with their bundles, riding a buffalo, or poling a boat—the self with its journey to make, its burden to carry, its hill to climb, but surrounded by beauty on every side. People are not as formidable as mountains; they do not live as long as the pines. Yet they too belong in the scheme of things as surely as do the birds and the clouds. And through them, as through the rest of the world, flows the everlasting *Tao*.

Taoist naturalism combined with a propensity for naturalness as well. Pomp and extravagance were regarded as silly. When Chuang Tzu's followers asked permission to give him a grand funeral, he replied: "Heaven and earth are my inner and outer coffins. The sun, moon, and stars are my drapery, and the whole creation my funeral procession. What more do I want?" Civilization was ridiculed and the primitive idealized. "Let us have a small country with few inhabitants," Lao Tzu proposed. "Let the people return to the use of knotted cords [for keeping records]. Let them obtain their food sweet, their clothing beautiful, their homes comfortable, their rustic tasks pleasurable." Travel was discouraged as pointless and conducive to idle curiosity. "The neighboring state might be so near at hand that one could hear the cocks crowing in it and dogs barking. But the people would grow old and die without ever having been there."[11]

[11] Fung Yu-lan's translation of the *Tao Te Ching*, chapter 80, in his *A Short History of*

It was this preference for naturalness and simplicity that most separated the Taoist from the Confucian. The basic objectives of the two schools did not differ widely, but the Taoists had small patience with the Confucian approach to them. All formalism, show, and ceremony left them cold. What could be hoped for from punctiliousness or the meticulous observance of propriety? The whole approach was artificial, a lacquered surface that was bound to prove brittle and repressive. Confucianism here was but one instance of the human tendency to approach life in regulated mode. All calculated systems, the very attempt to arrange life in shipshape order, is pointless. As different ways of slicing the same reality, none of them amounts to more than Three in the Morning. And what is Three in the Morning? Once, in the state of Sung, hard times forced a keeper of monkeys to reduce their rations. "From now on," he announced, "it will be three in the morning and four in the evening." Faced with howls of rebellion, the keeper agreed to negotiate, and eventually accepted his monkeys' demand that it be four in the morning and three in the evening. The monkeys gloried in their triumph.

Another feature of Taoism is its notion of the relativity of all values and, as its correlative, the identity of opposites. Here Taoism tied in with the traditional Chinese *yin/yang* symbol, which is pictured thus:

This polarity sums up all of life's basic oppositions: good/evil, active/passive, positive/negative, light/dark, summer/winter, male/female. But though the halves are in tension, they are not flatly opposed; they complement and balance each other. Each invades the other's hemisphere and takes up its abode in the deepest recess of its partner's domain. And in the end both find themselves resolved by the circle that surrounds them, the *Tao* in its eternal wholeness. In the context of that wholeness, the opposites appear as no more than phases in an endless cycling process, for each turns incessantly into its opposite, exchanging places with it. Life does not move onward and upward

Chinese Philosophy (Princeton, NJ: Princeton University Press, 1953), p. 20.

toward a fixed pinnacle or pole. It bends back upon itself to come, full circle, to the realization that all is one and all is well.

Those who meditate on this profound symbol, Taoists maintain, will find that it affords better access to the world's secrets than any length of words and discussion. Faithful to its import, Taoism eschews all sharp dichotomies. No perspective in this relative world can be considered as absolute. Who knows when the longest way 'round might not prove to be the shortest way home? Or consider the relativity of dream and wakefulness. Chuang Tzu dreamed that he was a butterfly, and during the dream had no notion that he had ever been anything else. When he awoke, however, he was astonished to find that he was Chuang Tzu. But this left him with a question. Was he really Chuang Tzu who had dreamed that he was a butterfly, or was he a butterfly that was now dreaming that it was Chuang Tzu?

All values and concepts, then, are ultimately relative to the mind that entertains them. When it was suggested to the wren and the cicada that there are birds that fly hundreds of miles without alighting, both quickly agreed that such a thing was impossible. "You and I know very well," they nodded, "that the furthest one can ever get, even by the most tremendous effort, is to that elm tree over there, and even this one cannot be sure of reaching every time. Often one finds oneself dragged back to earth long before one gets there. All these stories about flying hundreds of miles at a stretch are sheer nonsense."

In the Taoist perspective even good and evil are not head-on opposites. The West has tended to dichotomize the two, but Taoists are less categorical. They buttress their reserve with the story of a farmer whose horse ran away. His neighbor commiserated, only to be told, "Who knows what's good or bad?" It was true, for the next day the horse returned, bringing with it a drove of wild horses it had befriended. The neighbor reappeared, this time with congratulations for the windfall. He received the same response: "Who knows what is good or bad?" Again this proved true, for the next day the farmer's son tried to mount one of the wild horses and fell, breaking his leg. More commiserations from the neighbor, which elicited the question: "Who knows what is good or bad?" And for a fourth time the farmer's point prevailed, for the following day soldiers came by commandeering for the army, and the son was exempted because of his injury. If this all sounds very much like Zen, it should; for Buddhism processed through Taoism became Zen.

Taoism follows its principle of relativity to its logical limit by positioning life and death as complementing cycles in the *Tao*'s rhythm. When Chuang Tzu's wife died, his friend Hui-tzu visited him to express his condolences, only to find Chuang Tzu sitting on the ground with his legs spread wide apart, singing away and whacking out a tune on the back of a wooden bowl. "After all," said his friend, "she lived with you devotedly all these years, watched your eldest son grow to manhood, and grew old along with you. For you not to have shed a tear over her remains would have been bad enough, but singing and drumming away on a bowl—this is just too much!" "You misjudge," said Chuang Tzu. "When she died I was in despair, as any man well might be. But then I realized that before she was born she had no body, and it became clear to me that the same process of change that brought her to birth eventually brought her to death. If someone is tired and has gone to lie down, we do not pursue her with hooting and bawling. She whom I have lost has lain down to sleep for a while in the chamber between heaven and earth. To wail and groan while my wife is sleeping would be to deny nature's sovereign law. So I refrain."

Elsewhere Chuang Tzu expressed his confidence in the face of death directly:

> There is the globe,
> The foundation of my bodily existence.
> It wears me out with work and duties,
> It gives me rest in old age,
> It gives me peace in death.
> For the one who supplied me with what I needed in life
> Will also give me what I need in death.[12]

It is no surprise to find an outlook as averse to violence as Taoism verging on pacifism. There are passages in the *Tao Te Ching* that read almost like the Sermon on the Mount.

> One who would guide a leader of men in the uses of life
> Will warn him against the use of arms for conquest.
> Even the finest arms are an instrument of evil.
> An army's harvest is a waste of thorns. (ch. 30)

[12] Quoted in K. L. Reichelt's translation of the twenty-fifth chapter of the *Tao Te Ching* in his *Meditation and Piety in the Far East* (New York: Harper and Brothers, 1954), p. 102.

> Weapons are the tools of violence;
> all decent men detest them.
> Weapons are the tools of fear;
> a decent man will avoid them
> except in the direst necessity
> and, if compelled, will use them
> only with the utmost restraint.
> Peace is the highest value. . . .
> He enters a battle gravely,
> with sorrow and with great compassion,
> as if he were attending a funeral. (ch. 31)

That in China the scholar ranked at the top of the social scale may have been Confucius' doing, but Taoism is fully as responsible for placing the soldier at the bottom. "The way for a vital person to go is not the way of a soldier." Only one "who recognizes all people as members of his or her own body is qualified to guard them. . . . Heaven arms with compassion those whom she would not see destroyed."

War is a somber matter, and Taoism spoke to life's solemn, somber issues. Yet it always retained a quality of lightness verging on gaiety. There is a sophistication, an urbanity, a charm about the perspective that is infectious. "He who feels punctured," notes the *Tao Te Ching*, "must once have been a bubble." The economy, directness, and good humor in such a statement is typical of its entire outlook. In its freedom from a heavy-booted approach to life, Taoism is at one with the rest of China; but it is also, as we have seen, free of the Confucian tendency toward rigidity and formalism. Taoist literature is full of dialogues with Confucianists in which the latter come off as stuffy and pompous. An instance is the story of the Taoist Chuang Tzu and the Confucian Hui Tzu, who on an afternoon's stroll came to a bridge over the Hao River. "Look how the minnows dart hither and thither at will. Such is the pleasure fish enjoy," Chuang Tzu remarked. "You are not a fish," responded Hui Tzu. "How do you know what gives pleasure to fish?" "You are not I," said Chuang Tzu. "How do you know I don't know what gives pleasure to fish?"

Conclusion

Circling around each other like *yin* and *yang* themselves, Taoism and Confucianism represent the two indigenous poles of the Chinese character. Confucius represents the classical, Lao Tzu the romantic. Confucius stresses social responsibility, Lao Tzu praises spontaneity and naturalness. Confucius' focus is on the human, Lao Tzu's on what transcends the human. As the Chinese themselves say, Confucius roams within society, Lao Tzu wanders beyond. Something in life reaches out in each of these directions, and Chinese civilization would certainly have been poorer if either had not appeared.

There are books whose first reading casts a spell that is never quite undone, the reason being that they speak to the deepest "me" in the reader. For all who quicken at the thought that anywhere, at every time, the *Tao* is within us, the *Tao Te Ching* is such a book. Mostly it has been so for the Chinese, but an American poet can equally find it "the straightest, most logical explanation as yet advanced for the continuance of life, the most logical use yet advised for enjoying it."[13] Though obviously never practiced to perfection, its lessons of simplicity, openness, and wisdom have been for millions of Chinese a joyful guide.

> There is a being, wonderful, perfect;
> It existed before heaven and earth.
> How quiet it is!
> How spiritual it is!
> It stands alone and it does not change.
> It moves around and around, but does not on this account suffer.
> All life comes from it.
> It wraps everything with its love as in a garment, and
> yet it claims no honor, it does not demand to be Lord.
> I do not know its name, and so I call it Tao, the Way,
> and I rejoice in its power.[14]

[13] Bynner, *The Way of Life*, pp. 12-13.

[14] Adapted from K. L. Reichelt's translation of the twenty-fifth chapter of the *Tao Te Ching* in his *Meditation and Piety*, 41.

THE PRIVATE ENCOUNTER WITH THE MASTER*

Philip Kapleau

Since Dr. D. T. Suzuki introduced an intellectually-oriented Zen to the West—the inevitable first step—the literature of Zen has ballooned, now filling many library shelves. Yet this vast literary production contains few volumes on actual Zen training. Rarely examined is one crucial aspect of the training process—*dokusan* ("going alone"), the eyeball-to-eyeball encounter with the master (*roshi*) in the privacy of his teaching room. My book *The Three Pillars of Zen,* first published in 1965, sought to fill this lacuna by describing my own and other practitioners' experiences in *dokusan.* Now, after some twenty years as a teacher, I am in a position to speak about this encounter from a different perspective—to clarify its function and to tell what lies behind a teacher's words and actions.

The private encounter with the Zen master is one of the three pillars on which Zen training rests; the other two are meditation (*zazen*) and the master's commentary (*teisho*). No English word conveys the precise meaning and spirit of *dokusan,* only because no such mode of spiritual training has existed in our own culture until recent times. The private encounter is not an interview in which a would-be student answers questions about himself, explains why he wants to practice Zen, and perhaps asks a variety of questions unrelated to practice. Nor is it a simple, friendly meeting. Neither does it involve a discussion of Buddhist doctrine in the manner of the classroom. Still less is it a counseling session during which a student may seek advice on matters affecting personal relationships. In *dokusan* the teacher probes the student's understanding and realization, if any, and gives him pointers for future practice. With a more advanced student the "testing" is more active, as the teacher tries to evoke a demonstration of the student's understanding, not unlike the insertion of an irritant into an oyster to cause it to produce a pearl.

* Editor's Note: from *Zen: Tradition and Transition,* ed. Kenneth Kraft.

Individual instruction is a teaching method in Buddhism that is said to go back to the time of the Buddha, when monks assembled in caves for intensive training during the three-month rainy season. Later in China a more open form of encounter between teacher and students developed. In Japan, and in Korea too, the Zen masters added a new and vigorous dimension in which *dokusan* became less a matter of didactic instruction and more a form of testing. It is this style that is most common in Zen centers in the West today, with modifications that reflect our own cultural and psychological characteristics. Before discussing these inner aspects, let me describe some of *dokusan*'s outer, formal procedures.

Upon entering the *roshi*'s room the student, with hands palm to palm, first makes a standing bow and then proceeds to a mat in front of the *roshi*. There he or she prostrates once as a sign of respect and humility. Although prostration is traditional among Asians, I do not insist upon it. Eventually most students, even those in whom such a gesture raises shackles of resistance at first, come to see its value as a "horizontalizing of the mast of ego," and they perform it willingly.

Dokusan is announced in the *zendo* (meditation hall) with a clanging of the *roshi*'s handbell. Those who wish to go before him—and this is optional—quickly leave their seats in the *zendo* in order to get a place in the waiting line. They proceed to mats lined up before a small bell suspended from a wooden frame. When the *roshi* rings his handbell, the student at the head of the line strikes the bell in front of him twice with a padded wooden mallet and then enters the *roshi*'s chamber. The whole line then moves up one place. When the waiting sitters have all seen the *roshi*, the monitors in the *zendo* signal the next group to line up. And so on until all who wish private instruction have had it.

These procedures are more than ceremonial. Besides preserving a sense of order, they aid the *roshi* in determining the mind state of the student. Has he or she hit the bell firmly or with a glancing blow? Is the striking hasty or sluggish? Has the bell been struck too loudly or too softly, or is one strike noisier or quieter than the other? In short, how the bell is struck tells the *roshi*, who can hear the sound in his room, whether the student is a beginner or a more advanced student and what the condition of his or her mind is.

How long does an individual's meeting with the *roshi* take? It varies. Sometimes it may be only a minute or two, at other times as long as fifteen minutes or half an hour. The length is determined not by any arbitrary time limit but by the needs of the student. Much depends, too, on whether the meeting with the *roshi* is the student's first, which is usually lengthy, or whether the student is working on a first *koan* or a subsequent *koan*. During intensive meditation sessions (*sesshin*), there may be as many as forty or fifty participants. Since most of them want to avail themselves of every opportunity for private instruction, the *roshi* cannot in fairness entertain questions extraneous to a student's practice without penalizing the others waiting their turn. *Dokusan* is not the proper time to bring up personal matters or raise theoretical questions.

Of the three facets of Zen training mentioned above (*zazen*, the *roshi*'s commentary, and *dokusan*), *dokusan* offers the greatest opportunity for personal growth and spiritual awakening. Thus it is held three times a day during a seven-day *sesshin*, while the commentary is given only once daily. Although the three facets are not unrelated, they have different functions and purposes.

In *zazen*, the practice of looking into one's own mind, the student is on his own as he seeks to gain control over his wayward thoughts. As he faces a wall or divider, symbolic of his stubborn ego, neither the master nor anyone else can substitute for him. In this solitary voyage into the vast hidden world of mind, all of one's inner resources must be brought to bear by oneself on oneself. This process I have described previously as:

> a lonely trek through winding canyons of shame and fear, across deserts of ecstatic visions and tormenting phantasms, around volcanoes of oozing ego, and through jungles of folly and delusion in a ceaseless struggle to gain that oneness and emptiness of body and mind which ultimately lead to the lightning-and-thunder discovery that the universe and oneself are not remote and apart but an intimate, palpitating whole.[1]

In the commentary the *roshi* takes center stage for a solo performance. His talk of approximately an hour facing the Buddha altar is less a sermon on Buddhist doctrine or a philosophical discourse on the nature of ultimate reality than a vivid, straight-from-the-gut demonstration of reality itself. Charged with all the energy of his liberated mind, his talk inspires, instructs, and points the way to future effort.

[1] Philip Kapleau, *The Three Pillars of Zen* (Garden City: Anchor Press/Doubleday, rev. ed., 1980), p. 214.

In the private encounter the student comes on stage in a contrapuntal duet with the teacher. Often dreaded if he is a beginner yet eagerly sought by him if he is an advanced student, *dokusan* is his long-awaited confrontation with the teacher, his time to shine or simply to make himself like a sponge, soaking up the truth the teacher is thrusting before him. The juxtaposition of their postures reinforces the idea of confrontation (in the mild sense of the word), for they face each other with no more than two feet separating them. The teacher usually sits in the lotus posture on a round cushion placed on a square mat, while the student kneels on a mat, back erect, perhaps with a cushion between his buttocks and heels. Zen rejects asceticism, and the teacher does not insist on a prescribed position that may turn out to be painful for the student. With the back straight and the body-mind's center of gravity resting in the region two inches below the navel (the *tanden*), the student's mind is denuded of random thoughts. Thus he can more easily and quickly respond with his total being and not simply from the head.

The Master-Disciple Relationship in Zen

While everyone is free to practice *zazen* and listen to the *roshi*'s commentary, the essential nature of *dokusan* is the forming of a karmic bond between the *roshi* and a student, the significance of which is deep in Buddhism. So the personal encounter is not something to be taken lightly. Since what passes between the *roshi* and the student concerns matters of a deep and ultimate nature, only the truth must be spoken between them. For these reasons, many centers have a rule that one must become a personal student of the *roshi* before receiving private instruction from him. And because the relationship is a karmic one, it implies that the student will not lightly seek another teacher.

Let me clarify the differences between the master-disciple relationship (in a Zen context) and the teacher-student relationship (in a secular setting). In the ideal teacher-student relationship the student respects the teacher as the possessor of a certain body of knowledge or of a skill that the student would like to acquire, while the teacher values the student for his eagerness and his ability to absorb this knowledge. Their relationship is largely impersonal and limited; what sustains it is their common interest in a particular study. The master-disciple relationship of Zen is deeper and more personal because it is grounded in a karmic affinity. What moves the disciple in the direction of the master is not the master's knowledge but his compassion, enlightened wisdom, character, and warm personality—traits born of long discipline and training. The disciple senses that it is through these qualities that he will be able to complete himself and eventually come to full awakening.[2] At its highest level the relationship between master and disciple may even be stronger than the link between parent and child. In this bond the master assumes responsibility for the disciple's spiritual development, while the disciple undertakes responsibility for the master's economic and general well-being.

The direction a student's meeting with the *roshi* takes depends primarily on his aspiration. Does he want to train in Zen only to eradicate mental confusion, frustrations, or the bodily pains that usually spring from them? Is his interest in Zen primarily philosophical or literary? Or is his motivation simply to cultivate *samadhi* power for the practice of a martial art? All those worthwhile objectives can be accomplished through *zazen* properly practiced. From the standpoint of Zen Buddhism, however, they constitute low levels of aspiration. Only if one aspires to enlightenment itself is one's aspiration truly spiritual.

At a new student's first appearance before me I will question him carefully about his aspiration. If it is awakening, does he have the conviction that he can realize it? Does he have the determination to do so? And is he willing to dedicate himself to achieving it? If his answer to each of these questions is an unequivocal "Yes," he is usually assigned a *koan*, one with which he has an affinity. However, *koan*s are not assigned to a student with no previous experience of *zazen*. It is desirable that he first engage in breath exercises to gain control over his unruly thoughts. One must acquire what in Zen is called a "seat," the ability to deal calmly with the vicissitudes of one's life. Until one reaches this point, it is futile to try to grapple with a *koan*. If *koan* practice is attempted without adequate preparation, the student will quickly become frustrated or bored and give up on the *koan* and often on Zen itself.

A Zen student in training is constantly being tested, but in this one-to-one encounter the teacher utilizes specific modes of testing, all of which have different purposes. One kind, for example, involves a student who insists he has had an awakening and asks to be tested.

[2] Philip Kapleau, *Zen: Dawn in the West* (Garden City: Anchor Press/Doubleday, 1979), pp. 34-35.

"I've had an enlightenment experience. Please test me," he demands of the teacher. Although such an assertion already has a "smell" to it, it cannot safely be ignored. One who has had a valid awakening, even if shallow, does not say, "I am enlightened." Nor is enlightenment an *experience* to be grasped among other experiences; it is the ground of all experiences. The teacher will usually comply with a request for testing; otherwise a student may believe he is enlightened when he is not.

If it is common to believe mistakenly that one is enlightened, it can also happen that one has become enlightened and be unaware of it. That is why Dogen could say, "Do not think you will necessarily be aware of your own enlightenment." There may be understanding on a subconscious level that has not yet found its way into consciousness. So this is another reason why testing is vital.

What sort of testing questions does a teacher ask to establish whether a student has had a genuine awakening? Here are some I myself use:

"Where did you come from when you were born and where will you go when you die?"

"Are you in the universe or is the universe in you?"

"Why is this called a hand (extending hand)?"

"If you had to die right now, what would you do?"

A faltering, uncertain reply or even a simple "I think" can vitiate an entire answer. To be acceptable, the student's response must be spontaneous and sure; understanding must radiate from the eyes and body as well as from the mouth.

Sometimes a student who fails to give satisfactory responses to these questions will protest, "You're asking me Zen questions and I don't know enough about Zen to answer them. But I know I've become enlightened." With such a student I will say, "All right, tell me what happened." He may reply, "I felt as though everything disappeared and I was the only one in the universe." Such a statement can be persuasive if it carries conviction and is accompanied by telltale signs of transformation, but only testing can verify it. When asked "Who is it that knows he is the only one?" few can respond meaningfully. Where there is a deep penetration into truth, most people experience tears of joy. If not simply an emotional reaction, that response may eliminate the need for testing. Yet a student may easily deceive himself or herself. Certain blissful states, hallucinations, the oceanic feeling of oneness, trances, or the sudden cessation of thought—all of which can induce tears of elation and gratitude in one with a strong emotional nature—can be confused with enlightenment.

Testing is vital because there is a fine line between a profound intellectual awareness (based on an experience of insight) and a genuine awakening. In ordinary awakening one may barely open one's eyes, half asleep in a twilight zone, or one may open one's eyes fully and jump out of bed. With *kensho*, seeing into one's nature, one may see dimly or with great clarity; the gradations are many and subtle.

Another mode of testing is suddenly to jar a student physically or verbally when I sense his mind is ripe, in a state of absolute emptiness. Before I can determine that, however, I scan him carefully with my inner eye as he negotiates the rather long distance to the mat in front of me. Is he rigid and tense, or wobbly and tentative? Are his shoulders drooping or is he walking erect? Most important, what is the condition of his mind? If his head is bent forward and his body stiff and unsteady, the chances are his thoughts are chasing each other like a pack of monkeys stung by a swarm of bees. But if he is in a *samadhi* state, he will be walking as though not walking.

Again, as he sits in front of me I watch his face intently, especially the eyes. I don't think, "Should I test him, and if so, what kind of procedures should I use?" I must size him up in a split second and intuitively, unthinkingly, apply the incendiary that may ignite the dried tinder of his mind into the flames of self-transcendence. In this type of testing the *roshi* is like a hen, sensing the precise moment to peck at the egg to liberate the chick from its shell.

In a *sesshin* a student may give satisfactory responses to the testing questions early on and be unable to answer more than one or two of the same questions at a later time. Or the reverse may happen. Until the third day of a seven-day *sesshin*, when the energy is still building up, very little can be accomplished by testing in any event. After the third day, however, when the participants are buoyed and sustained by the *samadhi* power that has accumulated, they may suddenly find themselves able to respond to questions that heretofore baffled them. The human mind is extraordinarily subtle and complex, and there are no precise criteria by which to measure or anticipate its responses. Moreover, we know that the subconscious mind registers and preserves past impressions and experiences that have bypassed the conscious mind. In fact, Zen training can be called a process of bringing into consciousness what was formerly hidden in the subconscious mind. For these reasons a teacher will put the same testing questions to a student early in the *sesshin* and at a later time, varying the pace, to be certain the student's experiential understanding is real and unshakeable.

Let me illustrate further dimensions of the master-disciple encounter by citing two episodes from the traditional lore of Zen. A clever monk approached the great Zen master Chao-chou and asked, "If all the myriad things in the universe return to the One, to what does the One return?" Very likely the questioner was referring to a passage in the *Gandavyuha Sutra* that says, "All things of the three realms are reduced to the One Mind." The monk's question is like asking, "If everything returns to God, where does God return to?" or "What was God doing before he created the world?" When St. Augustine was asked this latter question he quipped, "Creating a hell for the person who asked the question!" That was clever, but had Augustine said it in *dokusan* he would have been instantly rung out.

To understand why, one needs to savor Chao-chou's response: "When I was in Ch'ing Province I had one hempen shirt made weighing seven pounds." What a seemingly irrelevant reply! But Chao-chou is actually right on target. Obviously the monk is trying to twist the lion's tail, to get Chao-chou to say something like "Emptiness" or "Nothingness," but the master avoids the trap and gives the monk a faultless demonstration of the truth of Zen. Philosophically the question is unanswerable, of course, as Chao-chou and the monk both know. By responding as he does the master not only avoids a meaningless abstraction, he also brings the questioner down to earth, to the concrete and the real, where Zen operates. What could be more real than this seven-pound hempen shirt that can be touched, worn, and experienced through direct contact? Notice, too, how Chao-chou equates oneness with the seven-pound shirt. "All myriad things" are in fact this one, this shirt: one equals seven, seven equals one, one equals all. Try to elaborate oneness, though, and you fall into concepts and abstractions. But fondle the shirt, wear it—become one with it—and you know it directly, concretely, intimately. Ultimate truth can be grasped only through direct experience, not by abstract thought.

This fact is dramatically illustrated in a second encounter, from a well-known *koan* in the *Gateless Barrier.* The flashpoint that touched off a conflagration in the monk's mind was, appropriately enough, the master's lighting a candle and then suddenly blowing it out. This climax had been preceded by a long discussion on the *Diamond Sutra* between Lung-tan, the master, and Te-shan, a scholar-monk. We can only speculate about the content of their talk, for the *koan* does not say. But since Te-shan was considered an authority on this scripture, lecturing widely on it, we can presume he questioned the master about it at great length and received the sort of responses that left him suspended in mid-air. When Lung-tan finally said, "It is getting late, you had better leave," Te-shan's mind was emptied of all the concepts he had been harboring. Peering out, he said, "It's dark outside." Thereupon the master lit a candle and handed it to him. As Te-shan went to take it, Lung-tan suddenly blew it out. With that Te-shan was enlightened.

What prompted the master to blow out the candle? Was it the sudden eruption into his conscious mind of Lao-tzu's observation, "When darkness is at its darkest that is the beginning of all light"? Did he intuitively sense that Te-shan was in a state of absorption to the point of self-forgetfulness, needing only a jolt to precipitate his mind into Self-awareness? His act was literally a "shot in the dark" that struck home.

Dokusan *and* Koan *Training*

We now need to consider in some detail a vital aspect of the private encounter—namely, how the *roshi* deals with students who are investigating *koan*s. This will be done by examining five principal concerns—most of which focus on *sesshin*, *dokusan*, or *koan*s—that Zen students and others have expressed over the years. Though some of these objections arise from a limited knowledge of Zen training, they often contain a kernel of truth. Undeniably, the pressures of a seven-day *sesshin* are intense, especially when keyed to *koan*s and the probing style of *dokusan*, and the system may have its drawbacks. But my experience as a teacher has convinced me that the advantages of strict *sesshin* training, with *koan*s and *dokusan*, far outweigh the disadvantages.

OBJECTION A: *KOAN*S ARE GRASPED SUPERFICIALLY

"Students these days go through whole books of *koan*s (such as the *Gateless Barrier* and the *Blue Cliff Record*) in a superficial manner, in what amounts to assembly-line fashion, without deeply penetrating any of the *koan*s. Contemporary *roshi*s, themselves the product of this 'once-over-lightly' system transmitted by their teachers, apply the same low standards to their own students, passing those who have merely tasted but not fully digested a *koan*. This insidious process begins with the initial breakthrough *koan*."

REPLY

To begin with, it must be recognized that the practice of passing a student who has not fully penetrated his or her *koan* is a calculated one and not the outcome of ignorance or a "one-more-notch-in-the-belt" complex. In former times, when students had more zeal and ardor, teachers would not sanction a student's enlightenment unless his penetration into the world of oneness (or emptiness or *Mu*) went to the very bottom. Today the distractions and insatiable demands of our complex, technological society, as well as the stresses of coping with rapid change, make such high standards virtually impossible to achieve. How many students nowadays will persist in their training for at least fifteen or twenty years—and hard training at that—until they have had deep awakening? How many contemporary Zen followers could even dream of vowing, as Gautarna Buddha and the masters of old did, "Though only my skin, sinews, and bones remain and my blood and flesh dry up and wither away, yet never from this seat will I stir until I have attained full enlightenment"? That kind of determination is too rare these days for a teacher to set his training standards by it. Americans are also handicapped in another way. We are a people impatient for a speedy outcome in whatever we undertake. The "quick fix" is the hallmark of our social, political, economic, and even religious life. If a particular course of action does not bring a quick solution, we soon tire of it and seek faster results elsewhere.

My teacher Yasutani Hakuun Roshi used to say that *koan*s are like offering a tired child sweets to induce him to walk on. This simple statement, however, does not reveal why *koan*s are such a lure to Zen practitioners. In seeking to *demonstrate* the spirit of the masters, as demanded by the *koan*s, the student can relate to the *koan*'s protagonists as flesh-and-blood human beings. A student working on *koan*s has a front-row seat to an ongoing drama in which he is both observer and participant. After several years of *zazen* focused on breath practices, he is now challenged by the *koan*s to use his mind actively but not analytically. Intellect must transcend itself, entering a wholly new realm in which the unitive mind, the creative intuition, is brought into play. The one-to-one relationship with the *roshi* enables the student to grasp the Mahayana Buddhist teachings embodied in the *koan*s in the most direct manner possible. And it affords an unparalleled opportunity to experience intimately the spirit and personality of the teacher.

Of course, none of these circumstances imply that masters should pass students who have not penetrated their *koan*s even partially. This point applies to a first *koan* as well as subsequent ones. With respect to a first *koan*, the line is often obscure between the darkness before insight and the glimmer of light radiating from a small penetration. Yet an experienced *roshi*, as we have seen, has many resources at his command by which to test students to be sure that a purported *kensho* is real. Should a *roshi* become lax, however, and sanction a student to go on to subsequent *koan*s when the student has not caught even a glimpse of his true nature, the end result is frustration for both of them. For the *roshi* it is a constant struggle to keep such a student's head above water as the latter flounders helplessly in a sea of *koan*s. Nor is the *roshi* in less of a predicament if he passes a student who has *barely* opened his Zen eye, for then he may have to extend him a helping hand at every turn as he wallows through the classic *koan* collections. In some cases, the *roshi* may find himself in the unenviable position of having to send a student back to the starting line, to *Mu* or another initial *koan*. For these reasons a wise *roshi* will prefer to err on the side of caution.

Generally speaking, a *koan* brings about awakening more quickly than other types of practice because it provides a tool for focusing one's efforts. The value of even a meager initial insight is that a student who has caught a glimpse of his essential nature is encouraged to persist in his training. Even a small *kensho* brings greater energy, equanimity, and light into one's life. Attaining *kensho* quickly through a *koan* is like vigorously shaking a tree to bring down unripe fruit. Just as green fruit cannot be eaten, so a tiny penetration will not radically transform one's life. But Zen training does not stop with a *kensho* experience, shallow or deep. Ripening takes place through work on subsequent *koan*s.

No experienced teacher would say to a student who has caught merely a glimpse of his essential nature, "You are enlightened," for such a pat on the back could reinvigorate an ego which has been only temporarily banished from its dominant position in the mind. Besides, until one has integrated this vision into one's life and is able to live by it, one cannot truly be called enlightened. Often the teacher describes to the student the extent and significance of his awakening in terms of the Ten Oxherding pictures, which depict the developing stages of enlightenment, or simply by using some objects at hand. I myself usually point to the square mat in front of me on which the student is sitting and say, "Let us suppose this mat is the world of enlightenment and that the carpet is the unenlightened world. Actually they are not two, but for purposes of comparison let us say they are. From the carpet you have gotten on to the extreme right-hand corner of the mat. There is a qualitative difference between being on the carpet and reaching the mat, even just the corner. Now, a deep penetration would be here," and I point halfway across the mat, "and full enlightenment might be here at the extreme left-hand side of the mat. With subsequent *koans* you will begin to work your way across the mat."

Then I add: "I must also emphasize that you have not yet fully penetrated your initial *koan*, as must be apparent to you." I take my baton and say, "The upper side of this stick represents your practice on subsequent *koans*, and the underside stands for your continuing efforts with *Mu*. Every time you pass a subsequent *koan* you reaffirm the world of oneness; that is, you see the world of *Mu*, beyond the dichotomy of subject and object, more clearly. As a result you will be able to deal with subsequent *koans* more surely. So the two practices are mutually reinforcing. Through subsequent *koans* your initial breakthrough can be enlarged and your inner vision expanded."

Passing a first *koan* is like finally taking hold of the bottom rung of a ladder from the floor of a deep pit into which you have fallen. To grasp this rung after trying for a long time gives you confidence that you can climb the rest of the rungs and escape to freedom. I never cease to marvel at the upsurge in mental and physical energy that occurs in students with even a shallow awakening.

OBJECTION B: *KOAN* TRAINING IS TOO HARSH

"Zen *koan* training is calculatingly harsh. In *sesshin* the monitors repeatedly work over the participants with a large stick. This practice reaches a crescendo of beatings and shouts just before the encounter with the *roshi*, culminating in the '*dokusan* rush,' better called a stampede. In *dokusan*, the *roshi* has a smaller stick, which he is not loath to apply to students' backs when they are bowing down before him. Or he will rebuff students with scathing words. How can such harsh practices be reconciled with the Buddhist ideal of compassion?"

REPLY

The encouragement stick (*kyosaku*) is still the favorite whipping boy of Zen's critics, who insist it is "a perversion of Buddhism." Experienced *sesshin*-goers, however, appreciate it as a welcome goad, especially during those long afternoons of *zazen* when the energies sink, drowsiness takes over, and the mind teems with unwelcome thoughts. One or two well-directed blows across the flat of the shoulders, at acupuncture meridians, will scatter the most tenacious thoughts and liberate stores of unsuspected energy. For those who are working hard on their practice, the strikings rarely hurt, just as giving the spurs to a fast-running horse will elicit a burst of speed without paining him. Unusually nervous sitters are hardly ever struck, for the monitors know that they will do better *zazen* without the encouragement stick. Outside of *sesshin* the stick is used only when a sitter requests it.

But why the heavy use of the *kyosaku* before *dokusan*? Long experience has shown that when the stick is used persistently just before the encounter with the *roshi*, the meeting is more effective. By emptying the mind of the contrails of irrelevant thoughts, it leads to a *samadhi*-like condition. An individual who reaches this "no-mind" state is verging on awakening and may need no more than a jolt by the *roshi*, verbal or physical, to precipitate his mind into Self-awareness. The sudden clanging of the *dokusan* bell affords release from the tension accumulated during the intensive effort at concentration. Simultaneously there is an uncontrollable urge to race to the *roshi*—to be tested by him or just to present oneself before him.

In the rush to *dokusan* and in *dokusan* itself the student expresses a spontaneity that is an essential element of Zen training. Spontaneity is that condition where one is unrestrained by calculation or preconceived notions of how to respond to circumstances. It implies the courage to plunge unreservedly into whatever activity one faces. Most people lead passive lives; they are not the actors but the acted upon. Because they have lost their inborn creativity as free-acting individuals, they can't "let go" unless impelled by strong emotion. In *dokusan* and in Zen spontaneity is never repressed.

What about the contention that heavy pressures are unreasonably brought to bear on students to achieve a breakthrough in seven days of *sesshin*? This raises a further question: Is genuine awakening possible in such a short time? Yes, given certain conditions. The seven-day seclusion is the cornerstone of Zen training; in it all the elements of Zen—intensive *zazen*, the *roshi*'s commentary, and individual instruction—are coordinated into a meaningful whole. With forty or fifty participants striving ardently day and night, *sesshin* turns into a powerhouse of focused energy. One could call *sesshin* a process of splitting the atom of the mind to release the stores of untapped energy lying dormant within. Because such energy is indispensable for *kensho*, the seven-day seclusion is unequaled as a means of achieving a breakthrough.

A disciplined *sesshin* is one in which the participants do not begin at different times or leave before the end. Freed from outer preoccupations, they can direct all their energies inwardly. During the entire seven days there is no talking or reading. The eyes are kept lowered so that random sights will not disturb concentration. Yasutani Roshi used to say that a taut, coordinated *sesshin* accomplishes what it would take from two to three years to achieve on one's own. Awakening to one's true nature is the most fundamental realization possible for a human being. Intense inner struggle is necessary to gain control over the mind and then, like a missile, to penetrate the barrier of the five senses and the discursive intellect. To enter this wholly new realm calls for energy, determination, and courage. Yasutani Roshi called it "a battle between the opposing forces of delusion and enlightenment." The Chinese Zen master Po-shan affirmed, "When working on Zen, one never reaches enlightenment merely by waiting for it. One must press forward with all one's mind to get this enlightenment." In the same spirit Zen master Dogen wrote, "The great way of the buddhas and the patriarchs involves the highest form of exertion. . . . This sustained exertion is not something which men of the world naturally love or desire, yet it is the last refuge of all."

Without force of one kind or another from the outside, not many can accomplish the formidable task of awakening in seven days of intensive meditation; despite a strong aspiration, few can mobilize their dormant energies through sheer willpower. Thus we have the encouragement stick and other forceful aids. Contrary to what many believe, the use of force is not characteristic only of the Zen sect; in Buddhism it goes back to the Buddha himself. In the *Satipatthana Sutta* he is quoted as saying:

> One should with clenched teeth and with tongue pressing on palate, subdue, crush, and overpower the mind by the mind, just as if a strong man, having taken a very weak man by the head and shoulders, were to subdue him, crush him, and overpower him. Then the harmful thoughts connected with desire, hate, and delusion will disappear.

So force is indispensable—if applied at the right time and in the right way.

In genuine Zen training—and in the use of the encouragement stick—compassion, force, and wisdom are joined. For love without force is weakness, and force without love is brutality. When Zen master Mu-chou slammed the door on the foot of Yün-men, who was trying to force his way into Mu-chou's room for instruction, Yün-men's leg was broken. With a cry of pain Yün-men came to enlightenment. Was Mu-chou compassionate or merely brutal? Later Yün-men castigated Tung-shan for his aimless wandering from teacher to teacher and thereby brought him to awakening. Was that Buddhist compassion or not? A student of mine, referring to the incident of the broken leg, once told me, "Roshi, if you broke both my legs and thereby brought me to awakening, I would be eternally grateful to you. After all, broken legs mend, while a lifetime of practice may not achieve enlightenment."

Pressure, it should be noted, is only one aspect of a Zen *sesshin.* Like a well-conducted symphony, *sesshin* has its calm, quiet moods and its crescendos. An able master, like a conductor, directs and blends the diverse movements and sees that none dominates. This variety is also evident in the private encounter. Sometimes the master quietly encourages, at other times he resorts to the "carrot and stick" approach, but without the stick overshadowing the carrot. On still other occasions he shoots fast questions at the student, demanding instant answers. In the *zendo,* too, there is variety. Sometimes the stick-wielding is heavy, sometimes light, and sometimes conspicuous by its absence. When used, it is *selectively* applied by the monitors, who know the limits of the individual sitters. Especially during the first three days of a *sesshin,* when the energies are building up, there is virtually no pressure exerted either by the teacher in *dokusan* or by the monitors in the *zendo.* It is only during the last four days of a *sesshin,* when the energies are running high, that the sitters are pressed to exert themselves to the utmost. They discover that they are capable of much more than they ever imagined.

OBJECTION C: *KOAN*S ARE ARTIFICIAL AND IRRELEVANT

"The Zen *koans* are artificial problems imposed from the outside by the teacher. They do not arise from the practitioner's own life situation but from stories of ancient Zen masters. Accordingly, they have little or no relevance to the complexities of contemporary life."

REPLY

Undoubtedly the best *koan* is one that naturally grows out of one's life situation. For example, a Buddhist might be gripped by the following problem: "If all beings without exception are intrinsically perfect, as the Buddha proclaimed, why is there so much imperfection, so much pain and suffering in the world?" Or a believer may question intensely:

"If I am fundamentally a Buddha, why do I act like anything but one?" Those driven by the need to dispel a fundamental contradiction between their faith in the truth of the Buddha's pronouncement and the evidence of their senses have a natural *koan*. Similarly, if the question, "Where did I come from when I was born and where will I go after I die?" gripped one constantly, it could be another natural *koan*. I emphasize "could" because not everyone would be motivated to resolve the matter of birth and death. A natural *koan* is a personal perplexity that gives one no rest.

Strictly speaking, the inquiry "Who am I?" is not a *koan*, for it lacks a contradictory element, the "bite" that wheedles the intellect into attempting a solution impossible for it. Yet it too can be effective as a spiritual dilemma. At the base of all seeking, whether couched in terms of the "I" or a *koan*-type paradox, is the desire for self-understanding. If students tell me that the Who? inquiry has been with them since childhood, and that they feel strongly drawn to it, I assign it to them and then give pointers on how to work with it.

In my book *Zen: Dawn in the West* I mention the case of a man who fought in World War II and saw extensive action in the Pacific theater. When he returned to the United States he was utterly beat. In his own words, "I could not work, sleep, or make love." One question obsessed him: "What is reality?" Although his formal education did not go beyond primary school and he had no philosophic or religious inclinations, this question kept biting into him. He would wake up in the middle of the night and the first thing that came into his mind was "What is reality?" Walking along a street he would bump into telephone poles, so absorbed was he in the question. After some six months in this state an explosion took place in him, followed by a tremendous joy. This was his enlightenment. His exhausting war experiences had provided him with a natural *koan*.

The traditional Zen *koans*, however foreign they may appear initially, can have just as much impact as a natural *koan*. The main purpose of an assigned *koan* is to awaken an aspiration to self-realization that is normally submerged. People are usually propelled into Zen training by profound dissatisfaction with life, a fear of living and a dread of dying. A *koan* provides a much-needed focus for their spiritual striving and eventually evokes a strong aspiration to awakening. It is emphatically untrue that *koans* have no relevance to one's daily life. On the contrary, they embody our deepest spiritual concerns; through the struggle to penetrate them they become very real and very intimate.

As Heinrich Zimmer points out in *Philosophies of India*, knowledge is the reward of action:

> For it is by doing things that one becomes transformed. Executing a symbolical gesture, actually living through, to the very limit, a particular role, one comes to realize the truth inherent in the role. Suffering its consequences, one fathoms and exhausts its contents.[3]

This passage also expresses the value of *koan* training. Because *koans* cannot be theorized about in the abstract, they compel us to feel and act, not merely to talk and think. They liberate us from the snare of language, which fits over experience like a straitjacket; they pry us loose from our tightly held dogmas and prejudices; they empty us of the false notion of self-and-other that distorts our inner vision and our view of the world. How can the realization of such a liberated state be called artificial or irrelevant?

OBJECTION D: ZEN MASTERS HAVE TOO MUCH POWER

"A Zen master is an authoritarian figure with absolute power, nowhere more so than in his teaching room, where all the procedures are weighted in his favor. With an imperious clang of his handbell, he may ring out a student at any time—even in the middle of a bow or a sentence. The bewildered student is given no explanation for this peremptory dismissal. In contrast, the student may not leave when *he* wishes to; he is completely subject to the whims of the master."

REPLY

A Zen *roshi* is not considered by his followers to be an incarnation of a god or some exalted holy figure. If even Shakyamuni Buddha is not looked upon as divine, how much more would that apply to a *roshi*. One source of his authority is his awakened understanding (and the wisdom and compassion flowing from it). Another source is the sanction to teach he received from his master. Obviously these qualities command a great deal of respect, but they do not compel unquestioning obedience. The Buddha himself affirmed:

> Do not believe anything on the mere authority of teachers or priests. Accept as true and as the guide to your life only that which accords

[3] Heinrich Zimmer, *Philosophies of India* (Princeton: Princeton University Press, 1969), p. 544.

> with your own reason and experience, after thorough investigation. Accept only that which contributes to the well-being of yourself and others.

In Zen there are built-in checks which help to restrain a *roshi* from dictatorial displays of power. The very presence of a twenty-five-hundred-year-old lineage acts as a corrective to individual grandiosity. Moreover, there is a tradition going back to the sixth century in China in which outstanding masters and patriarchs are mocked in a manner that is best described as "praise by slander." Listen to Zen master Wu-men describe Bodhidharma, the First Patriarch of Zen in China and the twenty-eighth in line from Shakyamuni: "That broken-toothed old barbarian who came so importantly from across the seas. He had only one disciple and even he was a cripple." The Buddha receives similar treatment: "Old Shakya put on a clumsy play and was no better than a child." There is wisdom in this attitude of disrespectful respect and respectful disrespect. Its purpose is to bring these great figures down to our level and to prevent us from deifying them. After all, Buddha-nature is common to the lowborn and the highborn, to saints and sinners; if we are willing to exert ourselves mightily as the ancients did, we too can realize our potential buddhahood. But if we look up at them adoringly, they seem so far above us that their achievement of buddhahood appears beyond our reach.

In Zen it is said that the primary role of the master is to protect students from his influence. A good teacher tries to guide himself accordingly. The *roshi*'s aim is not to control the lives of his students but to make them strong enough to lead their own lives with awareness, equanimity, and compassion. While it is also said in Zen that the *roshi* stands in place of the Buddha, this really means that he manifests the awakened Buddha-nature common to all. In any case, the authority of a *roshi* over his students extends for a limited period only. When they have completed their Zen training, approached his level of understanding, and "graduated," his authority over them ceases. What remains is the disciples' deep respect and gratitude toward their teacher.

Ken Wilber, who is familiar with Zen training methods, writes in his book *Eye to Eye*:

> I have been a participant-observer in almost a dozen non-problematic new religious movements, Buddhist, Hindu, Taoist. In none of those groups was I ever subjected to any harsh degree of authoritarian

> pressure (discipline, yes, pressure, no). In fact, the authoritarian pressure in these groups never even equaled that which I experienced in graduate school in biochemistry. The masters in these groups were looked upon as great teachers, not big daddies, and their authority was always that of a concerned physician, not totem boss.[4]

The contention that the *roshi*'s authority is total in the *dokusan* encounter, as purportedly shown by the fact that he may ring out a student at any time, is based on a misunderstanding of a vital function of private guidance. As pointed out earlier, to be effective a *roshi* must size up a student immediately and decide intuitively how best to help him or her. If the student's manner perhaps reflects an inflated pride, nothing will deflate the balloon of self-importance faster than a sudden wordless dismissal.

How well I remember the effect of this "fast-bell" treatment administered to me by Harada Sogaku Roshi early in my training in Japan. During a seven-day *sesshin* I had been having a series of *makyo* (hallucinations) in which I saw the universe dyed in the colors of Paul Klee, only more vivid, more intense, and, paradoxically, more colorless. I was the universe. Only I am, nothing else is. My excitement was unbounded. "This *must* be awakening," I told myself repeatedly in the *zendo.* As I sashayed into the Roshi's room, brimming with self-confidence and prepared to receive the Roshi's acclaim, he immediately rang me out. I was stunned. My first thought was, "So he doesn't want to sanction a foreigner's enlightenment!" At the next encounter again I waltzed in, my conceit somewhat diminished but still strong enough to communicate itself to the Roshi. As I was in the act of prostrating before him, he clanged his bell. "Out!" it commanded. Back at my mat in the *zendo* I was boiling mad. Two dismissals in a row with no explanation. This was too much! One more wordless dismissal and I was quitting, I told myself. At my third appearance that day I actually reached the mat in front of the Roshi, having already made my prostrations. As I sat glaring balefully at him, the Roshi suddenly seized his bell and rang me out again.

Back in the *zendo*, I began to reconsider my own behavior and whether it had any connection with all these peremptory dismissals. My anger started to evaporate, and some self-reflection and humility

[4] Ken Wilber, *Eye to Eye: The Quest for the New Paradigm* (Garden City: Anchor Press/Doubleday, 1983), p. 265.

began to emerge. "You've got too much ego, that's why you were rung out three times, you conceited idiot," I told myself wretchedly. "At your next meeting you must apologize to the Roshi and not even suggest you are enlightened, for obviously you're not." And I did just that.

To come to understand by oneself what is wrong with oneself is always more valuable than to be told it by someone else, even one's own teacher. All this, and more, such Zen treatment can accomplish. Were a student allowed to leave the *dokusan* room whenever *he* wanted to, the *roshi* would be deprived of this invaluable device. The *roshi* must be free to push a person down or raise him up, to encourage one and chastise another. The allegation that the personal encounter invests the *roshi* with unlimited authority and deprives the student of his rights could only be made by someone unfamiliar with the aims and functions of private instruction in Zen.

OBJECTION E: BASICALLY, THERE IS NOTHING TO TEACH

"Zen maintains that in an ultimate sense there is nothing to teach and nothing to learn, nothing to seek and nothing to find. As a Zen verse puts it, 'Without raising a foot we are there already. The tongue has not moved, but the teaching is finished.' If this is so, why is there private instruction? Why severe training? Why Zen itself?"

REPLY

It is true that in an ultimate sense there is nothing to teach or learn, nothing to know or do. Yet one is not entitled to say that unless one has actually realized down to one's bones the truth of those statements. For truly to know that there is nothing to know is to know a great deal. Spiritual traditions are full of such glittering truths as: "You cannot enter a place you never left"; "The Absolute is a sphere whose center is everywhere and whose circumference is nowhere"; "Who sees not God everywhere sees him truly nowhere"; or "Refrain from seeking buddhahood, since any search is condemned to fail."

These quotations reflect the awakened awareness of the masters. By simply reading them can we dispel our greed, anger, and deluded thinking, thereby transforming our lives? Hardly. This is not to say that reading and study are useless. What others have written about their own deep spiritual experiences can be valuable in showing the way and inspiring one in the spiritual quest—up to a point.

The time comes when we need to abandon the armchair for the sitting mat and undertake training under a genuine master. For the Way, to be a Way, must be walked. Religious doctrines remain mere concepts until translated into actions. It is by acting out the profound teachings that we are transformed. As the Buddha himself affirmed:

> It is indeed a fact that salvation cannot come from the mere sight of me. It demands strenuous efforts in the practice of meditation. . . . A man must take medicine to be cured: the mere sight of the physician is not enough.

It is to this end, then, that Zen masters Po-shan, Dogen, and the rest urge us to exert ourselves to the utmost. Why else the strenuous exertions of the Buddha and the patriarchs if not to see into their own nature? If there were nothing to do, "then Bodhidharma could just as well have written a note of two or three lines and sent it on to China," comments Zen master Hakuin wryly.[5] Instead Bodhidharma risked his life to make the hazardous journey to China and then spent nine years "facing the wall" in meditation at Shao-lin temple. Hakuin goes on to emphasize that, "It is an unparalleled ignorance to believe one can become a buddha without seeing into one's own nature."[6]

But having trained oneself in *zazen*, having gone to many four-, and seven-day *sesshin*s, having heard many commentaries by the master, having had numerous private encounters with him, and at last having caught a glimpse of one's true nature, one can finally assert with confidence: "Without raising a foot we are there already. The tongue has not moved, but the teaching is finished."

[5] Philip B. Yampolsky, *The Zen Master Hakuin: Selected Writings* (New York: Columbia University Press, 1971), p. 137.

[6] Ibid., p. 137.

AN INTRODUCTION TO JAINISM
Embodied Knowledge in a Non-Theistic Tradition

Lynna Dhanani

Om namo arihamtanam
om namo siddhanam
om namo ayariyanam
om namo uvajjhayanam
om namo loe savvasahunam

eso pamca namukkaro
savvapavapanasano
mamgalanam ya savvesim
padhamam havai mamgalam

Praise be to the Omniscient Ones
Praise be to the Liberated Bodiless Souls
Praise be to the Mendicant Leaders
Praise be to the Mendicant Teachers
Praise be to all Mendicants in the World

This *Mantra* of Fivefold Homage
Destroys all demerit
And is the first and foremost of all
Auspicious recitations

Implicit in the text of this *Panca-Namaskara Mantra*, known to Jains as the "The Great Mantra" (*maha-mantra*), is found the essence of the Jain way: liberation from worldly bondage (*moksa*) and the attainment of infinite knowledge (*kevalajnana*) resulting from the complete separation of the Pure Soul (*paramatman*) from karmic defilement. The five grades of religious prototypes (*paramesthin*) are given homage for their pursuit and achievement of *moksa* and their various roles in guiding others to the same. Similar to early Buddhism, Jain spirituality and devotion centers around the achievement of such a goal as opposed to worship centered on a Creator God or deity.

This non-theistic orientation toward reality can require special explanation for those most familiar with theistic and especially Abrahamic monotheistic perspectives. If the defining characteristic of theistic traditions is belief in God as the ultimate reality, the most natural and important starting point of comparison when turning to face a foreign tradition is knowing its unique way of conceiving of the supreme reality. In Jainism, it is the Pure Soul (*paramatman*), the realization of which occurs during the moment of liberation, that constitutes the supreme reality and goal. On the surface, the notion of *paramatman* and of God are contradictory, hence a long history of Jain polemical literature criticizing the idea of the existence of a Supreme Being. But beyond the dogmatic, unavoidably conceptual level of polemical argumentation, we want to ask, is there not a way in which God and *paramatman* may be seen to relate with one another on the most profound level, that of the essence and intention underlying conceptualization? One particularly fruitful interpretive framework for exploring this issue is provided by the teachings of the *religio perennis* as expounded in the writings of Frithjof Schuon, which enables us to place Jainism in a meaningful relationship with other faiths.

The *religio perennis* offers a sophisticated way of explaining the phenomenon of the existence of many religions under the perspective that the ultimate reality can in essence only be One, but without denying the specific nature and orientation of each individual religion. It is the fundamental principle of the *religio perennis* that every orthodox religion comprises within its framework the twofold requirement of discernment between the Permanent and the impermanent and a sacred means of attachment to the Permanent or Real. It is by means of this essentialized vision that it is able to move beyond the polemical rhetoric of theism versus non-theism. Specifically in regard to grasping the meeting point between these two major categories of faiths, the *religio perennis* asserts that what is most immanent in reality is ultimately identical or at least analogous to what is most transcendent, so that in the final analysis the concept of God and that of the *paramatman* may be seen to possess the same semantic value and reality.

In this article, we attempt to give an overview of the Jain religion and to delineate key principles of Jain doctrine and method using the comparative framework offered by the *religio perennis*. We use this method in part to clarify Jain tenets to those more familiar with theistic notions of reality. Whereas Ananda Coomaraswamy was the only perennialist to touch upon Jainism to some degree with his book *Jaina Art*, Frithjof Schuon's books and explications of *Vedanta* and Buddhism contain several fundamental principles and insights that are applicable to Jainism, despite Jain polemical history with these two traditions. Schuon goes clearly beyond simple parallelism or idealism and fully comprehends the complexity of any given religious tradition. In his words:

> It has been said more than once that total Truth is inscribed, in an immortal script, in the very substance of our Spirit; what the different Revelations do is to "crystallize" and "actualize," in different degrees according to the case, a nucleus of certitudes which not only abides forever in divine Omniscience, but also sleeps by refraction in the "naturally supernatural" kernel of the individual, as well as in that of each ethnic or historical collectivity or of the human species as a whole.

It is the goal of this article to describe this "nucleus of certitudes" in Jainism that most directly speaks of its own orthodoxy, and to use some of Schuon's ideas heuristically to introduce Jainism.

A Brief History

Over time, apparent misunderstandings have arisen over the origins of Jainism and its relationship with its "sister religions" of Hinduism and Buddhism. Over the thousands of years of its existence, Hinduism—a generic term covering a variety of doctrines and practices of Vedic and sometimes non-Vedic, yet Indian origin—has had the remarkable capacity to absorb various traditions as it own, without negating, in principle, what is true to each. Many have claimed that Jainism is an offshoot of Hinduism, considering it as a Hindu sect. What is important to realize here is the specific nature of Jainism. Similar to Buddhism, Jainism represents "as spontaneous and autonomous a reality as do the other great Revelations."

There has been an ongoing debate between Jainism and Vedic Hinduism as to which revelation preceded the other. What is historically known is that there was a tradition alongside that of Vedic Hinduism known as the *sramana dharma*. Essentially, the *sramana* tradition included in its fold the Jain and Buddhist traditions, which disagreed with the eternality of the *Vedas*, the need for ritual sacrifices, and the supremacy of the *brahmins*. Spiritual efforts were based almost solely upon self-perseverance and control of one's passions, hence its characteristic asceticism. Up until the fairly recent return of Buddhism to India (mainly by Tibetan monks and laity), Jainism has existed as the only *sramana* sect in India since approximately the thirteenth century, when Buddhism left the subcontinent altogether. What both the *sramana* and Vedic traditions share is a commonwealth of symbols arising from a similar spiritual, mythological, and cultural universe, each tradition having the capacity to borrow from the other and assimilate similar doctrines and methods that speak the same spiritual language or fulfill certain spiritual needs that surface periodically.

The word "Jain" comes from the word *jina*, derived from the Sanskrit verbal root *ji-* meaning "to conquer or overcome." In Jainism, the term *jina* came to designate the "Spiritual Victors," the *jina*s, the succession of human teachers, who, having conquered their passions and attained infinite knowledge, taught the way to eternal liberation, *moksa*, from worldly bondage. The *jina*s of Jainism, the twenty-four messengers of liberating knowledge, are also known as the *tirthankara*s. The Sanskrit root *tirtha* means "ford" or "crossing," *tirthankara* thus meaning "the one who crosses the ford of existence." René Guénon brings to light the significance of this symbolism in the following passage:

> The "crossing of the bridge" (which also may be the crossing of a ford) is found in nearly all traditions and more particularly in certain initiatic rituals as well. The crossing may likewise be made on a raft or boat, which then is linked with the very widespread symbolism of navigation. The river that must be crossed is more specifically the "river of death"; the shore which is left behind is the world subject to change, that is, the domain of manifested existence (most often considered in its human and corporeal state in particular, as it is from this state that we must actually set forth), and the "other shore" is *nirvana*, the state of the being which is definitively set free from death.

After years of hardship, austerities, and spiritual discipline, these wanderers, in their last birth, shed their karmic veils of existence and attained *moksa*, already destined to become *tirthankara*s. After attaining *moksa*, they taught the spiritual knowledge and discipline conferred on them by their enlightenment. "If you desire to cross the terrible ocean of worldly existence, O virtuous one, better you quickly board the boat of austerity and self-restraint."

Although little is known historically about the last twenty-two *tirthankara*s, we find that they are mentioned in different Hindu and Buddhist scriptures. The cult of Rsabha, the first *tirthankara*, was said to be extremely popular among Jains, and he is said to have lived for an extensive period ranging up to 600,000 years until he reached *moksa* on Mount Kailasa. The Hindu text the *Bhagavata Purana* mentions

Rsabha as an *amasavatara*, a "minor incarnation of Visnu." The lives of the last three *tirthankaras*, Nemi, Parsva, and especially Mahavira, "Great Hero," are known in greater detail. One sees references to a great number of *nigganthas* or "unattached" ascetics who followed Parsva's path of fourfold restraint mentioned in Buddhist texts. But it was Vardhamana Mahavira, the final *tirthankara* of Jainism, who came to recapitulate the teachings of the previous *jinas* and propound the doctrine and method of Jainism as we know it today.

Mahavira

Tradition speaks of Mahavira's birth taking place in 599 BC in the large city of Kundagrama in the realm of Vaisali (near modern day Patna in Bihar, Eastern India), where he was born into a warrior-caste (*ksatriya*) family. The two main sects in Jainism, the *Svetambaras* and *Digambaras*, differ as to whether certain life events of Mahavira actually occurred. The *Kalpasutra*, a scripture of the *Svetambara* sect, describes scenes from Mahavira's life and gives an account of his extraordinary birth, wherein the god Indra switches the embryo of Mahavira from the *brahmin* woman Devananda to the *ksatriya* queen, Trisala, though *Digambara* versions of this story deny this occurrence. During Queen Trisala's pregnancy, the appearance of fourteen heavenly symbols in a dream—for example, a lake adorned with lotuses—signified the coming of a great being. After these dreams were interpreted, both of Vardhamana's parents (Vardhamana being Mahavira's birth name), King Siddhartha and Queen Trisala, were aware that they were about to bear either a universal monarch (*cakravartin*) or a great sage. What is known is that he lived the life of a prince until the age of thirty, either marrying and having a daughter according to the *Svetambara* tradition or remaining unmarried in the *Digambara* rendition. In both traditions, he is invariably characterized by a strong aversion to worldliness.

Mahavira's thirtieth year marked the blessed moment in his life when he was visited by gods, who were said to have beckoned him to leave the world.

> Victory, victory to thee, gladdener of the world! Victory, victory to thee, fortunate one! Luck to thee, bull of the best *ksatriyas*! Awake, reverend lord of the world! Establish the *dharma-tirtha* (teaching of the holy path) for the sake of every living being in the entire universe; it will bring supreme benefit to all!

Thus spoke Laukantika, the god known as the "World-Ender." Different versions of the Great Renunciation exist. What is known is that after donning a divine cloth and pulling out his hair, Mahavira set out on foot, wandering for up to thirteen years seeking Truth while performing extreme austerities, fasting, and penance with deep concentration. After years of temptations and hardships at the hands of both men and gods, Mahavira reached *kevalajnana*, infinite and supreme knowledge, under the *sala* tree, close to his thirteenth year of exile from the world. Mahavira's enlightenment can be paralleled to that of the Buddha's, since "the enlightenment which occurred in the lifetime of [Sakyamuni] beneath the Bodhi tree is none other than what in more or less Western parlance would be called 'Revelation,' namely the reception of the Message or of the prophetic function." As Buddha brought the doctrine of suffering, Mahavira brought the doctrine of non-violence, *ahimsa*, and non-onesidedness, *anekantvada.*

Mahavira's Enlightenment and Community

Mahavira attained the Four Perfections or Four Infinities (*ananta-catustaya*) of Joy, Power, Supreme Apprehension, and Supreme Cognition. In Jainism, the enlightenment of the *tirthankara*s is characterized by such an exalted state of awareness that enlightenment is equated with omniscience, understood as the "ability to know and see everything in the universe at all times and in all possible modifications simultaneously, in other words a complete unfettering of the mind," thereby knowing the past, present, and future and being able to read the thought processes of others. Certain Buddhist schools and a few Vedic schools, such as the *Mimamsa*, criticized this idea of omniscience, but it nevertheless remained the ultimate category of knowledge in Jain scriptures.

After his enlightenment, Mahavira gave sermons to humans and animals simultaneously in all four directions, his speech being an emanation of divine sound. Mahavira and his first and direct disciples, the *ganadhara*s, who passed his teachings on to the community before and after Mahavira died, codified the rules of the fourfold *sangha* of male monks (*sadhu*s), female monks (*sadhvi*s), laymen and laywomen (*sravaka*s). Reluctant to use Sanskrit, the language of the spiritual elite, he preached in Prakrit, a language understood by the common people of his time, up until the day that he reached *nirvana*, in 527 BC at the age of seventy-two. As the tradition states, all souls who attain the perfection of the *jina* abide in the abode of the perfected beings (*siddhas*)—that "slightly bending place" that resides at the apex of cosmic existence.

Mahavira's message stated that man must take his own initiative in his deliverance and emphasized the need for a form of spiritual rigor that disengaged the soul from the snares of worldly and self-perpetuated bondage. The goal of renunciation in Jainism is to restore the soul to its true state; as the soul in its unadulterated form is said to exist in isolation from matter, the aspirant should seek to abstract himself—his awareness—from material sensations, in order to attain supreme isolation (*kevalajnana*). The following statement by Schuon explains the necessity for the comprehensive character of renunciation in Jainism:

> Renunciation would be purposeless were it not a case of grasping with our whole being—and not with the mind alone—what we really are, and above all of understanding what total Reality is, that "something" by virtue of which we exist, and from which we cannot for a moment escape. Renunciation aims at preventing man from becoming imprisoned in an ephemeral illusion, from identifying himself with it and finally perishing with it; it aims at helping him to free himself from the tyranny of dreams that leave no outlet. A sage never loses sight of the universal context of life; he does not give himself up to fragments of consciousness such as events agreeable or disagreeable, joyful or sad, for he is perpetually conscious of the whole, so much so that in the end the question of "renunciation" does not even exist for him any longer; he has ceased to be involved in fragmentary experience, he is not bound by it, he does not identify himself with it, nor is he consumed by it.

One could say that in Jainism the true position of the soul and the final goal are so parallel that in fact the state of renunciation for a Jain monastic is none other than abiding in the way things are, in the nature of things. Because of this preeminent importance placed on renunciation, those who were able to fully renounce the world were and continue to be considered the spiritual "elite."

Regarding the scriptures, the Jains believe that the sermons of the *jina* encapsulate "divine sound" (*divyadhvani*). *Artha*, the meaning that manifested from these divine sounds, was said to be translated into "canonical scriptures" (*sutra*) by the *ganadharas*. After an elaborate history of events took place, the scriptures as we know them today were written by Mahavira's later disciples, several centuries after his *nirvana*, compiled into some "sixty sets of texts" (*agamas*).

The writing of the scriptures were prompted from different councils, one of which eventually led to the major split in the community (*sangha*), between the "sky-clad" (nude) mendicants and (clothed) laity called the *Digambaras* and the "cotton-clad" *Svetambara* sect, each adhering to its own set of scripture and rule. The major points of contention existing between these two are whether one must be completely free of possessions, and therefore nude, in order to attain *moksa*; whether an embodied omniscient being engages in any worldly activity and bodily demands, such as eating; and finally whether a woman can attain liberation. The *Svetambaras* believe that the nineteenth *tirthankara* was a woman, and that women have the ability to attain freedom from bondage. The *Digambaras* contest this idea, since women are not allowed to be naked. Other divergences have taken place between the two sects, and the sect that was characterized as a combination of both *Digambara* and *Svetambara* practices, the Yapaniya, was short-lived. Nevertheless, each had its place in the context of the overarching tradition, which "has the function not only of communicating vital truths, but also of creating an environment adapted to the manifestation of spiritual modes of a particular character."

Mahavira's community spread rapidly in its earlier years through monastic initiation (*diksa*) and sermons, first in North India, and then later in the South. Jainism's popularity wavered over time due to its relationship with different political movements, spiritual figures, and outside communities. Several practices entered into Jainism that were foreign to its original structure, such as tantric yoga, the use of mystical diagrams (*yantras*), and devotional worship (*puja*) (which were incorporated into Jain ritual with the rise of the *bhakti* movement in India).

Jainism did not leave the subcontinent until the twentieth century, for two reasons: one, a strictness regarding travel and means of transportation stemming from the "extreme" form of non-violence practiced, and two, the rigorous spiritual demands of the religion on both mendicants and laity. Today, the six to seven million followers in India, East Africa, England, and America belong to various subdivisions within the *Svetambara* and *Digambara* sects. The main divisions existing in the *Svetambara* branch, for example, can be generally divided into the non-icon worshippers, the Sthanakvasis and Terapanthis, and the icon (*murti*) worshippers, the Murti-pujaks. Each have contributed to the wealth of Jain literature, art, and philosophy.

Situating Jainism's Non-Theism

Jainism's intrinsic orthodoxy rests on the foundations of a non-theism based solely on the truth of the permanent reality of the *paramatman*. Schuon addresses the validity of such a non-theistic perspective in the following passage from his chapter entitled "Orthodoxy and Originality of Buddhism": "One . . . does not have to ask whether [Buddhism's] 'non-theism' (not its 'atheism') is reconcilable, in its expression, with the Semitic theism or any other, but solely whether that 'non-theism' expresses the Truth or a sufficient and effective aspect of that Truth." Exoterically, Jainism is seemingly situated at the opposite pole from that of the Semitic traditions, since the transcendence of God in Islam, for example, implies a height, and "height suggests an abyss between man and God, because the servant is below and the Lord above." This can be resolved, however, in the light of the principle that a movement towards the higher, the most transcendent, is simultaneously a movement towards the inner, the most immanent. It is in the metaphysical identity between these two poles that faiths as different as Jainism and Abrahamic monotheism may be seen to meet—at the point that is simultaneously both God and supreme goal. We use the word "God" here to connote reality understood in its essence and totality. As Schuon explains,

> The word "God" does not and cannot admit of any restriction for the simple reason that God is "all that is purely principial" and that he is thus also—and *a fortiori*—"Beyond-Being"; this one may not know or may deny, but one cannot deny that God is "That which is supreme" and therefore also That which nothing can surpass.

In Schuon's terminology, "Beyond-Being" refers to God in His Essence or what is equivalent to the *paramatman*, the "supra-personal Self."

From this perspective, Schuon asserts that each tradition emphasizes a certain aspect of reality. For its part, Jainism emphasizes the immanence of divine knowledge and the soul as the locus of this knowledge. That what is understood as divine knowledge in Semitic traditions—more specifically in their esoteric circles—corresponds to pure consciousness—the most important quality of the soul in Jainism—negates, for the Jain, the necessity to posit either a God "out there" or a *Brahman*, a preexisting Self—God as Self—like that of *Advaita Vedanta*, vis-á-vis the *paramatman*. Everything within the religion being a function of this necessitates Jainism's rigorous asceticism and self purification; for "the inward unfolds on the basis of a certain nullifying of the outward, or on the basis of a mental or moral 'concentration.' The 'straight gate' is *a priori* a sacrificial annihilation, but it also and more profoundly signifies a beatific annihilation." In Jainism, this "beatific annihilation" corresponds to the level at which the soul exists in its natural state, characterized, in addition to consciousness and energy, by bliss (*ananda*).

Acharya Mahaprajna, the current leader of the Terapanthi sect, gives prime importance to the function of the intellect, the vehicle of awareness through which "the abstract changes into the concrete, the hidden becomes manifest, and the remote becomes close . . . the invisible turns into the visible and the inaccessible becomes accessible." By virtue of the centrality of the intellect in Jain doctrine, the defining characteristic of man or of what it means to be human is his intelligence and ability to know the abstract or other-worldly realities, therefore his capacity for pure intellection and pure knowledge (*kevalajnana*).

Doctrine (Siddhanta)

It is impossible in a few paragraphs to fully present the core elements of Jain doctrine, let alone its development from the time of the earliest *sutra*s on the subject. But if one comprehends the following structure of Jain ontology, one will have a fundamental understanding of the foundations of all later doctrinal developments. Jain doctrine remained fairly standard throughout history and has never seen a transition such as that from early Indian Buddhism, of which Theravada Buddhism is the best known example, to Mahayana Buddhism. Later elaborations of Jain doctrine only sought to further elucidate preexisting doctrine and avoided changing the ontological status of any of its components or sublimating the external world toward a non-dualism, as occurred in certain Mahayana Buddhist schools.

The first chapter of the *Tattvartha Sutra*—a scriptural text the compilation of which is attributed to the Jain monk Umasvati (second century CE) and one of the only texts accepted by both sects of Jainism—expounds the valid means of knowing, empirical (perceptual, inferential, analogical, and linguistic) and innate (spiritual knowledges, e.g., clairvoyance), that set the foundation for investigating the true nature of reality, on which proper conduct and faith are based. An explicit epistemological method gives those examining reality a reliable means of extracting meaning and of examining the relationships of phenomena in the world. After the general nature of an existent is known by these epistemological means, its specific nature is then understood through a series of "philosophical standpoints," the different perspectives by means of which an existent, by virtue of its multi-dimensionality, is viewed (a few examples of the different perspectives enumerated in the *Tattvartha Sutra* are the "common person's view," the "generic view," the "practical view," and the "etymological view"). Each standpoint "is a proposition established by logic," which relates either to a substance—the essence of a thing—or to its various modifications. The identification of substances gives unity and homogeneity to diversity. Jain doctrine combines philosophy, logic, and ontology in an integral fashion as instruments for understanding the real nature of things. It for these reasons that Jain scriptures are given to enumeration of existents and their respective natures.

As lower epistemological processes are considered valid, albeit limited, means of knowing reality—as opposed to innate knowledge, which opens up onto infinity—the world continues to be a real existent even after liberation. It is by virtue of this characteristic that Jain ontology is considered a realist and dualist metaphysics. It is realist in the sense that knowledge of ultimate reality does not exclude the reality of the existing world; the enlightened worldview includes knowledge of particulars. It is dualist in that the two prime categories of substances, soul and matter, are mutually exclusive.

These two categories correspond to the spiritual and the material and functional realms of existence. Soul and matter, more properly understood in this system as "non-soul," interact eternally in the cosmos. According to the *Tattvartha Sutra*, the following seven truths (*tattvas*) encapsulate the essential relationship obtaining between the spiritual and the material and functional realms. The understanding provided by these, therefore, constitutes the essential foundation upon which an "enlightened worldview" can be formed.

1. soul (*jiva*)
2. non-sentient phenomena (*ajiva*)
3. inflow of karmic matter (*asrava*)
4. bondage of soul with the inflow of karmic matter (*bandha*) (cognate with the word "to bind")
5. cessation of the inflow of karmic matter (*samvara*)
6. partial dissociation of the bound karmic matter from soul (*nirjara*)
7. total and absolute dissociation of the bound karmic matter from the soul (*moksa*)

Other scriptures mention nine categories of truth, including auspicious karmic matter, *punya*, and inauspicious karmic matter, *papa*, whereas these two categories are implied in item three and four of the *Tattvartha Sutra.* For the sake of clarity and time, we will group these "seven truths" into the first two categories of soul and non-soul, while keeping in mind that the category of non-soul is always understood in its relationship to the soul.

Jiva: *The Soul*

The Jain vision of the universe entails a cosmos divided into "space-points" (*pradesa*). Whereas souls occupy a limited number of these units, omniscient beings can occupy all of cosmic space. The *Tattvartha Sutra* classifies souls as either enlightened or "enlightened-oriented" and those bound by the cycle of eternal bondage, *samsara.* Worldly souls are broken down into further categories of different sensed beings, from micro-organisms to human beings. Such souls are bound by the laws of transmigration, which has no beginning or end. In this section, we will focus on the nature of the enlightened soul-type—that which realizes its own true nature, the soul as "liberating Substance." On this foundation rests the totality of Jain doctrine.

Whereas both souls and that which constitutes non-soul all belong to the genus of "substance" (*dravya*), the soul as substance is distinguished by sentience. The *Tattvartha Sutra* further breaks down sentience into knowledge and intuition. Such sentience or consciousness exists in all soul types, despite limitations imposed upon it by *karma*, which affects in turn the level of awareness and determines the type of being that comes into existence. Without this quality, the human soul, the most developed of all earthly species, would not be able to know, discern, and will. Several other attributes characterize the soul, two particularly important ones being energy (*virya*) and bliss or beatitude (*sukha*).

The qualities preexist in the substance eternally, although they are subject to change. The level of sentience or beatitude may decrease or increase, but the soul never exists without them. In other words, the substance in general acts as the substratum for all the manifold qualities, in regard to both the attributes of the most gross material objects and those of the soul. The nature of the soul is thus understood through the qualities or attributes. Every quality (*guna*) has its various modifications (*parinama*), which last for a particular time period. Although these modifications are not mere illusions but are said to have the character of existence, they are by nature impermanent, subject to origination and cessation, the quality of persistence belonging to substance alone. Jains use this point to distinguish their doctrine from *Advaita* and Buddhist doctrine, considering them as two extremes or absolutes. Whereas the *Advaita Vedanta* tradition claims that *maya*—the emanation from the changeless, eternal *brahman*—is illusory, the early Indian Buddhist tradition denies the permanence of substance and relegates it to continuous change. The Jains consider themselves between these two perspectives; they attribute permanence to substance and impermanence to the modifications, while considering both to be existing realities.

Liberated beings realize such qualities as bliss, knowledge, consciousness, and joy to their fullest extent and therefore realize the nature of the soul in its innermost essence. The indefinite number of souls that span the universe are in their essence the same immanent Reality that remains unconditioned by the existence of the lower realms of being and the world subject to change by its various modalities. Only the omniscient soul can view reality in its totality and thus comprehend all the attributes in the universe, whereas ordinary man can only perceive the parts of a whole. Padmanabh Jaini explains:

> Because the qualities are innumerable and their modes are infinite, stretching from the beginningless past to the endless future, it is not possible for an ordinary (non-omniscient) person to perceive the existent in its entirety. At a single moment he can be aware either of the persisting unity (*ekatva*) of the substance or the transient multiplicity (*anekatva*) of its modes. This complexity of the existent—its simultaneous unity and multiplicity, eternity and transience—finds expression in the Jaina term *anekanta*, manifold aspects, which purports to fully describe the existent's nature.

According to Jainism, a substance has multiple dimensions and therefore cannot be described absolutely according to only one particular mode and nature. Schuon often writes about manifestation as both discontinuous and continuous, on the principle that it is simultaneously remote from the source and yet projects something of its nature. This remoteness or distinction between quality and accident on the one hand and substance on the other, gives rise to a variance of forms and possibilities which the doctrine of non-absolutism, or multiple aspects (*anekantvada*), sets out to explain by a whole system of "qualified assertions" (*syadvada*) about an existent, taking into account its particular context. *Anekantvada* "denies absolute existence or absolute non-existence, absolute permanence or absolute impermanence and defends non-absolutism." It is by virtue of this method that Mahavira is said to have explained the nature and existence of the soul. In recent times, *anekantvada* has been increasingly used by Jains to explain the multiplicity of religious perspectives with full acceptance of them, whereas previously *anekantvada* was used to demonstrate the validity of Jain doctrine over other religious traditions in India, which, according to Jain thinkers, made absolute claims for what was actually a "partial view of reality" (*naya*).

Although a liberated soul can see things in their totality, such a soul does not disappear upon attainment of Siddhahood into a preexisting, supreme being, but remains forever a fully liberated soul without body. Schuon explains this reality in the following passage: "Even the being who has realized *Parinirvana*, that is, who is no longer limited by an exclusive divine Aspect, but is identified with the divine Essence, such a being is still and always, or rather eternally, 'himself,' for the divine Qualities clearly cannot but in some way be inherent in the Essence." The human state is the only state which permits of this lofty possibility, and it is to this end that the *Arahat*'s entire teachings are aimed.

The *Arhat* is an *Arihanta*, one who has killed the enemy, *Ari*, the active and destructive karmic forces found within his soul. He who has attained the four infinities has left samsaric existence already within bodily form; he is the *Siddha* adorned with the material body. We have already detailed the extraordinary life of Mahavira and the arduous spiritual discipline undertaken before reaching the stage of the *Arhat*. This "liberated being is rigidly self-conscious and in its pure consciousness, no object other than itself is reflected." Depicted in Jain iconography with the umbrella of wisdom over his head, the *Arhat* has at least 1008 Divine Names, such as *suddha*, "the one who is free from all eighteen degradations" (e.g. greed, etc.).

Ajiva: *The Non-Soul*

According to the *Tattvartha Sutra*, something is eternal if it "remains as it is and does not pass away." This definition must be understood before one can correctly understand the way in which things function in the Jain worldview. It is natural for followers of Western faiths to associate the concept of eternality with that of God. The Jain philosophical concept of eternality does not usurp the supremacy of the "spirit" over the "letter," but establishes a definite set of axioms that assists in understanding the forces that act upon the soul and its position in the total space in which it finds itself. The Jain cosmos continues without beginning or end, and souls either continuously transmigrate or attain liberation.

Since it is the nature of the cosmos to continue *ad infinitum*, space (*akasa*), the medium of motion (*dharma*), the medium of rest (*adharma*), time (*kala*), and matter (*pudgala*) exist co-eternally with the soul (*jiva*). Such *ajiva* function as either the efficient or material causes through which the *jiva* subsists and acts. Most of these entities are considered dimensionless and extensive, meeting at the "space-points" (*pradesa*) and thus pervading cosmic space (*loka-akasa*), as opposed to transcosmic space (*aloka-akasa*), an entity-less vacuum.

The way in which these entities function is understood as follows: Space (*akasa*) is the basis for all other substances. The medium of motion (*dharma*) and the medium of rest (*adharma*) function as the supporting cause for motion and for rest in relation to matter or body and to soul. Time (*kala*) has no extension in space like *dharma* and *adharma*, and is likened to droplets placed in each *pradesa*. By reason of inferring the existence of time from the workings of manifestation—from its quality of non-sentience and non-materialism and its modalities of origination, preservation, and cessation—some Jain thinkers categorized time as substance whereas others kept it as a separate category altogether. Like *kala*, matter (*pudgala*) also lacks dimensionality and extension, its basic unit being the indivisible atom, the ultimate cause for material bodies. Extensionality is introduced when atoms cluster, then having qualities such as taste and smell and modes such as subtlety and grossness. It is important to note that material clusters such as these are defined by quality and not by quantity as modern science would seek to do. Atoms combine with each other depending on their viscosity or dryness. Their lack of dimensionality allows them to combine, analogously to the way in which light interpenetrates from various lamps in a single room. Such aggregates then produce the visible elements, sounds, and shapes, in addition to the subtle, vital, and physical body that houses the soul. Intertwined with these material substances is the mass of karmic matter also originating from material or atomic clusters. This generalized *karma* permeates the cosmos. The soul's volition beyond that which is purely spiritual attracts karmic particles, causing the permutation and defilement of *karma* to occur by virtue of this very attraction. When the soul attains liberation, these substances continue to exist as realities, although the soul is no longer bound by them through karmic matter.

Karma, a self-existent entity which works according to its nature, renders a Creator unnecessary. Jains view *karma* as material particles that adulterate the soul and produce certain conditions, having neither sentiency nor any "Divine Will" acting upon them.

Every practicing Jain is familiar with the law of *karma*, that an action brings a concordant reaction from the macrocosm in accordance with one's inner microcosm, and therefore elicits either a series of bondages or else a spiritual severance from that which binds. This interaction between *karma* and *jiva* does not mean that the *jiva* is bound by a sort of fatalism or determinism. The very consciousness of our own bondage points to that which can release us from such bondage, which in Jainism translates into relentless dedication to Jain practice. The practice delineated by Mahavira is an answer to the following existential question expressed in the *Jnatadharmakatha Sutra*: "Oh Lord! How does the soul rise up from the karmic bondage to get liberated, and what makes it entangled and sink into bondage?"

The idea undergirding this question conveys one of the fundamental doctrinal bases for seeking liberation: a fear of a "hellish" continuation in samsaric existence, where pleasure and pain alternate ceaselessly. The Sanskrit term *samsara* has as its base the root *sr*, meaning "to go or to wander." The doctrine of *karma* is intricately interwoven with the theory of the reincarnation of the soul and transmigration. In Jain doctrine, the impact of *karma* and the workings of reincarnation cannot be fully understood without understanding their interrelationship. The state of reincarnation to which the soul transmigrates immediately after bodily death is determined by the consciousness affected by the accumulated *karma* appropriated during its lifetime. The swastika, an auspicious Jain symbol used in different Jain rituals, has in the four spaces between its projected lines four dots. These dots represent the regions through which the soul traverses within *samsara*: that of heaven, the region of the gods; hell, the region of the demons; the region of humans; and the region of plants and animals. A hierarchy of cosmic realms or degrees exists within each of these regions.

By the medieval period in India, such thinkers as Sadhu Devendra Suri, a *Svetambara* monk living in the thirteenth century, had systematized and elaborated upon the basic framework of *karma*. Descriptions about various *karma* and their modifications became extensive, categorically describing hundreds of different *karma* that affect the soul and the world. This, as Paul Dundas notes, was "a mark of Jain intellectual distinctiveness." For an idea of the way in which *karma* has been categorized, consider the following categorization of the eight most fundamental *karma*:

> *Karma* that obscures knowledge (*jnanavarana karma*); *karma* that obscures undifferentiated cognition (*darsanavarana karma*); *karma* which produces the feeling of joy and grief (*vedaniya karma*); *karma* which obstructs belief and conduct (*mohaniya karma*); *karma* which determines the duration of life (*ayus karma*); *karma* which gives the various factors of individuality (*nama karma*); *karma* which destines family surroundings (*gotra karma*); and finally, *karma* which hinders the *jiva* in its ability to resolve and enjoy (*antaraya karma*).

Each of these individual *karma* either obstructs the natural faculties of the soul or determines the various factors of the embodied state.

Of even greater importance in Jain doctrine is answering the question posed in the *Jnatadharmakatha Sutra* of how the soul becomes entrapped and how it frees itself of karmic bondage. When a particular trial presents itself, a specific *karma* has ripened. At that moment, one is left to choose, and the consequences of one's decisions will lead to either a new influx of *karma* (*asrava*), a full cessation (*samvara*), or a partial cessation (*nirjara*). The daily workings of one's life generate either auspicious (*punya*) or inauspicious (*papa*) *karma*, but this *karma* does not necessarily come to fruition in one's lifespan. By its nature, *karma* leaves imprints and traces on the soul that can have long-term consequences. Early in the Jain tradition, these imprints were described as coloring the soul, each coloring designating the degree of purity in the soul by virtue of its karmic stain. The actual coloring is termed *lesya*. Each *karma* has different aspects, such as a physical aspect (*dravya karma*) and a psychic aspect (*bhava karma*), and has a certain manner, duration, intensity, and quantity; its quantity can be divided into the three additional degrees of bondage (*bandh*), existence (*satta*), and realization (*udaya*).

Humans have the capacity, through the upward pull of spiritual exertion, of disassociating and detaching themselves from the exigencies of relative phenomena to which *karma* gives birth. The "Fourteen Spiritual Stages" or more precisely the "Stages of Quality" (*gunasthana*) found in *Digambara* texts after the common era and in later *sutras* of both sects, delineate stages of spiritual development that aspirants undergo. One passes from ignorance and delusion to a mixture of true and false beliefs, finally attaining the "enlightened worldview," an understanding of the real nature of the soul by virtue of the suppression of "view-deluding *karma*." This characterizes the fourth stage of advancement. Thereafter the soul seeks increasingly difficult levels of self-control and attains higher levels of meditation until the ideal attainment of the thirteenth stage, having eliminated all subtle bondage and having reached *kevalajnana*, supreme knowledge. The fourteenth stage is characterized by omniscience without embodiment, in which the final goal of Siddhahood is achieved. The practitioner fluctuates through different stages, and it is only when one stage is permanently fixed by an uncompromised awareness that he has truly realized it. The fact that such a demarcation of spiritual growth applied universally to all aspirants was itself an attestation in Jain doctrine to the "commonality of human experience."

Jain cosmography complements Jain doctrine and sums up in essence the Jain picture of the world outside and the soul's place within it. Early Jain miniature painting in *Svetambara* scriptures illustrates the universe by three worlds—the upper, middle, and lower—within different sections of a Cosmic Man (*loka-purusa*), standing in a vertical posture with arms outstretched and legs set apart. Everything from hell to heaven, from humans to the most elemental forces, are found in Cosmic Man, including the supreme state of Siddhahood found at the summit of all existence. Depictions of regions where *karma* affects different beings, where Mt. Meru stands at the center, and so forth, remind one not only of the macrocosm but also of the inner microcosm of man. The only goal of man's journey through the myriad dimensions of existence remains a state of Pure Self (*paramatman*) completely dissociated from the burdensome effects of karmic causality.

Method: Some Key Practices

Knowing must be in accordance with being, for "one cannot know That which alone is except with all that one is," as Schuon often states. The Jain way prescribes renunciation, the virtue of non-violence, and meditation to complement and actualize scriptural knowledge. Similar to Buddhism in perspective, Jainism does not emphasize the positive, symbolic nature of the manifested world, but rather sees in it imperfection and corruption. Whereas what is positive is consonant with the pure and imperishable substance of the *jiva*, the body and the world are subservient and dismissible in relation to the constant awareness of one's true nature. Jain scripture emphasizes the distinction between the world and the soul, matter and spirit, as exemplified in the following statement of the *Dasavaikalika Sutra*: "One, who does not know the self and the non-self, how can he know the path to self-control (*saiyama*)?"

Jain practice ultimately seeks to cultivate mastery over oneself through five main principles. These "Five Great Vows" (*mahavrata*) taught by Mahavira serve as the fundamental principles behind a majority of Jain practices and ritual, and are as follows:

1. *ahimsa*—non-violence (to other beings and to oneself)
2. *brahmacarya*—chastity (in word, thought, and deed)
3. *satya*—truth (as the foundation of all acts)
4. *asteya*—non-theft
5. *aparigraha*—simplicity or renunciation (in speech, thought, and action)

The *mahavrata* apply to the mendicants and the laity in varying degrees. Initiation into the monastic order makes incumbent upon the mendicant the full performance of all five vows, whereas the worldly affairs and married life of the laity make impossible their full application. The continuance of worldly life entails levels of violence, *himsa*, that would never be allowed of mendicants. Nevertheless, one finds many of the householders performing extreme austerities and living a life marked by ascetic discipline.

The vow of *ahimsa* is specially emphasized and indeed possesses a central significance, for it binds all vows together and thus gives Jain thought and practice its distinctiveness. Jains consider *ahimsa* as the great river of virtue whose tributaries are the other vows such as chastity and simplicity, gushing forth into the multiple domains of human affairs. Both remedy and effect, *ahimsa* annuls the contracting and ego-centered effect of *himsa*, violence against oneself and others (including animals and different sense beings) in thought, action, word, and deed, both gross and subtle.

In the West, many activist groups have recently incorporated the idea of *ahimsa* as a key to social change, to counteract the violence that so regularly occurs in our environment. Although the truth of *ahimsa* can be applied to all domains of life, the true practice of *ahimsa* in Jainism goes well beyond its social value. It serves as a gateway to knowledge, and in a certain sense is knowledge itself. As stated in the *Dasavaikalika Sutra*: "Knowledge of the living and the non-living alone will enable one to be compassionate towards all living creatures. Knowing this, all aspirants proceed from knowledge to eternal virtues. What can an ignorant one do? How does he know what is noble and what is evil?" From the source of *ahimsa* comes a spring of compassion and charity. However, such charity never leaves the bounds of knowledge *qua* truth (*satya*), for as Schuon specifies, "knowledge as such cannot be an instrument designed for charity any more than the Real can be subordinated to the illusory."

This concept of charity manifests itself in such situations as animal shelters built by the Terapanthi Jains in Rajasthan. These shelters are built to house animals, some of which arrive crippled from meat industries, and allow them to live out the rest of their lives in relative peace. Although the place in which they rest is kept clean and these animals are fed, the Jain keepers of the sanctuaries will not prevent a sick animal from dying or try to cure an injured animal. In their opinion, such interference in the natural course of events would amount to acting from emotional attachment to the animal. Not every Jain animal shelter in India works in this manner, but the mere fact that such shelters abide by such a philosophy illustrates the way in which *ahimsa* and *satya* complement each other and manifest in the practical affairs of Jain society.

The importance of *ahimsa* manifests in other ways as well in the daily life of a Jain. For the lay person, for example, it means participating in business that effects the least amount of violence towards all beings. Overall, it demands self-restraint and conscious action. Jain mendicants abide by a rigorous set of rules of conduct, where they must eat, sleep, pray, and even walk with full diligence and with an awareness that even walking kills several hundreds of minute beings. The Five Rules of Conduct (*samiti*)—the regulation of walking, of speaking, of begging, of taking or keeping, and disposal of wastes—are to instill a continued "self-awareness." One often sees Jains, either during devotional rites (*puja*), or as a daily act of conscious non-violence, wearing scarves around their mouths to refrain from unconsciously killing the minutest beings found in the air. This seemingly "extreme" behavior comes from a sense that every action, no matter how minute and subtle, has a karmic effect which can bind the soul and inhibit liberation, especially those that result in *himsa*. This imposes a great responsibility on the practitioner, as words, thoughts, and acts are all consequential. This responsibility extends to conscious eating for example, where, taking into consideration the sacredness of life and our delicate relationship to it, meat or animal products used from animal slaughter are considered to be completely unnecessary for basic human survival. From the Jain point of view, to cause an animal to suffer for one's own "needs" is one of the greatest forms of violence. According to the Jains, one should show compassion to all beings and oppression to the ego and the passional body.

Ahimsa penetrates the life of a Jain in so many diverse ways that its overarching meaning is impossible to describe in a few sentences. *Ahimsa* means, apart from restraint, performing salutary spiritual acts. One must persevere in spiritual effort and certain transforming ascetic practices. There is a great emphasis on undertaking different types of fasting (*upavasa*) to curb the passions and bodily wants. The great period of fasting for the layman, called *paryusan*, extends for eight days. One has the option of performing a partial fast during this time, although some people will forsake food and drink for the entire period of fasting. During *paryusan* and outside of this holy day, Jains ritually perform what is known as *pratikraman*, reciting litanies asking for forgiveness from all that they have harmed and done wrong. The *Panca-Namaskara Mantra* is commonly recited 108 times on a rosary (*mala*) and is considered the greatest of all Jain *mantra*s and prayers.

Alongside the Five Rules of Conduct exist the Three Rules of Preservation (*gupti*). These specify that one should guard over all bodily activity, speech, and thought. Apart from cultivating righteousness, the mendicant should constantly be engaged in pure reflection. In Jainism, there are twelve mental reflections into the nature of reality known as the *anupreksa* that were originally preached by Mahavira. According to Jaini, reflection on such realities "ostensibly increase [the spiritual aspirant's] detachment from the world, protect him from any tendencies toward heretical views, and spur his efforts towards final enlightenment." For example, the first and second *anupreksa* deal with the plasticity of everything surrounding man, and "the utter helplessness of beings in the face of death." The twelfth discusses "the absolutely true teachings of the Jinas (*dharma-svakhyatatva*), how they are most fundamentally expressed through the practice of *ahimsa*, and how they can lead one to the ultimate goal of eternal peace."

Since the outset of the tradition, meditation (*dhyana*) has remained the principal form of inner cultivation. One of the higher forms of meditation mentioned in the scriptures is known as *sukladhyana*, pure and unified concentration on one's own true Self. Several methods of yoga and meditation come from within the tradition, while a certain number of practices were borrowed from movements within Hinduism. These practices, including tantric diagrams and the practice of various *mantras* as mentioned previously, were assimilated into Jainism and took on a specifically Jain character.

Now that we have discussed the vows of *ahimsa* and *satya* in some detail, we will turn to the remaining vows of celibacy or chastity (*brahmacarya*), non-theft (*asteya*) and simplicity (*aparigraha*). These vows more readily characterize the monastic institution and the partial adherence to these vows by the lay are seen as what would be, ideally, a gradual transition into the monastic life. In all actuality, very few of the laity make such a transition, but remain hopeful of acquiring such an impetus in a future life by leading a morally and ethically upright life in the present. Even a weak fulfillment of the Five Great Vows is considered to help curb passional attachment. Devotion to the monastic community fulfills one of the major religious duties of the laity whereas religious education and giving of spiritual counsel are incumbent on the monastic community. The laity must be fully aware of all of the major vows and laws that comprise the life of mendicancy; it is their duty to serve and provide alms according to the monks' strict laws of conduct.

For the mendicants, the practice of such vows translates into several rules that must be followed to ensure that each vow is practiced to its fullest extent. One who gives up the world for the spiritual life, must in consequence give up any desire for sexuality, which in Jainism automatically implies passion. The monastic life implies a great harnessing of one's ego and passions, and Jain mendicants see the benefits of the spiritual life as compensating for what some see as a senselessly strict discipline or as something that goes against the sexual nature of the human being. In this connection, Schuon states that, "no path can afford to be too negative, for an overstrung bow will snap." Jainism does not have in mind to oppress the aspirant to the point of insanity, but to inculcate in him values and discipline that, in the Jain point of view, can lead him directly to the true realization of the nature of soul. Acharya Mahaprajna verifies this in the following passage, where he speaks of the compensation found within yogic practice at the expense of sexuality:

> Some psychologists believe that celibacy means repressing desires and such repression leads to insanity. According to them celibacy is a negative or prohibitive activity. . . . Indian thinkers regard celibacy as a creative power. It prohibits merely the external stimulants.

> Celibacy has an extensive creative power because it is the most effective means of developing and liberating the inner consciousness. . . . The yoga teachers speak of seven *cakra*s (ganglions) in the human body. Among them, the second one is called *swadhishthan*. It is a *kam cakra*—sex ganglion. When it is not developed, a man indulges in sex. When we unite it with *visuddha cakra*, the source of our feeling of happiness undergoes a change. . . . According to psychology, sex is sublimated. According to the science of yoga, the *kam cakra* undergoes ascension (vertical movement). Because of this ascension our mind establishes contact with natural bliss. No one can become a celibate after closing the doors of joy. Only by opening the doors of joy can one become a celibate.

Continuing with the remaining two vows, non-theft (*asteya*) is implemented into monastic ruling regulating the acquisition of necessary goods for one's basic survival, for example, begging for food. The rigidity of the rules governing the acquisition of alms leave one to wonder how in fact mendicants can successfully receive alms. For the *Digambara* mendicants, simplicity (*aparigraha*) is interpreted in its fullest sense as the complete abandonment of worldly belongings, save a water gourd to wash oneself after excretion and a small broom to gently sweep the path before oneself to prevent unintentional violence to insects. *Digambara*s abandon the wearing of clothes and the motivating principle behind wearing them, shame. *Svetambara* monks and nuns own the minimal amount of white clothing necessary and are given a "small broom, a begging bowl, a blanket, a staff, and some volumes of scripture" upon initiation. The early scriptures emphasize the proper execution of these vows and give rules pertaining to monastic behavior in relation to the social and biological world. The second book of the *Acaranga Sutra*, a *Svetambara* scripture, continuously emphasizes the importance of preventing the unintentional or intentional killing of various life-forms. The early scriptures, such as the *Acaranga*, give primacy to action and non-action over doctrine.

This basic overview of the five vows in no way exhausts the depth and diversity of Jain practice and sectarian differences. We can only offer a small window through which to understand the interrelationship of the various doctrinal and methodical principles, in order to give a picture of the organic structure of the tradition as a whole. The Jain ternary Right Knowledge (*samyak-jnana*), Right Faith or Insight (*samyak-darsana*), and Right Conduct (*samyak-caritra*), known as the "Three Jewels" (*ratnatraya*), essentially summarizes the Jain view of "lived" knowledge. The following passage from Acharya Mahaprajna expresses the nature of the Jain way through an elaboration on the *ratnatraya* and the difficulty of reaching the desired goal of emancipation:

> The sequential relationship between Right Faith and Right Conduct does not mean that the former automatically generates the latter. Right Conduct is acquired only when the soul becomes concentrated on itself—when self-knowledge is acquired. If [every soul] concentrated on itself, [assuming] self-knowledge and self-love . . . yield the same result, everyone concentrating on himself would . . . become free from all ignorance and passions. But this is not the case. Even after acquiring Right Faith, passions are not enfeebled and in the presence of passions Right Knowledge does not manifest itself. If one could acquire all having acquired Right Faith, the period of penance and spirituality would have become redundant. But this is not true of real life. The need for long spiritual practice remains even after attaining Right Faith. Even after acquiring perfection of Right Faith perfection of Right Knowledge is not achieved. Even after acquiring perfection of Right Knowledge perfect stoppage of karmic influx is not attained, and liberation is not possible without perfect cessation of karmic influx. There is no principle that perfection of Right Knowledge and perfect cessation of karmic influx are ensured by perfection of Right Faith. The principle is that perfection of Right Knowledge is impossible without perfection of Right Faith and perfect cessation of karmic influx is impossible without perfection of Right Knowledge.

Doctrinal knowledge is only useful to the extent that one realizes and implements its consequences in one's daily practice.

Conclusion

In this introductory essay we have attempted to make Jainism more accessible to those more familiar with theistic conceptions of the world and of God or ultimate reality through a perennialist approach such as that exemplified in the writings of Frithjof Schuon. To view a given religious perspective through the lens of fundamental, universal principles existing in all orthodox traditions—as Schuon does in his comparative treatments of Eastern and Western faiths—is to constructively use what is familiar to gain a deeper understanding of what is unfamiliar.

The Jain conception of God can be seen to equate to an impersonal essence found at the center of each existing soul (*jiva*) in the universe. "Creation" comes into being through the forces of space, time, motion, rest, matter and, by extension, *karma*, each of which is viewed by Jains as distinct ontological entities existing co-eternally with the soul and to which the soul is bound through its perpetual state of transmigration. The religion established by Mahavira, linked to the lineage of twenty-three previous *tirthankaras*, teaches the way out of perpetual bondage through strict adherence to the Five Great Vows—the foundation of intense ascetic practice incumbent on Jain mendicants and, to a lesser degree, the laity. The disassociation of the soul from karmic matter symbolizes the autonomous reality of the soul in the cosmic scheme of things. Jains have always envisaged their practice as being in accordance with the way things actually are and as a way of knowing and of being that conforms with what is deepest in one's nature. As Schuon has eloquently remarked, "Omniscience teaches us all this because it is in our nature to learn it, even as the swallows are taught to fly southwards and the plants to turn towards the light."

Works Cited

Acharya Mahaprajna. *I and Mine*. Ladnun, Rajasthan: Jain Vishva Bharati Institute, 1995.

Bhattacharya, Harisatya. *The Jaina Prayer*. Calcutta: University of Calcutta, 1964.

Cort, John E. "'Intellectual Ahimsa' Revisited: Jain Tolerance and Intolerance of Others," *Philosophy East and West* 50, no. 3 (July 2000).

Dundas, Paul. *The Jains*, 2nd ed. London: Routledge, 2002.

Guénon, René. *Fundamental Symbols: The Universal Language of Sacred Science*, trans. Alvin Moore Jr., ed. Martin Lings. Cambridge: Quinta Essentia, 1995.

Jain, Dulichand. *Pearls of Jaina Wisdom*. Varnasi: Parshvanath Vidya Peeth, 1997.

Jaini, Padmanabh S. *The Jaina Path of Purification*. Delhi: Motilal Banarsidass, 1979.

Schuon, Frithjof. *Language of the Self*, trans. Marco Pallis and Macleod Matheson. Madras: Ganesh, 1959.

——*Light on the Ancient Worlds*, trans. Lord Northbourne. Bloomington: World Wisdom Books, 1984.

——*Logic and Transcendence*, trans. Peter Townsend. London: Perennial Books, 1975.

——*Spiritual Perspectives and Human Facts*, trans. Peter Townsend. Pates Manor: Perennial Books, 1987.

——*Survey of Metaphysics and Esoterism*, trans. Gustavo Polit. Bloomington: World Wisdom Books, 1986.

——*Treasures of Buddhism.* Select Books: Bangalore, 1996.

Shah, Hemant. *Jain Theism: The Concept of God in Jainism.* Ahmedabad: Academy of Philosophy, 1997.

Umasvati. *That Which Is: Tattvartha Sutra*, trans. Nathmal Tatia. San Francisco: HarperCollins, 1994.

SANNYASA[*]

Swami Abhishiktananda

Sannyasa confronts us as a sign of that which is essentially beyond all signs—indeed, in its sheer transparency, it proclaims its own death as a sign. This is how it has been handed down from generation to generation by the dominant tradition of renunciation in India. This also is how it appears above all to those whose heart and mind is overwhelmed by the call to *sannyasa*, and to whom the Spirit has given a glimpse of that infinite Space that is within the heart.

However the *sannyasi* lives in the world of signs, of the divine manifestation, and this world of manifestation needs him, "the one beyond signs," so that it may realize the impossible possibility of a bridge between the two worlds; the *kesi* ["hairy one"; Vedic ascetic] bears up the two worlds, keeping them apart, and yet being the way through which man has access to the *brahma*-world (cf. Ch. Up., 8.4.1; Br. Up., 4.4.22).

These ascetics who flee the world and care nothing for its recognition are precisely the ones who uphold the world. They are like the Vedic *skambha* [tree trunk, symbolizing the axis of the world] which maintains the stability of the universe (cf. Atharvaveda 10.7 and 8). It is their renunciation which is symbolized by all the *yajna*s and *homa*s [sacrifices] offered by the priests. In them the primordial sacrifice of the *Purusa* is accomplished in the full reality of the Spirit. From their inward fire, the *agni* manifested in their austerity (*tapas*), all sacrificial fires are lit.

As far as they are concerned, being known or unknown is of no importance. They go their way in secret. There is no sign to identify them, they are *alinga* [without sign], *avyaktacara* [not manifested]. But society needs to know them. It needs to know that they are there, so that it may preserve a reminder of transcendence in the midst of the transient world.

[*] Editor's Note: from *The Further Shore*. Abhishiktananda was the adopted name of Father Henri Le Saux. *Sannyasa* is the Sanskrit term for renunciation.

For this reason, despite the risk of sclerosis in anything human that becomes an institution, it is none the less good for society to allow a place for monks and publicly to acknowledge their condition as "apart." Further, it is normally through the institution of monasticism that the Spirit reveals himself in making his call heard by those whom he chooses—even if, later on, this very same call thrusts them remorselessly beyond all signs. *Sannyasa-diksa* [initiation into renunciation] can never be made obligatory, but no more can it be denied to those who sincerely ask for it, not to gain prestige from its special status, but that they may be free to devote themselves more entirely to the quest for *Brahman*, "dedicated to *Brahman*, established in *Brahman*, in search of the supreme *Brahman*" (Prasna Up. 1.1)—in fact, "seeking God" (*quaerere Deum*), as St. Benedict says.

It would certainly be wrong to regard *sannyasa-diksa* as an empty sign with no real content. Its rich significance entitles it to be termed a *symbol* rather than a sign (to adopt the widely accepted distinction in contemporary thought, with which is related the recent treatment of the Christian sacraments as symbols). *Sannyasa-diksa* in fact carries all the concreteness of a symbol whose roots penetrate to the very source of being itself—so deeply that in some sense it bears within itself the very reality which it signifies. The sign of *sannyasa*—and equally that of *diksa*—stands then on the very frontier, the unattainable frontier, between two worlds, the world of manifestation and the world of the unmanifest Absolute. It is the mystery of the sacred, lived with the greatest possible interiority. It is a powerful means of grace—that grace which is nothing else than the Presence of the Absolute, the Eternal, the Unborn, existing at the heart of the realm of becoming, of time, of death and life; and a grace which is at the same time the irresistible drawing of the entire universe and its fullness towards the ultimate fullness of the Awakening to the Absolute, to the *Atman*. This sign, this grace is supremely the *tarana*, the raft by which man passes over to the "other shore," "the ultimate shore of the Beyond." Finally, it is even the *taraka*, the actual one who himself carries men across to the other shore, the one and only "ferryman," manifested in manifold ways in the form of all those *rishi*s [sages], *mahatma*s ["great souls"], gurus, and buddhas, who throughout history have themselves been awoken and in turn awake their brother-men.

While it is true that monastic life is transcendent in relation to any *dharma*, it is perfectly natural for the "profession" or initiation which marks the official entry on monastic life to be performed within the particular religious tradition into which each individual is born and in which he has grown up in the Spirit. As long as we remain at the level of signs, the best signs for us are normally those among which we first awoke as men, and as men devoted to God, even if later on those signs have to be purified and freed from their limitations and particularity. However, there is in Hindu *sannyasa* something so strong, such a burning savor of the Absolute, that it is irresistibly attractive to those who have discovered within themselves that ineffable mystery to which the Upanishads give their insistent testimony. Then, no matter which *dharma* happens to be theirs—and even more when they feel themselves unrelated to any *dharma*—they have a strong desire to be coopted into the great Indian tradition of *sannyasa*. Through the sign of the *vamsa* [genealogy], linking them with the ancient *rishis*, their hope is to discover more surely the unique Seer, *ekarsi*, who reposes in the depths of their heart.

Let us take first the case of Christian monks, who are already bound—and freed—by their religious profession. When they come into contact with their Hindu brother-monks and meet with the uncompromising ideal of *sannyasa*, they discover in their own dedication a compelling summons, even more interior than exterior, which no longer allows them any respite. They feel a natural urge to take the garb of the Indian *sannyasi* and to observe at least the most essential of their customs in matters of poverty, abstinence, *abhayam* [fearlessness], etc. Even more fundamentally, they surrender themselves to that freedom breathed in their hearts by the Spirit. In such case to receive a new *diksa* would be without meaning, since in the total surrender of their original profession, expressed in the prayer "*Suscipe*. . . ,"* the essential oblation was already made. Their case is comparable with that of the *paramahamsa* ["great swan"; one who has pure renunciation] who, when the full light shines within him, passes over, quite naturally and without further thought, to the condition of a *turiyatita* [beyond the fourth stage of life] or of an *avadhuta* [renunciate].

* Editor's Note: A Latin prayer composed by St. Ignatius of Loyola, the sixteenth century founder of the Jesuit Order. In English translation it reads: "Receive, O Lord, all my liberty. Take my memory, my understanding, and my entire will. Whatsoever I have or possess Thou hast bestowed upon me; I give it all back to Thee and surrender it wholly to be governed by Thy Will. Give me love for Thee alone along with Thy grace, and I am rich enough and ask for nothing more."

There are, however, others who come to India with no previous monastic or even religious affiliations and, when here, "awake," sometimes as a result of hearing the Scriptures, or more particularly through contact with a true guru, in whom they encounter a burning fire which consumes all their desires and previous aspirations. Then, whether or not they intend, or are allowed, to remain in India, or perhaps have to return to the country of their birth, they often dream of pronouncing their vow of renunciation in the Indian manner, and seek permission to do so, in order that they may be officially set apart from society and may thereafter spend their life in undivided attention to the mystery within. This raises a problem; for, although it is true that *sannyasa-diksa* means an end of all rites and a final passing beyond the world of signs, the fact remains that such a *diksa* is so intimately connected with Hindu ritual and tradition that it can have no meaning for those who do not belong to the Hindu *dharma.*

For a Hindu the initiation to *sannyasa* belongs to the series of rites which mark the stages in the life of the *dvija* (twice-born) from his conception to his being carried to the funeral-pyre. Indeed it actually anticipates the performance of that final *agnihotra* [sacrifice to/by fire] (cf. Ch. Up., 5.4-9). *Sannyasa-diksa* is therefore regularly accompanied by rites which signify the end of all rites; thus the candidate repeats the *gayatri* [Vedic mantra] one thousand times at each of the two *sandhya* [sunset and sunrise] which precede his initiation.

Further—at least in the case of a *krama-sannyasi* [one who takes renunciation as the final stage of life]—the ceremony concludes with the guru handing over to the disciple the paraphernalia of *sannyasa,* namely, the *danda* [wooden staff] and *kamandalu* [gourd], the *kaupinam* and the *kavi* covering. These insignia are barely intelligible outside the particular social and cultural context of India, and their handing over by the guru has little meaning in the case of a non-Indian *sannyasi* who will have to live outside India, despite the rich significance inherent in this ceremony.

One might dream of investing *sannyasa* with signs of universal significance, both as regards the rite and in the external appearance of the *sannyasi.* But by definition all signs are particular, belonging as they must to some given culture and milieu. Once again we are face to face with the paradox (or rather, the contradiction) at the heart of *sannyasa,* that it is at the same time not at home in any world (*aloka*) and also present to all worlds (*sarvaloka*), the sign of what is beyond signs.

Inevitably we are led back to the original *sannyasa* described in the ancient texts as "without sign" (*alinga*), "without rules" (*aniyama*).

The ambivalence of *sannyasa* is such that, in the last resort, when stripped of all rules and outward signs, it can no longer be differentiated from the spontaneous inner renunciation of any awakened man. Nothing external can serve as the sign of the *sannyasi*, just as there is nothing that could be the sign of a *jivan-mukta* [one liberated in this lifetime]. He may roam through the worlds like the *kesi* of the Rig-Veda, he may hide himself in caves and jungles, and equally he may live in the midst of the multitude and even share in the world's work without losing his solitude. The unperceptive will never notice him; only the *evamvid* (the one who knows *thus*) will recognize him, since he too abides in the depth of the Self. However, anyone who is already in the slightest degree awakened cannot fail to experience something of his radiance—a taste, a touch, a gleam of light—which only the interior sense can perceive, and which leaves behind it a truly wonderful impression.

If then there cannot possibly be any universally meaningful sign of *sannyasa*, and if social pressures compel the *sannyasi* ultimately to divest himself of all signs, is there any remaining justification for the retention of an outward form of initiation, since in any case its value is debatable from the point of view of what *sannyasa* essentially is?

The reasons given above for its retention still hold good. There is, first, the grace with which such an institution is unquestionably surrounded and endued. No doubt those whose approach is purely intellectual will question this; but those who have given or received the *diksa* testify to the grace which has flooded their being to its depths. All that they can say of it—and still more, all that they cannot possibly express in words—was made known to them from within through a profound and unforgettable experience.

Then there is the need of society itself for *sannyasi*s, who are known to be genuine, to live in its midst as witnesses to a transcendent presence, even if the signs of this presence cannot well be determined in advance and perhaps have to be thought out afresh every day, as circumstances continually change. We have to trust in the Spirit and to recognize that the monk—being a privileged witness to the Spirit—has ways of action and communication over and above those which pass through the senses. This is his real strength, which no obstacle can resist.

Moreover a public engagement in the presence of authorized witnesses will guard the *sannyasi* most effectively from the temptation to look back. When once the enthusiasm generated by his first spiritual experience has faded, and when he is no longer living in a situation which holds him to his spiritual quest, there is a real danger of his being carried away by his desires, which often appear under a plausible disguise. At the mental level, where a host of desires present themselves as they seek to force the gate of his heart, the memory of his commitment and of the transcendence of which it is the sign, will surely aid him powerfully in remaining steadfast, unshaken. When temptation assails him, and the solicitations of mind and sense are strong, the *sannyasi* can fall back on the remembrance of his vows; so, even if he cannot live on *bhiksa*, his food should always be as simple as possible, the bare minimum required to maintain his body, and never taken to gratify his palate; even if he can no longer wander from village to village and can find no forest hut for his shelter, his house must only be what is absolutely essential for his needs; even if he cannot wear *kavi* dress, even if he cannot make do with rags picked up on the roadside or live altogether without any clothing, his garment must be no more than what is needed to cover his body according to the simplest standards of his neighbors. Always he will remember that his essential obligation is to silence, solitude, meditation (*dhyana*), and this he can never abandon. The very fact that he is no longer marked by any particular outward sign will make him all the more careful to express his dedication through the way he lives. In the end the truest sign of what he is will be his essential freedom and his refusal to be dependent on anything or to seek security in anything whatever outside himself.

His commitment as a *sannyasi* will also safeguard him against the persuasion of others, his friends and relatives for instance, who with the best intentions will try to draw him back into the world, either permanently, or at least for the time being. Some will encourage him to marry; others will invite him into their homes. Some will tell him that he should write or give lectures; others will offer to build an *ashram* for him, where he would be able to teach conveniently. The time may perhaps come for him, when he will have a right to share with others what he has seen within; but first he needs to have passed long years—twelve, according to the tradition—in silence and solitude, forgotten by all and buried out of sight. This alone will eventually make him capable of speaking from experience of the Self;

for all speech about the Self which does not spring spontaneously out of the depths is delusion and a lie; the knowledge of the Self can only be learnt through interior recollection within the depth of the Self. Until the Spirit gives unmistakable signs that the hour has come—and one of the signs is the coming to him of seekers already "established in *Brahman*" (*Brahmanisthah*) his answer to all these invitations will be the same: "My vow does not permit me to do this."

There is another fact that is worth taking into consideration, even though it is limited to one particular religious tradition. Western monasticism, like all religious institutions, is at present facing a crisis, as it gropingly seeks to find a path forward; avoiding on one side a sterile medievalism, and on the other, a modernism which loses all sense of mystery. As has happened in the past, a genuine monastic revival will follow in the wake of a renewed eremitical life, of which many hopeful signs can be discerned. It is possible to imagine that in the West there might be a kind of blend between the tradition of the Desert (harking back to John the Baptist and the great Elijah, the typical monk-prophet of the Old Testament) and the tradition of *sannyasa*, deriving from the primeval *rishis* of India. In such a context those monks who have tasted here of the Upanishadic ideal would feel less out of place when they return to their own countries, for they can no longer adjust themselves to an exclusive spiritual tradition, and still less to any monastery, whether traditional or modernized. Further, in the West there is in fact no recognized initiation into the hermit-life, understood in terms of living "beyond signs." There may therefore be something to be said for communicating the grace of *sannyasa-diksa* to the eremitical life of the West, so that it may infuse into it something of the "great departure" (*mahaprasthana*) which is characteristic of our Indian *sannyasa*. That could only be done by those Christian westerners who have come to India and sat at the feet of a true guru. Discovering in the advaitic experience the fullness of Christ's mystery and universal presence, they will have finally abandoned everything in their symbolical plunge into the Ganga, and will have received from the guru, together with the fire-colored robe, the pressing command to depart to that "place" (*loka*) which is beyond all place, to the very Source. This would not mean the foundation of a new Order, for *sannyasa* is in no sense an "order" and the Spirit does not "found" anything, being rather the foundation of everything; all that is needed is a recognition of the signs of the Spirit's call and a method whereby those who are called may be enabled to answer their call. Evidently a *sannyasa* of this kind would in no way be limited by any forms, and would be open to whoever is called to it, whatever his cultural or religious background may be.

In this connection it is possible to dream of a kind of ecumenical *diksa*, a monastic profession to which both a Hindu *sannyasi* and a Christian monk would be witnesses. The first would transmit to the candidate the initiation which he himself received, and would coopt him into that mystery of *sannyasa* which has been manifested throughout the centuries by innumerable *mahatma*s and *sadhu*s [reninciates], descending from the original *rishi*s who first heard the inner call to the experience of the Self. The other would receive him into the company, no less numerous, of those who have heard the call of Christ to leave all for the sake of the Kingdom, beginning with those giants of the Desert, men like Antony, Hilarion, or Arsenius. Then, beyond that double *vamsa*, both together, in *advaita*, will lead him to the one who has called him, to the Spirit, the Inner Light which shines in the heart of all those who are called.

In such a situation the ritual handing on of *sannyasa* from guru to disciple, despite all, continues to have value at the level of signs—and nothing whatever is exempted from belonging to the world of signs—even though it is absolutely impossible to predict the manner in which that *sannyasa* would actually be lived. But it would be necessary that this handing on, while certainly inducting the candidate into the great tradition of the *rishi*s, should as far as possible be freed from anything that linked it too closely with Vedic myth and ritual. Just as one cannot determine in advance the outward conditions of *sannyasa* in a milieu that is different from the traditional Indian one, so equally one cannot lay down *a priori* what form such a *diksa* should take.

In any case it should contain a minimum of ceremonies, and should be modeled on the initiation of the *vidvat-sannyasi* [one who takes *sannyasa* as expression of Self-realization], since the type of candidate that is here in view would be (to follow the classification of the Sannyasa Upanishads) a *jnana-*, not a *krama-*, *sannyasi*. Indeed it is clear that a *sannyasa* so curtailed of forms could only be given to an aspirant on whom the awakening had already taken hold, and not to one who required the help of an "institution" in order to attain to this awakening. But in whatever form this *diksa* might be given, it should undoubtedly be based above all on the primitive Upanishadic tradition. For the ancient Upanishads, more clearly than any other texts, mark the passage from rites and myths to the experience of the self and of

Brahman who is the All (*sarvam*), and in so doing give freedom from all that adventitious man-made sacredness which the previous age of Vedas and Brahmanas had superimposed on the real Man, the *Purusa*, who is henceforth known in all his glory.

THE ABSOLUTE IN MAHAYANA BUDDHISM AND THE PURE LAND WAY*

John Paraskevopoulos

A perennial problem for Buddhists has always been the question of how to articulate the relationship that obtains between the Absolute and the Relative orders of reality, i.e., between *Nirvana* and *Samsara*. Although conceptions of *Nirvana* within the Buddhist tradition have changed over the centuries, it is safe to say that some of its features have remained constant throughout the doctrinal permutations of its different schools. Indeed, some modern scholars of Buddhism in the West have even questioned whether it is meaningful to speak of an Absolute in Buddhism at all claiming that such a notion is an illegitimate transposition of certain "substantialist" notions relating to the highest reality as found in its parent tradition, Hinduism. This paper will attempt to address the question of whether one can meaningfully speak of an Absolute in Buddhism, in what such a reality consists and what its implications are for understanding the highest goal of the Buddhist path. In doing so, this paper will be focusing chiefly on the Mahayana tradition and, in particular, on one of its principal metaphysical texts—*The Awakening of Faith*—in which we arguably find one of the most comprehensive treatments of the Ultimate Reality in the history of Buddhism. The paper will then address some of the implications of this discussion for understanding the Pure Land way—a spiritual path preeminently suited to the exigencies of the Decadent Age of the *Dharma* (Jp: *mappo*) in which we currently find ourselves.

In one of his early seminal works on Buddhism,[1] Edward Conze in discussing the question of whether early Buddhism can be considered atheistic, summarizes the earlier, Hinayana view, of *Nirvana* as follows:

* Editor's Note: from *Sacred Web 3*, 1999, pp. 121-138.

[1] Edward Conze, *Buddhism: Its Essence and Development* (Harper & Row, 1975), p. 40.

> We are told that *Nirvana* is permanent, stable, imperishable, immovable, ageless, deathless, unborn, and unbecome, that it is power, bliss and happiness, the secure refuge, the shelter, and the place of unassailable safety; that it is the real Truth and the supreme Reality; that it is the Good, the supreme goal and the one and only consummation of our life, the eternal, hidden and incomprehensible Peace.

which is contrasted with this world "i.e., everything conditioned and impermanent, which is emphatically regarded as wholly ill, as wholly pervaded with suffering, as something to be rejected totally, abandoned totally for the one goal of *Nirvana*."[2] In this sense, early Buddhism was radically dualistic in how it perceived these two realms—there was simply no connection between them. In other words, the individual can only attain *Nirvana* through the dissolution of this very individuality whence the doctrine of *anatta* or "no-self." Furthermore, there was also the tendency to view *Nirvana* as more of a state of realization than any kind of "being" given the apophatic reticence of early Buddhism to commit itself to any definitive declarations regarding this ineffable reality and, to some extent at least, its conscious desire to demarcate itself from the metaphysics of the Upanishads. However, to what extent the polemics between these two camps was simply an outcome of a mutual misunderstanding over the meaning and implications of the concept of *atman* is a moot point that warrants an entire treatise in itself.

The Mahayana Perspective

With the arising of the Mahayana as a discrete vehicle of the *Dharma* in its own right, one witnesses a growing tendency to universalize the concept of Buddhahood as a spiritual principle transcending the human personality of Shakyamuni (Gautama) Buddha and embodying a higher and permanent reality. Hence the concept of the "eternal" Buddha which we see promulgated in such central scriptures as the *Lotus Sutra* and in such fundamental doctrines as that of the *trikaya* or the Three Bodies of the Buddha with the *Dharmakaya* (Body of *Dharma*) effectively becoming tantamount to the Buddhist Absolute. Other currents of thought within the Mahayana developed this notion further preferring to view Buddha or *Nirvana* as an all-pervasive

[2] Conze, p. 21.

reality embracing all things including the totality of *Samsara*. In time, this growing tendency of attenuating the distinction between the two realms led eventually, especially in the *Madhayamika* school, to a full-blown identification which we find explicitly formulated in the famous dictum, "*Samsara* is *Nirvana*." From the fairly unqualified dualism of the Hinayana we now find a radical non-dualism at the apex of Mahayana thinking—and all this under the umbrella of "Buddhism." Such a revolution in thinking clearly serves to demonstrate the complexity and controversy inherent in the tradition's struggle to understand the reality of enlightenment.

Having very briefly charted the rudimentary outlines of the transition from the early Buddhist view of *Nirvana* to the more developed and comprehensive conception of the *Dharmakaya* developed by the Mahayanists, let us now delve a little deeper in to the nature of this Absolute. In one of his earliest works, D.T. Suzuki quotes the following passage on the *Dharmakaya* from the great *Avatamsaka Sutra*:[3]

> The *Dharmakaya*, though manifesting itself in the triple world, is free from impurities and desires. It unfolds itself here, there, and everywhere responding to the call of karma. It is not an individual reality, it is not a false existence, but is universal and pure. It comes from nowhere, it goes to nowhere; it does not assert itself, nor is it subject to annihilation. It is forever serene and eternal. It is the One, devoid of all determinations. This body of *Dharma* has no boundary, no quarters, but is embodied in all bodies. Its freedom or spontaneity is incomprehensible, its spiritual presence in things corporeal is incomprehensible. All forms of corporeality are involved therein, it is able to create all things. Assuming any concrete material body as required by the nature and condition of karma, it illuminates all creations. Though it is the treasure of intelligence, it is void of particularity. There is no place in the universe where this Body does not prevail. The universe becomes but this Body forever remains. It is free from all opposites and contraries, yet it is working in all things to lead them to *Nirvana*.

At once, we see a more dynamic and all-encompassing view of ultimate reality possessed of personality, compassion, and intelligence

[3] D.T. Suzuki, *Outlines of Mahayana Buddhism* (New York: Schocken, 1963), pp. 223-224.

which takes the initiative in the liberation of sentient beings. This is in quite stark contrast to the Hinayanistic *Nirvana* which is more of a static, indifferent, and dispassionate reality with no intimate connection to the world of birth-and-death. Nevertheless, both Buddhist traditions would agree that however conceived, *Nirvana* (which is really none other than the experiential dimension of the *Dharmakaya*) remains the ultimate goal of human endeavor and the only real source of human fulfillment and felicity. In any case, by "personifying" the Absolute and in forging a non-monastic path to its attainment, the Mahayana opened the gates of the *Dharma* to all people, especially the laity who had hitherto played a largely peripheral role in the spiritual life.

The Awakening of Faith

In many respects, the culmination of this cataphatic conception of the Absolute is to be found in a very short yet profoundly influential treatise known as *The Awakening of Faith in the Mahayana* traditionally attributed to Asvaghosha although only extant in Chinese. This work, which is often considered as a synthesis of the *Madhyamika*, *Vijnanavada*, and *Tathagata-garbha* traditions, has exercised its influence on the founders of all the major schools of the Mahayana who have venerated the text as an unimpeachable authority on the questions with which it deals. In that respect, it serves as a very useful and reliable compendium of Mahayana metaphysics containing, as it does in a small but terse compass, a range of sophisticated and subtle teaching which one would only come across elsewhere by consulting numerous other *sutra*s and *shastra*s where the same points are often made only obliquely.

The fundamental standpoint of *The Awakening of Faith* is its belief in the Absolute which it calls "Suchness" (*tathata*). As we have already seen, this reality has been called by many other names according to the perspective by which it is envisaged, viz. *Dharmakaya*, *Nirvana*, Buddha, *Sunyata*, *Bodhi*, etc. Now Suchness, the supreme reality according to this text, is both transcendent and immanent. In other words, it is completely beyond anything that we can imagine or conceive in our world of relativity and delusion with all its manifold limitations and yet, at the same time, it constitutes the very core of everything that exists—the deepest centre and "Ultimate Source"[4] of *Samsara* itself. A

[4] *The Awakening of Faith: Attributed to Asvaghosha*, translated, with commentary, by Yoshito S. Hakeda (New York: Columbia University Press, 1967), p. 92.

corollary of this is to say that the Absolute, which is formless, manifests itself through forms which, although finite and limited, are none other than the Absolute of which they are its reflections. This is one way of understanding the meaning of "*Samsara* is *Nirvana*." It is not, of course, to say that they are identical but rather that they are ultimately non-dual. In this way, the world around us is then seen as an admixture of the conditioned and the unconditioned. The most illustrious master of the Hua-yen school, Fa-tsang, was a great devotee of *The Awakening of Faith* on which he has written the most authoritative commentary. His own thought was deeply influenced by this text as is evidenced by the following passage from Francis Cook's book on Hua-yen Buddhism which is cited for the purpose of clarifying what was said earlier about the relationship between *Samsara* and *Nirvana*:[5]

> The very basis of Hua-yen thought seems to be a view of an Absolute which existed prior in time to a concrete world of things which it *became*. There it was said that any phenomenal object is a mixture of the True and the false, or the Unconditioned and conditioned (of course, the sum total of all things is this same mixture). Taking up the absolute side of things first, Fa-tsang says that it itself has two aspects. First, he says, it is immutable. This is not surprising because all religions claim immutability as the nature of the absolute. What kind of absolute would it be which changed like the ordinary things of the world? Being immutable, the absolute is forever unmoved, pure, eternal, still, and serene. This is, in fact, a common description of the absolute in all Mahayana forms of Buddhism. However, Fa-tsang next says something which not only seems to contradict this statement but which also is very unusual in Buddhism; he says that moved by certain conditions, this pure, unmoved eternal Reality changes and appears as the universe of phenomenal objects. However, like the gold which has become the ring, the immutable absolute remains the immutable absolute. Here the picture is apparently one of the emanation of the concrete universe from an immutable absolute with the result that things are a mixture of the absolute and the phenomenal.

This passage has been quoted at length to show the influence *The Awakening of Faith* had on a major school of Buddhism which although no longer extant continues to live through the doctrines and practices of the Zen school of which it is the intellectual complement.

[5] Francis H. Cook, *Hua-yen Buddhism: The Jewel Net of Indra* (Pennsylvania State University, 1977), p. 94.

When Cook talks about this "very unusual" statement by Fa-tsang he is referring to none other than the central thesis of *The Awakening of Faith* by which this eminent Hua-yen master was so greatly influenced. The important thing to note, however, is that it is not so much that this perspective is unusual as it is that it has been rendered so explicitly since it is a doctrinal position which must logically follow from the other fundamental tenets of Mahayana Buddhism.

Another distinctive feature of this text is its stress on the Absolute being both *sunya* ("empty") and *a-sunya* ("not empty"). Firstly, "Suchness is empty because from the very beginning it has never been related to any defiled states of existence, it is free from all marks of individual distinction of things and it has nothing to do with thoughts conceived by a deluded mind."[6] Considered in this way, "emptiness" should not be considered as "non-existent" but simply (as Yoshito Hakeda, in his commentary, notes) "devoid of a distinct, absolute, independent, permanent, individual entity or being as an irreducible component in a pluralistic world. . . . However, this negation does not exclude the possibility of Suchness being seen from a different viewpoint or order with which one is not accustomed. Hence, there is room to present Suchness, if it is done symbolically, as replete with attributes."[7] Asvaghosha, after pointing out that Suchness "was not brought into existence in the beginning nor will it cease to be at the end of time; it is eternal through and through" goes on to say:

> From the beginning, Suchness in its nature is fully provided with all excellent qualities; namely, it is endowed with the light of great wisdom, the qualities of illuminating the entire universe, of true cognition and mind pure in its self-nature; of eternity, bliss, Self, and purity; of refreshing coolness, immutability, and freedom. . . . These qualities are not independent from the essence of Suchness and are suprarational attributes of Buddhahood. Since it is endowed completely with all these and is not lacking anything, it is called the *tathagata-garbha* (when latent) and also the *Dharmakaya* of the *Tathagata*. . . . Though it has, in reality, all these excellent qualities, it does not have any characteristics of differentiation; it retains its identity and is of one flavor; Suchness is solely one . . . it is one without a second.[8]

[6] Hakeda, p. 34.

[7] Hakeda, p. 36.

[8] Hakeda, p. 65.

These are critical passages in helping us to understand the nature and function of Suchness. What we see is a concept of the Absolute as not only the fountainhead of all the happiness, joy, and beauty of which we only experience the pale shadows in this world but the source of enlightenment and saving activity of all Buddhas and *Bodhisattvas* directed towards suffering sentient beings in *Samsara*. It is therefore crucial to a proper understanding of Suchness not to view it under its other synonym, namely Emptiness or the Void, as meaning a mere nullity or non-existence—this would be to fall prey to the pitfalls of nihilism which the great Mahayana masters always warned us against. To be sure, Suchness is not the kind of existence which can be considered analogous to the realities with which we are familiar in this transitory world but rather is far more real than anything within the purview of our limited empirical existence. There is a great danger, especially when one reads certain modern studies of Buddhism in the West, in failing to recognize that the notion of "emptiness" about which one hears so much is not an emptiness or lack of reality as is sometimes curiously supposed but an emptiness of limitations, relativity, and delusion. In this respect, emptiness serves as an *upaya* to help rid people of misguided and blinkered views concerning the highest reality rather than being some kind of comprehensive statement regarding it. One is inclined to consider the punishing dialectics of Nagarjuna and his *Madhyamika* system as simply a form of intellectual therapy designed to remove the obstacles to a clearer understanding of Suchness—breaking through the ratiocinative and conventional ways in which we artificially construct what we believe to be reality and to promote a more direct and intuitive mode of awareness through *prajna* or "transcendental" wisdom. But such an exercise only stops half-way, otherwise the history of Buddhism would not have witnessed the rise of subsequent schools which endeavored to fill the gaps, so to speak, left by the purely negative and apophatic approach of the *Sunyata* perspective. There was a growing need for a more positive conception of the ultimate reality, a conception that addressed the fundamental needs of both the intelligence and the will in response to which arose, firstly, the *Vijnanavada* (also known as *Yogacara*) followed by the *Tathagata-garbha* schools of thought with their emphasis on the cataphatic dimension of the Absolute. Tantric Buddhism can also be considered a response to some of the perceived limitations with the early *Madhyamika* perspective. In any event, we now find a richer and more complex ontology which sought to integrate existence in its entirety—and at all its levels—with Suchness. No *dharma* or element of existence was considered to be outside its embrace or influence such that all reality was suffused with the presence of the Buddha—a notion unthinkable to the Hinayana which was in no real position to reconcile this world of suffering and delusion with the realm which delivered one from all such sorrow. Nevertheless, despite the paradoxical nature of the Mahayana's preferred way of viewing the Absolute, it felt that its more difficult perspective was thoroughly justified in view of what it considered to be a deeper awareness of the omnipresent activity of Suchness in our everyday world of samsaric existence.

The Pure Land Tradition

The rise of the Pure Land school of Mahayana Buddhism was largely contemporaneous with the flowering of the Mahayana itself and constituting one of its earliest manifestations. In one sense, it can be argued that the Pure Land way represented the most explicit example of the attempt to render the Buddhist Absolute as accessible as possible to ordinary people through the use of a wealth of rich and positive symbolism designed to heighten the aspiration for enlightenment. In this way, the Pure Land path can also be viewed as the best example of the *a-sunya* view of absolute reality, that is in contrast to the Madhyamikan view of Suchness as empty (*sunya*) or the "Void," it is seen in its fullness and plenitude as the inexhaustible font of all merits, virtues, wisdom, and compassion—an archetypal realm of perfection and beatitude. Hence the traditional descriptions of the Pure Land as being replete with the attributes of enlightenment through the evocative symbolism of jewels, music, colors, fragrances, etc. By employing ostensibly sensual imagery, the *sutras* are attempting to convey, in terms that could be readily understood, a sense of the blissfulness of *Nirvana*—in contrast, no doubt, to the imperfection that would have dominated the ordinary worldview of the average devotee. The Pure Land patriarch, T'an-luan, claimed that what distinguished Pure Land Buddhism from other schools is that the "*Dharmakaya* of *Dharma*-nature" (i.e., the formless Absolute) takes the initiative in relation to deluded and suffering beings manifesting itself as "*Dharmakaya* of Expediency" in the form of various Buddhas, *Bodhisattvas*, and Pure Lands but, in particular, the preeminent Buddha Amitabha ("Infinite Light"). This is the ultimate act of compassion for without this initiative, ordinary beings would remain stranded in *Samsara* with no hope of deliverance seeing as the clutches of ignorance and delusion in the

Decadent Age of the *Dharma* are considered too strong to allow for individual effort and initiative to suffice for the attainment of enlightenment.

The Decadent Age of the Dharma

The above reference to the "Decadent Age of the *Dharma*" calls for a short digression. Mahayana Buddhists entertain a qualitative view of time that is envisaged in relation to the lifetime of Shakyamuni Buddha. In other words, the spiritual, moral, and physical conditions on earth are seen to progressively deteriorate in direct proportion to the time that has elapsed since the Buddha's entry into the Great *Nirvana.* A number of distinct ages, since that time, are seen to reflect the successive stages in humanity's increasing darkness, turmoil, and spiritual incapacity. The Pure Land tradition considers the present period as the "Decadent Age" of the *Dharma* where—to quote the *Great Collection Sutra*—"out of billions of sentient beings who seek to perform practices and cultivate the way . . . not one will gain realization." Another quotation from this *sutra* serves to clarify this situation further:

> During the first five hundred-year period after the Buddha's *parinirvana*, my disciples will be resolute in acquiring wisdom. During the second five hundred-year period, they will be resolute in cultivating meditation. During the third five hundred-year period, they will be resolute in listening to the teaching and *sutra*-recitation. During the fourth five hundred-year period, they will be resolute in constructing towers and temples, practicing meritorious conduct, and performing penance. During the fifth five hundred-year period, they will be resolute in conflict and strife, which will become widespread with the good *dharma* being diminished. . . . This is now the last *dharma*-age; it is the evil world of the five defilements. This one gate—the Pure Land way—is the only path that affords passage.

The "five defilements" referred to above constitute the distinguishing characteristics of the age in which we currently live. They are (i) the impure or turbid age in which calamities occur incessantly; (ii) impurity of the view that ignores the principle of cause and effect; (iii) the impurity and defiling nature of evil passions; (iv) the degeneration of the minds and bodies of sentient beings; and (v) the shortening of the span of life of sentient beings as the result of prevailing evil passions and wrong views.

The famous *Lotus Sutra* also contains a description of this age which, in hindsight, has proven to be disturbingly prophetic:

> At the horrible time of the end, men will be malevolent, false, evil, and obtuse and they will imagine that they have reached perfection when it will be nothing of the sort.

The Pure Land masters considered that, under such conditions, the degree of spiritual attainment prevalent at the time of Shakyamuni was no longer considered possible in this age which is so far removed from his immediate presence and influence. Accordingly, they exhort us to take refuge in Amitabha Buddha (Jp. Amida*)* who compensates for our shortcomings by enabling us to reach *Nirvana* solely through the power of his Name.

The Name of Amitabha Buddha

Of all the forty-eight vows made by Amitabha Buddha, the eighteenth—the Primal Vow—is considered by far the most significant. It is to be found in *The Larger Sutra on the Buddha of Immeasurable Life* as follows:

> If when I attain Buddhahood, sentient beings in the lands of the ten directions who sincerely and joyfully entrust themselves to me, desire to be born in my land, and call my Name even ten times, should not be born there, may I not attain perfect Enlightenment. Excluded, however, are those who commit the five gravest offences and abuse the right *Dharma.*

The phrase "call my Name even ten times" referred to thinking on the Buddha in a general sense (*buddhanusmriti* in Sanskrit). This gradually developed into the actual invocation of his Name (*Namo mitabhaya Buddhaya* or *Namu Amida Butsu* in Japanese)—the *nembutsu*—which was considered a natural corollary of one's remembrance of the Buddha. As the Sacred Name of Amitabha Buddha was thought to contain the perfection and virtue of Enlightenment itself, its mere recitation was seen to have the power to bring to *Nirvana* all those who had complete faith in it.

In the age of *mappo*, the practice of *nembutsu* was considered easier to accomplish for ordinary lay people whose weak capacities prevented them from engaging in the more difficult and austere practices of traditional monastic Buddhism. Unlike such practices, the *nembutsu* was open to everyone because the Name is both easy to say and keep in mind, providing a more universally accessible means by which mindfulness of the Buddha can he maintained by those incapable of the rigors of monastic life.

As the Name was considered to have this great power to effect total liberation from the snares of *Samsara*, Pure Land adepts in both China and Japan would commit themselves to tens of thousands of recitations of *nembutsu* each day with a view to ensuring that their eventual salvation would be guaranteed. Shinran, the founder of the Jodo Shinshu school of Pure Land Buddhism, came to regard this attitude to the *nembutsu* as unsatisfactory and inconsistent with the intention of Amitabha Buddha's Primal Vow as he saw it as yet another form of "self-power" along the lines practiced by the older schools. After twenty years of monastic discipline at Mount Hiei, stronghold of the Tendai sect, Shinran abandoned this life in frustration, seeing that it could not help one so blinded by evil passions and ignorance as himself. As he considered his own "self" thoroughly polluted by the incessant cravings of his ego, Shinran sought refuge in the teaching of "Other-Power"—namely that of Amitabha Buddha, in whom he saw as the only hope for his salvation.

It was Shinran's view that to practice the *nembutsu* as a means of gaining reward was to fall prey to the same limitations that afflicted the traditional "self-power" schools which advocated taxing meditation, difficult austerities, and strict adherence to the monastic precepts. In other words, he did not believe that our limited and conditioned egos could bridge the vast gulf separating the finite self from the Infinite. After all, it would not be in the ego's own interests to want to contribute to its own destruction, which is why recourse to a power that transcends it is required. Therefore, to want to amass innumerable invocations of the *nembutsu* with a view to attaining birth into the Pure Land is, according to Shinran, to believe that our self-interested acts are actually capable of attaining the same level of enlightenment as the Buddha. To think thus is to harbor the worst of self-delusions since there is absolutely no common measure between the absolute perfection of Amitabha's *Nirvana* and the blind, misguided gropings of our impure selves.

The real significance of the *nembutsu* for Shinran was that its invocation—and the mindfulness of Amitabha that it expressed—was none other than the manifestation of true faith (*shinjin*) in the hearts of devotees. As *shinjin* can only be conferred by Amitabha, to practice *nembutsu* in the hope of "producing" it for oneself is futile. Amitabha's mind is incomparable, inconceivable, and inimitable, and its arising in the hearts of deluded beings is a pure grace which no merely human act can contrive. Similarly, no amount of bad karma can thwart the power of the Name as there is no good that surpasses it. To recite the *nembutsu* in a spontaneous and uncalculating way is to be imbued with Amitabha's pure mind of *shinjin*. It is a natural expression of our being embraced by his Light, despite our grave karmic defilements, and of our complete assurance of the eternal bliss of *Nirvana* when our time comes to leave this world of tribulation and sorrow.

When Shinran declared that the *nembutsu* was a manifestation of *shinjin* rather than simply a means of procuring spiritual benefits, he did not mean to suggest that the Name could no longer be regarded as having the power attributed to it by his Pure Land predecessors. The sacred Name of Amitabha Buddha is the vehicle by which we are able to transcend the world of *Samsara* and attain perfect enlightenment in the Pure Land. This capacity, seemingly incredible at first sight, is made possible by the fact that the power of the Absolute itself is fully invested in the Name and conferred to those who hear it, believe in it, and invoke it with complete faith in its saving power. To simply recite the *nembutsu* with no other motive than to attain blissful entry into *Nirvana* for oneself is doomed to failure because the incentive then appears to be solely one of self-gain uninformed by either gratitude to the Buddha or compassion for one's suffering fellow beings. As the *nembutsu* is not our good but that of the Buddha, it cannot possibly form the foundation for any meritorious act of our own.

When viewed in this way, the number of recitations of *nembutsu* is not relevant as it is the quality of the faith behind them that is important. Some will feel impelled to say the *nembutsu* constantly, others again only seldom. It should be noted, however, that invoking the Name, although a very important feature of Pure Land practice, is not the only way in which the *nembutsu* can be expressed. Chanting the *sutras*, worshipping and contemplating the Buddha, making offerings to Him etc., can also be considered as forms of *nembutsu* in which the mind of *shinjin* may find its expression. In any event, regardless of the form that *nembutsu* may take, it is always the working of Amitabha Buddha in us that is the true source of such practice and the ultimate guarantee of its efficacy.

The Activity of Suchness

Although the Pure Land school claims the dynamic and compassionate nature of Suchness as a major advance in Mahayana thinking, it is possible to find the seeds of this conception in *The Awakening of Faith* itself in its doctrine of "permeation" (*vasana*). Hence we find:[9]

> The essence of Suchness is, from the beginningless beginning, endowed with the perfect state of purity. It is provided with suprarational functions and the nature of manifesting itself. Because of these two reasons, it permeates perpetually into ignorance. Through the force of this permeation, it induces a man to loathe the suffering of *Samsara*, to seek bliss in *Nirvana* and, believing that he has the principle of Suchness within him, to make up his mind to exert himself. . . . The Buddhas and *Bodhisattva*s all desire to liberate all men, spontaneously permeating them with their spiritual influences and never forsaking them. Through the power of the wisdom which is one with Suchness, they manifest activities in response to the needs of men as they see and hear them.

This passage clearly shows the omnipresent activity of Suchness functioning as the immanent Absolute working in all things to bring them to enlightenment, to the extent that even an individual's aspiration to seek Buddhahood is brought about by the compassionate working of the *Tathagata*s irrespective of whether the aspirant is aware of this influence or not. In this respect, the "self-power" and "other-power" debate can be resolved if it is recognized that there is only one power—that of the Absolute—that pervades and supports all things and that one can either recognize and collaborate with it (which is to conform to the *Dharma*) or allow it to operate unnoticed (which is to continue living in a state of nescience)—either way, the working of Suchness, according to the Mahayana, will eventually bring all sentient beings to nirvanic fulfillment as there is no thing which does not constitute the Body of *Dharma* (*Dharmakaya*) and is thereby not fully embraced by its wisdom and compassion.

The Significance of Shinran

Finally, I would like to give some brief consideration to the thought of Shinran, founder of the Jodo Shinshu sect of Pure Land Buddhism, and his attempts to reconcile the traditional Pure Land teaching which he

[9] Hakeda, pp. 59, 63.

had inherited with the sapiential perspective of the Mahayana which he would have doubtlessly imbued as a Tendai monk for twenty years on Mt. Hiei. The long-established view of the Pure Land school was that the principal object of devotion was not the formless *Dharmakaya* itself but the Buddha of Infinite Light (*Amitabha*) who had formerly been a *bodhisattva* called Dharmakara who, out of compassion for the multitudes of suffering sentient beings, underwent aeons of self-sacrificing practice and austerities which enabled him to accrue sufficient merit to attain Buddhahood and establish a Pure Land, over which he presides, and which provides aspirants with an ideal environment in which to pursue the *Dharma* and attain enlightenment. For a long time, Amitabha was recognized as one of many Buddhas existing throughout the universe each with their own Pure Lands which have been generated from their practices and vows. Devotion to Amitabha, however, was considered particularly efficacious owing to the fact that his vows were intended specifically for ordinary beings with little or no spiritual capacity whereas other Buddhas had established certain difficult preconditions for admission to their Pure Lands.

Shinran, while not explicitly repudiating this traditional view, chose rather to universalize what he may have considered the mythological symbolism behind the Dharmakara story by grounding it in fundamental Mahayana principles partly in order to address strong criticisms by other sects which considered the Pure Land way unBuddhistic and partly, no doubt, because he had a profound awareness of a higher reality (which he often refers to as *jinen* or "as-it-isness") which he saw as working in all things and manifesting itself through innumerable compassionate guises such as Amitabha's Vows and his Pure Land. For Shinran, *jinen* signifies that which is beyond form and time and beyond the domain of human intellect and will. It is the *Dharma*-body as Suchness which "fills the hearts and minds of the ocean of all beings."[10] In one of his famous letters, Shinran makes the following observation:[11]

> The Supreme Buddha is formless and because of being formless is called *jinen*. When this Buddha is shown as being with form, it is not called the supreme *Nirvana* (Buddha). In order to make us realize

[10] *The Collected Works of Shinran: Volume II* (Jodo Shinshu Hongwanji-ha, 1997), p. 191.

[11] *Letters of Shinran: A Translation of Mattosho*, Shin Buddhism Translation Series, ed. Yoshifumi Ueda (Kyoto: Hongwanji International Centre, 1978), p. 30.

> that the true Buddha is formless, it is expressly called Amida Buddha; so I have been taught. Amida Buddha is the medium through which we are made to realize *jinen*.

This passage was written towards the end of Shinran's life and signals a revolutionary attitude in thinking about the Buddha within the Pure Land tradition. It is as if Shinran has stripped the complex and rich edifice of Pure Land spirituality down to its bare principles. This, however, is not reductionism on Shinran's part but an attempt to rehabilitate the "wisdom" aspect of the Mahayana which was in danger of possibly being overlooked by the rich *upaya*s offered by the great message of compassion which, in many ways, formed the centerpiece of the Pure Land message. One also finds in Shinran, and to a far greater extent than his own illustrious teacher Honen, a deep appreciation of the multifaceted nature of *Nirvana* and its activity:[12]

> *Nirvana* has innumerable names. It is impossible to give them in detail; I will list only a few. *Nirvana* is called extinction of passions, the uncreated, peaceful happiness, eternal bliss, true reality, *Dharmakaya*, *dharma*-nature, Suchness, oneness, and Buddha-nature. Buddha-nature is none other than *Tathagata*. This *Tathagata* pervades the countless worlds; it fills the hearts and minds of the ocean of all beings. Thus, plants, trees, and land all attain Buddhahood. Since it is with these hearts and minds of all sentient beings that they entrust themselves to the Vow of the *dharma*-body as compassionate means, this *shinjin* (faith) is none other than Buddha-nature. This Buddha-nature is *dharma*-nature. *Dharma*-nature is the *Dharmakaya*.

Shinran here is advocating a broader grasp of *Nirvana* than we see in any of his predecessors even though he was greatly influenced by them in arriving at his developed position. Amitabha, therefore, becomes the compassionate personification of Suchness itself and not the outcome of the innumerable practices of a particular quasi-historical individual over many *kalpa*s. Even Dharmakara himself, according to Shinran, emerges from the ocean of Suchness to make known the vows of the Buddha of Infinite Light through the *sutra*s of the Pure Land school. Furthermore, he takes the radical step of equating the Pure Land with *Nirvana* itself rather than treating it as a more favorable

12 *The Collected Works of Shinran: Volume I* (Jodo Shinshu Hongwanji-ha, 1997), p. 461.

abode for Buddhist practice, so that to attain birth in the Pure Land is tantamount to attaining enlightenment. Similarly, in relation to the central experience of the religious life according to Shinran, i.e., *shinjin* or faith, we no longer find just a rudimentary faith in the Buddha and his power to save but a recognition that this experience has its source in the very heart of reality itself—another way of saying that awareness of the Buddha's working through the experience of *shinjin* is none other than the activity of the Buddha himself in sentient beings.

Shinran was very conscious not to be seen as indulging in unorthodox innovations which is why he goes to such pains to cite authoritative scriptures in support of his views. On the one hand, he needed to convince the other Mahayana sects that his teaching was not an aberration of the *Dharma* and, on the other, he had to assure those within the Pure Land tradition that he was not being unfaithful to its perspective either. The extent to which he succeeded in accomplishing this difficult and challenging task is evidenced by the extraordinary flourishing of the Jodo Shinshu over the past seven hundred years. One of the principal texts that Shinran used in support of his views regarding the ultimate reality was the famous *Nirvana Sutra* which he practically quotes in its entirety in his magnum opus, *Kyogyoshinsho.* In order to reinforce the point about the unanimity between Shinran and the great Mahayana metaphysical tradition which he deeply venerated, a few important passages from the *Nirvana Sutra* will be quoted[13]—passages which Shinran cites with approval in the *Kyogyoshinsho* and which serve to demonstrate that not only is he thoroughly Mahayanistic in his view of the Absolute but that he accomplished a wonderful synthesis between the respective demands of wisdom and compassion in his propagation of the Pure Land faith:

> *Tathagata* is also thus—nonarising, nonperishing, unaging, undying, indestructible, and incorruptible; it is not a created existence. . . . All created things are impermanent. . . . Buddha nature is the uncreated; hence it is eternal.
>
> The *Tathagatas* are eternal and never changing; hence they are termed true reality.
>
> Although sentient beings are impermanent, still their Buddha-nature is eternal and unchanging.

[13] *Collected Works: Volume I*, pp. 181, 184, 185, 188.

> The *dharma*-body (of the *Tathagata*) is eternity, bliss, self, and purity.

Conclusion

In closing, I would like to reiterate the great importance of an adequate and satisfying conception of the Absolute as being indispensable to the Buddhist path. In a climate of increasing skepticism and reductionism, especially in certain Buddhist scholarly circles in the West, it is imperative that one does not lose sight of the fact that without such concepts as *Dharmakaya*, Suchness, *Nirvana*, *Sunyata*, etc. being grounded in a true reality which both transcends and suffuses all things, Buddhism is left without any foundations and stands on nothing, thereby losing all sapiential and soteriological efficacy. In the attempt by some to make Buddhism more fashionable by denying that it has anything much in common with views of ultimate reality in other spiritual traditions, it does itself a great disservice in failing to recognize clear parallels where they exist—parallels, indeed, which should not surprise anyone. To speak of all these terms to describe the Absolute as "symbolic" in an attempt to somehow downgrade the reality of the ultimate object of aspiration is sheer folly—of what exactly are they symbols? To be sure, these terms do not exhaust the fathomless depth of the reality to which they refer but, on the other hand, neither are they empty symbols created by us in order to fulfill some kind of nostalgic and delusory quest for the Infinite which has no basis. A spiritual path which cannot secure deliverance from that which is finite, imperfect, and illusory, to that which affords eternal blessedness and liberation from suffering and the painful clutches of samsaric existence, is simply not worthy of the name.

III

ART, SYMBOLISM, AND THE LANGUAGE OF SILENCE

One climbs halfway up the mountainside [of Elephanta] on magnificent stone steps until a wide gate opens on the right, in the volcanic rocks. This leads into one of the mightiest of early Indian rock temples. Heavy pillars hewn out of the rock support the roof. The eye slowly accustoms itself to the semi-darkness, gradually distinguishes awesome representations—carved into the wall—of the religious epics of India, until it reaches the imposing central recess. Here an image rises up out of the rock which I can only compare with the great representations of Christ in early Byzantine churches. It is a three-headed form, carved only as far as the breast, in threefold human size. . . . Still and powerful the central head looks down, with both the others in profile. Over the image rests a perfect peace and majesty. . . . Nowhere else have I found the secret of the transcendent world, the other world more grandly and perfectly expressed than in these three heads. . . . To see this place were alone worth a journey to India, while from the spirit of religion which has lived here, one may experience more in a single hour of contemplation than from all the books.

Rudolf Otto

HINDU ART*

Titus Burckhardt

The Hindu Temple

Among sedentary peoples, the sacred art *par excellence* is the building of a sanctuary, in which the Divine Spirit, invisibly present in the universe, will "dwell" in a direct and as it were "personal" sense. Spiritually speaking, a sanctuary is always situated at the center of the world, and it is this that makes it a *sacratum* in the true sense of the word: in such a place man is protected from the indeterminacy of space and time, since it is "here" and "now" that God is present to man. This is expressed in the design of the temple; by emphasizing the cardinal directions, it orders space in relation to its center. The design is a synthesis of the world: that which, in the universe, is in ceaseless movement, is transposed by sacred architecture into a permanent form. In the cosmos, time prevails over space: on the other hand, in the construction of the temple, time is as it were transmuted into space: the great rhythms of the visible cosmos, symbolizing the principal aspects of existence—aspects which, in the world of becoming, are disjointed and dispersed—are reassembled and fixed in the geometry of the building. Thus, through its regular and unalterable form, the temple represents the completion of the world, that is to say, its timeless aspect or final state, wherein all things repose in the equilibrium that precedes their reintegration in the undivided unity of Being. It is precisely because the sanctuary prefigures this transfiguration of the world—a transfiguration symbolized in Christianity by the "Heavenly Jerusalem"—that it is filled by the Divine Peace (*shekhina* in Hebrew, and *shanti* in Sanskrit).

This completion of the world which the temple prefigures is symbolized by its rectangular form, a form which opposes the circular form of a world subject to the cosmic movement. Whereas the spherical form of the sky is indefinite, and not accessible to any kind of measurement, the rectangular or cubical form of a sacred edifice expresses a positive and immutable law, and that is why all

* Editor's Note: from *The Essential Titus Burckhardt*, ed. William Stoddart.

sacred architecture, to whatever tradition it belongs, can be seen as a development of the fundamental theme of the transformation of the circle into the square. In the genesis of the Hindu Temple, the development of this theme is particularly clear, in all the richness of its metaphysical and spiritual contents.[1]

The "crystallization" of all cosmic realities in a geometrical symbol—which is like an inverted image of the timeless—is prefigured in the Hindu tradition by the construction of the Vedic altar. Its cubical shape represents the "body" of *Prajapati*, the total cosmic being.[2] *Prajapati* is the Principle in its manifested aspect; though this aspect includes the totality of the world, it appears as if fragmented by the diversity and mutability of the latter. In his Essence *Prajapati* is none other than *Purusha*, the immutable and indivisible Essence of man and the universe; according to the *Rig-Veda* (X.90), it is *Purusha* whom the *deva*s sacrificed at the beginning of the world, in order to constitute the various parts of the universe and the different kinds of living beings. This must not be understood as "pantheism," for *Purusha* is not divided in itself, nor is it "localized" in ephemeral beings; it is only its manifested and apparent form that is sacrificed, while its eternal nature remains as it ever was, so that it is both the sacrifice (the victim) and the goal of the sacrifice. Henceforth every sacrifice reproduces and in a sense compensates for the pre-temporal sacrifice of the *deva*s; the unity of the total being is symbolically and spiritually reconstituted by the rite.

[1] Nevertheless, the relation between these two fundamental symbols—the circle and the square—bear different meanings depending on the plane of reference. If the circle is the symbol of the undivided unity of the Principle, the square signifies its first and changeless determination, the universal law or Norm; in this case the circle indicates a reality superior to that suggested by the square. The same is true if the circle is related to the heavens, whose movement it reproduces, and the square is related to the earth, whose solid and relatively inert state it recapitulates: then the circle is to the square as the active is to the passive, or as life is to the body, for it is the heavens that engender actively, while the earth conceives and gives birth passively.

[2] The *deva*s immolated this primordial being at the beginning of the world and its disjointed limbs, which constitute the multiple aspects or parts of the cosmos, have to be symbolically reassembled. This recalls the dismemberment of the body of Osiris in the Egyptian myth. The myth of the immolation of *Prajapati* is analogous to the Sufi doctrine according to which God manifested the universe by virtue of His multiple Names.

The art of building an altar is more ancient and more universal than sacred architecture, for altars are used by both nomads and sedentaries, whereas temples exist only amongst the latter. The primitive sanctuary is the sacred area surrounding the altar; the rites employed for consecrating and delimiting this area were later transposed to the founding of a temple—*templum* in Latin originally meant the sacred precinct set apart for the *contemplation* of the cosmos. There are many indications to support the conclusion that these rites constitute a primordial inheritance linking the two great currents, nomads and sedentaries, whose lifestyles, in other respects, are so different.

A particularly eloquent testimony of this primordial legacy is the following description of the consecration of a fire altar by Hehaka Sapa (Black Elk), priest sage of the nomadic Sioux Indians: "Taking the ax, he (the officiant) pointed it towards the six directions, and then struck the ground to the West. Repeating the same movement, he struck the ground to the North, then in the same way to the East, and then to the South; he then raised the ax skywards and struck the ground in the center, twice for the earth, and twice for the Great Spirit. Having done this, he scratched the soil and, with a stick which he had purified in the smoke and offered to the six directions, he traced a line running from the West to the center, then from the East to the center, then from the North to the center, and finally from the South to the center; then he offered the stick to the heavens and touched the center, and then to the earth and touched the center. In this way the altar was made. In the manner described, we fixed in this place the center of the world, and this center, which in reality is everywhere, is the dwelling-place of the Great Spirit."[3]

As this example shows, the consecration of the altar consists in the evocation of the relationships that connect the principal aspects of the universe with its center. These aspects are: heaven, which in its generative activity is opposed to the earth (the passive and maternal principle), and the four directions or "winds," whose forces determine the cycle of the day and the succession of the seasons; they correspond to so many powers or aspects of the Universal Spirit.[4]

[3] See *The Sacred Pipe: Black Elk's Account of the Rites of the Oglala Sioux*, recorded by Joseph Epes Brown (Norman: University of Oklahoma Press, 1953 and 1989).

[4] See Frithjof Schuon, *The Feathered Sun* (Bloomington, Indiana: World Wisdom Books, 1990) and *Language of the Self* (Bloomington, Indiana: World Wisdom Books, 1999), the chapter "The Sacred Pipe of the Red Indians."

Whereas the normal shape of a temple is rectangular, the nomadic altar such as has been described is not square in outline, even though its origin is the quaternary of the celestial regions. This is explained by the "style" appropriate to the nomadic life; to nomads, buildings that are rectangular in shape express the fixation of death. Nomadic sanctuaries, made like tents or cabins of live branches, are generally round; their model is the dome of the sky. Likewise, nomadic encampments are arranged in circular form, and the same practice is sometimes found in the cities of nomadic peoples who have become sedentary, like the Parthians. Thus it is that the cosmic polarity of the circle and the square is reflected in the contrast between nomadic and sedentary peoples. The former recognize their ideal in the dynamic and limitless nature of the circle, whereas the latter see theirs in the static character and the regularity of the square.[5] But apart from these differences of approach, the conception of the sanctuary remains the same. Whether it be built of solid materials like the temples of sedentary peoples, or whether it be no more than a *sacratum* established temporarily like the nomadic altar, it is always situated at the center of the world. Hehaka Sapa says of this center that it is the dwelling-place of the Great Spirit, and that in reality it is everywhere. That is why a symbolical point of reference is sufficient for its realization.

The basic plan of a temple is derived from the procedure of orientation, which is a rite in the proper sense of the word, for it links the form of the sanctuary with that of the universe. An orientation rite is universal; it was practiced in the most diverse civilizations. It is mentioned in ancient Chinese books, and Vitruvius tells us that the Romans established their cities in this way. There are also numerous indications that the same procedure was used in medieval Europe. The three phases of this rite correspond to three fundamental geometrical

[5] Sometimes the static perfection of the square or the cube is combined with the dynamic symbolism of the circle. Such is the case with the Kaaba, one of the oldest sanctuaries in the world and an ancient center of the rite of circumambulation perpetuated by Islam. The Kaaba is situated on the "axis of the world" and its four corners are oriented towards the cardinal regions of the sky. The rite of circumambulation expresses with precision the relationship existing between the sanctuary and the celestial movement; it is accomplished seven times to correspond with the number of the celestial spheres. Abraham built the Kaaba where, according to legend, the Divine Presence (*Sakina*), in the form of a serpent, had led him; the serpent coiled itself round the building. This recalls the symbolism of the serpent, *Ananta* or *Shesha*, which moves round the precinct of the Hindu temple, itself the center of a rite of circumambulation.

figures: the circle, image of the solar cycle; the cross formed by the cardinal axes; and the square derived from it. These are the symbols of the Chinese Great Triad, Heaven-Man-Earth, Man, in this hierarchy, being the intermediary between Heaven, the active principle, and Earth, the passive principle just as the cross of the cardinal axes is the intermediary between the limitless cycle of the heavens and the terrestrial "square."

Chinese ideogram of the Great Triad: Heaven-Man-Earth

According to the Hindu tradition, the square obtained by the rite of orientation is the symbol of *Purusha* insofar as it is immanent in existence. *Purusha* is pictured in the shape of a man stretched out in the fundamental square, in the position of the victim in the Vedic sacrifice: his head is to the East, his feet to the West, and his two hands touch the North-East and South-East corners of the square. The fundamental diagram of the temple is thus a symbol of the Divine Presence in the world.

This symbolism is found among peoples who have no historical link with the Hindu world. The Osages, a tribe of the plains of North America, look upon the ritual arrangement of their camp as "the form and the spirit of a perfect man" who faces the East. In the Christian tradition, medieval liturgists such as Durant de Mende and Honorius d'Autun, compared the plan of the cathedral to the form of the crucified Christ: His head corresponds to the apse with its axis to the East; His outstretched arms are the transepts; His torso and legs are the nave; His heart lies at the main altar. This interpretation evokes the Hindu symbolism of *Purusha* incorporated in the plan of the temple. In both cases, the Man-God incarnated in the sacred building is the sacrifice which reconciles Heaven with earth.

Hindu Sculpture

The Hindu sculptor must know the rules of the sacred dance, which is the first of the figurative arts, since it has man himself as its means. Sculpture is thus related to two radically different arts: by its artisanal technique it is related to architecture, which is essentially static and transforms time into space, whereas the dance is essentially dynamic and transforms space into time, by absorbing the former into the continuity of rhythm. It is therefore not surprising that these two poles of Hindu art—sculpture and dancing—should have together engendered what is perhaps the most perfect fruit of Hindu art, the image of Shiva dancing.

The dance of Shiva expresses at once the production, conservation, and destruction of the world, considered as phases of the permanent activity of God. Shiva is the "Lord of the Dance" (*Nataraja*). He himself revealed the principles of the sacred dance to the sage Bharatamuni, who codified them in the *Bharata-Natya-Shastra*.[6]

The static laws of sculpture and the rhythm of the dance are combined to perfection in the classical statue of Shiva dancing. The movement is conceived as a rotation around a motionless axis; by its decomposition into four typical gestures, following one another like phases, it reposes so to speak in its own amplitude; it is in no way rigid, but its rhythm is continued in a static formula, like the waves of liquid in a vessel; time is integrated in the timeless. The limbs of the God are arranged in such a way that the worshiper who views the statue from in front grasps all the forms at a glance: they are inscribed in the plane of the flaming circle, symbol of *Prakriti* (Universal Substance), without their spatial polyvalence being in any way impaired. On the contrary, from whatever side one contemplates the statue, its static equilibrium remains perfect, like that of a tree outspread in space. The plastic precision of the detail is combined with the uninterrupted continuity of the gestures.

Shiva dances on the vanquished demon of chaotic matter, the subjective equivalent of which is spiritual indifference or forgetfulness of God (*apasmara*). In his outermost right hand he holds the drum whose beat corresponds to the creative act. By the gesture of his uplifted hand he announces peace, protecting what he has created. His lowered hand points to the foot which is lifted from the ground, as a sign of deliverance. In his outermost left hand he carries the flame which will destroy the world.

Images of Shiva dancing show sometimes the attributes of a god, sometimes those of an ascetic, or of both together, for God is beyond all forms, and He assumes form only so that He may become his own victim.

6 The "celestial" origin of the Hindu dance is indirectly proved by its extension in space and time: in a form adapted to Buddhism, it has influenced the choreographic style of Tibet and all eastern Asia including Japan; in Java it survived the Islamicization of the island; and through the medium of Gypsy dancing it seems even to have influenced Spanish dancing.

THE BUDDHA FIGURES AT POLONNARUWA*

Thomas Merton

Polonnaruwa with its vast area under trees. Fences. Few people. No beggars. A dirt road. Lost. Then we find Gal Vihara and the other monastic complex *stupas*. Cells. Distant mountains, like Yucatan.

The path dips down to Gal Vihara: a wide, quiet, hollow, surrounded with trees. A low outcrop of rock, with a cave cut into it, and beside the cave a big seated Buddha on the left, a reclining Buddha on the right, and Ananda, I guess, standing by the head of the reclining Buddha. In the cave, another seated Buddha. The vicar general, shying away from "paganism," hangs back and sits under a tree reading the guidebook. I am able to approach the Buddhas barefoot and undisturbed, my feet in wet grass, wet sand. Then the silence of the extraordinary faces. The great smiles. Huge and yet subtle. Filled with every possibility, questioning nothing, knowing everything, rejecting nothing, the peace not of emotional resignation but of Madhyamika, of *sunyata*, that has seen through every question without trying to discredit anyone or anything—*without refutation*—without establishing some other argument. For the doctrinaire, the mind that needs well-established positions, such peace, such silence, can be frightening. I was knocked over with a rush of relief and thankfulness at the *obvious* clarity of the figures, the clarity and fluidity of shape and line, the design of the monumental bodies composed into the rock shape and landscape, figure, rock and tree. And the sweep of bare rock sloping away on the other side of the hollow, where you can go back and see different aspects of the figures.

Looking at these figures I was suddenly, almost forcibly, jerked clean out of the habitual, half-tied vision of things, and an inner clearness, clarity, as if exploding from the rocks themselves, became evident and obvious. The queer *evidence* of the reclining figure, the smile, the sad smile of Ananda standing with arms folded (much more "imperative" than Da Vinci's *Mona Lisa* because completely simple and straightforward). The thing about all this is that there is no puzzle,

* Editor's Note: from *The Asian Journal of Thomas Merton*, ed. N. Burton et al.

no problem, and really no "mystery." All problems are resolved and everything is clear, simply because what matters is clear. The rock, all matter, all life, is charged with *dharmakaya* . . . everything is emptiness and everything is compassion. I don't know when in my life I have ever had such a sense of beauty and spiritual validity running together in one aesthetic illumination. Surely, with Mahabalipuram and Polonnaruwa my Asian pilgrimage has come clear and purified itself. I mean, I know and have seen what I was obscurely looking for. I don't know what else remains but I have now seen and have pierced through the surface and have got beyond the shadow and the disguise. This is Asia in its purity, not covered over with garbage, Asian or European or American, and it is clear, pure, complete. It says everything; it needs nothing. And because it needs nothing it can afford to be silent, unnoticed, undiscovered. It does not need to be discovered. It is we, Asians included, who need to discover it.

TIBETAN SACRED MUSIC*

Anagarika Govinda

The soul-stirring quality of Tibetan ritual music which accompanies and often precedes the liturgy is not based on melody but on rhythm and pure sound-values: the latter in the sense that the different instruments do not try to imitate the variations and movements of a human song or its emotions, but each of them represents the tonal value of a fundamental quality of nature, in which the human voice is merely one of the many vibrations that make up the symphony of the universe. This symphony does not follow the laws of Western musical harmony, and yet it achieves an effect that is far from disharmonious, because each sound has its fixed place and corresponds to the others in a way that establishes an unmistakable parallelism on different levels.

I am not a musician, so as to be able to describe or to analyze Tibetan music in technical terms. But I am deeply moved by music, and therefore I can only describe my own reaction. Moreover, the few references I have read about Tibetan sacred music are so scanty and inadequate that I have come to the conclusion that either Western terminology is unsuitable to express the nature of Tibetan music or that those who have attempted to give an idea of it were not able to enter into its spirit.

To do this one has to experience the religious as well as the natural background from which this music grew, and this is only possible if one has lived in those surroundings and has taken part in the spiritual and emotional life of which this music is the most immediate expression. Tibetan Buddhism regards man not as a solitary figure but always in connection with and against a universal background. In the same way Tibetan ritual music is not concerned with the emotions of temporal individuality, but with the ever-present, timeless qualities of universal life, in which our personal joys and sorrows do not exist, so that we feel in communion with the very sources of reality in the deepest core of our being. To bring us in touch with this realm is the very purpose of meditation as well as of Tibetan ritual music, which is built upon the

* Editor's Note: Chapter 7 of *The Way of the White Clouds.*

deepest vibrations that an instrument or a human voice can produce: sounds that seem to come from the womb of the earth or from the depth of space like rolling thunder, the mantric sound of nature, which symbolize the creative vibrations of the universe, the origin of all things. They form the foundation as well as the background from which the modulations of the higher voices and the plaintive notes of the reed instruments rise like the forms of sentient life from the elementary forces of nature—which are nowhere more apparent than in the gigantic mountain ranges and in the vast, lonely highlands of Tibet.

Just as the bass-voice of the precentor forms the basis of the choir, from which the liturgy starts and to which it sinks back in a peculiarly sliding way at the end of each part of the recitation, in the same way the huge twelve-foot *radong*s form the basis and the starting-point of the orchestral music. They are always in pairs and are alternately blown in such a way that the sounds of the one merge into the other without breaking its continuity and at the same time producing the effect of gradually swelling and ebbing tides of an ocean of sound. And on the surface of this ocean the breeze of individual life creates and plays with a multitude of waves and wavelets which, like the high-pitched tremolo of the oboes, add vivacity and melody to the vastness of the ocean, whose sound seems to be that of the all-embracing OM, the prototype of all mantric sounds.

It is in imitation of this sound that *mantra*s are recited in that peculiar, deep bass-voice with which the Umdzé begins and conducts the liturgy. The liturgy, after all, is mainly mantric in character, especially the opening and closing passages of each section. Certain important *mantra*s are accompanied by hand-bells and *damaru*s (small, hour-glass-shaped hand-drums, which can be played with one hand).

In contrast to the more or less static sound of the *radong*s, the bass-drums and the big cymbals introduce a dynamic element into the orchestra. Not only does the rhythm change according to the meter of the recitation, but—what is more important from the musical and emotional point of view, as it creates a feeling of liberation and a release from a slowly mounting tension—towards the end of each section the rhythm is accelerated until it merges into one great finale, in which the big cymbals by a peculiar rotating movement produce triumphantly upsurging sound, rising above the thundering rumble of the bass-drums, and ending in a mighty clash. After this a new slow rhythm marks the beginning of another section of the liturgy.

If the *radong* or the human bass-voice represent the primeval cosmic sound, in which we experience the infinity of space, the drum represents the infinity of life and movement, governed by the supreme law of its inherent rhythm, in which we experience the alternating cycles of creation and dissolution, culminating in manifestation and liberation.

While melody plays only the ephemeral part of the passing moods of individual life, the rhythm (of the bass-drum in particular) gives the real significance and structure to the music. With the drum, therefore, the Tibetan (and perhaps the East in general) associates quite different emotions than the West, where it is not regarded as a basic or independent musical instrument. The importance of the drum from the very beginnings of Indian civilization may be seen from one of the most significant similes of the Buddha, in which he compared the eternal law of the universe (*dharma*) with the rhythm of the drum, when in his first utterance after the attainment of enlightenment he spoke of "the drum of immortality" (*amata-dundubhin*) which he wanted to make heard throughout the world.

Since I could not follow yet the details of the liturgy and the particular service which was conducted that morning in the presence and under the guidance of Tomo Géshé Rimpoché, my whole attention was given to the effects of the music and the meaning it conveyed to me. The inspiring atmosphere, which prevailed all through the service, put me into a state of greater receptiveness than ever before. I had attended during the last weeks many liturgic services and ceremonies in the temple, but never had I witnessed them in such perfection and complete harmony. All who took part in it seemed to be moved by the same spirit—united, as I felt, in the bigger consciousness of the great Guru, so that they acted and chanted in perfect unison, as if merged into *one* body.

All this moved me all the more as during the last years in Ceylon I had been starved of all musical inspiration, which is entirely absent in Southern Buddhism (*Theravada*) on account of the mistaken view that music is merely a form of sense-pleasure. In consequence of this the religious life had taken on a dry, intellectual form of expression, in which together with the lower also the higher emotions were suppressed and all negative virtues were fostered to the extent that no great personality could arise—i.e., rise above the level of the accepted norm. Book-knowledge had become more important than experience, the letter more important than the spirit.

No wonder, therefore, that it was believed that no *Arahans* (realized saints) could arise after the first millennium of the Buddhist era, in other words, that for the last 1,500 years the Buddhadharma in Ceylon had existed only in theory, or at the best as a belief, since (according to the Sinhalese themselves) Ceylon had not produced a single saint during this long period and it was no more possible to enter into the higher states of *dhyana* or direct spiritual insight. It was, therefore, impossible even to discuss deeper experiences of meditation, as it was regarded preposterous to assume that anybody could actually realize any of the states of higher consciousness of which the sacred texts speak so often. Thus Buddhism had become a matter of the past, a creed or a distant ideal towards which one could strive by leading a moral life and committing to heart as many sacred texts as possible.

THE SYMBOLISM OF THE TAOIST GARDEN*

Jean Cooper

The development of the typical Chinese garden with its full *yin-yang* symbolism was essentially Taoist in origin. The Han Emperors had earlier created vast artificial landscapes or parks with mountains, ravines, forests, rivers, lakes, and open spaces to provide a habitat for hordes of game for hunting, but during the time of the Six Dynasties and the T'ang, when Taoism prevailed, there developed the quiet intimacy of the Taoist garden, intended to reflect heaven on earth. It became a symbol of Paradise where all life was protected and sheltered. The park had been given over to the grandiose, the artificial, extravagant, and luxurious, to the hunter and aggressor; the Taoist garden was a place of naturalness and simplicity, a haven for the sage, scholar, and nature lover.

Both landscape painting and garden-making owe their development to the Taoist philosophers who derived their inspiration from Nature as the Mother of All Things, the womb of life, eternal renewal, with her rhythms and moods. What was said of the painting of a landscape applied equally to the creation of a garden: "Chinese painters intuitively felt these same forms to be the visible, material manifestations of a higher all-embracing Reality; the Word made—not flesh—but Living Nature."[1] Or: "The Sages cherish the Tao within them, while they respond to the objective world. . . . As to landscapes, they both have material existence and reach to the realms of the Spirit. . . . The virtuous follow the Tao by spiritual insight and the wise take the same approach. Landscapes capture the Tao by their forms and the virtuous take pleasure in them. Is this not almost the same thing? . . . The Divine Spirit is infinite, yet it dwells in forms and inspires likeness, and thus truth enters into forms and signs."[2] But while landscapes portrayed the vastness and grandeur of Nature, the garden revealed her intimate aspect.

* Editor's Note: from *Studies in Comparative Religion*, 11:4, 1977.

[1] Michael Sullivan, "The Birth of Landscape Painting in China."

[2] From the *Hua shan-shui hsü*. Preface to *Landscape Painting* by Tsung Ping.

All forms of art are the outward and visible expression of *Ch'i*, the Cosmic Breath or Energy, with which all creation must be in accord, whether it be painting, poetry, music, or the creation of a garden. Indeed, all these arts developed side by side, for the Chinese scholar was expected to be capable of interpreting the same inspiration in all three arts together and the place of both their inspiration and expression was most usually the garden, this term being applied also to the rural retreat of a sage or hermit where in some remote and beautiful scenery a hut had been built and round it trees planted. In a well-designed garden it should be difficult to distinguish between the work of man and Nature. One should "borrow scenery from Nature" and the ideal place was "among trees in the mountains." Wherever it was, the garden was a place of quiet, meditation, and communion with Nature, whether in wild scenery beside a waterfall, or a trickling stream, or in a bamboo grove, or the courtyard of a city dwelling.

The garden is "the natural home of man" and house and garden were situated according to *feng-shui* (wind and water) influences in harmony with the currents of *Ch'i*; these were held in balance in both the house and garden, as in Nature, by the *yin-yang* forces. The *yin* lunar and *yang* solar powers were represented by the *yin* valleys and waters and the *yang* mountains and sky with all their endless *yang* and *yin* qualities such as sunshine and shadow, height and depth, heat and cold.

However small the space utilized, the garden was never laid out as a flat expanse from which all could be viewed at once. This removal of any definite boundary made for succession, expansion, rhythm, and a sense of unlimited time and space. The garden, like Nature, is ever-changing, a place of light and shade with a life-breath (*Ch'i yün*) which is in harmony with the rhythms of the seasons and their contrasts in weather. Irregularity of line also suggests movement and life. "Everything that is ruled and symmetrical is alien to free nature."[3] Or, as it has been said: "The awareness of change, the interaction symbolized by the *yin-yang* theory, has caused Chinese gardeners to seek irregular and unexpected features which appeal more to the imagination than to the reasoning faculty of the beholder. There were certain rules and principles for gardening, but these did not lead to any conformity. The basic elements were the same for landscape painting,

[3] From the *Yüan Yeh*, a Ming treatise on gardening.

shan shui or 'mountain and water'"[4] which might be imposing scenery or simply a pond and rocks. The smallest space could be converted into an effect of depth, infinite extension, and mysterious distance; groves, rockeries, bushes, winding paths, all helped to lure on beyond the immediate scene. As Rowley says of Western and Chinese art: "We restrict space to a single vista as though seen through an open door; they suggest the unlimited space of nature as though they had stepped through that open door."[5]

The entire garden must be considered in association and relationship with all things in Nature. Chang Ch'ao says: "Planting flowers serves to invite butterflies, piling up rocks serves to invite the clouds, planting pine trees serves to invite the wind, . . . planting banana trees serves to invite the rain, and planting willow trees serves to invite the cicada." These are all traditional symbolic associations.

In the past in China, though man was the mediator between Heaven and Earth, he was not the measure of the universe; his place was simply to maintain the balance and harmony between the *yin* and the *yang*. It was Nature which was the Whole, and controlling cosmic power. The garden helped man in his work of maintaining harmony; it also had an ethical significance and influence. According to Ch'ien Lung it had "a refreshing effect upon the mind and regulated the feelings" preventing man from becoming "engrossed in sensual pleasures and losing strength of will." Its pleasures were simple, natural, and spiritual. A Suchou poet wrote of the garden: "One should enter it in a peaceful and receptive mood; one should use one's observation to note the plan and pattern of the garden, for the different parts have not been arbitrarily assembled, but carefully weighed against each other like the pairs of inscribed tablets placed in the pavilions,[6] and when one has thoroughly comprehended the tangible forms of objects one should endeavor to attain an inner communication with the soul of the garden and try to understand the mysterious forces governing the landscape and making it cohere."

The garden was for all seasons with their changing moods and colors, flowers and trees, so the pavilion and open gallery were necessary for

[4] Yang Yap and A. Cotterell, *The Early Civilization of China.*

[5] *Principles of Chinese Painting.*

[6] Pairs of tablets were inscribed with parallel quotations which corresponded in tonal value and content.

enjoyment in the heat of summer or the cold of winter and became an integral part of the scenery. Even in winter one sat out in the pavilion to admire the beauties of the snow and to watch the budding of the almond and plum blossom. A portable brazier of glowing charcoal kept one warm and a large brazier was used to melt the snow to make tea. The garden was particularly evocative by moonlight and the new and full moons, times of spiritual power, had their own festivals, especially the festival of the mid-autumn moon. Other festivals were also celebrated in the pavilion or garden; the vernal equinox, observed on the twelfth day of the second month of the Chinese year, was known as the Birthday of the Flowers.

Pavilions and galleries obviously had to blend with their surroundings. The *Yüan Yeh* says: "Buildings should be placed so as to harmonize with the natural formation of the ground." When pavilions were connected by galleries these followed the rise and fall and curves of the land or winding of the waters which were often crossed by bridges, bringing in all the symbolism of the crossing of the waters, of transition, of communication between one realm or plane and another, as well as of man as mediator, occupying the central position between the great powers. Added beauty and symbolism was introduced in the "moon bridge," a lovely half-circle which when reflected in the clear water below formed the perfect circle of the full moon.

Roofs were curved and painted and the lattice work of the balustrades was lacquered and painted in harmonizing and symbolic colors. Harmony and proportion had to be maintained but symmetry was alien to Nature, thus the garden contained no such thing as clipped lawns or hedges or stiff geometrically designed flower beds, or flowers marshaled in rows or patterns. And "landscaping" had to absorb buildings and, like planted trees, make them look as if they had grown there. "One erects a pavilion where the view opens and plants flowers that smile in the face of the spring breeze."[7] It was a place for both relaxation and active enjoyment, for solitary meditation and study, or for convivial gatherings for friends to meet and drink tea or wine or take *al fresco* meals. There they composed poetry and music, painted, practiced calligraphy or discussed philosophy. One amusement was to compose a poem in the time that it took a floating wine cup and saucer to drift from one end to the other on a meandering water-course set in the floor of the pavilion. A poet failing to complete his poem in the

[7] The *Yüan Yeh*.

time had to catch and empty the cup. These water-courses could also be constructed in symbolic forms such as the swastika, or the cross-form of the Chinese character for the number ten, or in the shape of a lotus or open flower. Sometimes the water tumbled over small waterfalls or rocks.

Pavilions were given names such as the Pavilion of the Hanging Rainbow, the Fragrance of the Lotus, the Secret Clouds, the Eight Harmonious Tones, Invitation, or Contemplation, of the Moon, Welcoming Spring, Pleasant Coolness, and so on. In some gardens there were Halls of the Moon; these were constructed in the shape of a hemisphere, the vaulted ceiling painted to represent the nocturnal sky with innumerable small windows of colored glass depicting the moon and stars. The total effect was one of the subdued light of a summer's night. Sometimes the floor was planted with flowers, but more usually it contained running water, the moon and water being closely allied: "The moon washes its soul in the clear waters," but although moon and waters are both *yin* water is symbolically related to the sun since the waters catch and reflect back the sun's light, the *yang*. These halls could be large enough for holding banquets or of a smallness suitable for intimate sitting about in conversation or listening to music and poetry. Here, in the garden, where heaven and earth meet, music and poetry become the natural form of the expression of harmony.

While the pavilion was built in and for the garden and was open to it, this breaking down of the distinction between in and out of doors applied also to the dwelling house which was not only sited for *feng-shui* but for fitting as naturally as possible into the scenery and giving access so immediately to the garden that there seemed no dividing line. Doors either did not exist or were left open. (Socially, closed doors were not considered courteous since they implied exclusion, while the open door symbolized the welcome extended by the essentially outgoing Chinese temperament with its spontaneous and natural relationships developed over the ages in the highly socialized life of a large family). Doors were often only a means of enhancing a view into the garden or to the scenery beyond, such as the moon door, a beautifully placed circle framing some special outlook. Not only was every aspect used to its full natural advantage but "if one can take advantage of a neighbor's view one should not cut off the communication, for such a 'borrowed prospect' is very acceptable."[8]

[8] Ibid.

The house opened on to the garden and the garden came into the house; rooms opened on to the courtyards where flowering trees grew and ferns and flowers fringed a central pool, usually with golden carp swimming in it, for the garden was a place for animal and bird life also. Indeed, animals and plants were not considered the only 'living' things; everything shares in the cosmic power and mountains and rivers also 'live.' Nor was it at all unusual for the house to go out into the garden, for the lover of nature would move a bed out of doors, beside some special tree, shrub, or flower which was coming into bloom, so that no stage of its development and beauty would be lost; or one would sit up all night to enjoy the effect of the moonlight. "The moonlight lies like glittering water over the countryside. The wind sighs in the trees and gently touches the lute and the book that lie on the couch. The dark rippled mirror of the water swallows the half-moon. When day dawns one is awakened by the fresh breeze; it reaches the bed and all the dust of the world is blown out of one's mind."[9]

The garden was not, however, merely aesthetic but creative and a reminder of, and contact with, the creative forces and the great cycle of the seasons, birth, maturity, decay, death and rebirth.

The merging of the native Taoism with imported Buddhism in Ch'an, or Zen, carried on the tradition of the intimate relationship between man and Nature. Ch'an Buddhism and gardens were two facets of Chinese inspiration which were adopted and carried on by the Japanese, but in later decadent times the original symbolism of the garden as a reflection of Paradise was lost and gardens became mere pleasure grounds, except where attached to monasteries in which much of the symbolism was taken over and where the association with meditation remained. In those gardens of effete times artificial extravagances crept in; windows were made in shapes which bore no relationship to symbols, such as teapots, animals, vases, and fans, even if some of these forms had, in fact, a symbolic content. But these aberrations were stigmatized by the *Yüan Yeh* as "stupid and vulgar" and "intelligent people should be careful in such matters." (Shades of plastic cranes and gnomes!)

The garden was a reflection of the macrocosm and embodied all the *yin-yang* dualisms projected in manifestation. Mountains, valleys, rivers, lakes, were all represented. As Cheng Pan ch'iao said: "The

[9] Ibid.

enjoyment of life should come from a view regarding the universe as a garden . . . so that all beings live according to their nature and great indeed is such happiness."

The importance of water in the Chinese garden was not only due to *yin-yang* symbolism but to the wide significance of water itself as, next to the Dragon, the greatest Taoist symbol. It is strength in weakness, fluidity, adaptability, coolness of judgment, gentle persuasion, and passionlessness. While mountains and rocks are the bones of the body and the earth its flesh, rivers and streams are the arteries and blood, life-giver and fertilizer. Flowing water and still water symbolized movement and repose and the complementary opposites, and water-worn stones represented the interaction of the soft and the hard. Still water also takes on all the symbolism of the mirror.

Water could be made by forming lakes and rivers in the earth excavated for making mountains, though mountains were most frequently represented by rocks, hollow and weather-worn, fretted out by the restless sea or the elements or formed from the strange shapes of petrified trees. These rocks were carefully selected for their color, texture, grain, and shape; some were upright and towering, others, larger at the top than at the base, gave the effect of disappearing into the clouds, others, lying down, took fantastic animal shapes, some gave out a note when struck, others were mute. Sometimes the rocks formed grottoes, but whatever the shape they always appeared as natural to the setting and were as near to the form of wild mountain crags as possible, giving the impression of Nature, untamed and capricious. (In this "naturalness" it must be remarked that the mountains of China in the Yangtze gorges, the far West, and the Southern provinces have been worked by nature herself into fantastic and sometimes grotesque shapes.) "Try to make your mountains resemble real mountains. Follow Nature's plan" but "do not forget they have to be built by human hands."[10]

Symbolically, the mountain is of course the world axis, but in the Chinese garden it also represented the *yang* power in Nature with the waters as the *yin*; the "mountain" is traditionally placed in the middle of a lake or pond, the rock being the stable and eternal, the water the flowing and temporal. This mountain-and-water (*shan shui*) symbolism also obtains in landscape painting. The rock and the shadow it casts are

[10] Ibid.

also *yang* and *yin.* Rocks are "silent, unmovable, and detached from life, like refined scholars." Their ruggedness also suggests the challenging and dangerous element in the mountains and in life.

In larger gardens the mountains were sufficiently high for the formation of small valleys and dales, with winging streams opening out into lakes on which boat journeys could be taken and where the water could be spanned by bridges. Sometimes a series of islands or rocks were so connected. Tunnels in the rocks gave the same effect and carried the same symbolism as bridges in passing from one world to another. But "even a little mountain may give rise to many effects . . . a small stone may evoke many feelings."[11] Shen Fu says: "In the designing of a rockery or the training of flower trees one should try to show the small in the large and the large in the small and provide for the real in the unreal and the unreal in the real. One reveals and conceals alternately, making it sometimes apparent and sometimes hidden."

Both the *yang* mountain and the *yin* tree are axial and so represent stability and balance between the two great powers; they also offer a line of communication for man between the celestial *yang* forces coming down to earth and the earthly *yin* forces reaching up to heaven, with man again as central and responsible for the maintenance of balance and harmony in responding equally to the *yin* and *yang* powers.

Trees were an essential feature of both the domestic and hermitage garden, particularly the latter where they were often the only addition made by man to the natural scenery and their variety was almost as important as the trees themselves. While all trees are beautiful and symbolize the femininc power, some were especially noted for their *yin-yang* qualities. Though *yin* as a tree, the pine and cedar express *yang* masculine dignity and rigidity in contrast to the feminine gracefulness, pliability, and charm of the willow, both these trees were considered necessary to maintain the *yin-yang* harmony. Flowering trees such as the almond, cherry, plum, and peach were esteemed—one should say loved—for their beauty and their symbolism. The almond, as the first flower of the year, is in many traditions the Awakener, watchfulness. As flowering in winter it is also courage in adversity. The cherry depicts delicacy of feeling and purity of feeling on the *yin* side and nobility on the *yang.* The plum, a symbol of winter and beauty signified strength

[11] Ibid.

and longevity and the hermit. It is one of the favorite subjects for artists and the plum, pine, and bamboo were called "the three friends of winter." The almond and plum are both symbolic of new life coming in spring, but the plum should have a gnarled trunk and branches, called sleeping dragons, as the *yang* to offset the delicate blossoms of the *yin;* they also represent the old and new together. Just as lovers of the garden would move their beds out under trees, so we read of artists who wandered all night in the moonlight to catch every phase of the beauty of "the dry limbs clad in jade-white blooms."

The peach holds a special position as the tree of the Taoist genii or Immortals; it is the Tree of Life at the center of Paradise. It is also the Tree of Immortality and one bite of the fruit growing on the tree in Paradise confers immediate immortality. Peach stones were apotropaic and were beautifully and symbolically carved and kept, or worn, as amulets and talismans. The tree is a symbol of spring, youth, marriage, wealth, and longevity.

Preeminent among flowers were the lotus, peony, and chrysanthemum. The peony is the only purely *yang* flower. Flowers, with their cup shape, naturally depict the *yin* receptive aspect in nature, but the peony is a royal flower, flaunting the red, fiery, masculine color; it is also nobility, glory, riches. The chrysanthemum, on the other hand, is a flower of quiet retirement, the beloved flower of the cultured scholar, the retired official, who was of course also a scholar, the philosopher, and poet. It was so much cultivated in retirement that it became a symbol of that life and of leisure. It signifies longevity as being that which survives the cold and as autumnal it is harvest and wealth, but it is primarily ease, leisure, joviality, and enjoyment. Yüan Chung-lang said that the retired and the scholar were fortunate in having "the enjoyment of the hills and water, flowers and bamboo" largely to themselves since "luckily they lie outside the scope of the strugglers for fame and power who are so busy with their engrossing pursuits that they have no time for such enjoyment."

But the lotus, a universal symbol in the East (its symbolism is taken on by the lily and sometimes the rose in the West) is "the flower that was in the Beginning, the glorious lily of the Great Waters . . . that wherein existence comes to be and passes away." It is both *yin* and *yang* and contains within itself the balance of the two powers; it is solar as blooming in the sun and lunar as rising from the dark of the waters of pre-cosmic chaos. As the combination of air and water it symbolizes spirit and matter; its roots bedded in the darkness of the mud depict indissolubility; its stem, the umbilical cord of life, attaches man to his origins and is also a world axis; rising through the opaque waters of the manifest world, the leaves and flowers reach and unfold in the air and sunlight, typifying potentiality in the bud and spiritual expansion and realization in the flower; its seeds, moving on the waters are creation. The lotus is associated with the wheel both as the solar matrix and the sun-wheel of cycles of existence. Iamblichus calls it perfection, since its leaves, flowers, and fruit form the circle. As lunar-solar, *yin-yang*, the lotus is also the androgyne, the self-existent. It has an inexhaustible symbolism in Hinduism, Taoism, and Buddhism alike. Again it appears as both solar and lunar associated with sun gods such as Surya and lunar goddesses such as Lakshmi; solar with Amitabha and lunar with Kwan-yin and androgynous in Kwannon. The lotus is the Golden Flower of Taoism, the crystallization and experience of light, the Tao. While on the spiritual level it represents the whole of birth, growth, development, and potentiality, on the mundane level it depicts the scholar-gentleman who comes in contact with mud and dirty water but is uncontaminated by it. Apart from its almost endless symbolism, the lotus is a flower of great beauty and highly evocative; as Osvald Sirén says, a sheet of lotus blossom "emanates a peculiar magic, an atmosphere that intoxicates like fragrant incense and lulls like the rhythms of a rising and falling *mantra*."[12]

Ancient China understood many things which are only now reaching the West and being hailed as new discoveries. She anticipated by centuries the "discovery" that flowers and plants have feelings. Yüan Chung-lang knew that they have their likes and dislikes and compatibilities among other vegetation and that they respond to care and appreciation in more than a material way. The flowers in a Chinese garden were genuinely loved, but not in any "precious" aestheticism, rather in an intimate relationship between living individuals. He said that "flowers have their moods of happiness and sorrow and their time of sleep. . . . When they seem drunk, or quiet and tired, and when the day is misty, that is the sorrowful mood of flowers. . . . When they bask in the sunlight and their delicate bodies are protected from the wind, that is the happy mood of flowers. . . . When the ancient people knew a flower was about to bud they would move their beds and pillows and sleep under it watching how the flower passed from infancy to

[12] *Gardens of China.*

maturity and finally dropped off and died. . . . As for all forms of noisy behavior and common vulgar prattle, they are an insult to the spirits of flowers. One should rather sit dumb like a fool than offend them."[13] Among things which flowers dislike are: too many guests; ugly women putting flowers in their hair; dogs fighting; writing poems by consulting a rhyming dictionary; books kept in bad condition; spurious paintings; and common monks talking Zen! On the other hand they do like a visiting monk who understands tea!

Picked flowers and vases of flowers should never be regarded as normal, only as a temporary expedient employed by those living in cities and unnatural places deprived of the hills and lakes or any garden.

For the town-dweller or for one kept indoors of necessity the miniature garden was created; though it was also seen in pavilions it was most usually on the tables of scholars. It, too, symbolized Paradise, the Isles of the Blessed, or the Abode of the Immortals reflected in miniature perfection with the whole range of the *yin-yang* symbolism. Exceptionally beautiful stones or shells were used and there were miniature grottoes, trees, bamboos, and grasses growing among the mountains, valleys, and waters. The making of these gardens was an art in itself; just as Wang Wei maintained that the artist can bring all Nature into the space of a small painting, so the creator of a garden, large, small, or miniature can concentrate the cosmos within its bounds.

Enclosing the whole garden in the city, or where the extent of the garden was limited, was the wall which was used not only as a boundary but as a setting for trees, shrubs, and flowers; it could also provide an aperture which opened up some special view. In the city, where space was restricted, walls were often a garden in themselves, sometimes built with considerable width with a roof-garden effect or with trees and shrubs planted on top and flowers and ferns in the crevices below. Enclosing walls also helped to make the city garden a place where one could find "stillness in turmoil." Apart from the symbolism of the enclosed garden the walls brought in the *yin-yang* significance of the interplay of light and shade.

Today China joins the industrial nations of the world in "exploiting" Nature. Hideous concrete blocks of flats, offices, and factories insulate man from any contact with the yellow earth and, sadly, Seyyed Hossein

[13] The treatise of P'ing Shih.

Nasr's words can be applied: "There is nearly total disequilibrium between modern man and nature as attested by nearly every expression of modern civilization which seeks to offer a challenge to nature rather than to cooperate with it. . . . The harmony between man and nature has been destroyed."[14] The *yin-yang* balance has been betrayed.

[14] *Man and Nature*, Allen & Unwin.

THE SUBSTANCE OF THE TEACHING*

Gustie Herrigel

When one studies the "true teaching," one becomes more clearly aware of the characteristically Oriental conception of freedom. In the East, inner freedom is understood to mean adapting yourself to forms which have the significance of cosmic laws. By adapting himself to them, the pupil takes his place in a coherent world order. The triadic pattern that underlies flower-setting is nothing less than a cosmic principle. Only by adapting himself to this principle can the floral artist reach the solid ground where his creative powers can develop to the full. He is then free to depict the schematic relationships in a living way. Neither mindless imitation of this schema, nor a misplaced originality that thrusts it aside unthinkingly, would be the right thing. Both would be looked upon as a transgression against the "true teaching" and the spirit of flower-setting.

Hence, as repeatedly emphasized, inner discipline, adaptability, and the capacity for self-denial are demanded of the pupil. On these qualities, which become more and more self-evident, the teacher sets the greatest value from the beginning; they seem to him more important than a light, skilful hand or good taste.

Although self-renunciation and dissolution in the spiritual principle of the world are regarded in the East as the highest good and constitute the deepest meaning of life, this does not mean that a work born of such an attitude must be completely impersonal. Even the Eastern artist cannot prevent his work from showing traces of individuality—indeed, this is an essential part of it—yet his individuality should not disturb the spirit of the work but must be fully absorbed by it. This means that the artist should not make a deliberate attempt to give his work a personal note. Only so far as this streams into the work unintentionally and fuses spontaneously with the law of its being in perfect unity, is it justified and even has a profound meaning.

What we see here, in the modest domain of flower arrangement, is characteristic of all Eastern art and particularly of the Zen Buddhist

* Editor's Note: from *Zen in the Art of Flower Arrangement.*

outlook on life. Everything ultimately depends on what is outside and beyond the opposites, on the spirit, and on man's capacity not only to dissolve himself in it through passionate self-immersion, but also to live out of it with equal composure. This is not a negation or a flight from the world.

From whatever side the Westerner seeks access to the spiritual life of the East, he will encounter quite special difficulties. Almost always he is in danger of wanting to penetrate intellectually into what lies beyond the intellect, into something that is given to Eastern man directly, and which he experiences in unquestioning reality. The difficulty of coming to an intellectual understanding is further exacerbated by the fact that the Oriental seldom feels any desire to explain his experience in intellectual terms. Consequently, there is often a deep gulf between what he says with words and what he really means by them. Mostly he has to content himself with bare hints and images, if he does not take refuge in paradox. To find the right approach and *not* regard understanding of what the teacher says as understanding of the thing itself, demands much intuitive patience from the Westerner, and constantly renewed attempts somehow to guess and experience what it is all about. Even though there are many things in flower-setting that can be said and shown, yet behind everything that can be visibly represented there stands, waiting to be experienced by everyone, the mystery and deep ground of existence.

It should be evident from what has been said that flower arrangement is concerned with this inner, spiritual principle. But one must be quite clear that the right attitude has nothing to do with mood. That which underlies this art and needs to be experienced is in itself formless, but it takes on form as soon as you try to represent it symbolically. And it is just this spiritual form that constitutes the essence of flower arrangement. By adhering strictly to the cosmic pattern, the artist learns, in accordance with the Eastern attitude of pure, unpurposing surrender to the laws of the cosmos, to experience them through and through. At the same time he breaks through to the depths of his own being, which rests on those same laws.

Here without doubt is the key to an understanding of Eastern art and the spiritual life of the East in general: in this "looking away from oneself," in the utter "unpurposingness" of its highest spiritual achievements. Thus the painter brushes his strokes not as though *he* painted them, but as though they painted themselves from the primal "Ground." Thus, too, the flowers are not brought into harmony by looking at them first from one side and then from the other, by experimenting and comparing—only the beginner does that—rather, the eye is directed inwards. Not the slightest intention of arranging them "beautifully" must disturb this self-immersion, not even the desire to become "purposeless on purpose." If you succeed in producing this frame of mind and in keeping it pure, then only does the hand unconsciously follow spontaneous impulses. This attitude only *looks* passive; according to the Eastern view, it is in reality the source of that inner strength.

Stages of Knowledge

It goes without saying that there are stages along "the flowers' way" which the Master can recognize and knows how to interpret. He shows the pupil the degree of knowledge he has now attained. Often he can read the beginner's character with uncanny accuracy from the way he arranges his flowers and does his work.

Spontaneity and individuality seldom appear during the initial stages. Only through patient practice and continual inner transformation does habit gradually wear away, until the work manifests the "pure form." At higher stages of development the pupil's "originality" can venture forth more freely, till finally it becomes more and more purified and blends with the "pure truth" in the perfect unity of art and nature.

Thus the "truth" finds, in the essential nature of the artist, the theatre in which it takes on visible form. To embody the truth of "Heaven itself"—this is the highest task, whose solution is granted only to the best poets and painters. And if he is successful, the flower artist will find it rising out of himself with unforced naturalness, like a gift that can never be lost.

Yet behind the visible forms there is always the form that cannot be expressed and cannot be represented, the eternal mystery, which he struggles in vain to apprehend, unless it reveal itself unhoped for.

SACREDNESS*

Jean Biès

Something still exists in India that guarantees the duration of civilizations, and when forgotten, it hastens their end: the meaning of mystery and the sacred from which we have freed ourselves. Only the obtuse ignorance of principles and symbols joined with the obscure suicidal willingness lurking in its veins, can still let the West consider itself an adult since its evacuation of the mystery—at a time when the growing immensity of this mystery is proclaimed by science; and its destruction of the sacred—whose disappearance leads to the familiar ecological, cultural, and psychic calamities.

The loss of this double meaning drags man to his downfall because the mystery and the sacred live in man: within him, one and the other are the intuition of his depth and dignity, the sentiment of the immutable, the majestic, the formidable, the infinite. Comparatively, they are the souvenir of the Absolute that came to perfume existence; they prevent mediocrity and sordidness, teach the value of each gesture and each word, and respect for each object. Before starting each meal, the Hindu presents an offering, which is already a mastery of the senses. He apologizes to the earth before plowing a furrow that will injure it and kill thousands of creatures. He calls for inspiration before writing (even if just a letter) in order to prepare himself mentally for writing fairly. I was watching one of them very carefully fold the pelt of a panther. He spoke to me about his appreciation of it: it protected him from the nocturnal cold, supported him when he meditated. It offered him unselfish aid: how could he simply heap this instrument of salvation into a corner?

The Westerner who no longer prays to God would find it truly demeaning to pray to the tree he plans to assassinate. And yet, the tree is venerated as the image of the cosmos: the trunk characterizes the axis of the world, the branches, the universe that gravitates around it; the image of *Brahman*, which, as stated in the *Veda*, "occupies the center of the world, is surrounded by all the gods as the branches surround

* Editor's Note: from *Returning to the Essential*.

the trunk"; in short, the image of man uniting heaven and earth in his verticality. For man to so fiercely and unrelentingly persecute His Lordship the Tree, how much hatred must he have accumulated against the world, against God, against his brothers, against himself; a hatred that can only be fabricated by the individual of a world that is *too* civilized, and who sees ruin as a necessity! I have never witnessed the destruction of forests here; I have even seen the road circumvent age-old trees. I suspect that the Hindu who must cut one down—and this must be done according to astrologically exact moments—still wishes good luck to the genie who lives in it and offers him the same prayer as in the past: "May the god who lives in this tree depart (the *yaksha*, the vegetal entity) and let us not bear the blame for having forced him out!"

But where I most clearly perceive the difference between the East and the West is where it should be the least perceptible: in the spiritual. By cheapening the supernatural or simply poetic elements and replacing them with ideological prattling or vain sentimentality, by imposing the worship of the administrative rigidity of the terrestrial city, the West pretends to make God "accessible to all," and in fact, closes the door on him. On the contrary—the *puja*—exactly like the Byzantine liturgy closing the "royal doors" of the iconostasis—encircles itself with reverential precautions and at certain times screens from view the image of the divinity, drawing the curtain, these eyelids of the altar, in front of it. The *puja* spares no effort for the sounds, fragrances, and colors for purifying the senses, and invites the entire body to participate in the festival of the spirit. The Divine only allows the speculation of His actual presence as He is mysteriously veiled, as He delicately allows Himself to be seen, desired. Tossed as nourishment to the stark white of false obviousness, He retracts, He no longer exists.

Perhaps in defiance of memory, but also with the vulgar absence of any sense of secrecy, the West has increasingly entrusted everything it could to the written word; to the point where someone's remarks are only taken into consideration if they are duly documented on paper. Our defiance of spoken matters has resulted in the mutual defiance of one another and consequently we have cheerfully lost the highest revelations that were always conveyed by word of mouth. In the East, written words vanish into thin air while spoken words remain. One still strolls in the gardens of Orality. Even though the volume of Hindu Scriptures is several times that of the Bible, huge continents of words from the beginning of the ages exist alongside the body of solidified doctrines that are destined to traverse the darkest periods of the Dark Age with their anonymity; better concealed because they are deeper, because they are more dangerous also, and about which no one knows anything; except for the disciple whose master gives him some parcels of this learning that personally concern him.

Even written texts are nostalgic for the time when they were spoken, for the state where these guardians of supreme truths were still as immaterial, invisible, and intangible as the Spirit they portray; they do not take up any space, do not lend themselves to any commentary, that is to say, to any inception of cerebral processing. They are still entrusted to recitation as if to return them to their original verbality, and also so as to avoid any deviation or betrayal. Also, their memorization is done in a curious manner that I readily believe is protohistoric. In the Tiruvannamalai Temple, I saw twelve-year-old *brahmins* learning the *Veda* by heart—with the heart—and, I must say, by gorge—with the gorge, because before wanting to *understand*, the simplicity of *learning* is required. Therefore, they recite each hymn forward then backward, by pronouncing the first syllable, then the second, by repeating the second, then the first, continuing onto the third, returning back to the first two, going down to the fourth, and so on and so forth, in a series of meticulous advances and retreats, slow conquests, and incessant recapitulations; syllable after syllable, phoneme after phoneme, they manage to permanently engrave themselves with each verse until they have learned thousands of them! This mnemotechnical method, which paradoxically develops automatic reflexes rather than hampering them, furthers learning with the help of physical swaying and develops a veritable laryngo-oral memory; the doctrine is not learned mentally, but is incorporated into the entire being. This recalls the way of monastical chanting where repeating the same words gathers together the spirit and the voice for penetrating the essence of what they name rather than their intellectual meaning. While watching these young *brahmins*, I said to myself that it was almost how Christ "learned" the Torah: Palestinian pedagogy recognized the priority of the oral over the written, practiced similar body movements and similar impregnations of the *Targum* by emphasizing repetitive echoes.

How can the value and significance of repetition be understood by a Westerner possessed by the need for accrued speed and continual changes due to his own dissatisfaction, pregnant instability, and anguish, and who instead of seeing in these sonorous meditations an exercise in concentration and deepening, a source of appeasement, or a time for putting things in order and holy sleep, only sees another occasion for yawning? To say that I had been spellbound by the *bhajan*s would be holding myself to an easy and inexact formula. Instead, I was seized by a double synthesis: the one of action (because singing is an action) and the one of contemplation (because one sings the divine Names); the one of the multiple (the inflections of the voice and the nuance of rhythms change each time) and of unity (the same *mantra* is continuously repeated). The West has completely forgotten that repeating over and over, repeating a divine Name over and over, is to identify oneself with this Name and consequently to God himself since, as Ramakrishna said, "God and his Name are identical." The West has collected loads of the last refuse of litanies and has thrown them into the great cleansing fires in its need for periodically refusing the sacred. On the other hand, how I love to rediscover the *mantra* and all its radiance in the Hesychastic "Prayer of the Heart," this *japa-yoga* of Christianity, both one and the other corresponding to a veritable manducation of the Word!

It is true that the West has not forgotten that the repetition of one thing intensifies its presence and efficiency, and that it has found replacement products that are better attuned to its nature: advertising campaigns and political slogans. Here the complete subversive conspiracy of an epic is surprised in its cold and cynical organization. What are the most basic political slogans, the deliverance of advertising's jargon, if not the parodies of sacramental words and *mantra*s—with exactly the opposite effects: the explosion of hatred, the blaze of appetites?

The same is true of both auditive and visual resources. The same parallel can be established on the one hand between rosaces, icons, and *mandala*s, and on the other between commercial advertising or caricatures that present the features, but not the faces of a lower humanity. Thus, the West has imperceptibly become an immense counter liturgy based on everything that is capable of destroying beauty, closing off all chances of elevation, of excelling. The *Kali Yuga* is not only the time when there is no longer anything but problems without solutions, nor the time when the sacred ceases to exist. It is the time when everything that fundamentally opposes the spiritual passes itself off as spiritual. And it succeeds. The *Kali Yuga* strikes the hour when "the chosen themselves are seduced." Such a quotation from the *Emerald Tablet* brings this out: "Everything that is down below is like everything that is up above, but upside down."

Attention and rigor are exactly what is unwanted by the dispersion and superficiality of such a world. They do, however, preside over the reading of the Holy Scriptures, or rather their psalmody. The Vedic psalmody is sung with concern for the exact pronunciation of a language whose words are still the things they represent. One single error committed and everything must be started over for fear of violating the integrality of the text, and by consequence, of troubling the harmony of the cosmic ocean; because this simple drop, subtly diluted, will gradually contaminate it completely, and its poison will eat away at the shores of the universe. This is what the guardians of tradition knew and know. Yet modern science has discovered that certain resonances pollute with the remote action of one vibration over another. The example is given of the sonorous repercussion following an atomic explosion in a faraway lake; this led to the pollution of the sea's water. From the time when dragons spoke, Vritra, defying the king of the gods, dealt with Indrashatru, "Conqueror of Indra"; but mispronouncing the words, he said "Conquered by Indra," and this led to his downfall. We know what is revealed by our *lapsus* lingo; it is commonly known that they can also deteriorate our internal economy.

India's loyalty is devoted less to the past—in which it is only sterilely conservative—than to certain primordial, unalterable and trans-temporal principles that have originated in something other than autonomous reason. With tiny deviations and minute betrayals, these misunderstood then forgotten principles have led humanity to the present inextricable situation, to a growing servitude and an intensification of means of destruction, even if the official ideologies try to substantiate the contrary. This uninterrupted continuity, which is bathed in eternity, will always astound the West who is plunged into the course of History, that is to say, into a time that is cut off from its roots, made up of a chaotic succession of events and cracks.

One of the strongest threads of this continuity is found in Sanskrit, a language that has remained unchanged for the past three thousand years and is still spoken and written. It is as if the West still used Homeric vocabulary and syntax and wrote in the language of Agamemnon. Likewise, for Chinese in China, notwithstanding its revolution, this linguistic fixedness got the better of all the surface transformations; and, for the same reason, I am not sure that what Valéry said about the death of civilizations[1] is applicable to these two countries with nevertheless diverging destinations.

Fixedness does not mean being at a standstill. It can be the guarantee of stability and, as demonstrated, even ferment for vitality. For example, and again unlike us, whereas the Bible has been completed once and for all, I was surprised to learn that new texts are regularly added to the existing scriptural corpus and enrich the *Smriti* with successive developments; it is as if the recent biblical editions had been complemented with the Dead Sea Scrolls or the Visions of Anne Catherine Emmerich. Thus, in the eighteenth century, the *Dharma-Shastra*, including some that go back to the Vedic times, were added to the previous ones. Only an infinite respect for the sacred can authorize such boldness or familiarity with it.

I also wonder if our distinction between the sacred and the profane is not the fruit of the dualist tree. Instead, I see that here the sacred impregnates India all the way to the profane, and better yet, that the profane does not exist. This is why certain explosive mixtures just do not exist for Hindus, for whom the lyricism of incantations is not at all bothered by the humming of sewing machines in temples. Undoubtedly, it is also why Hinduism has never needed to be organized into a Church that is the holder of peremptory dogmas authoritatively dealt out, the distributor of anathema, and obsessed with heresy. Here is plenary tolerance! Hinduism has been content to proclaim human diversity, freedom of difference, and subjective reality; it has not split everything into error and truth, but it has discerned an entire scale of evaluations that come closer and closer to the truth; it has digested the religions, systems, "points of view," in keeping spiritual practice as a priority over speculations and theological mental calculations. Neither has it turned saintliness into an *inferiority complex*, nor has it hidden the existence of the "liberated while living" behind a shameful illness: even today, anyone can visit them, listen to their teachings, live however one pleases. The skeptic simply has to go to India to see the sages, as well as the tigers, strolling in their natural state.

[1] Translator's Note: "We perceive that a civilization is as fragile as a life" (Paul Valéry, *The Crisis of the Mind*, 1919).

IV

EASTERN LIGHT ON MODERN PREDICAMENTS

"East and West" imports a cultural rather than a geographical antithesis: an opposition of the traditional or ordinary way of life that survives in the East to the modern and irregular way of life that now prevails in the West. It is because such an opposition as this could not have been felt before the Renaissance that we say that the problem is one that presents itself only accidentally in terms of geography; it is one of times much more than of places.

Ananda Coomaraswamy

SRI RAMAKRISHNA AND RELIGIOUS TOLERANCE*

Ananda Coomaraswamy

"They call Him by a multitude of names, Who is but One"; "A single Fire that burns on many altars"; "Even as He sheweth, so is He named"; these are affirmations taken from the sacrificial hymns of the *Rg Veda*. "As He is approached, so He becomes"; "It is because of His great abundance—or because He can be so variously participated in—that they call Him by so many names." By way of comment, we cite St. Thomas Aquinas, "The many aspects of these names are not empty and vain, for there corresponds to all of them one single reality represented by them in a manifold and imperfect manner" (*Sum. Theol.* 1.13.4 and 2). Nothing, perhaps, so strangely impresses or bewilders a Christian student of Saint Ramakrishna's life as the fact that this Hindu of the Hindus, without in any way repudiating his Hinduism, but for the moment forgetting it, about 1866 completely surrendered himself to the Islamic way, repeated the name of Allah, wore the costume, and ate the food of a Muslim. This self-surrender to what we should call in India the waters of another current of the single river of truth resulted only in a direct experience of the beatific vision, not less authentic than before. Seven years later, Ramakrishna in the same way proved experimentally the truth of Christianity. He was now for a time completely absorbed in the idea of Christ, and had no room for any other thought. You might have supposed him a convert. What really resulted was that he could now affirm on the basis of personal experience, "I have also practiced all religions, Hinduism, Islam, Christianity, and I have also followed the paths of the different Hindu sects. . . . The lake has many shores. At one the Hindu draws water in a pitcher, and calls it *jala*, at another the Muslim in leather bottles, and calls it *pani*, at a third the Christian finds what he calls 'water.'"

* Editor's Note: A lecture in New York in March, 1936, on the centenary of the sage's birth, reprinted in *Coomaraswamy: Selected Papers, Vol. 2: Metaphysics*, ed. Roger Lipsey.

Such an understanding may be rare, but is absolutely normal in the East: as the *Bhagavad Gita* expresses it, "There is no deity that I am not, and in case any man be truly the worshipper of any deity whatever, it is I that am the cause of his devotion and its fruit. . . . However men approach Me, even so do I welcome them, for the path men take from every side is Mine." Similarly the *Bhaktamala* (cf. G. A. Grierson, ed., London, 1909): "No one is ignorant of the doctrines of his own religion. . . . Therefore let every man, so far as in him lieth, help the reading of the Scriptures, whether those of his own church, or those of another." And similarly also in Islam, "My heart has become capable of every form . . . it is a convent for Christian monks, a temple for idols, the place of pilgrimage at Mecca, the tables of the Torah, the book of the Koran: I follow the religion of Love, whichever way His camels take."

Such an understanding is rarer still, and one may say abnormal to the Western type of humanity. If the modern Christian does not quite endorse the conduct of Charlemagne's heroes at Saragossa—"The synagogues they enter and the mosques, whose every wall with mallet and axes they shatter: they break in pieces small the idols. . . . The heathen folk in crowds to the font baptismal are driven, to take Christ's yoke upon them. . . . Thus out of heathen darkness have five-score thousand been redeemed, and be now true Christians," it is at least quite certain that for every man that has died by religious persecution in India, ten thousand have died in Europe, and equally certain that the activity of Christian missions still quite frankly endorses a program of conversion by force—the force of money, not indeed paid out in cash, but expended on education and medical aid bestowed with ulterior motives. "Force," as Lafcadio Hearn once wrote, "the principal instrument of Christian propagandism in the past, is still the force behind our missions." No greater offenders are to be found than missionaries against the commandment, "Thou shalt not bear false witness against thy neighbor." I do not, however, at all wish to dwell upon this point of view, but rather to point out that although religious tolerance in Europe has never, as in Asia, been founded upon the belief that all religions are true, but rather founded on a growing indifference to all religious doctrines, an intellectual basis for a willing tolerance of other forms of belief is by no means wanting in Christianity. John, indeed, speaks of the "True Light that lighteth every man." Even St. Thomas admits that some of the Gentiles who lived before Christ's temporal birth may have been saved. For as Clement of Alexandria had long since said, "There was always a natural manifestation of the one Almighty God, amongst all right-thinking men." Eckhart speaks of "One of our most ancient philosophers who found the truth long, long before God's birth, ere ever there was Christian faith at all as it is now," and again much more boldly, "He to whom God is different in one thing from another and to whom God is dearer in one thing than another, that man is a barbarian, still in the wilds, a child."

Note that "Merlyn made the round table in tokenying of the roundenes of the world for by the round table is the world sygnefyed by ryghte. For all the world crysten and hethen repayren unto the round table . . . (that) by them which should be felawes of the round table the truth of the Sancgreal should be well knowen" (Malory, *Morte D'arthur*, XIV.2). The truth is with Blake when he says, "The religions of all nations are derived from each nation's different reception of the poetic genius[1] which is everywhere called the spirit of prophecy. . . . As all men are alike (though infinitely various), so all religions, and as all similars have one source." The Vedic and Christian traditions are never tired of employing "Truth," "Being," and "Beauty," as preeminently fitting, essential names of God. Now we are well aware that in this human world there cannot be a conceptual knowledge or expression of truth except in some way; just as there can be no perceptible beauty except of some kind. What is true in all truths, or what is beautiful in all beauties, cannot itself be any one of these truths or beauties. As Dionysius says, "If anyone in seeing God understood what he saw, he saw not God himself, but one of those things that are His." Belief in Revelation or Audition does not mean that the very words in which the truth is expressed in any case contain the truth, but rather that they point to it, for as St. Thomas says, "Everything has truth of nature according to the *degree* in which it imitates the knowledge of God"; "our intellect considers God *according to* the mode derived from creatures"; and finally, "the thing known is in the knower *according* to the mode of the knower." All concepts of God, even the most nearly adequate, are thus man-made; as we say in India, "He takes the forms that are imagined by His worshippers." Very surely He is not to be thought of as confined by or fully expressed by any of these forms, Who is Himself the single form of every form, and transcendent with respect to each and every form; it is from this point of view that many

[1] Vedic *kavitva*.

a Christian teacher has affirmed that "Nothing true can be said of God." The value of concepts, of any expression verbal or visible, *per verbum in intellectu conceptum*, is one of use; the concept is of value not as a thing in itself, but as dispositive to an essential vision, *not* in any likeness. The beauty of the formula, the verbal or visual icon, poignant as it may be in Christian gospel or Vedic liturgy, is not an end in itself but, referred to him who uses it, is an invitation. The purpose of any art, and no less of that highest art of theology, in which all other arts, whether literary or plastic, subsist *per excellentiam*, is to teach, to delight, and above all to move (Augustine's *docere, delectare, movere*). An exclusive attachment to any one dogma, any one group of verbal or visual symbols, however pertinent, is an act of idolatry; the Truth itself is inexpressible.

If the image is His whose image it is, the colors and the art are ours. Whoever claims that his own manner of understanding and statement is the only true one is moved not by the vision of God, but by spiritual pride. Such a believer, as Ibn Arabi says, "praises none but himself, for his God is made by himself, and to praise the work is to praise the maker of it: its excellence or imperfection belongs to the maker. For this reason he blames the beliefs of others, which he would not do if he were just. . . . If he understood the saying of Junayd, 'The color of the water is the color of the vessel containing it,' he would not interfere with others, but would perceive God in every form and every belief. He has opinion, not knowledge: therefore God said, 'I am in my servant's opinion of Me,' that is, 'I do not manifest myself to him save in the form of his belief.' God is absolute or unrestricted as He pleases; and the God of religious belief is subject to limitations, for He is the God who is contained in the heart of His servant." The Oriental Gnostic has no fault to find with any Catholic doctrine; judged by Vedic standards, one can say that Christianity is true and lovely, true so far as any formulation can be true, lovely in so far as any thing, as distinguished from One who is no thing, can be lovely.

Moreover, it can be positively affirmed that every notable Christian doctrine is also explicitly propounded in every other dialect of the primordial tradition: I refer to such doctrines as those of the eternal and temporal births, that of the single essence and two natures, that of the Father's impassibility, that of the significance of sacrifice, that of transubstantiation, that of the nature of the distinction between the contemplative and active lives and of both from the life of pleasure, that of eternity from aeviternity and time, and so forth. Literally hundreds of texts could be cited from Christian and Islamic, Vedic, Taoist, and other scriptures and their patristic expositions, in close and sometimes literally verbal agreement. To cite a trio of instances at random, whereas Damascene has to say that "He Who Is, is the principal of all names applied to God," in the *Katha Upanisad* we have "He is, by that alone is He to be apprehended"; whereas St. Thomas says, "These things are said to be under the sun which are generated and corrupted," the *Satapatha Brahmana* affirms that "Everything under the sun is in the power of death"; and whereas Dionysius speaks of That "which not to see or know is really to see and know," the *Jaiminiya Upanisad Brahmana* has it that "The thought of God is his by whom it is unthought, or if he thinks the thought he does not understand." All traditional teaching employs side by side the *via affirmativa* and the *via remotionis*, and in this sense is in agreement with Boethius that "Faith is a mean between contrary heresies." Sin is defined by the Thomist and in India in one and the same way as a "departure from the order to the end." All tradition is agreed that the last end of man is happiness.

On the other hand, while there can be only one metaphysics, there must be not merely a variety of religions, but a hierarchy of religions, in which the truth is more or less adequately expressed, according to the intellectual capacities of those whose religions they are. Nor do I mean to deny that there can be heterodox doctrines, properly to be condemned as heresies, but only that any and every belief is a heresy if it be regarded as the truth, and not merely as a signpost of the truth. Pantheism, for example, is equally a heresy from Christian, Islamic, and Hindu points of view; a confusion of things as they are in themselves with things as they are in God, of the essence of the participant with the participated Essence, is an egregious error, and yet not so great an error as to assume that the being of things as they are in themselves is altogether their own being. The distinction of essence from nature of the *Samkhya* system is true from a certain point of view, and yet false when regarded from the standpoint of a higher synthesis, as in the *Vedanta*, and similarly in Christianity, where from one point of view essence and nature are the universe apart, and yet in the simplicity of the First Cause are one impartite substance.

It is perfectly legitimate to feel that a given religion is more adequately true than another; to hold, for example, that Catholicism is more adequately true than Protestantism, or Hinduism than Buddhism. Real distinctions can be drawn: Christianity maintains, for example, that metaphysics, though the highest of the other sciences, is inferior to the sacred science of theology; Hinduism is primarily metaphysical, and only secondarily religious, hence the controversies as to the true significance of "deification," and hence it is that however much a Hindu may find himself in enthusiastic agreement with the angelic and celestial doctors (Thomas and Bonaventura), he is more at home with certain giants of Christian thought whose orthodoxy is suspect, I mean Eriugena, Eckhart, Boehme, Blake, and more at home with Plotinus than with the representatives of exoteric Christian orthodoxy; more at home with St. John than with St. James, more in sympathy with Christian Platonism than with Christian Aristotelianism, scarcely at all in sympathy with Protestant theologies, and far more in sympathy with Qabbalistic interpretations of Genesis and Exodus than with any historical approach. So that we do not for a moment mean to maintain the impropriety of all dogmatic controversy. We must bear in mind that even within the framework of a presumably homogeneous faith it is taken for granted that one and the same truths must be presented in various ways suited to the audience, and that this is not a matter of contradictory statement, but of "convenient means." What we do maintain is that all paths converge; that the Wayfarer, having already trodden a given path, will under all normal circumstances sooner reach that point at which all progress ends—"On reaching God, all progress ends"—than if he retrace his steps and start afresh.

What we must not forget is that no one can finally pronounce upon the truth of a given religion who has not lived it, as Ramakrishna lived both Christianity and Islam, as well as Hinduism; and that once convinced that only one's own truth is true, "It is," as Professor C. A. Briggs of Drew University lately remarked, "the easiest thing imaginable to take the concepts of other faiths, abstract them from their contexts, and demolish them." For example, how easily the Islamic definition of Christianity as a polytheistic religion could be deduced from the considered statement of St. Thomas, that "We do not say *the only* God, because deity is common to several" (*Sum. Theol.* 1.31.2c). In the same way, a pantheistic definition of Christianity could easily be deduced from St. Thomas' "A thing has being by participation. . . . We must consider . . . the emanation of all being from the universal cause, which is God" (*Sum. Theol.* 1.44.1 *ad* 1 and 45 1c).

What is then, in the last analysis, the value of comparative religion? Certainly not to convince us that one mode of belief is the preparation for another, or to lead to a decision as to which is "best." One might as well regard ancient or exotic styles of art as preparations for and aspirations towards one's own. Nor can the value of this discipline be thought of as one conducing to the development of a single universally acceptable syncretic faith embodying all that is "best" in every faith; such a "faith" as this would be a mechanical and lifeless monstrosity, by no means a stream of living water, but a sort of religious Esperanto. Comparative religion can demonstrate that all religions spring from a common source; are, as Jeremias says, the "dialects of a single spiritual speech." We cannot, therefore, take the formulae of one religion and insert them in another without incongruity. One can recognize that many formulae are identical in different religions; confront, for example, St. Thomas, "Creation, which is the emanation of all being from the not-being, which is no thing" (*Sum. Theol.* 1.45.1c) with the Vedic "Being is engendered from nonbeing" (*asatah sad ajayata, Rg Veda* X.72.3), and such comparisons can be validly employed (even by the most orthodox) as what St. Thomas calls "extrinsic and probable proofs" of the validity of a given dogma.

But of greater value than this is the clarification that results when the formulae of one tradition are collated with those of another. For, as we have already seen, every tradition is necessarily a partial representation of the truth intended by tradition universally considered; in each tradition something is suppressed, or reserved, or obscure which in another may be found more extensively, more logically, or more brilliantly developed. What then is clear and full in one tradition can be used to develop the meaning of what may be hardly more than alluded to in another. Or even if in one tradition a given doctrine has been definitely named, a realization of the significance of this definition may lead to the recognition and correlation of a whole series of affirmations in another tradition, in all of which the same doctrine is implicit, but which had previously been overlooked in their relation to one another. It is thus a great advantage to be able to make use of the expression *Vedic exemplarism*; or conversely, to speak of Christian *yoga* immediately brings out the analogy between St. Bernard's *consideratio*, *contemplatio*, and *raptus* with Sanskrit *dharana*, *dhyana*, and *samadhi*.

To many Christians, no doubt, Sri Ramakrishna's primary attachment to the cult of the Great Mother gives offense. Nothing is, indeed, more usual than to consider that Christianity, whether for better or worse, adheres to purely masculine interpretations of divine being; the Christian speaks of a Father, but not of a Mother in Heaven, whereas in India the ancient love of the Magna Mater maintains itself at the present day on equal terms with that of the Propator. And yet the doctrine of the maternity of the divine nature is repeatedly, however reservedly, affirmed in Christian theology, fundamentally in that of the "two natures," more explicitly in that of the temporal *and* eternal nativities, and in that of the Generation of the Son as a vital operation from conjoint principles—"Processio Verbi in divinis dicitur generatio . . . quae est operatio vitae . . et propter hoc proprie dicitur genitum et Filius" (*Sum. Theol.* 1.27.2; cf. 1.98.2c, "In every act of generation there is an active and a passive principle."). It is inasmuch as "eternal filiation does not depend on a temporal mother" (*Sum. Theol.* III.35.5 *ad* 2) that Eckhart can speak of the "act of fecundation latent in eternity," and say that "it is God who has the treasure and the bride in Him," that the "Godhead wantons with the Word," and that "His birth in *Mary ghostly* was to God better pleasing than His nativity of her in the flesh." One sees that when St. Thomas speaks of "that Nature by which the Father begets" (*Sum. Theol.* 1.41.5), the reference is really to the Magna Mater, the Vedic Aditi, not to mention other names of the One Madonna, and sees what is really meant by the otherwise obscure assertion that notwithstanding primary matter "recedes from likeness to God, yet . . . it *retains* a certain likeness to the divine being" (*Sum. Theol.* 1.14.11 *ad* 3). Natura Naturata indeed "retains" a certain likeness to "Natura Naturans, Creatrix, Deus": Mother Earth to Mother Nature, Mary in the flesh to Mary ghostly. One need only consider Genesis 1:27, "To the image of God He created him; male and female He created them," in connection with Galatians 3:28, "according to the image of Him that created him, where there is neither male nor female," to realize that whereas Essence and Nature *in divinis* are one simple substance without composition, the very fact that the conjoint principles can be separately exemplified is proof that the Supreme Identity can be truly spoken of either as Father or as Mother, or as Father-Mother, just as in the Vedas the Divine "Parents" are indifferently "Fathers" (*pitara*) or "Mothers" (*matara*), or as "That One, spirated, despirated" (*tad ekam anit avatam, Rg Veda* X.129.2, where no gender is implied; cf. Eckhart's "Where these two abysms hang, equally spirated, despirated, there is the Supreme Being").

Thus we may go so far as to assert on behalf of a true "comparative religion," that however a religion may be self-sufficient if it be followed to the very end to which it is directed, there can hardly be supposed a way so plain that it could not here and there be better illuminated by other lights than that of the pilgrim's private lantern, the light of any lantern being only a refraction of the Light of lights. A diversity of routes is not merely appropriate to a diversity of travelers, who are neither all alike, nor start from one and the same point, but may be of incalculable aid to any traveler who can rightly read the map; for where all roads converge, there can be none of them that does not help to clarify the true position of the center of the maze, "short of which we are still in a duality." Hence we say that the very implications of the phrase "religious tolerance" are to be avoided: diversity of faith is not a matter for unwilling "toleration," but of divine appointment. And this will hold good even if we sincerely believe that other faiths are inferior to our own, and in this sense relatively "evil": for as Augustine says, "The admirable beauty of the universe is made up of all things. In which even what is called evil, well-ordered and in its place, is the eminent commendation of what is good" (*Enchiridion* XIII), whom St. Thomas quotes with approval, adding that "The universe, the present creation being supposed, cannot be better, because of the most beautiful order given to things by God" (*Sum. Theol.* 1.48.1 and 1.25.6 *ad* 3). As Augustine also says, "There is no evil in things, but only in the sinner's misuse of them" (*De doctrina christiana* III.12). As to the sinner's "misuse," who can assure us of that, with respect to which it has been said, "Judge not, that ye be not judged"?

In the matter of direction towards the Kingdom of Heaven "within you,"[2] the modern world is far more lacking in the will to seek, than likely to be led astray by false direction. From the Satanic point of view there could hardly be imagined a better activity than to be engaged in the "conversion of the heathen" from one to another body of dogmas: that, surely, was not what was meant by the injunction, "Go thou and preach the Kingdom of God"—or was He mistaken, when He said, "The Kingdom of Heaven is within you"?

[2] Sanskrit *hrdayakase, antarbhutasya khe.*

WHO SPEAKS FOR THE EAST?*

Rama Coomaraswamy

Anyone attempting to discuss "cross-cultural" relations between East and West must be prepared to answer the fundamental questions as to just what is meant by "culture" and just what is envisioned by such terms as "East" and "West." I as a product of both the East and the West would like to share a few thoughts on this topic.

Now, the term "culture" is extremely difficult to define. It can in no sense be synonymous with "education" as it is usually understood for we have all met people with the highest academic qualifications that we would agree are lacking in it. Conversely, an artist or a musician who has had no formal education can clearly be "cultured." Nor can the term be correlated with material success any more than it can be with the extremes of poverty. Few in recent times have attempted to come to terms with the meaning of this concept, and I should like to take as one authority an individual whom I think we would all accept as being "cultured": T. S. Eliot.

The first important assertion that Eliot makes in his book *Notes Towards the Definition of Culture* is that "no culture has appeared or developed except together with a religion." Indeed, he goes on to ask "whether what we call culture, and what we call the religion of a people are not different aspects of the same thing: the culture being (so to speak), the incarnation of the religion of a people." However much some of us in the West may like to pride ourselves on being "a-religious" or even "irreligious," I think we would all agree that until very recent times what was understood by Eastern culture would fall within the definitions that Eliot gives. Thus in common parlance we tend to speak of Islamic, Buddhist, Hindu, or American Indian culture regardless of any local accidental variants that are of ethnic or national origin. As if to prove the point, let us note that prior to the present century, it is virtually impossible to point to a work of art from the East that is without religious significance.

* Editor's Note: from a talk given at the East-West Center associated with the University of Hawaii, published in *Studies in Comparative Religion*, 11:2, 1977.

T. S. Eliot makes still further comment. For one, he states that culture is never the possession of a small elite, but rather the expression of a whole people, and for another that culture "is not merely the sum of several activities, but a *way of life*," which latter phrase he italicizes. Here again, we find in the traditional East a valid manifestation of his criteria. Anyone who has had the privilege of living in the more remote—and "less spoiled" parts of India cannot but be struck by the fact that the *way of life* of the people—at all levels of society—is intrinsically an expression of both the culture and the religion.

Now, I have said nothing about contemporary Western culture, for apart from the fact that almost no one would call it "Christian," it is much more difficult to define. None of us would dispute the material advantages and scientific advances that prevail in the West, but few would argue that these characterize its culture. Certainly, no one would point to the great industrial complexes, the skyscrapers, and the large banking enterprises as examples of Western culture any more than one can say that the waterfront hotels on Hawaii are representative of Hawaiian culture. In so far as the West is "a-religious" and has departed from its Judeo-Christian roots—a situation that is incidentally of very recent origin—other criteria than those that Eliot postulates must be used. There are those who see culture as synonymous with the beguiling pastime of going to the theatre, to concerts, and to museums. What often passes for "cultured" in the West is an intimate knowledge and appreciation of what is called "the fine arts." Yet in all this, there is nothing that can be called "religious"—nor is it the "possession" of more than a small and rather well-to-do group of individuals. Certainly, it is not in any sense a *way of life.*

Yet, despite this, what passes for modern culture can be said to "incarnate" what the greater majority of contemporary men have placed their "faith" in. There are in the West certain fundamental concepts that have been so taken for granted as to be almost axiomatic. Thus modern man and his "culture" reflect his belief in the concept of "progress," in the "evolving" of man through some sort of "dynamic process" into a continuously better state of existence; a belief that he has achieved the highest form of "civilization" yet discovered, and if there are still a few flaws to be found, we have but to wait a while, for modern science will bring about that perfect millennium that is just around the corner. He believes in no absolute truths, and as the poet Auden says somewhere, the very democratic system of modern government is based on the premise that all truth is relative—that one man's opinion is as good as another's. Above all, it is a belief that it is in this world that man finds his meaning and his purpose; that morality is necessitated by what is called "social contract"; that virtue is "enlightened self-interest" and that the most altruistic expression of all this is the euphemism of "serving mankind." I grant that this viewpoint is not espoused by all, but the greater majority of contemporary men hold to such attitudes with a "fideism" that borders on the "superstitious."

Now, if we turn our attention to the traditional world, such a humanistic and liberal doctrinal exposition would be anathema. However much we might disagree with the premises of Eastern culture, we would have to admit that it never envisioned this world as anything more than a preparation for the next. There is in Lahore a bridge dating back to Mogul times over which can be read the following inscription:

> Shaykh Isa (Jesus) said, "This world is a bridge, pass over quickly and build no house upon it."

Traditional Eastern culture is not anthropocentric, but theocentric, and holds that man is a metaphysical or spiritual being—or if not, then just an animal. It seeks not the psychological goal of "ego-satisfaction" but rather teaches that man's ego is nothing but an ephemeral chimera; he equates egoity with pride (a deadly sin!) and holds with Saint Paul that man must "hate" this aspect of soul if he is to know God. If contemporary man proclaims that all truth is relative, traditional man in both East and West believes in an absolute Truth revealed to him by God or a Divine Messenger, and preserved for him in both his Scriptures and his Traditions. This being so, he sees morality as pre-dispositive to the spiritual life, virtue as the "normal" expression of man's true nature, and the unfolding of time, not as a progressive evolving towards some earthly millennium or "point Omega," but rather as a continuous departure from the "center" as a result of which mankind becomes more and more degraded as he increasingly loses sight of the spiritual lights that are his "birthright." He seeks to serve, not man *qua* man, but God, and serves his neighbor because he takes literally the words of Lord Buddha:

> He who nurses the sick, nurses me.

We are living, as he sees it, in the end of the *Kali Yuga* or *dark age*, a time when the Truth is obscured and when "scoffers" prevail, "walking after their own lusts." Faith for him is an aristocratic virtue, and as an old gloss of Plato states, "unbelief is for the mob." Above all, he believes in sanctity, and hence it follows that sainthood is his highest aspiration. I could best summarize this attitude by quoting a contemporary American Indian medicine man:

> We wish to walk in the footsteps of our fathers, to be blessed by the same rites he performed, and to live in a sacred manner.

I have been careful throughout to characterize contemporary Western values as "modern" and Eastern values as "traditional." In doing so, I have painted a picture of two irreconcilable worlds. One must not forget that there was once a time when the Western world also adhered to the same traditional system of values. The contrast between traditional Christian beliefs and those of modern man are just as stark and are well summarized in the words of the American Indian chief Ohiyesa who said:

> It is my personal belief, after thirty-five years' experience of it, that there is no such thing as "Christian civilization." I believe that Christianity and modern civilization are opposed and irreconcilable, and that the spirit of Christianity and of our ancient religion is essentially the same.

Unfortunately, modern Western values have become increasingly prevalent in the East. As evidence of this I would point out that it is most unusual to find an English speaking Oriental who seriously holds to any of the above-noted traditional convictions. Admittedly he might defend the artistic achievements of his culture, or at least some of them. Yet typically he would have nothing but contempt for his relatives who still persisted in following the rules of caste, who still made daily visits to the temple, who still painted their bodies with ritual marks, and who persisted in reciting their "beads" or sacred texts with belief. He would almost certainly describe them as "backward" and "uneducated"—not blessed with the advantages of "progress"—and accuse them of "not being in step with the times."

Inevitably, in an article of this sort, one is forced to oversimplify. Clearly there is a spectrum between those who embrace the Traditional or "orthodox" viewpoint, and those who proclaim themselves, rather like the rabbit in Aesop's fable who lost his tail, to be "modern." But is it any different in the West? Should an Oriental be traveling in Europe and ask for an exposition of Western culture, the answer given by a mediaeval monk would be vastly different than that given by a contemporary Unitarian. And which, may I ask would speak for the West? It follows then, and here I quote my father Ananda K. Coomaraswamy, directly, that:

> The problem of the "spiritual East" versus the "material West" is very easily mistaken. I have repeatedly emphasized that it is only accidentally a geographical or racial problem. The real clash is of traditional with anti-traditional concepts or ideological with material or sensate points of view. . . . I think it undeniable that the *modern* world (which happens to still be a Western world, however fast the East is being Westernized) is one of "impoverished reality," one *entleert* (empty) of meaning, or values. Our contemporary trust in *Progress* is a veritable *fideism* as naive as is to be found.

You have, in your kindness, invited me to write, not only because I am a product of both East and West, but above all because you are honoring my father. Thus it is that in addressing you I have tried to give you the framework within which my father's writing may have real meaning. If I entitled my article "Who Speaks for the East?", it is because I feel it is important for you to understand that his function had nothing to do with speaking for any economic, political, or geographical entity. He spoke only for Traditional man, and it mattered not to him whether this man was Hindu, Muslim, American Indian, or Christian.[1] As such, he was admittedly "dogmatic" for he regarded Truth "as a matter of certainty, not of opinion." He was also "orthodox" in the sense that the Catholic Encyclopedia defines the word, for he held to "right belief or purity of faith." He clearly stated:

> I am not a reformer or a propagandist. I don't think for myself. . . . I am not putting forward any new or private doctrines or interpretations. . . . I spend my time trying to understand some things that I regard as immutable truths; in the first place, for my own sake, and secondly for that of those who can make use of my results. For me, there are certain axioms, principles, or values beyond question; my interest is not in thinking up new ones, but in the application of those that are.

[1] He was personally a Hindu and was invested with the *yajnopavite* (sacred thread) as a young man. At the time of his death he had resigned from the Museum of Fine Arts in Boston and was returning to India to embrace the religious life. His ashes were returned to the Ganges at Banares.

If, in conclusion, I can convey to you anything that my father would have said, it is that we must all return to the basic principles that underlie the Traditional view of life. The Traditional life, he taught, is one that incorporated the various concepts I have listed above at all levels of society, and hence it follows that it is truly the cultured life, one that must be lived, not studied. It is one that sees all activity as sacred because it is ordered to man's proper last end. It is one that is admittedly not perfect, for even in the Garden of Eden is to be found the serpent and it recognizes that each generation and each individual must in the last analysis make his own choices for good and evil. It is however the only form of society in which the "full potential of man is recognized and not just his potential freedom to rise to the top of the economic ladder."[2]

He therefore advocated that form of society which demanded that every individual be a special kind of artist and saw as false the concept that only special people such as painters, musicians, and writers should be "creative" while the remainder were to be laborers and to live as *shudras* or untouchables. Unlike the factory worker or bank clerk who works for money (or perhaps, just to survive), the artist's pleasure is in doing *well* the work to which he is called. If he earns a living, it is in order that he might go on working. (This is not dissimilar to the man who eats in order to live, rather than that of the glutton—the man who lives in order that he may eat). As Plato taught, the man who is not an artist has no true place in the social order.

Thus it follows that it is a society that holds that "man does not live by bread alone . . . but by the very Word . . . of God," for if the artist is one who makes things properly, he is also one who lives both a contemplative and an active life. Such a life does not demand of us that we return to mediaeval patterns of living, even though they were incomparably superior to those we now live with—rather it is a

[2] Those who believe that a return to traditional values would result in economic deprivation are simply unaware of historical fact, or else, have accepted the distortions of contemporary historians. Prior to her contact with the modern world, India was hardly a destitute nation. Indeed, it was her wealth that attracted the Western adventurers. Similarly, the American Indian was hardly deprived of the necessities of life in his natural condition. Anyone who argues for the modernization of India must realize that he is asking the village potter, an independent craftsman and artist, to become a "wage-slave" in a factory. Even the "moderns" would have to admit this to be a "crime against humanity."

return to the principles that underlay mediaeval Christendom as much as Hinduism. If the principles are correct "other things will be added unto us." Nor did my father advocate a position that can in any sense be considered "syncretist," for while my father admitted that many paths lead to the same summit, he also held that man can travel but one path at a time. Certainly, one can appreciate other cultures and traditions, but one cannot live them all simultaneously. One must live within that tradition to which one is called by circumstance. The only tragedy is that of modern or contemporary man who lives by no Tradition whatsoever, and therefore has no way to travel "home." It is he who is condemned to live on the "husks" that are fit only for swine.

Above all, as he was often fond of saying, it is really a question of putting first things first, a matter of "seeking first the Kingdom of God and His Righteousness." Such a principle was not for him a sociological anachronism; rather, it was the endeavor of his life, the purport of his writing, and, I think we may assume, his ultimate achievement.

SOME REFLECTIONS ON TIME*

Aldous Huxley

Time destroys all that it creates, and the end of every temporal sequence is, for the entity involved in it, some form of death. Death is wholly transcended only when time is transcended; immortality is for the consciousness that has broken through the temporal into the timeless. For all other consciousnesses there is at best a survival or a rebirth; and these entail further temporal sequences and the periodical recurrence of yet other deaths and dissolutions. In all the traditional philosophies and religions of the world, time is regarded as the enemy and the deceiver, the prison and the torture chamber. It is only as an instrument, as the means to something else, that it possesses a positive value; for time provides the embodied soul with opportunities for transcending time; every instant of every temporal sequence is potentially the door through which we can, if we so desire, break through into the eternal. All temporal goods are means to an end beyond themselves; they are not to be treated as ends in their own right. Material goods are to be prized because they support the body which, in our present existence, is necessary to the achievement of man's final end. Moral goods have many and very obvious utilitarian values; but their highest and ultimate value consists in the fact that they are means to that selflessness, which is the precondition of the realization of the eternal. The goods of the intellect are truths and, in the last analysis, these are valuable in so far as they remove God-eclipsing delusions and prejudices. Aesthetic goods are precious because they are symbolic of, and analogous to, the unitive knowledge of timeless reality. To regard any of these temporal goods as self-sufficient and final ends is to commit idolatry. And idolatry, which is fundamentally unrealistic and inappropriate to the facts of the universe, results at the best in self-stultification and at the worst in disaster.

Movement in time is irreversibly in one direction. "We live forwards," as Kierkegaard said, "but we can only understand backwards." Moreover, the flux of duration is indefinite and inconclusive, a

* Editor's Note: from *Vedanta for Modern Man*, ed. Christopher Isherwood.

perpetual lapse possessing in itself no pattern, no possibility of balance or symmetry. Nature, it is true, imposes upon this perpetual perishing a certain appearance of pattern and symmetry. Thus, days alternate with nights, the seasons recur with regularity, plants and animals have their life cycles and are succeeded by offspring like themselves. But all these patternings and symmetries and recurrences are characteristic, not of time as it is in itself, but of space and matter as they are associated with time in our consciousness. Days and nights and seasons exist because certain heavenly bodies move in a certain way. If it took the earth not a year but a century to move round the sun, our sense of the intrinsic formlessness of time, of its irrevocable one-way lapse towards the death of all the entities involved in it, would be much more acute than it is at present; for most of us, in those hypothetical circumstances, would never live to see all the four seasons of the long year and would have no experience of that recurrence and renewal, those cosmic variations on known themes, which, under the present astronomical dispensation, disguise the essential nature of time by endowing it, or seeming to endow it, with some of the qualities of space. Now, space is a symbol of eternity; for in space there is freedom, there is reversibility of movement, and there is nothing in the nature of a space, as there is in that of time, which condemns those involved in it to inevitable death and dissolution. Moreover, when space contains material bodies, the possibility of orderliness, balance, symmetry, and pattern arises—the possibility, in a word, of that Beauty which, along with Goodness and Truth, takes its place in the trinity of manifested Godhead. In this context a highly significant point should be noted. In all the arts whose raw material is of a temporal nature, the primary aim of the artist is to spatialize time. The poet, the dramatist, the novelist, the musician□each takes a fragment of the perpetual perishing, in which we are doomed to undertake our one-way journey toward death, and tries to endow it with some of the qualities of space: namely, symmetry, balance, and orderliness (the beauty-producing characteristics of a space containing material bodies), together with multidimensionality and the quality of permitting free movement in all directions. This spatialization of time is achieved in poetry and music by the employment of recurrent rhythms and cadences, by the confinement of the material within conventional forms, such as that of the sonnet or the sonata, and by the imposition upon the chosen fragment of temporal indefiniteness of a beginning, a middle, and an end. What is called "construction" in the drama and the narrative serves the same spatializing purpose. The aim in all cases is to give a form to the essentially formless, to impose symmetry and order upon what is actually an indefinite flux toward death. The fact that all the arts that deal with temporal sequences have always attempted to spatialize time indicates very clearly the nature of man's natural and spontaneous reaction to time, and throws a light on the significance of space as a symbol of that timeless state, towards which, through all the impediments of ignorance, the human spirit consciously or unconsciously aspires.

There has been an attempt on the part of certain Western philosophers of the last few generations to raise time from the position to which the traditional religions and the normal sentiments of humanity had assigned it. Thus, under the influence of evolutionary theories, time is regarded as the creator of the highest values, so that even God is emergent—the product of the one-way flux of perpetual perishing, not (as in the traditional religions) as the timeless witness of time, transcendent to it and, because of that transcendence, capable of immanence within it. Closely allied to the theory of emergence is the Bergsonian view that "duration" is the primary and ultimate reality and that the "life-force" exists exclusively in the flux. On another line we have the Hegelian and Marxian philosophies of history, which is spelled with a capital H and hypostatized as a temporal providence working for the realization of the kingdom of heaven on earth—this kingdom of heaven on earth being, in Hegel's view, a glorified version of the Prussian state and in the view of Marx, who was exiled by the authorities of that state, of the dictatorship of the proletariat, leading "inevitably" by the process of the dialectic to the classless society. These views of history make the assumption that the divine, or history, or the cosmic process, or *Geist*, or whatever the entity which uses time for its purposes may be called, is concerned with humanity in the mass, not with man and woman as individuals—and not with humanity at any given moment, but with humanity as a succession of generations.

Now, there seems to be absolutely no reason for supposing that this is the case—absolutely no reason for supposing that there is a collective soul of succeeding generations capable of experiencing, comprehending, and acting upon the impulsions transmitted by *Geist*, history, life-force, and all the rest. On the contrary, all the evidence points to the fact that it is the individual soul, incarnated at a particular moment of time, which alone can establish contact with the divine, to say nothing of other souls. The belief (which is based on obvious and self-evident facts) that humanity is represented at any given moment by the persons who constitute the mass, and that all the values of humanity reside in those persons, is regarded as absurdly shallow by these philosophers of history. But the tree is known by its fruits. Those who believe in the primacy of persons and who think that the final end of all persons is to transcend time and realize that which is eternal and timeless, are always, like the Hindus, the Buddhists, the Taoists, the primitive Christians, advocates of nonviolence, gentleness, peace, and tolerance. Those, on the contrary, who like to be "deep" in the manner of Hegel and Marx, who think that "history" deals with humanity-in-the-mass and humanity-as-successive-generations, not with individual men and women here and now, are indifferent to human life and personal values, worship the Molochs which they call the state and society, and are cheerfully prepared to sacrifice successive generations of real, concrete persons for the sake of the entirely hypothetical happiness which, on no grounds whatsoever, they think will be the lot of humanity in the distant future. The politics of those who regard eternity as the ultimate reality are concerned with the present and with the ways and means of organizing the present world in such a way that it will impose the fewest possible obstacles in the way of individual liberation from time and ignorance; those, on the contrary, who regard time as the ultimate reality are concerned primarily with the future and regard the present world and its inhabitants as mere rubble, cannon fodder, and potential slave labor to be exploited, terrorized, liquidated, or blown to smithereens, in order that persons who may never be born, in a future time about which nothing can be known with the smallest degree of certainty, may have the kind of a wonderful time which present-day revolutionaries and war-makers think they ought to have. If the lunacy were not criminal, one would be tempted to laugh.

GANDHI AND THE ONE-EYED GIANT*

Thomas Merton

The white man, says Laurens Van der Post[1] came into Africa (and Asia and America for that matter) like a one-eyed giant, bringing with him the characteristic split and blindness which were at once his strength, his torment, and his ruin. With his self-isolated and self-scrutinizing individual mind, Western man was master of concepts and abstractions. He was the king of quantity and the driver of those forces over which quantitative knowledge gave him supremacy without understanding. Because he ruled matter without understanding it, he faced his bodily self as an object which he could not comprehend though he could analyze and tamper with its every part. He submitted to passions which, though he no longer regarded them as devils, were nevertheless inscrutable and objective forces flying at him from the dark outside the little circle illumined by a pragmatic and self-complacent moral reason. The one-eyed giant had science without wisdom, and he broke in upon ancient civilizations which (like the medieval West) had wisdom without science: wisdom which transcends and unites, wisdom which dwells in body and soul together and which, more by means of myth, of rite, of contemplation, than by scientific experiment, open the door to a life in which the individual is not lost in the cosmos and in society but found in them. Wisdom which made all life sacred and meaningful—even that which later ages came to call secular and profane.

It is true that neither the ancient wisdoms nor the modern sciences are complete in themselves. They do not stand alone. They call for

* Editor's Note: from *Gandhi on Non-Violence.*

[1] See the important book, *The Dark Eye in Africa*, with its thesis that the white man's spiritual rejection and contempt for the African is the result of his rejection of what is deepest and most vital in himself. Having "lost his own soul," the materialistic and cunning exploiter of the colonies destroyed the soul of the native. The "one-eyed giant" has "outer vision" only, no "inner vision." Therefore, though he tries to take precautions to avoid spiritual disaster for himself and the races he has subjugated, these precautions are "without perspective" and in "the wrong dimension of reality."

one another. Wisdom without science is unable to penetrate the full sapiential meaning of the created and material cosmos. Science without wisdom leaves man enslaved to a world of unrelated objects in which there is no way of discovering (or creating) order and deep significance in man's own pointless existence. The vocation of modern man was to bring about their union in preparation for a new age. The marriage was wrecked on the rocks of the white man's dualism and of the inertia, the incomprehension, of ancient and primitive societies. We enter the post-modern (perhaps the post-historic!) era in total disunity and confusion. But while the white man has always, naturally, blamed the traditional ancient cultures and the primitive "savage" whom he never understood, it is certainly clear that if the union of science and wisdom has so far not been successful it is not because the East would not listen to the West: the East has been all too willing to listen. The West has not been able to listen to the East, to Africa, and to the now practically extinct voice of primitive America. As a result of this the ancient wisdoms have themselves fallen into disrepute and Asia no longer dares listen to herself!

The split of the European mind has become universal. All men (says L. L. Whyte) are caught in the "fundamental division between deliberate activity organized by static concepts, and the instinctive and spontaneous life."[2] This dissociation, which was fruitful in the Renaissance, has now reached a point of mad development, of "behavior patterns unrelated to organic needs" and a "relentless passion for quantity" . . . "uncontrolled industrialism and excess of analytical thought" . . . "without the catharsis of rhythmic relaxation or satisfying achievement."[3]

> This [Whyte continues] is the moment of uninhibited perversions which can now ally themselves with technical power . . . in a brief period of dominance. This short reign of Antichrist depends on the fusion of two principles which are both vicious because they represent only a part of European or Western human nature: instinctive vitality distorted into sadism, and differentiating human vitality distorted into quantitative expansion.[4]

[2] L. L. Whyte, *The Next Development in Man* (New York, 1948), p. 122.

[3] Ibid., pp. 148, 149, 151.

[4] Ibid., p. 169.

Whyte was writing this in the days of Hitler, Mussolini, and Stalin, at the beginning of the Second World War. The "short" reign of Antichrist would soon, he believed, give way to a reign of light, peace, harmony, and reconstruction. The end of the war would begin a better era. Or at least so he hoped, though not without reservations, for he added: "One more dark decade would disprove my judgment, revealing a rot deeper than I have seen."[5] We are now in the third dark decade since his words were written.

Ananda Coomaraswamy, writing about the same time as L. L. Whyte, viewed the sickness of civilization in more religious terms, and with much the same seriousness. The problem of the whole world was the problem of Western man: for everywhere the one spiritual illness was now rampant, and malignancies, which in the West were perhaps endemic, were proliferating in the most alarming fashion in the East and in Africa.

"East and West," Coomaraswamy wrote, "are at cross purposes only because the West is determined, i.e., at once resolved and economically 'determined,' to keep on going it knows not where, and it calls the rudderless voyage 'Progress.'"[6]

He wrote before the days of Red China and of postwar Japan, both of which now lead scores of other nations in carrying the logic of the Western split to its most extreme dissociation. Today it is not only the West that is "determined" on its rudderless voyage; all, down to the newest African nation, are in the same centrifugal flight, and the itinerary points to outer space.

The question remains the same. It is a crisis of *sanity* first of all. The problems of the nations are the problems of mentally deranged people, but magnified a thousand times because they have the full, straight-faced approbation of a schizoid society, schizoid national structures, schizoid military and business complexes, and, need one add, schizoid religious sects. "We are at war with ourselves," said Coomaraswamy, "and therefore at war with one another. Western man is unbalanced, and the question, Can he recover himself? is a very real one."[7]

The question is all the more urgent now that it concerns not only Western man but everybody.

[5] Ibid., p. 288.

[6] *Am I My Brother's Keeper?* (New York, 1947), p. 67.

[7] Ibid., p. 64.

There have of course been spurious attempts to bring East and West together. One need not review all the infatuated theosophies of the nineteenth century. Nor need one bother to criticize the laughable syncretisms which have occupied the talents of publicists (more often Eastern than Western) in which Jesus, Buddha, Confucius, Tolstoy, Marx, Nietzsche, and anyone else you like join in the cosmic dance which turns out to be not Shiva's but just anybody's. However, the comparison of Eastern and Western religious philosophy is, in our time, reaching a certain level of seriousness and this is one small and hopeful sign. The materials for a synthesis of science and wisdom are not lacking.

One of the most significant facts about the life and vocation of Gandhi was his discovery of the East through the West. Like so many others of India, Gandhi received a completely Western education as a young man. He had to a great extent renounced the beliefs, the traditions, the habits of thought, of India. He spoke, thought, and acted like an Englishman, except of course that an Englishman was precisely what he could never, by any miracle, become. He was an alienated Asian whose sole function in life was to be perfectly English without being English at all: to prove the superiority of the West by betraying his own heritage and his own self, thinking as a white man without ceasing to be "a Nigger." The beauty of this (at least to Western minds) was that it showed Western culture to be a pearl of such great price that one could reasonably sell the whole of Asia in order to acquire it, even though the acquisition was not that of a new being, or even of a new identity, but only of a new suit.

Gandhi was unusual in this. Instead of being fooled by the Western costume, and instead of being persuaded that he no longer really existed as an Asian, he recognized that the West had something good about it that was good not because it was Western but because it was also Eastern: that is to say, it was *universal.* So he turned his face and his heart once again to India, and saw what was really there. It was through his acquaintance with writers like Tolstoy and Thoreau, and then his reading of the New Testament, that Gandhi rediscovered his own tradition and his Hindu *dharma* (religion, duty). More than a tradition, more than a wisdom handed down in books or celebrated in temples, Gandhi discovered India in discovering himself. Hence it is very important indeed to understand Gandhi's political life, and particularly his non-violence, in the light of this radical discovery from which everything else received its meaning. Gandhi's dedicated struggle for Indian freedom and his insistence on non-violent means in the struggle—both resulted from his new understanding of India and of himself after his contact with a *universally valid* spiritual tradition which he saw to be common to both East and West.

The Christianity, the spiritual and religious humanism, of the West opened his eyes to forces of wisdom and of love which were closer to his own heart because they were expressed in the symbols and philosophic language of his own people, and they could be used immediately to awaken this sleeping and enslaved people to an awareness of its own identity and of its historic vocation. He neither accepted Christianity nor rejected it; he took all that he found in Christian thought that seemed relevant to him as a Hindu. The rest was, at least for the time being, of merely external interest.

Here was no syncretism and no indifferentism. Gandhi had the deepest respect for Christianity, for Christ and the Gospel. In following his way of *satyagraha** he believed he was following the Law of Christ, and it would be difficult to prove that this belief was entirely mistaken—or that it was in any degree insincere.

One of the great lessons of Gandhi's life remains this: through the spiritual traditions of the West he, an Indian, discovered his Indian heritage and with it his own "right mind." And in his fidelity to his own heritage and its spiritual sanity, he was able to show men of the West and of the whole world a way to recover their own "right mind" in their own tradition, thus manifesting the fact that there are certain indisputable and essential values—religious, ethical, ascetic, spiritual, and philosophical—which man has everywhere needed and which he has in the past managed to acquire, values without which he cannot live, values which are now in large measure lost to him so that, unequipped to face life in a fully human manner, he now runs the risk of destroying himself entirely.

Call these values what you will, "natural religion" or "natural law," Christianity admits their existence at least as preambles to faith and grace, if not sometimes vastly more (Romans 2:14-15, Acts 17:22-31). These values are universal, and it is hard to see how there can be any "catholicity" (*cath-holos* means "all-embracing") that even implicitly

* A term coined by Gandhi. Its root meaning is "holding on to truth," and, by extension, resistance by non-violent means.

excludes them. One of the marks of catholicity is precisely that values which are everywhere natural to man are fulfilled on the highest level in the Law of the Spirit. And in Christian charity. A "charity" that excludes these values cannot claim the title of Christian love.

In rediscovering India and his own "right mind," Gandhi was not excavating from libraries the obscure disputed questions of Vedantic scholasticism (though he did not reject *Vedanta*). He was, on the contrary, identifying himself fully with the Indian people, that is to say not with the Westernized upper classes nor with the *brahmin* caste, but rather with the starving masses and in particular with the outcaste "untouchables," or *Harijan.*

This again is a supremely important fact, without which Gandhi's non-violence is incomprehensible. The awakening of the Indian mind in Gandhi was not simply the awakening of his own spirit to the possibilities of a distinctly Hindu form of "interior life." It was not just a question of Yoga *asanas* and Vedantic spiritual disciplines for his own perfection. Gandhi realized that *the people of India were awakening in him.* The masses who had been totally silent for thousands of years had now found a voice in him. It was not "Indian thought" or "Indian spirituality" that was stirring in him, but India herself. It was the spiritual consciousness of a people that awakened in the spirit of one person. But the message of the Indian spirit, of Indian wisdom, was not for India alone. It was for the entire world. Hence Gandhi's message was valid for India and for himself in so far as it represented *the awakening of a new world.*

Yet this renewed spiritual consciousness of India was entirely different from the totalitarian and nationalist consciousnesses that came alive in the West and in the East (Japan) to the point of furious and warlike vitality. The Indian mind that was awakening in Gandhi was inclusive not exclusive. It was at once Indian and universal. It was not a mind of hate, of intolerance, of accusation, of rejection, of division. It was a mind of love, of understanding, of infinite capaciousness. Where the extreme nationalisms of Western Fascism and of Japan were symptoms of paranoid fury, exploding into alienation, division, and destruction, the spirit which Gandhi discovered in himself was reaching out to unity, love, and peace. It was a spirit which was, he believed, strong enough to heal every division.

In Gandhi's mind, non-violence was not simply a political tactic which was supremely useful and efficacious in liberating his people from foreign rule, in order that India might then concentrate on realizing its own national identity. On the contrary, the spirit of non-violence sprang from *an inner realization of spiritual unity in himself.* The whole Gandhian concept of non-violent action and *satyagraha* is incomprehensible if it is thought to be a means of achieving unity rather than as *the fruit of inner unity already achieved.*

Indeed this is the explanation for Gandhi's apparent failure (which became evident to him at the end of his own life). He saw that his followers had not reached the inner unity that he had realized in himself, and that their *satyagraha* was to a great extent a pretense, since they believed it to be a means to achieve unity and freedom, while he saw that it must necessarily be the *fruit of inner freedom.*

The first thing of all and the most important of all was the inner unity, the overcoming and healing of inner division, the consequent spiritual and personal freedom, of which national autonomy and liberty would only be consequences. However, when *satyagraha* was seen only as a useful technique for attaining a pragmatic end, political independence, it remained almost meaningless. As soon as the short-term end was achieved, *satyagraha* was discarded. No inner peace was achieved, no inner unity, only the same divisions, the conflicts and the scandals that were ripping the rest of the world to pieces.

This, then, is the second crucially important principle that we discover in Gandhi. Contrary to what has been thought in recent centuries in the West, the spiritual or interior life is not an exclusively private affair. (In reality, the deepest and most authentic Western traditions are at one with those of the East on this point.) The spiritual life of one person is simply the life of all manifesting itself in him. While it is very necessary to emphasize the truth that as the person deepens his own thought in silence he enters into a deeper understanding of and communion with the spirit of his entire people (or of his Church), it is also important to remember that as he becomes engaged in the crucial struggles of his people, in seeking justice and truth together with his brother, he tends to liberate the truth in himself by seeking true liberty for all. Thus Plato taught that "to philosophize and concern oneself with politics is one and the same thing, and to wrestle with the sophist means at the same time to defend the city against tyranny."[8]

[8] A. Koyré, *Discovering Plato* (New York, 1945), p. 108.

So true was this that Socrates would not turn his back on the equivocation of his fellow citizens and their betrayal of truth, even when their hatred of reason meant his own death.

The "spiritual space" created by the Polis was still, in any event, the only place for the philosopher. True, in an imperfect city a fully human life was not possible, and hence *a fortiori* the perfect philosophical life was out of the question. "The philosopher has no place in the city except at its helm." Yet if he is not only silenced but even condemned unjustly to death, it remains his function as philosopher to teach the city truth by his death rather than fly into exile or withdraw into private life, since a purely private existence could not be fully "philosophical." This was Gandhi's view also, and we know that he had no illusions about the perfection of the Indian Polis.

Gandhi's career was eminently active rather than contemplative. Yet his fidelity in maintaining intact the contemplative element that is necessary in *every* life was well known. However, even his days of silence and retirement were not days of mere "privacy"; they belonged to India and he owed them to India, because his "spiritual life" was simply his participation in the life and *dharma* of his people. Their liberation and the recovery of their political unity would be meaningless unless their liberty and unity had a dimension that was primarily spiritual and religious. The liberation of India was to Gandhi a *religious* duty because for him the liberation of India was only a step to the liberation of all mankind from the tyranny of violence in others, but chiefly in themselves. So Gandhi could say, "When the practice of *ahimsa* becomes universal, God will reign on earth as He does in heaven."

The life of the Indian sage, or guru, is in any case public to the point of being excruciating. Day and night Gandhi was surrounded not only by respect but by worship. Somewhere in *The Human Condition* Hannah Arendt speaks of the Greek citizen's "merciless exposure to the Polis." It was in the life of the Polis that the citizen manifested his deeds and his courage, above all his reason. "No activity can become excellent if the world does not provide a proper space for its exercise."[9]

[9] Hannah Arendt, *The Human Condition* (Chicago, 1958), p. 49.

This does not mean that the classical idea allows no "space" for what is hidden and private. There is the economy of private life in the home. But this is not the proper sphere of man's activities as a being of logic, of courage, and of wisdom. It is in the public and political realm that he shares words and deeds, thus contributing his share of action and thought to the fabric of human affairs. Now, the public and political realm is that where issues are decided in a way worthy of free man: by persuasion and words, not by violence. Violence is essentially wordless, and it can begin only where thought and rational communication have broken down. Any society which is geared for violent action is by that very fact systematically unreasonable and inarticulate. Thought is not encouraged, and the exchange of ideas is eschewed as filled with all manner of risk. Words are kept at a minimum, at least as far as their variety and content may be concerned, though they may pour over the armed multitude in cataracts: they are simply organized and inarticulate noise destined to arrest thought and release violence, inhibiting all desire to communicate with the enemy in any other way than by destructive impact.

Though there are at best only analogies between the Greek concept of the Polis and the entirely hierarchical structure of ancient Indian society, it is instructive to see how these basic ideas are illustrated in Gandhi. It cannot too often be repeated that with him non-violence was not a simply marginal and quasi-fanatical indulgence of personal religious feeling. It belonged to the *very nature* of *political life*, and a society whose politics are habitually violent, inarticulate, and unreasonable is a subpolitical and therefore subhuman society. This of course was a truth that Gandhi had learned not from books but from experience—in South Africa!

In any case Gandhi's public life was one of maximum exposure, and he kept it so. *For him the public realm was not secular, it was sacred.* To be involved in it was then to be involved in the sacred *dharma* of the Indian people. Surrender to the demands of that *dharma*, to the sacred needs of the *Harijan* (outcastes, untouchables) and of all India, was purely and simply surrender to God and to His will, manifested in the midst of the people. When friends tried to dissuade Gandhi from fasting for the people (and Gandhi's fasts were completely public, political acts in the highest sense of the word) he replied: "God's voice has been increasingly audible as years have rolled by. He has never forsaken me even in my darkest hour. He has saved me often against myself and left me not a vestige of independence. The greater the surrender to Him, the greater has been my joy."[10] Yet it would be a mistake to think of these fasts only as means of applying political (in the lowest and current sense) pressure to achieve short-term ends.

Fasting remained primarily an act of worship and an act of witness to universal truth. It formed part of the Hindu *dharma* and therefore of India's witness to the religious truths implicit in the very structure of cosmic reality. Hence for Gandhi to speak, write, fast, and exercise non-violent resistance in behalf of the *Harijan* and of Indian freedom was at the same time to bear witness to the chief truth of Hinduism: "The belief that ALL life (not only human beings but all sentient beings) is one, i.e., all life coming from the One universal source, call it *Allah*, God, or *Parameshwara*. . . ."[11]

Gandhi adds an interesting commentary to this. His immediate conclusion is one that is full of social and moral consequences: "Hinduism excludes all exploitation" (hence it follows implicitly that the caste structure in so far as it rested upon a basis of crass injustice toward the *Harijan* was in fact a denial of the basic truth of Hinduism). Gandhi's sense of the Hindu *dharma* demanded, then, that this be made clear and that all Hindus should collaborate in setting things right. This fundamental re-establishment of justice was essential if India was to have the inner unity, strength, and freedom to profit by its own political liberation.

At the same time, the cooperation of the whole Indian people in the sacrificial and religious art of non-violent self-liberation was a necessary sign to the rest of the world—a witness that would enable all peoples, especially those subject to colonialist exploitation, to take the same measures for the restoration of the order willed by God.

Gandhi continues:

> There is no limit whatsoever to the measure of sacrifice that one may make in order to realize this *oneness with all life*, but certainly the immensity of the ideal sets a limit to your wants. That, you will see, is the antithesis of the position of the modern civilization which says "Increase your wants." Those who hold that belief think

[10] *Hindu Dharma* (Ahmedabad, 1958), p. 93.

[11] Ibid., p. 35.

> that increase of wants means an increase of knowledge whereby you understand the Infinite better. On the contrary, Hinduism rules out indulgence and multiplication of wants, as these hamper one's growth to the ultimate identity with the Universal Self.[12]

Gandhi therefore did not identify the "private" sphere with the "sacred" and did not cut himself off from public activity as "secular." Yet he did on the other hand look upon certain cultures and social structures as basically "secular" in the sense that their most fundamental preconceptions were irreligious (even though they might, on occasion, appeal to the support of religious clichés). Some of the most characteristic and least understood elements in his non-violent mystique follow from this principle which implies a rejection of the basic idea of the affluent industrial society. A society that lives by organized greed or by systematic terrorism and oppression (they come to much the same thing in the end) will always tend to be violent because it is in a state of persistent disorder and moral confusion. The first principle of valid political action in such a society then becomes *non-cooperation* with its disorder, its injustices, and more particularly with its deep commitment to untruth. *Satyagraha* is meaningless if it is not based on the awareness of profound inner contradiction in all societies based on force. "It is not possible for a modern state based on force non-violently to resist forces of disorder, whether external or internal." Hence *satyagraha* according to Gandhi cannot seriously accept claims, advanced by a basically violent society that hopes to preserve order and peace by the threat of maximum destruction and total hate. *Satyagraha* must begin by putting itself against this claim in order that the seriousness of one's dedication to truth may be put to the test. It is not possible for the truly non-violent man simply to ignore the inherent falsity and inner contradictions of a violent society. On the contrary, it is for him a religious and human duty to confront the untruth in that society with his own witness in order that the falsity may become evident to everyone. The first job of a *satyagraha* is to bring the real situation to light even if he has to suffer and die in order that injustice be unmasked and appear for what it really is.

All the political acts of Gandhi were, then, at the same time spiritual and religious acts in fulfillment of the Hindu *dharma*. They were

[12] Ibid., p. 36.

meaningful on at least three different levels at once: first as acts of religious worship, second as symbolic and educative acts bringing the Indian people to a realization of their true needs and their place in the life of the world, and finally they had a universal import as manifestations of urgent truths, the unmasking of political falsehood, awakening all men to the demands of the time and to the need for renewal and unity on a world scale.

In Gandhi the voice of Asia, not the Asia of the Vedas and Sutras only, but the Asia of the hungry and silent masses, was speaking and still speaks to the whole world with a prophetic message. This message, uttered on dusty Indian roads, remains more meaningful than those specious promises that have come from the great capitals of the earth. As Father Monchanin, the French priest and scholar who became a hermit in India, declared at Gandhi's death: "When we hear the voice of Gandhi we hear the voice of his Mother [India] and of his nurse. We hear the voice of all the peasant masses bending over the rice fields of India."[13]

"Man cannot be free if he does not know that he is subject to necessity, because his freedom is always won in his never wholly successful attempts to liberate himself from necessity."[14]

We have seen that Gandhi's political philosophy was based on this principle, because his religious intuition of the Hindu *dharma* saw all life as one in a sacred cosmic family in which each member helped to elevate the whole from a selfish and destructive to a spiritual and productive level through sacrificial participation in the common needs and struggles of all. Hence the cornerstone of all Gandhi's life, action, and thought was the respect for the sacredness of life and the conviction that "love is the law of our being." For he said, "If love or non-violence be not the law of our being, the whole of my argument falls to pieces." Note he also says that "Truth is the law of our being." But obviously Gandhi's life was without meaning unless we take into account the fact that it was lived in the face of untruth and hatred, the persistent and flagrant denial of love.

[13] "Allocution du P. Monchanin 20 fevrier 1948," in Appendix to C. Drevet, *Pour Connaître la pensée de Gandhi*, 2e edition (Paris, 1954), p. 224.

[14] Hannah Arendt, *The Human Condition*, p. 121.

Sometimes the idea of non-violence is taken to be the result of a purely sentimental evasion of unpleasant reality. Foggy clichés about Oriental metaphysics leave complacent Westerners with the idea that for the East (and as everyone knows, the Easterners are all "quietists" besides being "enigmatic") nothing really exists anyway. All is illusion, and suffering itself is illusion. Non-violence becomes a way of "making violence stop" by sitting down in front of it and wishing it was not there. This, together with the refusal to eat meat or to kill ants, indeed even mosquitoes, is supposedly thought to create an aura of benevolence which may effectively inhibit the violence of Englishmen (who are in any case kind to dogs, etc.) but cannot be expected to work against Nazis and Russians. So much for Western evaluations!

Gandhi knew the reality of hatred and untruth because he had felt them in his own flesh: indeed he succumbed to them when he was assassinated on January 30, 1948. Gandhi's non-violence was therefore not a sentimental evasion or denial of the reality of evil. It was a clear-sighted acceptance of the necessity to use the force and the presence of evil as a fulcrum for good and for liberation.

All forms of necessity can contribute to man's freedom. There is material and economic need. There is spiritual need. The greatest of man's spiritual needs is the need to be delivered from the evil and falsity that are in himself and in his society. Tyranny, which makes a sagacious use of every human need and indeed artificially creates more of them in order to exploit them all to the limit, recognizes the importance of guilt. And modern tyrannies have all explicitly or implicitly in one way or another emphasized the *irreversibility of evil* in order to build their power upon it.

For instance, it is not unusual in all political life, whether totalitarian or democratic, to incriminate the political novice in order to test his mettle and make sure of his commitment. He must be willing to get his hands dirty, and if he is not willing he must be framed so that he will have a record that can, when necessary, be used against him. Then he will be a committed man. He will henceforth cooperate with acts which might have given him pause if he were not himself marked with guilt. Who is he to complain of certain shady actions, certain discreet deals, certain white lies, when he knows what is in his own file at headquarters?

It is no accident that Hitler believed firmly in the unforgivableness of sin. This is indeed fundamental to the whole mentality of Nazism, with its avidity for final solutions and its concern that all uncertainties be eliminated.

Hitler's world was built on the central dogma of the irreversibility of evil. Just as there could be no quarter for the Jews, so the acts that eliminated them were equally irreversible and there could really be no excuse for the Nazis themselves. Even the arguments of an Eichmann, pleading obedience, suggest deep faith in an irreversible order which could not be changed but only obeyed. Such was the finality of Hitler's acts and orders that all the trials of all the Nazis who have been caught, whether they have been executed or liberated or put in prison for short terms, have changed absolutely nothing. It is clear that Hitler was in one thing a brilliant success: everything he did bears the stamp of complete and paranoid finality.

In St. Thomas Aquinas, we find a totally different view of evil. Evil is not only reversible but it is the proper motive of that mercy by which it is overcome and changed into good. Replying to the objection that moral evil is not the motive for mercy since the evil of sin deserves indignation and punishment rather than mercy and forgiveness, St. Thomas says that on the contrary *sin itself is already a punishment* "and in this respect we feel sorrow and compassion for sinners."[15] In order to do this we have to be able to *experience their sin as if it were our own.* But those who "consider themselves happy and whose *sense of power depends on the idea that they are beyond suffering any evil* are not able to have mercy on others" by experiencing the evil of others as their own.[16]

This is a splendid analysis of the mentality of power and greed which makes evil irreversible! Such a mentality lacks the interior strength necessary to assume the suffering of another as its own and thus to change his condition by forgiveness and acceptance. Instead of seeing the sin of another as punishment and suffering, and as motive for compassion, it looks on that evil as a despicable moral blemish which must be eliminated and punished, removed from sight and from experience. Only the admission of defect and fallibility in oneself makes it possible for one to become merciful to others.

St. Thomas continues this remarkable analysis by considering those who are "obsessed" with the notion of insult, either because they have

[15] *Summa Theologica*, II, IIae, q. 30, art. 1, ad. 1.

[16] Ibid., art. 2.

suffered a humiliation or because they intend to humiliate another.

> They are provoked to anger and aggression, which are virile passions. These make a man think that he is in danger of suffering some future evil (which he intends to resist). When men are so disposed, they do not have mercy on others. Likewise the proud do not have mercy because they despise others and look upon them as evil, taking it for granted that these people deserve to suffer whatever they have to suffer.[17]

A belief in the finality and irreversibility of evil implies a refusal to accept the precariousness and the risk that attend all finite good in this life. Indeed, the good that men do is always in the realm of the uncertain and of the fluid, because the needs and sufferings of men, the sins and failures of men, are constant, and love triumphs, at least in this life, not by eliminating evil once for all but by resisting and overcoming it anew every day. The good is not assured once for all by one heroic act. It must be recaptured over and over again. St. Peter looked for a limit to forgiveness. Seven times, and then the sin was irreversible! But Christ told him that forgiveness must be repeated over and over again, without end.

The "fabric" of society is not finished. It is always "in becoming." It is on the loom, and it is made up of constantly changing relationships. Non-violence takes account precisely of this dynamic and non-final state of all relationships among men, for non-violence seeks to change relationships that are evil into others that are good, or at least less bad.

Hence non-violence implies a kind of bravery far different from violence. In the use of force, one simplifies the situation by assuming that the evil to be overcome is clear-cut, definite, and irreversible. Hence there remains but one thing: to eliminate it. Any dialogue with the sinner, any question of the irreversibility of his act, only means faltering and failure. Failure to eliminate evil is itself a defeat. Anything that even remotely risks such defeat is in itself capitulation to evil. The irreversibility of evil then reaches out to contaminate *even the tolerant thought* of the hesitant crusader who, momentarily, doubts the total evil of the enemy he is about to eliminate.

[17] Ibid., ad. 3. Cf. St. Thomas Aquinas on the "mood of Nemesis" which "rejoices in the belief that others justly suffer and grieves when good comes to the unworthy," art. 3, ad. 2.

Such tolerance is already complicity and guilt, and must be eliminated in its turn. As soon as it is detected it becomes irreversible.

Fortitude, then, equals fanaticism. It grows with unreason. Reasoning itself is by its very nature tinged with betrayal.

Conscience does indeed make cowards. It makes Judases. Conscience must be eliminated.

This is the familiar mental machinery of tyrannical oppression. By reducing necessities to simple and irreversible forms it simplifies existence, eliminating questions that tend to embarrass minds and slacken the "progress" of the relentless and intolerant apparatus. Sin is thus prevented from entering into the living dialectic of society. And yet a dialectic that ignores the presence of evil is itself dead because it is untrue. The greatest of tyrannies are all therefore based on the postulate that *there should never be any sin.* That therefore what happened either was not a sin ("Dallas has no sins," as we all were quasi-officially informed at the end of 1963) or else it has been immediately wiped out (by a lynch mob, or a Jack Ruby). Since sin is what should never be, then it must never be, therefore *it will never be.* The most awful tyranny is that of the proximate Utopia where the last sins are currently being eliminated and where, tomorrow, there will be no more sins because all the sinners will have been wiped out.

> Non-violence has a different logic. It recognizes that sin is an everyday occurrence which is in the very nature of action's constant establishment of new relationships within a web of relations, and it needs forgiving, dismissing, in order to make it possible for life to go on by constantly releasing men from what they have done unknowingly. Only through this constant mutual release from what they do can men remain free agents, only by their constant willingness to change their minds and start again can they be trusted with so great a power as that to begin something new.[18]

This remarkable statement of Hannah Arendt's shows the inherent relation between non-violence and the renewal of India for which Gandhi lived and died. A violent change would not have been a serious change at all. To punish and destroy the oppressor is merely to initiate a new cycle of violence and oppression. The only real liberation is that which *liberates both the oppressor and the oppressed* at the same time from the same tyrannical automatism of the violent process which

[18] Hannah Arendt, *The Human Condition*, p. 240.

contains in itself the curse of irreversibility. "The freedom contained in Jesus' teaching of forgiveness is the *freedom from vengeance* [italics mine], which encloses both doer and sufferer in the relentless automatism of the action process, which by itself need never come to an end."[19]

True freedom is then inseparable from the inner strength which can assume the common burden of evil which weighs both on oneself and one's adversary. False freedom is only a manifestation of the weakness that cannot bear even one's own evil until it is projected onto the other and seen as exclusively his. The highest form of spiritual freedom is, as Gandhi believed, to be sought in the strength of heart which is capable of liberating the oppressed and the oppressor together. But in any event, the oppressed must be able to be free within himself, so that he may begin to gain strength to pity his oppressor. Without that capacity for pity, neither of them will be able to recognize the truth of their situation: a common relationship in a common complex of sins.

When asked if it was lawful to overcome force with force, Erasmus answered that this might be permissible according to "Imperial laws" but he wondered how it could be relevant for a Christian, who is bound to follow the law of Christ,

> granted that human laws do not punish what they have permitted. Yet what is Christ your leader going to do if you defraud this law. . . . If your enemy is hungry, give him to eat. . . . In so doing you will heap coals of fire upon his head, that is to say, you will enkindle the fire of love in him.

To the objection that rendering good for evil only lays one open to greater evil, Erasmus replied:

> If you can avoid evil by suffering it yourself, do so. Try to help your enemy by overcoming him with kindness and meekness. If this does not help, then it is better that one perish than both of you. It is better that you be enriched with the advantage of patience than to render evil for evil. It is not enough to practice the golden rule in this matter. The greater your position the more ready you ought to be to forgive another's crime.[20]

[19] Ibid., p. 241.

[20] *Handbook of the Militant Christian*, trans. with an Introduction by John P. Dolan (Notre Dame, 1962).

Here, as usual in Erasmus, one finds no platitudes. The apparently simple suggestion that one can avoid evil by suffering it contains an arresting paradox. One can overcome evil by taking it upon oneself, whereas if one flies from it he is not certain to escape and may, even if he seems to escape, be overwhelmed. The only way truly to "overcome" an enemy is to help him become other than an enemy. This is the kind of wisdom we find in Gandhi. It is the wisdom of the Gospels.

It is also the wisdom of the Apostolic Fathers. We read in the *Shepherd of Hermas*:

> For, if you are long-suffering, the Holy Spirit dwelling in you will be clear, unobscured by any other spirit of evil. Dwelling in a spacious place, He will rejoice and be glad with the lodging in which He finds Himself. Thus, He will serve God with abundant cheerfulness, because He has His well-being within Himself. However, if violent anger enters, the good spirit in His sensitiveness is immediately confined, since He has not a clean habitation. So, He tries to withdraw from the place. . . . For, the Lord dwells amid long-suffering, but the Devil has his abode in anger. . . . Take a little wormwood and pour it into a jar of honey. Is not the honey spoiled altogether? Even a great quantity of honey is ruined by the smallest amount of wormwood and its sweetness is lost. It is no longer pleasant to the owner, because it has been mixed and it is no longer enjoyable. Now, if no wormwood is put into the honey, it turns out to be sweet and becomes useful for the owner. You see, then, that long-suffering is very sweet, far more than honey, and useful to the Lord. His dwelling is in long-suffering.[21]

Gandhi took upon himself the evil of India, not in a spirit of masochism or with the spiritual frivolity of self-punishment that believes itself to have a magic efficacy over sin. Nothing is more deeply serious than the Gandhian fast unto death for the recognition of the *Harijan* and for their admission to the temple, in a word their integration into the sacred public life of the Indian people.

He did not seek to reproach and confound others with the spectacle of his own penitence for their sin. He wanted them to recognize from his example that they could learn to bear and overcome the evil that was in them if they were willing to do as he did. Gandhi's symbolic acts (which were meaningful as symbols only because they marked his own flesh with the stamp of their acute reality) were aimed at three

[21] *Shepherd of Hermas* (New York, 1948), pp. 267, 268.

kinds of liberation. First, he wanted to deliver Indian religious wisdom from the sclerosis and blindness into which it had sunk by reason of the gross injustices of a system which had become untrue to itself. Second, he wanted to liberate the untouchables, the *Harijan*, not only from political and economic oppression, but from the incubus of their own self-hate and their despair. And, finally, he wished to liberate the oppressors themselves from their blind and hopeless dependence on the system which kept things as they were, and which consequently enslaved everybody both spiritually and materially.

What is most striking in this concept of Gandhi's is its breadth, its integrity, and its unity. This is his lesson and his legacy to the world: The evils we suffer cannot be eliminated by a violent attack in which one sector of humanity flies at another in destructive fury. Our evils are common and the solution of them can only be common. But we are not ready to undertake this common task because we are not ourselves. Consequently the first duty of every man is to return to his own "right mind" in order that society itself may be sane.

Coomaraswamy, in an important article,[22] once outlined the meaning of the process called *metanoia*, or recovery of one's right mind, the passage from ignorance of self to enlightened moral awareness. "Repentance," he said, quoting Hermas,[23] "is a great understanding" (and by no means an emotional crisis!). It is the ability to cast off the intolerable burden of the past act, no longer seen as irreversible. But obviously no man enclosed in himself can utter an omnipotent word of command and abolish his own sin. The "knowledge" and "understanding" which is truly the "great [and repentant, liberated] understanding" is therefore "understanding-with" or "*con*-scientia" (conscience). "A kind of synthesis or agreement by which our internal conflict is resolved and 'all the knots of the heart are loosed.'" It is to understand "with" our inmost self "*in a union transcending consciousness of a within or a without.*"

This is obviously something much deeper than a mere interiority or a form of pious and introverted recollection. It is supra-conscious and supra-personal. And it obviously implies the ability to come into unity with the *prajnatman* (the solar spirit), or what the Greek Fathers would call the *pneuma*.

[22] "On Being in One's Right Mind," *Review of Religion*, November, 1942.

[23] *Shepherd of Hermas*, Fourth Mandate, II. 1, p. 265.

We find St. Thomas speaking somewhat in these terms in an interesting question in the *Summa* on blindness of mind.[24] There is, he says, a principle of intellectual vision in man, and man can give his attention to this principle or turn away from it. He turns away either by willful refusal to acknowledge its authority, or by becoming absorbed in the love of other things which he prefers to the intellectual light. And St. Thomas quotes Psalm 57:9: "*Fire hath fallen on them* (the fire of desire) *and they shall not see the sun.*"

The *Shepherd of Hermas* speaks of the Spirit of Truth as a trust given by God to man, living and dwelling in him in order to be returned to the Lord undefiled by any lie. "Love truth and let nothing but the truth issue from your mouth, in order that the spirit which God has settled in this flesh of yours may be found truthful in the sight of men. . . . Liars ignore the Lord and defraud Him since they do not return the Spirit received from Him, namely a Spirit in which there is no lie." Hearing this, Hermas weeps and declares: "I have not yet spoken a true word in all my life!" And the Angel then tells him that this declaration is the beginning of truth in himself.[25] Of course in this context truth and forgiveness go together, and there must be *one* truth and one forgiveness both for myself and my brothers. Both truth and mercy are falsified when I judge by a double standard.

The capacity for forgiveness and for understanding in this highest sense makes men able to transcend the limitations of that self which is the subject of evil. St. Cyprian says, "If no one can be without sin . . . how necessary and how beneficent is divine clemency which, since it recognizes that even those who are healed still retain some wounds, has granted health-giving remedies to be used in curing the wounds that remain to be healed."[26] But this is not a merely mental operation, a manipulation of "pure intentions" and the excitation of subjective benevolence toward offenders. It means an immolation of one's empirical self, by mercy and sacrifice, in order to save and liberate oneself and the other. Coomaraswamy here quotes the *Maitri Upanishad*: "When the mind has been immolated in its own source for love of truth, THEN THE FALSE CONTROLS OF ACTIONS

[24] *Utrum caecitas mentis sit peccatum*, Summa Theologica, II, IIae, q. 15, art. 1.

[25] *Shepherd of Hermas*, pp. 262-263.

[26] Migne, *Patrologia Latina*, 4:604.

DONE WHEN IT WAS DELUDED BY SENSIBILIA LIKEWISE PASS AWAY." This is the mystical basis of Gandhi's doctrine of freedom in truth as end, and of *satyagraha* (the vow of truth) as the means of attaining the end. Coomaraswamy also quotes a few lines from Jakob Boehme which throw light on this idea which is, of course, fundamentally Christian. Boehme says:

> Thou shalt do nothing but forsake thy own will, viz., that which thou callest "I" or "thyself." By which means all thy evil properties will grow weak, faint, and ready to die, then thou wilt sink down again into that one thing from which thou art originally sprung.

To forgive others and to forget their offense is to enter with them into the healing mystery of death and resurrection in Christ, to return to the source of the Spirit which is the Heart of Christ. And by this forgiveness we are ourselves cleansed: *Unde vulneratus fueras, inde curare*, says Cyprian.[27]

It should be quite obvious that *satyagraha* has nothing in it of Western middle-class banality. It does not mean "honesty is the best policy," because it is far more than honesty and it is infinitely more than a policy. One does not obey the *prajnatman*, or intellectual principle, the "spirit of truth," simply in order to get something out of one's obedience.

The truth may turn out in terms of the current moods and trends of a blind society to be supremely unprofitable. In that case, when truth becomes absolutely the worst policy, one follows it anyway, even when it leads to death.

The "vivisection" of liberated India into two hostile states was in fact the rending of Gandhi's own heart. Though India was technically "free," it was not free because it was not united. It was indeed placed in a situation of mortal danger, in which the perpetual threat of violence made true freedom and true unity impossible.

It remained for Gandhi to start all over again as a solitary. "The interior voice tells me to go on fighting against the whole world, even though I am alone. It tells me not to fear this world but to advance, having in myself nothing but the fear of God." At the same time he did not give up hope for India, because the truth of the Hindu *dharma*

[27] "Let that by which you were wounded become your own cure" (Migne, *Patrologia Latina*, *De Zelo et Livore*, 4:649).

remained what it had always been, and if India wished to fulfill the conditions of fidelity to her *dharma*, she could recover this truth.

"A man ends by becoming what he thinks," Gandhi said, "and it will be the same for India if she remains firmly attached to Truth by means of Love [*satyagraha*]." But he himself recognized that politically his battle had really been lost. Without complacency, without self-pity, he faced the truth that there was only one thing left. He must lay down his life for India, and he was in fact killed by a brother "whom he had failed to convince."

Whether we may think he succeeded or failed, Gandhi never ceased to believe in the possibility of a love of truth so strong and so pure that it would leave an "indelible impress" upon the most recalcitrant enemy, and awaken in him a response of love and truth. Such an attitude cannot be understood within the context of pragmatism, because what matters is the devotion to truth which it implies, not its actual impact on other men.

In retrospect one wonders how deeply India herself understood Gandhi and believed in him. Tagore himself, one of the greatest Indian minds of our time, doubted the Mahatma and leveled against him the accusation with which we are all too familiar in the West. "Non-cooperation" (with the British) seemed to Tagore to be nothing but negation, defeatism, passivity, and so on. The standard and lasting objection to Gandhi has always been that he was retreating into the past. He is accused of not seeing that there was no alternative for India but acceptance of the values and methods of the West with all their implications, including the rejection of what was most fundamentally and characteristically Eastern.

Thus, for Tagore, the refusal to attend English Government schools (suggested by Gandhi) was nothing more than a withdrawal into a kind of Hindu ghetto. One should do all one possibly could to acquire the techniques and attitudes of Western man, and then turn these against the oppressor. This has been the formula adopted wholeheartedly, for example, by Communist China.

Gandhi's idea was quite different. "Non-cooperation," he declared, "is a protest against an unwitting and unwilling participation in evil." The institutions of colonialism were in reality not intended to elevate and liberate the Indian. On the contrary, "the Government schools have unmanned us, rendered us helpless and Godless. They have filled us with discontent, and providing no remedy for the discontent have made us despondent. They have made us what we were intended to become: clerks and interpreters."[28]

How clear this has since become in the predicament of the new nations of Asia and Africa, suddenly liberated from colonial tutelage! Having accepted the white man's "culture" in their status as vassals, and still remaining intellectual and spiritual vassals after their liberation, they have entered a world of frustration, self-contradiction, resentment, and violence because the guilt of the colonial powers has been inherited, by them, as a tenfold self-hate, an incapacity to understand themselves, and a limitless fear and suspicion of everyone else. This is neither liberty nor civilization. It is the barbarism of post-historic man! A barbarism that can be avoided only by principles and policies like those of Gandhi or John XXIII.

Gandhi knew enough to see that to be "civilized" by force was in reality to be reduced oneself to barbarism, while the "civilizer" himself was barbarized. Can anyone deny that this has happened? In conclusion, Gandhi's "vow of truth" and all the other *ashram* vows, which were the *necessary preamble to the awakening of a mature political consciousness*, must be seen for what they are: not simply ascetic or devotional indulgences that may possibly suit the fancy of a few religious pacifists and confused poets, but precepts fundamentally necessary if man is to recover his right mind.

Gandhi's principles are, then, extremely pertinent today, more pertinent even than when they were conceived and worked out in practice in the *ashrams*, villages, and highways of India. They are pertinent for everybody, but especially for those who are interested in implementing the principles expressed by another great religious mind, Pope John XXIII, in *Pacem in Terris.* Indeed this encyclical has the breadth and depth, the universality and tolerance, of Gandhi's own peace-minded outlook. Peace cannot be built on exclusivism, absolutism, and intolerance. But neither can it be built on vague liberal slogans and pious programs gestated in the smoke of confabulation. There can be no peace on earth without the kind of inner change that brings man back to his "right mind."

Gandhi's observations on the prerequisites and the disciplines involved by *satyagraha*, the vow of truth, are required reading for anyone who is seriously interested in man's fate in the nuclear age.

[28] *The Gandhi Reader*, ed. by Homer A. Jack (New York, 1961), p. 219.

HINDU COSMOLOGY AND MODERN SCIENCE*
Some Remarks

Ian Watson

I

Every philosophy, as a wisdom-system (that is, metaphysic) has a cluster of doctrines which in one sense define it. Indian thought, especially Hindu *Vedanta*, has, not one, but several sets of variously related clusters, according to whether the system is expressing itself as epistemology, ontology, cosmology, soteriology, anthropology—or whatever. And there are more—but these will do.

A number of these may be familiar, but one or two will like-ly be strangers. "Epistemology" (*logos* of *epistemé*) is no doubt familiar as "the theory of knowledge"; "ontology" (*logos* of *ontos*), perhaps as the Existentialist-cum-Phenomenologist "study of being" (roughly what Aristotelians have wrongly taken "metaphysics" *as a whole* to be[1]); and "anthropology" (*logos* of *anthropos*), as "a study of the nature of persons," usually, though wholly misleading, called "philosophical psychology" or "philosophy of mind." But—"cosmology"? "soteriology"? These, unless we are historians of science or theologians, are not terms with which we are very likely to be very familiar—leastwise, not as bits or branches of "philosophy."

II

By "cosmology" is meant, the quest for wisdom and truth about the cosmos, as a whole—the *logos* of *kosmos*. This quest relates in some sense to that espoused by modern science. But, because of a certain

* Editor's Note: from *Studies in Comparative Religion*, 7:3, 1973.

[1] I have in mind writers like Theophrastus, whose wholly Aristotelian interpretation of Aristotle has been transmitted to us with the title, "Metaphysics." It is too little recognized that Aristotle himself likely never used the word "metaphysics."

general difference in approach, because, that is, Hindu *Vedanta* is what I will term "principial" and not "materialist-individualist," it employs different techniques in its effort to articulate, and to teach, an adequate understanding of the supposed largely observable cosmos. Moreover, it admits different, indeed *more* areas to count as, authentically, the subject-matter to be accommodated by any such "understanding." It includes, for instance, what in the West is known derisively as "the Occult" (i.e., "the hidden")—astrology, palmistry, necromancy, psychomancy, and so on.

Generally speaking, the intentions of Indian cosmology and of modern science in the West are roughly identical: both seek an explanation, descriptive where possible, of the basics of the more or less observable cosmos. But because there exist differences elsewhere in the general metaphysics, how these general intentions are carried through differs *in kind* from one approach to the other. For *modern science*, the quest, on at least many understandings of this discipline from within it, is for *basic particles*, or anyway, components, on the assumption that these basics *must* be—usually "physical," though, if we accept "psychology," on some understandings occasionally "mental," *stuff* somehow, usually, though not necessarily, assumed to be observable. *Hindu cosmology* is, on the other hand, a quest for *basic principles*, thought of as real, though non-substantial (i.e., non-stuffist, whether the stuff be physical or mental), *sources*, *occasions*, *grounds*, or (perhaps best) *ultimate explanations* of all substantial (or, stuff)—manifestation; this latter being then considered only *seemingly* or *relatively real*.

Indeed, I believe a largely ignored vast importance of Hindu *Vedanta* is that, if properly interpreted, it can offer a viable alternative to modern science as an explanatory system of the ultimate nature of the cosmos. To do this, one vital beginning will be a proper interpretation of the doctrine of the *gunas*, as "principial non-substantial basics," or, as the name implies, "principial properties (or qualities)" which, at a highly ultimate level, determine the behavioral-tendencies (*vasanas*) inherent in all subsequent manifestations. Their influence, in other words, is *wholly responsible* for all behavior, said "behavior" *simply being* their manifest expression. Put simply, and in Western terms, this doctrine is, at a certain high, though not *wholly* ultimate level, descriptive of the basics explanatory of the behavior of all things.

The *gunas* are, of course, threefold: *Sattva*, or the Light Principle, whose influence or manifest expression is latent in what, in the West, we would call "the tendency" to behave upward; that is, towards the most fulfilling or ultimate expression of the nature of the being in question, which, in the case of persons[2] will be a conscious realization of one's person (*jivatma*) at its best, most wholly developed or fulfilled. Secondly, *Tamas*, or the Darkness Principle, whose influence or manifest expression is latent in the tendency to behave downward, or away from this ultimate, or most fulfilling realization; and thirdly, *Rajas*, or the Light-Darkness Principle, whose influence, as manifest expression, results in the vascillation between fulfilling, improving, or developing movement, and non-fulfilling (or &c) movement, known only too well to us all.

These principial basics are, in other words, advanced as explanatory of *all* behavior in a way which, in some at least helpful degree, parallels that which in science is meant by (for instance), "ultimate particles having velocity and mass, or perhaps velocity only"; or perhaps more closely, notions such as "directed energies" or "directed drives," considered in some way to be substantial. Whether, on the other hand, these "principial basics" are *ad hoc*, or anyway, any *less ad hoc* than these things are in modern science, rests with appropriate investigation. And this involves investigating, and therefore *entering* that "beyond situation," said to result in that appropriately odd experience on the basis of which the *risis* who advance these doctrines have done so. I will however not at this point say more about this doctrine: for here is not the relevant place. It is after all meant only as an illustration of the more general point that, in order to understand how Hindu *Vedanta can* offer a viable alternative to modern science as an ultimate explanatory system, it is, in the very beginning, of vital importance to recognize the difference between the "principial" approach of the former, and the "substantial" or "stuffist" approach of the latter.

III

That the ultimate cosmic-bits, or basics, *must* be "physical stuff,"[3] as modern science usually says, is a simple assumption, to some extent based upon an earlier, epistemological assumption that knowledge

[2] I refer of course to *jivatma*.

[3] I here mean to include "stuff" such as "magnetic fields," "radio waves"; indeed, "energy" generally.

can only be of individuals, or particulars, at least in the sense that any knowledge-claim is true (or false) in virtue of its application (or not), to, or its being about, some individual, or cluster of them. There may be a sense in which *a law* is "knowledge": but always only because it applies ultimately in some way to a certain cluster of possible or actual individuals or particulars.

To isolate knowledge on the basis of this assumption, and in this way, is of course to isolate it usually to sense-organ using perception, or, on occasion, also to what vaguely is called "discursive reasoning" when, as happens of course very rarely amongst scientists,[4] the possibility of *a priori* knowledge is admitted.

And if, as Hindu *Vedanta* does, the above is recognized not merely to be an assumption, but *also rejected* on the grounds that some other approach to knowledge can be advanced which is demonstrably prior, in the sense of, more adequate to disclosure of the nature of reality, and hence of the explanatory basics in question, then there is *virtually no problem whatever* in doing the switch, and abandoning the model and approach of modern science entirely. "Entirely" as *ultimate*, that is: for the approach would naturally remain a highly useful operational intermediary. Whilst the methods of modern science may, on this understanding, *not* give ultimate information, they may well furnish most useful information for the ontological level of the subject-matter of their single manifestation form—that is, for that level at which this subject-matter (that of observable and/or thinkable individuals) is real. An understanding of the cosmos, even of reality,[5] as if it were "substantially physical" or, as we often say "material," is clearly of great assistance when, as often, we are forced to approach and deal with it as if it were.

Nonetheless, this possibility of substituting the world-approach, or (perhaps better) reality-approach of Hindu *Vedanta* for that of modern science is part of the reason for the contemporary interest, among a certain significant Western minority, in this wisdom tradition. For it at least offers the prospect of a metaphysically rigorous alternative to one illusion from which many consider themselves long since disabused. I

[4] I naturally exclude the mathematicians—or at least, the "pure" ones.

[5] By "reality" I mean, either the Ultimate Itself, or, if speaking of the cosmos only, the sum of explanatory basics whose more basic explanation *is* "the Ultimate," *being* Its initial, or nearly initial, self-expression.

speak of the possibility of a materialist-science interpreting the cosmos such that good sense can be made of, and an adequate program outlined for, self-development—for, that is, the betterment of persons, and of humanity.

IV

But of course—that there *is* this alternative is one thing: investigating it is wholly another. And, speaking finally, whether it *is* a more adequate approach to the nature of the explanatory basics of the cosmos than that of modern science will, as above, be wholly determined only by engaging in those activities on the basis of which the *risis* who advance it claim it to be so. And whilst I will not at this point go into the *details* of the activities in question, quite as there are in science two general ways of examining truth claims, so are there here—*doing* the activities in question (*dhyana*, &c), quite as one might *do* science to assess it; and accepting as *evidence for* the suggested truth the fact that certain appropriately revealing consequences follow if one does accept, and live in terms of, these claims, so far as they can be applied to one's living as principles in this way.

What of course happens these days is this: that the findings of modern science are accepted by most *on spec*, that is, on grounds of their being advanced by authorities in the field; whereas, the findings of those who claim to present evidence demonstrating the lack of ultimacy about science *are not accepted at all.* And this is no more than sheer bias in favor of one authority over another; bias, moreover, which does *not* stop short of dismissing the findings of the latter without in the slightest examining them in ways appropriate at all. No bias could go further—and indeed, none these days does.

ON THE PATH, OFF THE TRAIL*

Gary Snyder

Work in Place of Place

Place is one kind of place. Another field is the work we do, our calling, our path in life. Membership in a place includes membership in a community. Membership in a work association—whether it's a guild or a union or a religious or mercantile order—is membership in a network. Networks cut across communities with their own kind of territoriality, analogous to the long migrations of geese and hawks.

Metaphors of path and trail are from the days when journeys were on foot or by horse with packstock, when our whole human world was a network of paths. There were paths everywhere: convenient, worn, clear, sometimes even set with distance posts or stones to measure *li*, or *versts*, or *yojana*. In the forested mountains north of Kyoto I came on mossy stone measuring posts almost lost in the dense bamboo-grass ground cover. They marked (I learned much later) the dried-herring-by-backpack trade route from the Japan Sea to the old capital. There are famous trails, the John Muir trail on the crest of the High Sierra, the Natchez Trace, the Silk Road.

A path is something that can be followed, it takes you somewhere. "Linear." What would a path stand against? "No path." Off the path, off the trail. So what's *off* the path? In a sense everything *else* is off the path. The relentless complexity of the world is off to the side of the trail. For hunters and herders trails weren't always so useful. For a forager, the path is *not* where you walk for long. Wild herbs, camas bulbs, quail, dye plants, are away from the path. The whole range of items that fulfill our needs is out there. We must wander through it to learn and memorize the field—rolling, crinkled, eroded, gullied, ridged (wrinkled like the brain)—holding the map in mind. This is the economic-visualization-meditation exercise of the Inupiaq and Athapaskans of Alaska of this very day. For the forager, the beaten path shows nothing new, and one may come home empty-handed.

* Editor's Note: from *The Practice of the Wild.*

In the imagery of that oldest of agrarian civilizations, China, the path or the road has been given a particularly strong place. From the earliest days of Chinese civilization, natural and practical processes have been described in the language of path or way. Such connections are explicit in the cryptic Chinese text that seems to have gathered all the earlier lore and restated it for later history—the *Dao De Jing*, "The Classic of the Way and the Power." The word *dao* itself means way, road, trail, or to lead/follow. Philosophically it means the nature and way of truth. (The terminology of Daoism was adopted by early Chinese Buddhist translators. To be either a Buddhist or Daoist was to be a "person of the way.") Another extension of the meaning of *dao* is the practice of an art or craft. In Japanese, *dao* is pronounced *do*—as in *kado*, "the way of flowers," *bushido*, "way of the warrior," or *sado*, "tea ceremony."

In all the traditional arts and crafts there has been customary apprenticeship. Boys or girls of fourteen or so were apprenticed to a potter, or a company of carpenters, or weavers, dyers, vernacular pharmacologists, metallurgists, cooks, and so forth. The youngsters left home to go and sleep in the back of the potting shed and would be given the single task of mixing clay for three years, say, or sharpening chisels for three years for the carpenters. It was often unpleasant. The apprentice had to submit to the idiosyncrasies and downright meanness of the teacher and not complain. It was understood that the teacher would test one's patience and fortitude endlessly. One could not think of turning back, but just take it, go deep, and have no other interests. For an apprentice there was just this one study. Then the apprentice was gradually inducted into some not so obvious moves, standards of craft, and in-house working secrets. They also began to experience—right then, at the beginning—what it was to be "one with your work." The student hopes not only to learn the mechanics of the trade but to absorb some of the teacher's power, the *mana*—a power that goes beyond any ordinary understanding or skill.

In the Zhuang-zi (Chuang-tzu) book, a third-century B.C. witty radical Daoist text, perhaps a century or so after the *Dao De Jing*, there are a number of craft and "knack" passages:

> The Cook Ting cut up an ox for Lord Wenhui with dance-like grace and ease. "I go along with the natural makeup, strike in the big hollows, guide the knife through the big openings, and follow things as they are. So I never touch the smallest ligament or tendon, much less a main joint. . . . I've had this knife of mine for nineteen

> years and I've cut up thousands of oxen with it, and yet the blade is as good as though it had just come from the grindstone. There are spaces between the joints, and the blade of the knife has really no thickness. If you insert what has no thickness into such spaces, then there's plenty of room. . . . That's why after nineteen years the blade of my knife is still as good as when it first came from the grindstone." "Excellent!" said Lord Wenhui. "I have heard the words of Cook Ting and learned how to care for life!" (Burton Watson translation)

These stories not only bridge the spiritual and the practical, but also tease us with an image of how totally accomplished one might become if one gave one's whole life up to a work.

The occidental approach to the arts—since the rise of the bourgeoisie, if we like—is to downplay the aspect of accomplishment and push everyone to be continually doing something new. This puts a considerable burden on the workers of every generation, a double burden since they think they must dismiss the work of the generation before and then do something supposedly better and different. The emphasis on mastering the tools, on repetitive practice and training, has become very slight. In a society that follows tradition, creativity is understood as something that comes almost by accident, is unpredictable, and is a gift to certain individuals only. It cannot be programmed into the curriculum. It is better in small quantities. We should be grateful when it comes along, but don't count on it. Then when it *does* appear it's the real thing. It takes a powerful impulse for a student-apprentice who has been told for eight or ten years to "always do what was done before," as in the production tradition of folk pottery, to turn it a new way. What happens then? The old guys in this tradition look and say, "Ha! You did something new! Good for you!"

When the master artisans reach their mid-forties they begin to take on apprentices themselves and pass their skills along. They might also take up a few other interests (a little calligraphy on the side), go on pilgrimages, broaden themselves. If there is a next step (and strictly speaking there need not be one, for the skill of the accomplished craftsperson and the production of impeccable work that reflects the best of the tradition is certainly enough in one life-time), it is to "go beyond training" for the final flower, which is not guaranteed by effort alone. There is a point beyond which training and practice cannot take you. Zeami, the superlative fourteenth-century Noh drama playwright and director who was also a Zen priest, spoke of this moment as "surprise." This is the surprise of discovering oneself needing no self, one with the work, moving in disciplined ease and grace. One knows what it is to *be* a spinning ball of clay, a curl of pure white wood off the edge of a chisel—or one of the many hands of Kannon the *Bodhisattva* of Compassion. At this point one can be free, with the work and from the work.

No matter how humble in social status, the skilled worker has dignity and pride—and his or her skills are needed and respected. This is not to be taken as any sort of justification for feudalism: it is simply a description of one side of how things worked in earlier times. The Far Eastern craft-and-training mystique eventually reached every corner of Japanese culture from noodle-making (the movie *Tampopo*) to big business to the high-culture arts. One of the vectors of this spread was Zen Buddhism.

Zen is the crispest example of the "self-help" (*jiriki*) wing of Mahayana Buddhism. Its community life and discipline is rather like an apprenticeship program in a traditional craft. The arts and crafts have long admired Zen training as a model of hard, clean, worthy schooling. I'll describe my experience as a *koji* (lay adept) at the monastery of Daitoku-ji, a Rinzai Zen sect temple in Kyoto, in the sixties. We sat cross-legged in meditation a minimum of five hours a day. In the breaks everyone did physical work—gardening, pickling, firewood cutting, cleaning the baths, taking turns in the kitchen. There were interviews with the teacher, Oda Sesso Roshi, at least twice a day. At that moment we were expected to make a presentation of our grasp of the *koan* that had been assigned us.

We were expected to memorize certain *sutra*s and conduct a number of small rituals. Daily life proceeded by an etiquette and a vocabulary that was truly archaic. A steady schedule of meditation and work was folded into weekly, monthly, and annual cycles of ceremonies and observations which went back to Song-dynasty China and in part clear back to the India of Shakyamuni's time. Sleep was short, the food was meager, the rooms spare and unheated, but this (in the sixties) was as true in the worker's or farmer's world as it was in the monastery.

(Novices were told to leave their pasts behind and to become one-pointed and unexceptional in all ways except the intention to enter this narrow gate of concentration on their *koan. Hone o oru*, as the saying goes—"break your bones," a phrase also used (in Japan) by workingmen, by the martial arts halls, and in modern sports and mountaineering.)

We also worked with lay supporters, often farmers, in downright convivial ways. We would stand out back in the vegetable gardens with locals discussing everything from new seed species to baseball to funerals. There were weekly begging walks down city streets and country lanes chanting and pacing along, our faces hidden under a big basket hat (waterproofed and dyed brown with persimmon juice). In fall the community made special begging trips for radishes or rice to country regions three or four ranges of hills away.

But for all its regularity, the monastic schedule could be broken for special events: on one occasion we all traveled by train to a gathering of hundreds of monks at a small but exquisite country temple for the celebration of its founding exactly five hundred years before. Our group came to be kitchen-workers: we labored for days chopping, cooking, washing, and arranging alongside the farm wives of the district. When the big feast was served we were the servers. That night, after the hundreds of guests had left, the kitchen-workers and laborers had their own feast and party, and old farmers and their wives traded crazy funny dances and songs with the Zen monks.

Freedom at Work

During one of the long meditation retreats called *sesshin*, the Roshi lectured on the phrase "The perfect way is without difficulty. Strive hard!" This is the fundamental paradox of the way. One can be called on not to spare one's very bones in the intensity of effort, but at the same time we must be reminded that the path itself offers no hindrance, and there is a suggestion that the effort itself can lead one astray. Mere effort can heap up learning, or power, or formal accomplishment. Native abilities may be nourished by discipline, but discipline alone will not get one into the territory of "free and easy wandering" (a Zhuang-zi term). One must take care not to be victimized by one's penchant for self-discipline and hard work. One's lesser talents may lead to success in craft or business, but then one might never find out what one's more playful capacities might have been. "We study the self to forget the self," said Dogen. "When you forget the self, you become one with the ten thousand things." Ten thousand things means all of the phenomenal world. When we are open that world can occupy us.

Yet we are still called on to wrestle with the curious phenomenon of the complex human self, needed but excessive, which resists letting the world in. Meditation practice gives us a way to scrape, soften, tan it. The intent of the *koan* theme is to provide the student with a brick to knock on the gate, to get through and beyond that first barrier. There are many further *koans* that work deeper into non-dualistic seeing and being—enabling the student (as the tradition would like to have it) to ultimately be mindful, graceful, grateful, and skillful in daily life; to go beyond the dichotomy of natural and "worked." In a sense it's a practice of "an art of life."

The *Dao De Jing* itself gives us the most subtle interpretation of what the way might mean. It starts out by saying this: "The way that can be followed ('wayed') is not the constant way." *Dao ke dao fei chang dao.* First line, first chapter. It is saying: "A path that can be followed is not a *spiritual* path." The actuality of things cannot be confined within so linear an image as a road. The intention of training can only be accomplished when the "follower" has been forgotten. The way is without difficulty—it does not itself propose obstacles to us, it is open in all directions. We do, however, get in our own way—so the Old Teacher said "Strive hard!"

There are also teachers who say: "Don't try to prove something hard to yourself, it's a waste of time; your ego and intellect will be getting in your way; let all such fantastic aspirations go." They would say, at this very moment, just *be* the very mind that reads *this* word and effortlessly knows it—and you will have grasped the Great Matter. Such were the instructions of Ramana Maharshi, Krishnamurti, and the Zen Master Bankei. This was Alan Watts' version of Zen. One whole school of Buddhism takes this position Jodo-shin, or Pure Land Buddhism, which elegant old Morimoto Roshi (who spoke Osaka dialect) said "is the only school of Buddhism that can scold Zen." It can scold it, he said, for trying too hard, for considering itself too special, and for being proud. One must have respect for the nakedness of these teachings and their ultimate correctness. Pure Land Buddhism is the purest. It resolutely resists any and all programs of self-improvement and stands only by *tariki*, which means "other-help." The "other" that might help is mythologically described as "Amida Buddha." Amida is no other than "emptiness"—the mind without conceptions or intentions, the Buddha-mind. In other words: "Give up trying to improve yourself, let the true self be your self." These teachings are frustrating for motivated people in that no real instruction is offered the hapless seeker.

Then there have always been countless unacknowledged *Bodhisattvas* who did not go through any formal spiritual training or philosophical quest. They were seasoned and shaped in the confusion, suffering, injustice, promise, and contradictions of life. They are the unselfish, big-hearted, brave, compassionate, self-effacing, ordinary people who in fact have always held the human family together.

There are paths that can be followed, and there is a path that cannot—it is not a path, it is the wilderness. There is a "going" but no goer, no destination, only the whole field. I first stumbled a bit off the trail in the mountains of the Pacific Northwest, at twenty-two, while a fire lookout in the North Cascades. I then determined that I would study Zen in Japan. I had a glimpse of it again looking down the aisle of a library in a Zen temple at age thirty and it helped me realize that I should not live as a monk. I moved near the monastery and participated in the meditation, the ceremonies, and the farm-work as a layperson.

I returned to North America in 1969 with my then wife and first-born son and soon we moved to the Sierra Nevada. In addition to the work with farms, trees, and politics my neighbors and I have tried to keep up some formal Buddhist practice. We have deliberately kept it lay and nonprofessional. The Japanese Zen world of the last few centuries has become so expert and professional in the matter of strict training that it has lost to a great extent the capacity to surprise itself. The entirely dedicated and good-hearted Zen priests of Japan will defend their roles as specialists by pointing out that ordinary people cannot get into the finer points of the teachings because they cannot give enough time to it. This need not be the case for the lay-person, who can be as intent on his or her Buddhist practice as any worker, artisan, or artist would be with their work.

The structure of the original Buddhist order was inspired by the tribal governance of the Shakya ("Oak Tree") nation—a tiny republic somewhat like the League of the Iroquois—with democratic rules of voting (Gard, 1949; 1956). Gautama the Buddha was born a Shakya—hence his appellation Shakyamuni, "sage of the Shakyas." The Buddhist *sangha* is thus modeled on the political forms of a neolithic-derived community.

So our models for practice, training, and dedication need not be limited to monasteries or vocational training, but can also look to original communities with their traditions of work and sharing. There are additional insights that come only from the non-monastic experience of work, family, loss, love, failure. And there are all the ecological-economical connections of humans with other living beings, which cannot be ignored for long, pushing us toward a profound consideration of planting and harvesting, breeding and slaughtering. All of us are apprenticed to the same teacher that the religious institutions originally worked with: reality.

Reality-insight says get a sense of immediate politics and history, get control of your own time; master the twenty-four hours. Do it well, without self-pity. It is as hard to get the children herded into the carpool and down the road to the bus as it is to chant *sutras* in the Buddha-hall on a cold morning. One move is not better than the other, each can be quite boring, and they both have the virtuous quality of repetition. Repetition and ritual and their good results come in many forms. Changing the filter, wiping noses, going to meetings, picking up around the house, washing dishes, checking the dipstick—don't let yourself think these are distracting you from your more serious pursuits. Such a round of chores is not a set of difficulties we hope to escape from so that we may do our "practice" which will put us on a "path"—it *is* our path. It can be its own fulfillment, too, for who would want to set enlightenment against non-enlightenment when each is its own full reality, its own complete delusion. Dogen was fond of saying that "practice *is* the path." It's easier to understand this when we see that the "perfect way" is not a path that leads somewhere easily defined, to some goal that is at the end of a progression. Mountaineers climb peaks for the great view, the cooperation and comradeship, the lively hardship—but mostly because it *puts you out there* where the unknown happens, where you encounter surprise.

The truly experienced person, the refined person, *delights in the ordinary.* Such a person will find the tedious work around the house or office as full of challenge and play as any metaphor of mountaineering might suggest. I would say the real *play* is in the act of going totally off the trail—away from any trace of human or animal regularity aimed at some practical or spiritual purpose. One goes out onto the "trail that cannot be followed" which leads everywhere and nowhere, a limitless fabric of possibilities, elegant variations a millionfold on the same themes, yet each point unique. Every boulder on a talus slope is different, no two needles on a fir tree are identical. How could one part be more central, more important, than any other? One will never come onto the three-foot-high heaped-up nest of a Bushy-tailed Woodrat, made of twigs and stones and leaves, unless one plunges into the manzanita thickets. Strive hard!

We find some ease and comfort in our house, by the hearth, and on the paths nearby. We find there too the tedium of chores and the staleness of repetitive trivial affairs. But the rule of impermanence means that nothing is repeated for long. The ephemerality of all our acts puts us into a kind of wilderness-in-time. We live within the nets of inorganic and biological processes that nourish everything, bumping down underground rivers or glinting as spiderwebs in the sky. Life and matter at play, chilly and rough, hairy and tasty. This is of a larger order than the little enclaves of provisional orderliness that we call ways. It *is* the Way.

Our skills and works are but tiny reflections of the wild world that is innately and loosely orderly. There is nothing like stepping away from the road and heading into a new part of the watershed. Not for the sake of newness, but for the sense of coming home to our whole terrain. "Off the trail" is another name for the Way, and sauntering off the trail is the practice of the wild. That is also where—paradoxically—we do our best work. But we need paths and trails and will always be maintaining them. You first must be on the path, before you can turn and walk into the wild.

THE IMAGINED COMMUNITY*

Diana Eck

At the closing session of the World's Parliament of Religions in 1893, its president and one of the chief visionaries of the Parliament, Charles Bonney, declared, "Henceforth the religions of the world will make war not on each other, but on the giant evils that afflict mankind!"[1] None of us can read these words without a sigh of sadness and perhaps a tinge of cynicism. The past one hundred years have scarcely borne out Bonney's vision. Interfaith cooperation has gotten a good start, but interfaith violence has kept pace. The world's religious traditions still manage to provide fuel for the world's strife. The giant evils that afflict humankind have grown as rapidly as our dreams; the chasms between the cultural, racial, and religious families of humankind have opened as quickly as the bridges we have built to span them. Each day's newspapers remind us that Sikhs and Hindus struggle with one another in India, Christians and Muslims in the Philippines and Nigeria, Jews and African-American Muslims in the United States, Catholics and Protestants in Northern Ireland. These struggles are not wholly religious in origin, but they are made more difficult and complex by the extensive use of religious language and symbolism. The encounter of people of differing faiths in the world today, for better and for worse, is one of the most important facts of our time.

There are many ways of describing the world scene in the late twentieth century. There are alarming statistics on population growth and the growth of dire poverty and illiteracy. There are statistics on the growth of carbon dioxide emissions, on the pollution of the seas, the stripping of the forests, the extinction of species of plant and animal life. There are statistics on the high rate of infant mortality, on disease and death in children, on prostitution and the sexual enslavement of women, on the worldwide growth of vast populations of refugees.

* Editor's Note: Chapter 8 of *Encountering God: A Spiritual Journey from Bozeman to Banaras.*

[1] Barrows, *The World's Parliament of Religions*, vol. 2, p. 1560.

Above all, there is the growing recognition that these problems are all interrelated. The one word which increasingly describes the complexity and relatedness of the world is *interdependent*. The problems cannot be isolated one from the other and neither can the people who hope to solve them.

The 1987 publication of *Our Common Future*, the report of the United Nations World Commission on Environment and Development, makes clear the ecological interdependence of the world—the transnational consequences of acid rain, deforestation, nuclear testing, flooding, and desertification. The overuse of land, the creation of vast deserts, and the cycles of famine are not just Africa's problem; the erosion of the ozone layer above the Antarctic is not just Antarctica's problem; the effects of the nuclear disaster at Chernobyl are not just Russia's problem. More than any single issue, the environmental crisis has enabled a much more nuanced understanding of what this word *interdependence* means. It means we as a whole suffer the consequences of the part, and as a whole we must address the solution. None of us can "go it alone" as peoples or nations to solve these problems. A glimpse of Earth, "the blue planet," beamed back from space should be enough to convince us that there is no longer any such thing as "alone" in this interdependent world.

In a set of lectures given in the late 1930s, the Indian philosopher Radhakrishnan, then at Oxford University, saw the beginnings of the world's interdependence and raised the question of its implications:

> For the first time in the history of our planet its inhabitants have become one whole, each and every part of which is affected by the fortunes of every other. Science and technology, without aiming at this result, have achieved the unity. Economic and political phenomena are increasingly imposing on us the obligation to treat the world as a unit. Currencies are linked, commerce is international, political fortunes are interdependent. And yet the sense that mankind must become a community is still a casual whim, a vague aspiration, not generally accepted as a conscious ideal or an urgent practical necessity moving us to feel the dignity of a common citizenship and the call of a common duty.[2]

Radhakrishnan spoke of the "ferment of restlessness" created by modernity. "The world has found itself as one body," he said. "But

[2] S. Radhakrishnan, *Eastern Religions and Western Thought* (New York: Oxford University Press, 1959), p. 2.

physical unity and economic interdependence are not by themselves sufficient to create a universal human community. . . . The cause of the present tension and disorder is the lack of adjustment between the process of life, which is one of increasing interdependence, and the 'ideology' of life, the integrating habits of mind, loyalties, and affections embodied in our laws and institutions. . . . The supreme task of our generation is to give a soul to the growing world consciousness."[3]

Interdependence describes not only the inextricable relatedness of nations and economies, but also that of peoples, religious traditions, and cultures. Religious interdependence is a reality of our world and interreligious dialogue a necessity, an instrument of our common work to transform the world in which we live. Interreligious dialogue is a basic communication network and it has an extensive ethical and practical agenda. Terms like "peace" and "justice" will become nothing but the well-intentioned yet meaningless slogans of our separate tribes if they are not understood to involve a serious commitment toward working in partnership with people of other faiths.

The phrase "global village" has become a common way of referring to the ever-smaller world in which we live. But what does it mean in human terms? If our world were a village of a thousand people, who would *we* be? The World Development Forum tells us that there would be 329 Christians, 174 Muslims, 131 Hindus, 61 Buddhists, 52 Animists, 3 Jews, 34 members of other religions, such as Sikhs, Jains, Zoroastrians, and Baha'is, and 216 would be without any religion. In this village, there would be 564 Asians, 210 Europeans, 86 Africans, 80 South Americans, and 60 North Americans. And in this same village, 60 persons would have half the income, 500 would be hungry, 600 would live in shantytowns, and 700 would be illiterate.[4]

For North American Christians, most of whom would be among the sixty in the world with half the income, it is a sobering reality. We like to think that we would not tolerate such economic inequity in our own village, so how is it that we tolerate it in the world? We are not simply evil or uncaring. The answer to such a question has to do with a single word—the word *we*. The casual *we* for most of us does not include the 50 percent hungry, the 60 percent in shantytowns,

[3] Ibid., pp. vii–viii.

[4] World Development Forum, cited in *Encyclopedia Britannica Book of the Year,* 1990.

and the 70 percent illiterate. Most of us construct our *we* without including *them.* Thinking of the world close up, as if it were a village of one thousand people, forces us to confront what we mean when we say "we." As Wilfred Cantwell Smith used to say, the meaning of that word *we* constitutes one of the most important facts about any people.[5] Is it we Christians, we Protestants, we Americans, we scholars, we human beings? Our *we* will include different people at different times and we need to signal this in our writing and speaking. Sometimes in these pages I have meant we Christians, sometimes we people of religious faith, sometimes we human beings whether or not we are explicitly involved in a religious tradition.

Here I ask of all of us, how often does our *we* come to include people of other faiths, other nations, other races? How often does our *we* link rather than divide? Our relation with the "other" may move, as Smith puts it, through a number of phases. First we talk *about* them—an objective "other." Then perhaps we talk *to* them, or more personally, we talk to you. Developing a real dialogue, we talk *with* you. And finally, we all talk with one another about us, all of us. This is the crucial stage to which our interreligious dialogue must take us if we are to be up to the task of creating communication adequate for an interdependent world.[6]

There is *we* language in every religious tradition, for the *we* issue is not simply a sociological matter but a theological issue, inextricably related to our deepest religious values. Hindus speak of the whole world as a single family—*va-sudhaiva kutumbakam.* Buddhists speak of the *sangha* of the four directions; Muslims find ways of interpreting the *umma*, the Muslim community, in a broader and more open sense to include all people who have aligned their lives toward God. Jews speak of God's covenant with Noah as a covenant with all who keep basic moral precepts. There may be isolationists and survivalists who see the future in terms of the widening of the distance between *we* and *them.* But in every tradition there are also these currents of thinking that are attempts to steer toward a wider *we*, a *we* that links rather than divides.

[5] W. C. Smith, "Objectivity and the Humane Sciences," in *Religious Diversity: Essays by Wilfred Cantwell Smith*, ed. W. G. Oxtoby (New York: Harper & Row, 1976), p. 178.

[6] Ibid.

In the Christian tradition, there is the language of the *oikos*, the household. The Gospel of John speaks of the household of God in which there are many rooms, many mansions. From this term *oikos* comes the word *oikoumene* (or *ecumene*), which means the household of the "whole inhabited earth." It is not surprising that the Christian ecumenical movement found this term expressive of the worldwide reach of the church, a worldwide household. And yet clearly the "whole inhabited earth" is not Christian. In the Office on Interreligious Relations at the WCC headquarters in Geneva, a poster bears the reminder "*Oikoumene* is the whole inhabited earth—Not just the Christian part of it."

The word *ecumenical* is also related to those other household words *economics* and *ecology*. Both are reminders of the household dynamics that hold the whole world together. Economy is the management of a household or of a society ordered after the manner of a household. In a household, if 6 percent of the people had half the wealth, that 6 percent would not be seen as successful, but as unjust. Ecology is concerned with understanding the interrelated household of living and non-living beings. Even the most seemingly insignificant or humble being is critical to the balance of the larger whole. To think ecumenically, ecologically, and economically is to think about the world and its interrelations with the same loyalty and care that one brings to the consideration of one's own household.

Here again, India has cast up a teacher who has pointed the way to a larger sense of *we* for me and for many Christians—M. K. Gandhi. Gandhi's life is a good example of the potential meanings of pluralism. He was both committed to his own Hindu tradition and open to dialogue with others. The dialogue went beyond mutual understanding to real mutual transformation. In relation to Christians especially, he both taught and learned a great deal. His reverence for the way of Christ became part of who he was as a Hindu, but he did not become a Christian. He not only sought to recast and enlarge the *we*, he sought to create communities on the basis of that larger *we* and to commit their energies to the transformation of society.

Gandhi's Re-creation of the We

For years I acquiesced in the commonly held notion that there was nothing left of Gandhi in India but his name and his portrait, much revered and much forgotten. During the early years of my work in Banaras, I lived among Hindus in the most old-fashioned of Hindu cities. There were times when I imagined that I could have been living in the seventeenth century. When I finished my book on Banaras, I took a deep breath of twentieth-century Indian air, spent more time in Delhi, and began meeting people who were more my own contemporaries and counterparts—intellectuals, activists, and feminists. To my surprise, I discovered that many of these people thought of themselves as Gandhians.

There was Devaki Jain, an economist and feminist who had established a network of support for hundreds of grassroots agencies all over India that address themselves to the needs of women, who are the poorest of the poor. There was her husband, Lakshmi, who for years had been head of the All-India Handicrafts Board, generating cottage industry at the village level. They were conscious daily of what it meant to be consumers; they did not wear or buy anything, if they could help it, that was not produced or sold by the poor. Then there was Ela Bhatt, founder of the Self-Employed Women's Association in Ahmedabad, which organized self-employed women into cooperatives, occupational networks, and credit unions. "Self-employed" meant street vendors, paper scavengers, kerosene vendors, home spinners, cigarette rollers—all women who had previously had nothing and no one to rely on as social and financial support in times of crisis, sickness, or indebtedness. There was the formidable and venerable Kamaladevi Chattopadhyaya, who had been one of the first women to join Gandhi on the Salt March and who was one of the founders of the modern women's movement in India. And there was Radha Bhatt, who headed a Gandhian *ashram* in the Kumaon areas of the Himalayas, a productive community of girls and women dedicated to basic education, self-sufficiency, and environmental education. In the next valley over, the environmentalist Sundarlal Bahuguna helped to launch the Chipko movement, which has effectively stopped the widespread deforestation and erosion by the lumber companies, using the only power the villagers had at their disposal—fearlessness. They embraced the trees, saying, "Let the axes fall first upon our backs."

I began to realize that the Gandhian movement in India was perhaps small, but it was active and very much alive. While some were concerned with electoral politics, most were involved with what Gandhi had called "constructive work," meaning work for real change at the village level. Like Gandhi, they were concerned with the transformation of society, not simply with replacing the names and faces in government offices, so to those who look only at what governments do they were relatively invisible. I recalled that it was Gandhi, more than any one else in the Indian freedom movement, who insisted that India's freedom could not be brought about simply by changing who was in power. Gandhi had always been critical of what he called "British rule without the British"; freedom could only come by deep-seated change within the Indian people themselves. In 1914 Gandhi wrote, "The English have not taken India, we have given it to them. They are not in India because of their strength, but because we keep them."[7] He believed that India would be free in the most important sense the moment people began to think of themselves as free and to act as free.

In reconstituting the *we*, Gandhi was ahead of his time in speaking of solidarity with the poor and oppressed. He was the advance guard of what would later be liberation theology, with its "preferential option for the poor." It is little wonder that he has been read and studied by those who have directed their lives to human liberation—Howard Thurman, Martin Luther King, Jr., Adolfo Perez Esquivel, Ernesto Cardenal, Nelson Mandela. At the Gandhi *samadhi* in Delhi, the place of Gandhi's cremation and last rites, there is an inscription known as "Gandhi's talisman" chiseled in the marble. "I will give you a talisman. Whenever you are in doubt or when the self becomes too much with you, try the following expedient: Recall the face of the poorest and the most helpless person whom you may have seen and ask yourself if the step you contemplate is going to be of any use to him."

What attracted me to Gandhi was the fact that he took seriously and personally the teachings of the Sermon on the Mount, which he thought should "revolutionize the whole of life," but which most Christians praise and do not practice: identifying with the poor, loving one's enemies, absorbing insults, and returning love. Gandhi said, "If, then, I had to face only the Sermon on the Mount and my own interpretation of it, I should not hesitate to say: 'Oh yes, I am a Christian.'. . . But I can tell you that, in my humble opinion, much of what passes as Christianity is a negation of the Sermon on the Mount."[8] Gandhi considered himself a follower of Jesus, but he did

[7] M. K. Gandhi, *Hind Swaraj*, new edition (Ahmedabad, India: Navjivan Publishing House, 1938), p. 38.

[8] M. K. Gandhi, *The Message of Jesus Christ* (Bombay: Bharatiya Vidya Bhavan, 1964), p. 24.

not respect the dogmatism he saw in much of the Christian tradition. He did not like the preachers who had stood in his native town of Rajkot pouring abuse on the Hindu gods; he did not like the arrogance of some forms of Christian mission, holding Truth tight-fistedly as if it were an exclusive possession, and a club at that. For Gandhi, Truth, or God, cannot be the exclusive possession of any one people, but is the very transcendence of ourselves that calls us into relationship with others. Gandhi also did not like the materialism he saw in Christian culture, nor the violence. And he did not think all of this was worthy of the teachings of Christ.

In re-creating the *we*, Gandhi began at the household level or with the village of one thousand people; his vision was to extend the ethics, the care, and the common sense of the household to the whole of humankind. He began with the symbols of the domestic, the immediate, the near at hand. In religion, this means that the locus of religious life is not to be sought afar, by leaving home and society to journey to the far shore, the horizon, the frontier. The proper arena for religious life is not the Himalayas or the hermitage—not out there, but right here in the interrelatedness and struggles of the household and the village, on the "frontiers of encounter." This is where the *we* must be reconstituted: in how one behaves as well as in what one believes. Gandhi's favorite Christian hymn was "Lead Kindly Light," which includes the words "Guide Thou my feet. . . . I do not ask to see . . . the distant scene. . . . One step enough for me." That last line, "one step enough for me," became something of a slogan for Gandhi's distinctive style of leadership; he saw each step of the process to be as important as the horizon toward which it was aimed, for each step of the process creates the result.

Gandhi's *we* included the poor and the oppressed. In Gandhi's world this included, among others, the indentured laborers of South Africa, the landless farmers of rural northern India, and the "untouchables," whom he called Harijans, "children of God." "It is a mystery to me how anyone can feel himself honored by the humiliation of a fellow being," he said. Gandhian thinking about the deeply rooted sense of purity and pollution that produced untouchability in Hindu India was revolutionary. He did not simply protest. There was no march on Delhi to eliminate untouchability. He did something far more radical: he cleaned the latrines himself, he volunteered in the hospital and emptied bed-pans, he took on the work of untouchables. He invited others to do the same. He publicly ate with untouchables. He adopted an untouchable girl as his own and insisted that an untouchable family become part of the Sabarmati Ashram. He spoke of himself as "touchable by birth, and untouchable by choice."

Similarly, when it came to the life-and-death issue of food and clothing, Gandhi did not speak of charity, but of the transformation of the life of the rich to identify with the basic needs of the poor. Many think of Gandhi's personal austerity, including his food and dress, as one of his idiosyncrasies. For Gandhi, however, what one eats and what one wears are the very first political decisions one makes. The "personal" is the "political." In Gandhi's view there is no point in speaking of the oppression of the poor or of economic injustice as a matter of public policy if all of us continue to support the status quo through the personal choices we make every day. He chose to eat little and simply—no more than five articles of food a day. He chose to dress simply—in the cotton *dhoti* and sandals of villagers.

His book *Hind Swaraj* ("Indian Home Rule") sets out many of the themes of Gandhi's political and economic thought. For Gandhi, home rule truly begins at home. It is not "British rule without the British." It begins the moment we set our own house in order, clean up our own latrines, spin our own cloth, and free ourselves of the oppression that is within us. When Gandhi came to leadership in the Indian National Congress in the early 1920s, it was a movement of English-educated Indians in suits and bowler hats, looking very much like their British counterparts. How could most of village India, poor as it was, participate in such a movement? They could participate only if the English-educated lawyers would give up their suits made of cloth spun in Lancashire and take up the hand spinning and hand weaving that had been destroyed by the British Raj. Gandhi did not launch a verbal or legislative campaign against the imported cotton goods that had decimated the Indian handloom industry. From the rural women of Gujarat he learned hand spinning with the simplest of spinning wheels. From 1925 on, membership dues in the Indian National Congress were to be paid not in cash, but in homespun yarn made and worn by every member. Spinning became the declaration of India's freedom as well as the evidence of the freedom movement's solidarity with the poor.

Gandhi redefined the inclusive *we* not just in theory, but in practice. The *ashram* communities he created—Phoenix Farm and Tolstoy Farm in South Africa, Sabarmati and Sevagram *ashrams* in India—were attempts to expand radically the meaning of "family" and to extend the ethics of the family to a larger community inclusive of caste, religion, and race. In the *ashram*s everyone shared domestic duties—cooking, sweeping, cleaning latrines, and emptying chamberpots. The *we* included women and men, Hindus and Muslims, Christians and Jews, *brahmin*s and untouchables. "Distinctions of caste were not observed," he wrote. "Untouchability had not only no place in Ashram, but its eradication from Hindu society was one of our principal objectives. Emancipation of women from some customary bonds was insisted upon from the first. Therefore women in the Ashram enjoy full freedom. Then again, it was an Ashram rule that persons following a particular faith should have the same feeling for followers of other faiths as for their co-religionists."[9]

Gandhi saw the *ashram* as a religious community. But for him the *ashram* was not a "retreat" from the world, as the teaching *ashram*s of ancient India had been, but rather a microcosm and crucible for a new world. Gandhi used to say that everywhere religious devotees and tillers of the soil get up early. "Four a.m. is not early," he said in his instructions to his community, "but the latest time when we must be up and doing."[10] Getting "up and doing" included a foundation of daily prayer, which began and ended each day's schedule in the *ashram.* Gandhi's daily prayer meetings, usually held in the open air, attracted hundreds of people. Since people from many religious traditions were part of the *ashram* communities, the prayer meetings included readings from the Qur'an, the Gita, and the Bible; they included Christian hymns and Sikh *bhajan*s. This tradition is still very much a part of the Gandhian way. At the headquarters of the Self-Employed Women's Association in Ahmedabad, I joined in the women's daily morning prayer, which included both Hindu and Muslim readings. At Lakshmi Ashram in the Himalayas, I was up in the half-light of a Himalayan dawn and made my way down the trail to the community room where the girls assembled for *prarthana,* daily prayers, their "morning watch." There was song as well as prayer before breakfast. The little girls discovered that I knew "Lead Kindly Light" and insisted that I sing it each day as my contribution to the service.

[9] M. K. Gandhi, *Ashram Observances in Action* (Ahmedabad, India: Navjivan Publishing House, 1955), p. 8.

[10] Ibid., p. 24.

Finally, for Gandhi the *we* had to include one's enemies and opponents. This was the basis of his nonviolence, or *ahimsa.* Gandhi was not one to avoid a nonviolent fight, but he never cast a fight in terms of the humiliation and defeat of the opponent. He saw clearly that if conflict is cast in terms of winning or losing, of *us* prevailing over *them,* then there will be no way forward toward a transformed community. Even if one wins absolutely, one still has a defeated enemy. The next round of the conflict is only postponed. In Gandhi's evolving philosophy of nonviolence, this is a crucial point. Gandhi refused to concede that the adversary—whether the opponent in a legal case, the opponent in a political battle, or the opponent in combat—would forever remain polarized as the "other." If the polarization is not broken, then what we call "winning" is still losing, for we are still left with an opponent, an enemy. The supposed triumph of the victor and the defeat of the vanquished are illusory in the village of one thousand people. The vanquished do not disappear. Violence in a village claims everyone as its victims, winners and losers alike, as the urban unrest of American cities has so vividly shown.

Breaking the cycle of violence requires recreating the *we.* Gandhi never forgot that there was a person on the other side of a given conflict. When Gandhi was imprisoned by Jan Smuts in South Africa, he made Smuts a pair of leather sandals with his own hands during his time in prison and presented them as a gift when he was released. In India, when Gandhi was about to undertake the Salt March in defiance of the tax on salt, a tax which he knew fell more heavily on the poor, he wrote a striking letter to Lord Irwin, begging him to repeal the tax, reminding the viceroy of the tremendous inequities between the British administration and the villagers it taxed.

> Take your own salary. It is over 21,000 rupees [about $7,000] per month . . . against India's average income of less than two annas [four cents] per day. Thus you are getting over five thousand times India's average income. On bended knee, I ask you to ponder over this phenomenon. I have taken a personal illustration to drive home a painful truth. I have too great a regard for you as a man to wish to hurt your feelings. I know that you do not need the salary you get. Probably the whole of your salary goes for charity. But a system that provides for such an arrangement deserves to be summarily scrapped. . . . My ambition is no less than to convert the British people through nonviolence, and make them see the wrong they have done India. I do

> not seek to harm your people. I want to serve them even as I want to serve my own. . . . [signed] Your sincere friend, M. K. Gandhi.[11]

Gandhi refused to demonize his opponent as a person, even when he was in profound disagreement with everything the opponent stood for. For him, only in the give and take of relationship would it be possible to construct a world which both could affirm.

Across the road from the Gandhi *samadhi* in New Delhi is a museum containing an assortment of exhibits. There is a photograph of his cremation, the day the crowd roared, "*Gandhi amar ho gaye*"—"Gandhi has become immortal!" There is a photograph of his niece Manu, who, like others, called this immortal Gandhi "Bapu," meaning not "father," but the familiar, "daddy." Like many, she found his qualities strikingly maternal and she titled her book *Bapu, My Mother.* In addition to the photographs, there are exhibits in glass cases: "*He Ram.* These Bloodstained Clothes were worn by Bapu-ji on his Last Day, 30-1-1948," "One of the Three Fatal Bullets that took away Bapu-ji from us." In one case the items Gandhi owned at the time of his death are collected: his glasses, his spare *dhoti* and shawl, his sandals, a pocket watch, a pincushion, and a pen. In viewing this exhibit, I was not at all amused by the old joke about how much money it took to keep Gandhi in poverty. There was a leanness here that was truly sacred. It is this same leanness and economy that was truly universal and has spoken to people widely separated in culture, language, and religion.

Above the door of the room of exhibits is a reminder of the pluralism that Gandhi so energetically fostered: "I do not want my house to be walled in on all sides and my windows to be shut. I want the cultures of all lands to be blown about my house as freely as possible. Mine is not the religion of the prison house." The tragedy of India's partition and the ongoing communal competition and violence in India do not diminish the credibility of Gandhi's vision, but rather make the need for such a wider sense of *we* all the more plain.

Interrelated Traditions and Lives

Were I asked to describe the religious situation of the world today, in the late twentieth century, it would be virtually impossible to do so by focusing on each tradition as a separate entity, for the histories of

[11] Quoted in Louis Fischer, *The Life of Mahatma Gandhi* (New York: Harper and Brothers Collier Books, 1950), pp. 270–71.

all of the religious traditions are intertwined despite the fact that they are often treated as separate chapters in books on "world religions." Korean Christians both distance themselves from and are shaped by the shamanistic and Buddhist traditions of Korea. In Japan, Christians struggle with how to venerate ancestors, a matter of such critical importance that the Roman Catholic Church has prepared guidelines on the veneration of ancestors for Japanese Catholics. Hindus in India are undergoing a new period of self-definition in relation to Muslims and Sikhs. Muslims in North America are developing a new form of religiousness shaped by the denominational structure so typical of American Protestant, Catholic, and Jewish religious life. Native American people struggle with the appropriation of Native American symbols, rituals, and language in the context of Christian churches and in the context of the New Age movement. Buddhism is developing distinctive forms and lineages in North America, with many of its teachers women and many Jewish in origin. The rivers of our religious traditions roll on. Our religions are not complete, not finished, not able to pass on a finished "product" to the next generation. Our traditions are not isolated, but interrelated and interdependent. Both the interreligious dialogue and the interreligious conflict of the world today make us keenly aware of our constant and close interaction.

Individually we participate in one another's history as well. Gandhi is again a good example. He was very much influenced by his sojourn as a law student in England, where he read the Bible from cover to cover and was especially attracted to the Gospels, where he first read the *Bhagavad Gita* in the English translation by Edwin Arnold. In England he first met Christians who impressed him far more than the missionaries who had stood on the street corner in his native Rajkot, in Gujarat, insulting the Hindu tradition. Some Christians tried to convert him, impressed by Gandhi's eagerness to learn as much as he could about Christianity. He was honest. He could appreciate the centrality of Jesus as the distinctive testimony of Christians, but not as an objective fact that would deny his own experience as a Hindu. And yet to many Christians who met him, Gandhi as a Hindu revealed something of the true message of Christ. As the missionary E. Stanley Jones put it, "Never in human history has so much light been shed on the Cross, as has been through this one man, and that man not even called a Christian."[12]

[12] E. Stanley Jones, *Mahatma Gandhi: An Interpretation*, quoted in I. Jesudasan, *A Gandhian Theology of Liberation* (Maryknoll, N.Y.: Orbis Books, 1984), p. 133.

Reciprocally, African-American church delegates Howard and Sue Thurman and Edward Carroll visited Gandhi in India in 1935 and discussed Gandhi's use of direct nonviolent action. They brought what they learned of Gandhian campaigns like the Salt March back to the African-American church community in the United States. In 1936, Benjamin E. Mays, later to be a mentor of Martin Luther King, Jr., visited with Gandhi in India. While King's acquaintance with Gandhi is usually traced to a lecture he heard in 1950 by Mordecai Johnson, then president of Howard University, it is clear that the African-American community's acquaintance with Gandhi and their knowledge of the potential power of nonviolence was already decades old by that time.[13] As King put it at the time of the Montgomery bus boycott, "Christ furnished the spirit and the motivation, while Gandhi furnished the method."[14] Just as the Christian tradition participated in the development of Gandhi's ideas, so did Gandhi's Hindu tradition participate in the formation of King's style of leadership and in the civil rights movement as a whole.

The process of interparticipation continues in countless ways. There are many religious exchanges, like the intermonastic exchanges of today—Zen teachers teaching Catholic monks and Catholic monks leading sessions in Zen monasteries. There are student exchanges: a twenty-year-old Jewish woman lives with a Muslim family in Banaras; a Nigerian Muslim law student studies at Harvard Law School. There are scholarly exchanges and academic studies that begin to reshape religious understanding on both sides. When I first met Yves Raguin, who had lived in Taiwan since 1934, he told me, "Chinese Buddhism and Christianity have met in me. The Gospel cannot help but take on new dimensions as it encounters each culture. In teaching Christianity and Buddhism to students in Chinese, I know that when I take a Chinese word to express what we mean by 'God' it will still carry the overtones and undertones of its own cultural heritage and long history." In my own case, there is no doubt that by writing an interpretive study of the city of Banaras I have participated as a Christian, in a small way, in the history of the Hindu tradition. It is also true that my Hindu

[13] Sudarshan Kapur, *Raising Up a Prophet* (Boston: Beacon Press, 1992). Kapur documents the coverage of Gandhi in the African-American press from the 1920s on.

[14] Martin Luther King, Jr., *Stride Toward Freedom* (New York: Harper and Brothers, 1958), p. 85.

friends and teachers have participated in the history of the Christian tradition through their influence on me and my thinking. The point is not difficult to grasp, but very important: our religious traditions already intersect and interpenetrate through the lives of countless men and women.[15] As the Reverend Murray Rogers so clearly put it, speaking of his experience with people of other faiths in Hong Kong, Jerusalem, and North India, "the 'I' and 'they' have almost disappeared, and in their place it is 'we.'"[16]

The Interreligious Movement: Going It Together

Clearly interdependence is a fact of our global life. Even so, the world is not yet interrelated in the sense of actively and intentionally creating the international, intercultural, and interreligious relationships that will sustain a world in which we depend upon one another as much as we do. We share our communities and our world with men and women who worship in various ways, who base their judgments on differing authorities, who recognize differing revelations, who speak of God in strikingly different ways or do not speak of God at all. Our task is to learn to collaborate with one another on issues that none of us can solve alone.[17] The challenge could not have been stated more clearly than it was by the Jewish philosopher Abraham Joshua Heschel: "In the world of economics, science, and technology, cooperation exists and continues to grow. Even political states, though different in culture and competing with one another, maintain diplomatic relations and strive for coexistence. Only religions are not on speaking terms."[18]

At the closing session of the World's Parliament of Religions in 1893, the suggestion was made by one of the Unitarian conveners that the representatives of the world's traditions meet again in 1900 "on the banks of the Ganges in the ancient city of Benares."[19] But following

[15] See W. C. Smith, "Participation: The Changing Christian Role in Other Cultures," in *Religious Diversity*, pp. 118-37.

[16] Murray Rogers, "On the Pilgrim Path," in *Spirituality in Interfaith Dialogue*, p. 15.

[17] See *The Faith of Other Men*, p. 92.

[18] Abraham Joshua Heschel, "No Religion is an Island," in Harold Kasimow and Byron L. Sherwin, eds., *No Religion is an Island: Abraham Joshua Heschel and InterreligiousDialogue* (Maryknoll, N.Y.: Orbis Books, 1991), p. 11.

[19] Rev. Jenkin Lloyd Jones, quoted in Marcus Braybrooke, *Pilgrimage of Hope: One Hundred Years of Global Interfaith Dialogue* (London: SCM Press, 1992), p. 25. I am

the Parliament, at the turn of the century, the momentum to sustain a movement toward dialogue had not yet gathered. The whole idea of intentionally bringing people of various religious traditions together for colloquy was truly something new under the sun. Even Akbar, the broad-minded sixteenth-century Indian Mughal emperor who had convened men of various faiths for discussion in his private audience hall, had used the influence of his court to create a syncretistic new religion, the Din-i-Ilahi, rather than simply to foster a climate of mutual understanding through dialogue. The envisioned Banaras meeting to follow up on the Parliament did not take place. There was instead a meeting in Boston in 1900 of the International Council of Unitarian and Other Liberal Religious Thinkers and Workers. It came to include a few Muslims, Jews, Catholics, and reformist Hindu Brahmo Samajis, and in subsequent years its international congresses addressed questions such as justice for women and the expansion of narrow patriotism to a wider human loyalty. Two world wars in the twentieth century impeded the progress of organized interreligious efforts such as this one and underlined their importance.

Interreligious dialogue was certainly not on the agenda of the churches during the first half of the twentieth century. The prevailing energy was for mission, not for dialogue. The real breakthrough came in the 1960s. At the Second Vatican Council, the Roman Catholic Church focused attention on interreligious relations, published *Nostra Aetate*, and established the Secretariat on Non-Christians, now called the Pontifical Council for Interreligious Dialogue. In 1968, the General Assembly of the World Council of Churches, meeting in Uppsala, for the first time addressed the question of other faiths in a section called "Seeking Community: The Common Search of People of Various Faiths, Cultures, and Ideologies."

In 1970, the Central Committee of the WCC, meeting at Addis Ababa, declared interreligious dialogue to be "the common pilgrimage of the churches" and the first major multilateral dialogue meeting took place at Ajaltoun in Lebanon. Since then, the WCC Sub-unit on Dialogue, now the Office on Interreligious Relations, has worked at building relations with people of other faiths and at addressing the fears and hesitancies of the member churches. The WCC's *Guidelines*

indebted to the comprehensive work of Marcus Braybrooke on the early history of the various interreligious movements.

on Dialogue provides encouragement for churches to enter into active dialogue with neighbors of other faiths. *Ecumenical Considerations on Jewish-Christian Dialogue* and *Ecumenical Considerations on Christian-Muslim Relations* articulate the special histories and sensitivities that will shape relations with Jews and Muslims respectively. The study guide called *My Neighbor's Faith and Mine*, published now in fourteen languages and in use all over the world, aims at enabling Christians to think afresh about the theological implications of their relations with neighbors of other faiths. While the study guide has raised controversy and has even been "banned" by one national church council, its publication, according to one observer, "would have been unthinkable in the hallowed halls of the Christian *oikoumene* twenty years ago."[20]

Today interreligious dialogue is on the agenda not only of the churches, but also of Jewish, Muslim, Hindu, and Buddhist organizations. The International Jewish Committee on Interreligious Consultation (IJCIC) brings representatives from a variety of Jewish organizations into a single instrument for interfaith relations. The World Muslim League, based in Riyadh, Saudi Arabia, has an office for interfaith relations and its leader has exchanged visits with the National Council of Churches in the United States. The World Buddhist Fellowship, based in Thailand, and the U.S.–based International Network of Engaged Buddhists bring the energy of Buddhists to bear on global issues. There is now what one interfaith consultation called "a new momentum in all faiths to strengthen and give clearer voice to those elements in their traditions which drive toward recognizing our need for one another."[21] At that meeting, which took place in Mauritius under the auspices of the World Council of Churches, Christians, Jews, Muslims and Buddhists, Hindus, Native Americans, and African traditionalists affirmed together, "The world is one of inescapable interdependence in all realms. The threat to human life and to the whole earth urges upon all a growing recognition that no one faith can go it alone."[22]

There is no question that religious traditions have been part of the problem as one surveys the divisions and conflicts of the present world;

[20] Samartha, *One Christ—Many Religions*, p. 3.

[21] *The Meaning of Life: A Multifaith Consultation* (Geneva: World Council of Churches, 1983), pp. 2-3.

[22] Ibid.

and there is no question that religious traditions will also have to be part of the solution. The very concerns to which people of the various religious traditions address themselves—militarism and violence, the degradation of the environment, the violation of human rights, the transnational networks of drugs and prostitution, the need for a new international economic order—are increasingly seen to be concerns that cannot be addressed in a meaningful way, let alone solved, by any one people or any one nation alone. These are issues that demand the creation of new ways of thinking, new blueprints for working together, and new styles of international leadership. On a very practical level, they require the creation of a workable worldwide infrastructure of relationships.

Given that we cannot go it alone, the question of how to "go it together" is both critical and urgent. There are now many organizational expressions of a growing interreligious movement—global, regional, and local. The oldest of the international interreligious organizations is the International Association for Religious Freedom (IARF), which began with that congress of "religious liberals" in Boston in 1900. In Britain, the World Congress of Faiths was launched in 1936 to bring people of various religions together and make dialogue "a concern for the many rather than a dream of a few." The Temple of Understanding, based in New York since the mid-1960s, has sponsored a series of "spiritual summit conferences" and has taken a further step to bring religious leaders together with government and parliamentary leaders under the auspices of the Global Forum of Spiritual and Parliamentary Leaders for Human Survival. The World Conference on Religion and Peace (WCRP), formed in 1968, has worked explicitly on peace and disarmament issues as a non-governmental organization of the United Nations. It has regional chapters throughout the world and it construes its commitment to peace widely, focusing energy on such issues as the Vietnamese "boat people," the Cambodian refugees, and the UN Convention on the Rights of the Child.

Like many worldwide movements, the interreligious movement has force and energy, but no single center. At the local level, in the United States there has been a notable rise of interreligious councils as the religious landscape of cities and towns becomes more diverse. When the construction of the Buddhist Hsi Lai Temple in Hacienda Heights, California, was stalled in five years of zoning battles, it was the Interreligious Council of Southern California that came to the support of the Chinese Buddhist community. In Houston, when a mosque was firebombed in the wake of an airline hijacking in the Middle East in 1985, the association called the Houston Metropolitan Ministries was challenged to become a broader interfaith forum actively engaged with the Islamic Society of Greater Houston. In 1988, the Buddhist community of Boulder, Colorado, submitted an application to join the local Council of Churches and a serious discussion about the new religious landscape of Boulder ensued. All over the United States local councils of churches have become councils of churches and synagogues, and are now wrestling with what it means to become interreligious councils. In October of 1988, people representing various religious traditions and local interreligious councils came together in Wichita, Kansas, to create the North American Interfaith Network (NAIN) in order to coordinate and facilitate an interfaith movement that is already growing.

Interfaith services of prayer are on the rise, especially at times of community or international crisis. During the war in the Persian Gulf, for example, there was a burst of local bridge building as many Jews and Christians discovered for the first time the mosques in their own cities. There were many interfaith prayer services, including one at the Hsi Lai Temple in Hacienda Heights where people of all faiths gathered in the great hall dominated by Amida Buddha. For the most part such services follow a pattern of sequential readings or prayer, each participant contributing in the style and distinctive vocabulary of his or her own tradition. The most ambitious of such symbolic events was the Assisi World Day of Prayer called by Pope John Paul II in 1986, which brought together religious leaders from every tradition, including the elders and spiritual leaders of native peoples of the Americas and Africa. Even in the planning stages, the great public visibility of the Assisi event began to elicit a backlash. The Vatican received a number of critical responses from Christians who insisted that "praying together" went too far. The Vatican then clarified its intent by issuing a carefully worded statement that the religious leaders of various traditions would be coming together to pray, they would not be coming to pray together. To underline this nuance, the event was organized so that after an initial convocation the Buddhists, Hindus, Muslims, Christians, etc., went their separate ways to separate locations for their prayers and meditations.

The question of whether we all can pray together, whether we can only be together while we pray separately, or whether there should be any interfaith worship at all is one that is boiling on the front burner of many interreligious councils. In Britain, it has been raised by the Inter-Faith Consultative Group of the Church of England in a recent publication entitled *Multi-Faith Worship?* Prayer quite aside, even the ritual implications of interfaith encounters raise questions. The Inter-Faith Consultative Group poses a number of cases. For example:

> The Sikhs have opened a community welfare centre next to their gurudwara, with the encouragement of some local clergy. Wanting to build on this link, they decide to invite the Bishop to visit the gurudwara at *Baisakhi,* the next major festival. This is the first time the Sikhs have issued such an invitation to a local church leader. *How can the Bishop discover what will be expected of him in the temple? He will have to cover his head and remove his shoes, but will he acknowledge the presence of the Sikh scriptures with a reverent bow, and if so, will he be endorsing their validity?*

Such situations and questions have unleashed a storm of controversy in England and have been debated in newspaper columns and radio programs. Should the imam speak in the Remembrance Day services for those who lost their lives in war? Should there be a commonly agreed upon order of service or should it be a Christian service in which Muslims and Hindus participate as guests? May the new Sikh mayor have a service in the parish church marking his first year of office? In the United States such matters have not become public issues. That time may be coming, however. On state occasions such as the inauguration of a president, Protestant, Catholic, and Jewish clergy have offered invocations, prayers, and benedictions. Given the growing number of Muslims in the United States, soon to be equal to the number of Jews, one can well anticipate that before long a Muslim imam will be asked to participate in such a state event, just as imams have already participated in opening daily sessions of the U.S. Congress and various state legislatures. These shifts in the public iconic expression of American religious pluralism will make visible a reality for which many Christian Americans are as yet unprepared.

Both the global village and the urban cosmopolis make clear that interreligious dialogue can no longer be regarded as the arcane speculative interest of a few liberal thinkers in the various religious traditions. It is at the very heart of a workable society. Dialogue begins with the questions that arise from the common context of our lives together. Education, good government, health, families, AIDS, violence, and the response to violence—these are the subjects of interreligious dialogue. What about humanity's relation to nature? What is an ethical issue? What is the meaning of justice? What criteria should we bring to the making of just decisions? These are the questions of interreligious dialogue. The nascent interreligious movement will need to gain strength and visibility in the coming years in order to become part of the essential infrastructure of an interdependent world. And it will need to deepen and mature far beyond general expressions of fellowship and common vision.

Keeping One Another's Image

Among the implications of religious interdependence is that we each depend upon the "other" to know us as we would like to be known. We are therefore the keepers of one another's image. In the village of a thousand people, there is no way we can avoid facing up to the need for basic education about our neighbors. Yet as most of us look down the roster of religious communities in this village, we note how little, even now, we understand one another. What are the five pillars of Islam and what do they mean to a Muslim? Who was the Buddha—a man or a god? What does it mean for the Jewish people to speak of being "chosen"? Why do Christians speak of eating the body and drinking the blood of Christ? We can scarcely address the problems that beset the world without first tackling the basic ignorance, the fear, and the misunderstanding that separate us from one another.

Remember the claim of John Henry Barrows that the Parliament of Religions would be "the first school of comparative religions, wherein devout men of all faiths may speak for themselves without hindrance, without criticism, and without compromise, and tell what they believe and why they believe it."[23] That event in 1893 did indeed give impetus to the academic study of religion in American colleges and universities, but the public schools in the United States still lag far behind in being able to teach basic world religions as part of the social studies and history curriculum; other countries do better and do worse, but nowhere is our basic religious knowledge up to the level of our basic knowledge of mathematics or biology. Gandhi called the sympathetic study of the world's religions a "sacred duty": "I hold that it is the duty of every cultured man or woman to read sympathetically the scriptures of the world. If we are to respect others' religions as we

[23] Barrows, *The World's Parliament of Religions*, vol. I, pp. 72-79.

would have them to respect our own, a friendly study of the world's religions is a sacred duty."[24]

The knowledge of one another's traditions is not simply to inform our curiosity about the beliefs or customs of our neighbors. People of every religious tradition depend upon one another to interpret one another fairly and accurately. We are the keepers of one another's image. This is one of the most critical aspects of our interdependence and it is a sacred trust. We all depend upon one another not to tell lies, not to spread hatred, not to purvey a sensational or distorted image of one another. We all depend upon one another to correct those lies and distortions when they are made. There is no community that can do this entirely for itself. There is no amount of public vigilance and no amount of propaganda that can enable Christians, Muslims, or Buddhists to portray themselves as they would like to be understood.

In 1966, the Jewish philosopher Abraham Joshua Heschel delivered an address entitled "No Religion is an Island," in which he outlined the implications of our religious interdependence: "The religions of the world are no more self-sufficient, no more independent, no more isolated than individuals or nations. Energies, experiences, and ideas that come to life outside the boundaries of a particular religion or all religions continue to challenge and to affect every religion. Horizons are wider, dangers are greater. . . . No religion is an island. We are all involved with one another. Spiritual betrayal on the part of one of us affects the faith of all of us."[25] Spiritual betrayal may take many forms, but perhaps the most common is simply an inattention to hurt and defamation when it affects the image and well-being of another community. Such common daily betrayals have enabled the purveyors of hatred to ignite the fires of the pogrom, "ethnic cleansing," and the Holocaust.

Whether we like it or not, all of us bear witness to each other in an interdependent world. For those of us in the traditions of Moses, the commandment not to bear false witness against our neighbors is at stake every time we speak of our neighbors. We bear false witness against our neighbors because we do not know them. Or we bear false witness because we think it puts us in a better light to do so. We are tempted to compare the most refined aspects of our own tradition with the most crude aspects of the other. But the problem is that our

[24] M. K. Gandhi, *Young India,* 2 September 1926.

[25] Heschel, "No Religion is an Island," p. 6.

testimonies about one another are reciprocal. If Muslims are dependent upon Christians for a faithful image of their tradition, Christians are also dependent upon Muslims for the kind of image of Christianity that is presented in Muslim schools and mosque-based education programs.

Not only are we all keepers of one another's image, we are also guardians of one another's rights. In one critical sense the village of a thousand people is misleading. No village is quite like it. No religious tradition is a majority everywhere, and no tradition a minority everywhere. We are all minorities somewhere, with the vulnerabilities and defensiveness that minority status might entail. And we are majorities somewhere, with the insensitivities, the presumption, and the power that goes with it. There are Muslim minorities in Europe and North America concerned about the rights of Muslims in public schools, city councils, and penal institutions; there are Christian minorities in the Sudan, Bangladesh, and Pakistan concerned about the consequences for them if the governments establish Islamic *sharia* as the normative law of the land. There are Hindu minorities in Fiji and Malaysia, Buddhist minorities in Russia and France. Human rights and religious liberty cannot be guarded in one place and disregarded in another.

An important step in recognizing this kind of interdependence is being able to speak out when a religious tradition not one's own has been attacked or distorted. Taking offense when one's own rights have been attacked is expected. Groups like the Anti-Defamation League of the B'nai B'rith are formed explicitly to guard the well-being of the community in the public arena. But what is the context in which people and communities speak out for the rights of peoples of other faiths when there is a violation or offense? Why should it be the burden of Jews alone to speak out if a Roman Catholic convent is built right on the border of Auschwitz or if the Nation of Islam publishes an accusatory tract on Jewish complicity in black oppression? Why should Muslims have to be the first to speak out if a mosque is threatened or attacked with arson or if a newspaper publishes an article portraying Muslims as fanatical? Why should we think it primarily the Hindu community that is hurt if a temple is desecrated or its divine images broken? Being able to feel the hurt of one another and to speak out on behalf of one another is one of the great spiritual challenges of an interdependent world.

At a 1987 WCC consultation in New Delhi on "Religious Identity in a Multireligious Society," people of three religious traditions spoke of the urgent need for this kind of mutual guardianship in the South Asian situation. It goes without saying that communities will try to protect their own civil, religious, and human rights. On this they agreed. But Sri Lankan theologian Wesley Ariarajah asks, "How can we have solidarity *across* religious barriers? It is sad that there has been no Buddhist group fighting for the rights of Tamils in Sri Lanka, and no Tamils speaking out for the Sinhalese." Veena Das, a Hindu professor at Delhi University, made a similar point. "In the riots of November 1984, after Mrs. Gandhi's assassination, the violence and killing unleashed upon Sikhs was not simply an offense to the Sikhs, but an offense to us all." Mohinder Singh, a Sikh, said it too: "When we look in the paper and see, as we do daily, that 20 or 25 people were killed today in violence in the Punjab, we must not say that they were Sikhs or they were Hindus. We must not simply scan the list of victims and breathe a sigh of relief that our relatives or friends are not among them. All of these victims of violence are our relatives, our kin."[26]

Being keepers of one another's image and guardians of one another's rights are not roles that we as religious communities can either accept or reject. They are assigned by the very nature of our world and we perform them, either well or badly, either with neglect or vigilance.

Criteria and Criticism

Any real engagement with people of another faith will bring into play our deepest criteria of truth and value. If people of different traditions engage energetically in dialogue, what criteria are there, finally, for truth? The pluralist is often accused of being unable to answer that question, but that is precisely the point. It is a question without an a priori universal answer. Whatever answer there might be must emerge from the very process of dialogue that the askers of the question usually want to challenge. People of every religious tradition and people of none have irreducible criteria which they employ to navigate the waters of decision making, and deep values that provide a rudder and sense of direction. In each tradition these are articulated in different ways, and they may indeed be different values. That is not the real problem. Deepest values do not have to be modified until they all

[26] Kenneth Cracknell, ed., *Religious Identities in a Multi-Faith World.* Report of a multi-faith dialogue organized by the dialogue subunit of the WCC, New Delhi, November 1987 (Geneva: WCC, 1988). The citations are from the conference discussion.

converge; all the bumps in the road do not have to be flattened. What we must be able to do, however, is to recognize and clearly articulate our deep guiding values, our criteria, and place them in clear, critical conversation with others. At its deepest level, the dialogue that will undergird a pluralist society is the encounter of commitments as well as the encounter of criteria.

Gandhi had one clear guiding value, one foundational criterion—*ahimsa*, or nonviolence. It was not a doctrine or a belief; it was not something he held to because he felt it was divinely revealed. It was the irreducible basis of his life, founded on his deepest conviction that Truth is both within and beyond all religious traditions and all human knowing. One can hold it openly and invite the allegiance of others, even unto death, but one cannot hold it tight-fistedly and kill in its name.

There was no wishy-washy relativism in Gandhi, but a very clear criterion for discerning Truth as best he could and acting accordingly. Not everyone would agree with Gandhi. What about Auschwitz and Bergen Belsen? What about apartheid, racism, and the systemic violence that it perpetrates? What about the power of sixty to control the wealth of the village of one thousand? Will the criterion of *ahimsa* prove adequate as we grapple together with any of these issues? We need to ask these questions and struggle together to answer them. Others bring their own irreducible criteria. The plumb line of justice from the Hebrew prophets. The criterion of love from the Gospels. The twin criteria of compassion and wisdom from the Buddha's teachings. We cannot begin by insisting upon common criteria. And yet we cannot avoid serious dialogue about the issues of race, oppression, injustice, and violence simply because we do not have common criteria. If foundational criteria for a common ethic emerge, it will be because people of all religious traditions have risked this encounter.

I remember a moment of dawning consciousness at a week-long interreligious meeting of women activists on "Women, Religion, and Social Change" held at Harvard in June of 1983. There were Muslim, Christian, and Jewish women, Hindus, Buddhists, and Native Americans. During one long day, women from South Africa, Central America, and the Middle East spoke of the issue of justice in their own contexts. The two women from Japan seemed more and more frustrated with the discussion and were whispering to one another. Finally one of them raised her hand. "What really do you mean by 'justice'? Why does everything come back again to 'justice'?" I was dumbfounded. What do you mean, What do we mean by 'justice'? I and most of the women there presupposed the importance of justice as a basic criterion of value. "How do you say 'justice' in Japanese?" I asked, as if that were a response. They conferred and said there was no such term. I remember my feeling, somewhere between disbelief and disapproval. No "justice" in Japanese? I said, "But if you had to tell your families at home what we have been talking about—the racism and violence in South Africa, for example, and the need for 'justice,' or fairness, what would you say? What would right relations be called?" They conferred again and said, "The word in Japanese would be something like what you mean by 'harmony.'" That was the beginning of a very revealing discussion. Is justice harmony? Is harmony justice? What do we mean by these words? What might the Japanese mean? What if justice produces no harmony? And what if harmony produces no justice? Our very criteria of value are at stake here.

Criticism is, so far, terra incognita on the map of interreligious dialogue. And yet the way forward on the most difficult issues in the village of one thousand people will not be found simply by settling for what we can all agree upon. A sense of ethics must be won through the difficult process of dialogue, built from ongoing relationship. Both within and between religious communities, criticism must finally be safe and accepted if there is to be relationship and if knowledge of one another is to be more than superficial. It is well known that absolutism cannot abide criticism, which is one reason that absolutists and exclusivists will not place themselves in the interchange of dialogue. But if even the pluralists and inclusivists within each tradition do not welcome criticism in dialogue, then the dialogue becomes merely another form of dogmatism. Dialogue is not a debate, but a search for a wider understanding of Truth.

Self-criticism within any religious tradition is sensitive and often difficult. Absolutism and fanaticism fan the flames of these sensitivities. Gandhi once defined communalism as the nurturing of a sense of concern and loyalty that stops short at the borders of one's own community. The term *communalism* is used mostly in India, but the phenomenon of religious chauvinism it names is readily visible throughout the world today. The communalist consciousness does not welcome criticism from within, and the linking of communalism to violence makes internal criticism all the more dangerous. Sikhs who have opposed Sikh extremism or communalism have been killed by other Sikhs, just as Gandhi, who opposed Hindu communalism, was killed by another Hindu. Communalism flourishes only by effectively halting self-criticism. Extremists often gain power not by intimidation of the people of other communities, but by the intimidation and silencing of the moderate voices within their own communities.

It is a challenge to every community of faith to benefit from the dynamic of internal self-criticism. As a historian of religion, I think it is safe to say that there is no religious tradition in which there is only one view and one voice. One of the reasons that interreligious dialogue among women has been so successful is that women know that they do not speak in the name of some invisible authority or magisterium. Women are quite aware that as women they do not speak with the imprimatur of "the tradition."[27] Meeting at the boundaries comes naturally for those who have long felt marginalized. And in some traditions today those who are working toward a truly pluralist society are among the marginalized. As one of the participants in a dialogue meeting in New Delhi put it, "It is easier for me to talk of interreligious dialogue outside the community than to speak of honest dialogue within the community." Many have indeed found a strong sense of *we* that crosses religious lines and engages a sense of common purpose that is sometimes even stronger than the sense of the *we* within their own religious community.

Beyond this difficult question of intra-community dialogue and self-criticism there is the further question of the critique of one another's traditions. Having come to understand the caste system, at least as best I can, may I express my critique of it? Can I really understand the Jewish critique that Christian anti-Semitism is rooted right in the Gospels? Sometimes even if we can accept self-criticism we cannot abide the criticism of another. The history of conflict and of stereotype is often too painful. But the question is nonetheless legitimate. Is there also a role in dialogue for the criticism of one another? Or are we simply too thin-skinned to speak words of mutual criticism across the sensitive lines of religious traditions? Can we call another to accountability, at

[27] See Diana L. Eck and Devaki Jain, eds., *Speaking of Faith: Global Perspectives on Women, Religion, and Social Change* (Philadelphia: New Society, 1985) for the proceedings of such a women's dialogue at Harvard; the Women in Interfaith Dialogue meeting called by the World Council of Churches in Toronto (1988) was made into a series of eight hour-long television programs, called *Faithful Women*, by the National Film Board of Canada.

least in terms of that person's own criteria of value? Can we challenge one another's criteria? Can we say no harmony without justice? Can we say no justice without harmony?

Arun Shourie is an Indian journalist whose book *Religion in Politics* reflects on the complexities of this issue in the recent history of communal conflict in India. In a chapter entitled "On Taking Offence," he documents the readiness to take offense and the slowness to forget it in contemporary India: "How very often it is that when someone of our faith criticizes some aspect of our religion, the criticism seems to us to be perfectly in order, even scholarly, but how the identical criticism, if it has been made by someone who happens to have been born into a different religion, sends us up the wall. We must grow up. We must discard this defensive militancy."[28] Criticism is difficult, however, if people do not have the ongoing responsibility and opportunity for relationship and reparation that makes criticism a form of growth and not a form of violence. If interreligious dialogue is to move beyond occasional meetings and congresses to become what Wesley Ariarajah calls "a culture of dialogue," it must create a context of ongoing relatedness and trust in which self-criticism and mutual criticism are acceptable and valuable parts of the interreligious exchange.

Mutual criticism and self-criticism also involve apology, reparation, what Jews call *tikkun olam*, "the mending of the world." Forgetting and leaving it behind will not do. There must be some mending. In 1987, the Christian bishops and church officials of the Pacific Northwest wrote a remarkable joint letter that I wish the prophet Seattle himself could have seen. It is addressed "To the Tribal Councils and Traditional Spiritual Leaders of the Indian and Eskimo Peoples of the Pacific Northwest." It is an example of one kind of mending:

> Dear Brothers and Sisters,
> This is a formal apology on behalf of our churches for their long-standing participation in the destruction of traditional Native American spiritual practices. We call upon our people for recognition and respect for your traditional ways of life and for protection of your sacred places and ceremonial objects. We have frequently been unconscious and insensitive and have not come to your aid when you have been victimized by unjust Federal policies and practices.

[28] Arun Shourie, *Religion in Politics* (New Delhi: Roli Books International, 1987), p. 21.

> In many other circumstances we reflected the rampant racism and prejudice of the dominant culture with which we too willingly identified. During the 200th Anniversary year of the United States Constitution we, as leaders of our churches in the Pacific Northwest, extend our apology. We ask your forgiveness and blessing. . . . We offer our commitment to support you in the righting of previous wrongs: To protect your peoples' efforts to enhance native spiritual teachings; to encourage the members of our churches to stand in solidarity with you on these important religious issues; to provide advocacy and mediation, when appropriate, for ongoing negotiations with State agencies and Federal officials regarding these matters. . . . May the God of Abraham and Sarah, and the Spirit who lives in both the cedar and the Salmon People be honored and celebrated.[29]

The speech of dialogue must come to include not only words of faith and witness, but words of self-criticism and apology, and words of forgiveness and mutuality. One of the things I have always liked about Gandhi was his criticism of Christianity. It no doubt annoyed many Christians in his day and others might have thought it in bad taste. Though I would like to respond to his critique, I see his willingness to offer it as a gesture of truthful love. Essentially, he criticized Christianity not by his own yardstick, but by using the very criteria of love and service that he saw in Jesus. There was nothing self-serving or angry about it. Just honest. Gandhi pointed out the inconsistencies between Jesus' concern for the poor and the neglect of the poor in Christian countries, between Jesus' nonviolence and the aggression of Christian countries. Gandhi did not reserve his critique for Christianity alone; he was equally hard on the rigidity of the caste system, and of the empty ritualism and excessive concern for ritual purity in the Hindu tradition.

Gandhi was clearly a man who could criticize and still love. He was also critical of himself, which is no doubt why one of his foremost interpreters, Erik Erikson, was able to step out of his scholarly role right in the middle of his book *Gandhi's Truth* to do one of the most unconventional things a biographer has ever done—write a critical letter to his subject. Erikson had to get some things off his chest before he could leave Gandhi's formative years in South Africa and follow

[29] "A Public Declaration to the Tribal Councils and Traditional Spiritual Leaders of the Indian and Eskimo Peoples of the Pacific Northwest," *The NARF Legal Review*, Winter 1988.

him into his prophetic and even saintly years in India. Erikson wanted to see more of a search for *inner* truth in Gandhi, more awareness of the ambivalence of love and anger. He was upset by Gandhi's dissembling over his treatment of his wife, Kasturba, as he opened up his family and home in South Africa to a motley community of strangers. Gandhi had forced Kasturba to help with emptying the chamberpots. He had shown her the door when she revolted at his new open-house universalism. Erikson, the psychoanalyst, writes, "Non-violence, inward and outward, can become a true force only where ethics replaces moralism. And ethics, to me, is marked by an insightful assent to human values, whereas moralism is blind obedience; and ethics is transmitted with informed persuasion, rather than enforced with absolute interdicts. Whether the increasing multitudes of men can ever develop and transmit such an ethical attitude I do not know; but I do know that we are committed to it, and that the young are waiting for our support in attempting it."[30]

Imagining Communities

Benedict Anderson, in *Imagined Communities*, investigates the process through which nations imagine themselves and imagine others. Indeed it is through this imaginative process that nations come into being. Imagination is key, for we must take note that "the members of even the smallest nation will never know most of their fellow-members, meet them, or even hear of them, yet in the minds of each lives the image of their communion."[31] The images by which we imagine ourselves to be American, Estonian, Czech, or Chinese are very powerful. America was the "melting pot," China was the "Middle Kingdom." These imagined communities can be invested with a great deal of content for a time, and they can also disintegrate, as is clear now in the 1990s, when we are reconfiguring the world without the Soviet Union and all it was imagined to be.

Thinking about "imagined communities" in the context of our interdependent world raises many fascinating and important questions. It is clear that the most powerful mapping of the world and its boundaries is done not by armies, but by the power of the imagination which

[30] Erik Erikson, *Gandhi's Truth* (New York: W.W. Norton, 1969), p. 251.

[31] Benedict Anderson, *Imagined Communities* (London: Verso, 1983), p. 6.

creates and bears for us a sense of *we*—national, religious, cultural, multicultural. As imagined communities, religious traditions are more ancient and more tenacious than modern nation-states. Hindus and Jews in different ways link their imagined communities to a powerful sense of land. Hindus also posit the image of a four-petaled world lotus, with India being the southern petal. Muslims have a strong sense of center, spiritual but not "ecclesiastical," anchoring a worldwide community of faith. In a very different way, the Catholic Church has a strong sense of center, so much so that "Rome" and "the Vatican" convey a whole ecclesial order and authority. The Buddhist tradition is highly de-centered, with its imagined communities more ethnic than universal. The Oglala of the Great Plains think of themselves as one people among the "Seven Fireplaces" of the Sioux. The Aboriginals of Australia link their imagined community to the land and time they call The Dreaming.

The body is a common image of the interrelatedness of the imagined community. For both Christians and Hindus, the body is the image of the interdependent whole. In the Christian tradition, the "body of Christ" is the church, one body with many members. The eye cannot say to the hand, nor the head to the feet, "I have no need of you" (I Cor. 12). In the celebrated Vedic hymn called the *Purusha Sukta* (Rig Veda X.90), the whole created order—temporal, moral, and social—is seen to be the body of the cosmic person, Purusha, divided up in the beginning, at the time of creation. While the body is a holistic image for community and in that sense is positive, it is also a hierarchical image. There is a head and there are feet; no matter how valuable the feet are made to feel, there is a hierarchy. An image inherently hierarchical will not be adequate to imagine our interrelations as communities of faith in an interdependent world.

In developing a sense of *we* that is wider than the *we* of culture, religion, or clan, it will be important to have an image of what kind of human relatedness we wish to bring into being. People of each religious tradition have dreams of what the world should ideally be and how we should all be related to one another even though we are not all the same. Glimpsing one another's dreams is an important step in beginning to reimagine the *we*. Do we imagine ourselves to be separate but equal communities, concerned primarily with guarding one another's rights in a purely civic construction of relatedness? Do we imagine ourselves to be related as parts of an extended family, or as many families of faith? Do we imagine ourselves to be religious communities competing in goodness and in righteousness, as the Qur'an puts it? Imaging a wider *we* does not mean leaving our separate communities behind, but finding increasingly generative ways of living together as a community of communities. To do this, we all must imagine together who *we* are.

Both Gandhi and Martin Luther King, Jr., are among the many for whom the image of the household suggests our close relatedness. King introduced his talk "The World House" with these words:

> Some years ago a famous novelist died. Among his papers was found a list of suggested plots for future stories, the most prominently underscored being this one: "A widely separated family inherits a house in which they have to live together." This is the great new problem of mankind. We have inherited a large house, a great "world house" in which we have to live together—black and white, Easterner and Westerner, Gentile and Jew, Catholic and Protestant, Moslem and Hindu—a family unduly separated in ideas, culture, and interest, who, because we can never again live apart, must learn somehow to live with each other in peace.[32]

A household gathers together a large and usually complex extended family, with all the diversity of temperament and personality that human beings have. The imagined community of the household includes both hospitality and mutuality. A household may also have its hierarchies, but they are not the built-in hierarchies of the body. They will be open to challenge and negotiation. There is no household without its arguments, but its foundation is undergirding love and its language the two-way language of dialogue. Can we imagine the world, locally and globally, as such a household? Can we imagine the diversity of religious faith and tradition as such a household?

The household as an imagined community makes even more proximate the inequalities of the village of one thousand people. The rich will see the suffering and hunger of the poor in the very rooms of our common habitation. The household elicits from us the true recognition that, as King put it, "in a real sense, all life is interrelated. The agony of the poor impoverishes the rich; the betterment of the poor enriches the rich. We are inevitably our brother's keeper because we are our brother's brother. Whatever affects one directly affects

[32] Martin Luther King, Jr., *Where Do We Go from Here: Chaos or Community?* (Boston: Beacon Press, 1967), p. 167.

all indirectly."[33] To imagine such a household will require what King called a "revolution of values." "A genuine revolution of values means in the final analysis that our loyalties must become ecumenical rather than sectional. Every nation must now develop an overriding loyalty to mankind as a whole in order to preserve the best in their individual societies."[34]

Part of the revolution of values is a revolution of attitudes, a revolution of theological attitudes being foremost among them. A household cannot function on the underlying premise of exclusivity, though each community within the household may be exclusive in some things, such as its central rituals. A household cannot finally function on the underlying foundation of inclusivism either, for it will have to be *our* household as human beings, not ours as Christians, Muslims, or Buddhists, to which everyone else is welcome. No one community can set the terms for the whole. The underlying foundation of the world household will finally have to be pluralism.

In a household, people meet and live with one another at close range. The Hindu and the Christian know the Muslim and the Buddhist, who rise before dawn for prayer or meditation. Each community hears and overhears the prayers and sermons, the songs and silences of the others. Their privacy is respected. Occasionally there are invitations to join in. There are some joint celebrations. Each community also hears and overhears the hypocrisy of the others. As in any household, we come to know one another at our best and at our worst. We cannot sustain our pretenses to perfection.

Whether globally or locally, the household provides the context for understanding one another, not as strangers, but as neighbors. Mutual understanding may well lead to mutual transformation, as each of us begins to catch a glimpse of the glory as seen by the other. And above all, it provides the context in which the commitments of our faith can enable us to join with one another to solve the problems of our interdependent world.

Many religious traditions have their own distinctive visions of the imagined community of diverse peoples. In the Christian tradition, the dominant image of the community coming into being is the Kingdom of God—the world that God intends, the world of which we must be

[33] Ibid., p. 181.

[34] Ibid., p. 190.

co-creators. The New Testament is filled with images of the Kingdom. This "imagined community" is not finally the Christian community, but the community of the whole inhabited earth. In Jesus' time, as in ours, the term *kingdom* was intended somewhat paradoxically. Jesus overturned the regal understanding and expectation of "kingdom," for what was envisioned by Jesus was not like any earthly kingdom. This imagined community would not be imposed from above and ruled from on high, but would grow from the smallest seeds, like big bushes from tiny mustard seeds. It would be a kingdom inherited not by the rich and powerful, but by the poor, the widows, the homeless, and the strangers. This community would not secure its identity by dominion or exclusion, but was imagined to be an open house for all the peoples of the earth, coming from the East and West, North and South, to eat at table together. This imagined community is not off in the future in some heavenly place and time, but among us in community in this very world and within us. It is not some other place, but this place transformed by justice and filled to the brim with peace. The Kingdom of God is much wider than the church. It is the Kingdom of God, not of the Christian church. The role of the immediate followers of Christ in bringing this to be is not imagined in grandiose language, but in the most humble of domestic language. We are to be like yeast in the bread dough, like salt in the food, like a light to the path.

At the end of the final book of the Bible, the book of Revelation, is another imaginative vision. At the center of this vision is a holy city where it is forever daytime. The gates of the city stand open in every direction and are never shut. Through them come people from throughout the world, bringing into the city the "glory and the honor of the nations" (Rev. 21-22). Saint John's vision draws upon the earlier imaginative vision of the prophet Ezekiel, who also saw the city and the temple. In Ezekiel's vision, from underneath the main door of the sanctum of the temple, facing East, a stream is flowing. At first it is ankle deep, then knee deep. Gradually it becomes a great river. Its waters are the waters of life, pouring forth from the temple and bringing life, abundance, and healing wherever they flow. Saint John, too, saw that river, flowing with living waters, though in the city John saw there was no temple at all, but God alone. "Then the angel showed me the river of the water of life, bright as crystal, flowing from the throne of God and of the Lamb through the middle of the street of the city. On either side of the river is the tree of life . . . and the leaves of the tree are for the healing of the nations." And the water of life is free. "Let anyone who wishes take the water of life as a gift."

It is a beautiful image. There is no temple, only the river of the water of life and healing flowing from the very presence of God. Having journeyed from Bozeman to Banaras, I know that this image of the river of life is not our image alone. I cannot read the final chapters of Saint John's imaginative vision without seeing the Ganges in my mind's eye. For Hindus it is the River of Heaven, flowing from the foot of Vishnu, falling to the head of Shiva, touching the earth on top of its highest mountain, Mount Meru, and then generously splitting into four channels to flow in four directions, watering the whole of the earth with streams of blessing. The stream of the River of Heaven I know best flows south into India and even today skirts the sacred city of Banaras where pilgrims come to bathe at dawn. But surely the Jordan is one of those streams of the River of Heaven—and the Gallatin as well.

SOURCES AND ACKNOWLEDGMENTS

We thank the following authors, editors, and publishers for their consent to publish the articles and excerpts in this anthology.

Frithjof Schuon, "What Can the East Offer to the West?":
Language of the Self, Ganesh & Co, 1959, pp. 225-230.

René Guénon, "Oriental Metaphysics":
The Sword of Gnosis, ed. Jacob Needleman, Penguin, 1974, pp. 40-56.

Ananda Coomaraswamy, "The *Vedanta* and Western Tradition":
Coomaraswamy: Selected Papers, Vol. 2. Metaphysics, ed. Roger Lipsey, Princeton, 1977, pp. 3-22. Reproduced with the permission of Rama Coomaraswamy.

His Holiness the Dalai Lama, "A Wish for Harmony":
© His Holiness the Dalai Lama, and World Community for Christian Meditation, 1996, pp. 38-43. Excerpt from *The Good Heart: A Buddhist Perspective on the Teaching of Jesus*, with permission of Wisdom Publications, 199 Elm St., Somerville MA 02144 U.S.A, www.wisdompubs.org.

Whitall Perry, "Anti-Theology and the Riddles of Alcyone":
Challenges to a Secular Society, Foundation for Traditional Studies, 1996, pp. 65-79.

Marco Pallis, "The Tibetan Tradition: Its Presiding Idea":
The Way and the Mountain, Peter Owen, 1961, pp. 177-205.

Huston Smith, "Taoism":
The World's Religions, HarperSanFrancisco, 1991, pp. 196-220.

Philip Kapleau, "The Private Encounter with the Master":
Zen: Tradition and Transition, ed. Kenneth Kraft, Rider, 1988, pp. 44-69. Reproduced with permission of Kenneth Kraft and Grove Atlantic.

Lynna Dhanani, "An Introduction to Jainism":
Previously unpublished.

Swami Abhishiktananda, "*Sannyasa*":
The Further Shore, ISPCK, 1984, pp. 42-49.

John Paraskevopoulos, "Conceptions of the Absolute in Mahayana Buddhism and the Pure Land Way":
Sacred Web 3, 1999, pp. 121-138.

Titus Burckhardt, "Hindu Art":
The Essential Titus Burckhardt, ed. William Stoddart, World Wisdom, 2003, pp. 94-99.

Thomas Merton, "The Buddha Images at Polonnaruwa":
The Asian Journal of Thomas Merton, ed. Naomi Burton, et al., New Directions, 1975, pp. 233-236. © 1975, Trustees of the Thomas Merton Legacy Trust, reprinted by permission of New Directions Publishing Corp.

Anagarika Govinda, "Tibetan Sacred Music":
The Way of the White Clouds, Shambhala, 1970, pp. 29-31.

Jean Cooper, "The Symbolism of the Taoist Garden":
Studies in Comparative Religion, 11:4, Autumn 1977, pp. 224-234.

Gustie Herrigel, "The Substance of the Teaching":
Zen in the Art of Flower Arrangement, Routledge & Kegan Paul, 1958, pp. 117-124. Reproduced with permission of Souvenir Press.

Jean Biès, "Sacredness":
Returning to the Essential, World Wisdom, 2003, pp. 133-138.

Ananda Coomaraswamy, "Sri Ramakrishna and Religious Tolerance":
Coomaraswamy: Selected Papers, Vol. 2. Metaphysics, ed. Roger Lipsey, Princeton, 1977, pp. 34-42. Reproduced with the permission of Rama Coomaraswamy.

Rama Coomaraswamy. "Who Speaks for the East?":
Studies in Comparative Religion, 11:2, Spring 1977, pp. 85-91.

Aldous Huxley, "Some Reflections on Time":
Vedanta for Modern Man, ed. Christopher Isherwood, New American Library, 1972, pp. 138-142.

Thomas Merton, "Gandhi and the One-Eyed Giant":

Gandhi on Non-Violence, New Directions, 1965, pp. 1-20.

Ian Watson, "Hindu Cosmology and Modern Science":
Studies in Comparative Religion, 7:3, Summer 1973, pp. 174-177.

Gary Snyder, "On the Path, Off the Trail":
The Practice of the Wild, North Point Press, 1990, pp. 144-154. Reproduced with the permission of Shoemaker & Hoard, publishers of the 2004 edition.

Diana Eck, "The Imagined Community":
Encountering God: A Spiritual Journey from Bozeman to Banaras, Beacon Press, 1993, pp. 200-231.

SOURCES OF EPIGRAPH QUOTES

I. *Rig Veda* VIII.58.2, quoted in Whitall Perry, *A Treasury of Traditional Wisdom*, London: Allen & Unwin, 1971, pp. 777-778.

Sri Krishna in the *Bhagavad Gita*, translation taken from Ananda Coomaraswamy, "Sri Ramakrishna and Religious Tolerance," in *Coomaraswamy 2: Selected Papers: Metaphysics*, ed. Roger Lipsey, Princeton: Princeton University Press, 1977, p. 35.

II. *Svetasvatara Upanishad*, III.8.

III. Letter, Bombay, January 4, 1928, quoted in Philip Almond, *Rudolf Otto: An Introduction to His Philosophical Theology*, Chapel Hill: University of North Carolina Press, 1984, pp. 23-24. (An alternative translation can be found in Rudolf Otto, *Autobiographical and Social Essays*, ed. Gregory D. Alles, Berlin: Mouton de Gruyter, 1996, pp. 94-95.)

IV. Ananda Coomaraswamy, *The Bugbear of Literacy*, Bedfont: Perennial Books, 1979, p. 80.

NOTES ON CONTRIBUTORS

Swami Abhishiktananda (Henri Le Saux) was born in Britanny in 1910 and entered a Benedictine monastery in 1929. In 1948 he joined Father Jules Monchanin in establishing a Christian *ashram* in southern India and was later associated with Father Bede Griffiths at Saccidananda Ashram. He spent the later years of his life as a wandering monk, eventually founding a hermitage on the banks of the Ganges at Uttarkashi, in the Himalayas. He was deeply engaged in the encounter of Christianity and Hinduism, and was the author of many books including *Saccidananda: A Christian Experience of Advaita*, *The Secret of Arunachala*, and *The Further Shore.* A collection of several of his essays appeared posthumously as *The Eyes of Light.*

Jean Biès, the author of more than twenty books of philosophy, comparative religion, poetry, and travel, is former professor of Greek Literature at the University of Pau, France. A Chevalier of the French Legion of Honor and recipient of the High Prize of the Society of French Poets, since 1962 he and his wife have lived in a country home, "Saint Michel la Grange," at the foot of the Pyrenees. World Wisdom recently published an anthology of his writings entitled *Returning to the Essential.*

Titus Burckhardt, a German Swiss, was born in Florence in 1908 and died in Lausanne in 1984. He was one of the most authoritative exponents of the perennialist school. His lifelong task was the elucidation of timeless metaphysical, cosmological, and iconographical principles and the illumination of the manifold religious and cultural forms which gave them concrete expression. He was a major voice of the *philosophia perennis*, that "wisdom uncreate" that is expressed in Platonism, Vedanta, Sufism, Taoism, and other authentic esoteric or sapiential teachings. *The Essential Titus Burckhardt*, a compilation of some of his writings, was published by World Wisdom in 2003.

Ananda Coomaraswamy was born in 1877 in Ceylon. He was a multi-talented researcher, scientist, linguist, expert on art and culture, philosopher, museum curator, and author. Coomaraswamy was the first well-known writer of the modern era to expound the importance of traditional arts, culture, and thought as more than simply relics of a bygone past. His elucidation of traditional arts and crafts, and his exegesis of classical, Christian, and Indian metaphysics marked him as one of the twentieth century's most authoritative and influential exponents of the perennial philosophy. *The Essential Ananda K. Coomaraswamy* was published by World Wisdom in 2004.

Rama Coomaraswamy was educated in both England and India where he received a traditional education in Sanskrit and Hindi. He later studied medicine in the USA where he practiced as a surgeon. He was the author of many articles and books on theological subjects, including *The Destruction of the Christian Tradition*, an updated and revised edition of which was published by World Wisdom in 2006. He was the son of Ananda K. Coomaraswamy and edited his father's letters and several collections of his essays, including *The Essential Ananda K. Coomaraswamy*, published by World Wisdom in 2004. Rama Coomasraswamy died in July, 2006.

Jean Cooper was born in China where she spent much of her childhood. She wrote and lectured extensively in the U.K. on philosophy, comparative religion, and symbolism, and was the author of a wide range of books on spiritual topics, including *Taoism: The Way of the Mystic*, *Yin and Yang*, and *Symbolism: The Universal Language*, but is perhaps best known for her classic reference work, *An Illustrated Encyclopedia of Traditional Symbols.*

His Holiness Tenzin Gyatso, the 14th Dalai Lama of Tibet, is both the spiritual and temporal leader of the Tibetan people. Following the invasion of Tibet by the communist-inspired Chinese Army in 1959 and the impending threat on his life, he escaped into exile and has since resided in Dharamsala, the seat of the Tibetan Government-in-exile. He is a recipient of the Nobel Peace Prize and an author of numerous books and essays, including *Kindness, Clarity, and Insight*, *A Human Approach to World Peace*, and *Ocean of Wisdom.*

Lynna Dhanani holds a Master of Arts degree in South Asian and comparative religions from the University of Virginia. Her main areas of interest are Jainism, Indian philosophy and aesthetics, and comparative Hindu/Islamic philosophy and mysticism. She is studying Sanskrit and Persian, and contributed an article to *Dossier H: Frithjof Schuon.*

Diana Eck is Professor of Comparative Religion and Indian Studies at Harvard University, and has been closely involved in interfaith dialogue, especially through the World Council of Churches. She is the author of *Encountering God: A Spiritual Journey from Bozeman to Banaras* and *Banaras, City of Light*, and is a recipient of the National Humanities Medal.

Anagarika Govinda was born as Ernst Hoffman in Saxony in 1898. He studied architecture and philosophy at Freiburg University where he also developed his interests in painting and archaeology. In 1928 Hoffmann entered the *sangha* and moved to the Island Hermitage in Ceylon where he took his Buddhist name. Several years later he committed himself to the Tibetan tradition and spent thirty years in the sub-continent before moving to the USA. Lama Govinda died in 1985. He was the author of many works on Tibetan Buddhism, as well as an account of his pilgrimage through central and Western Tibet, *The Way of the White Clouds.*

René Guénon was a writer of extraordinary power and insight. In the early decades of the twentieth century, Guénon urged the imperative necessity of a recovery of integral metaphysics in the face of the onslaughts of modernity, and delivered an irrefutable indictment of the assumptions and values of the modern world, perhaps most powerfully in his master-work, *The Reign of Quantity and the Signs of the Times.* Guénon died in 1951. His writings have exercised a profound influence on many later perennialists.

Gustie Herrigel spent many years in Japan with her husband Eugen Herrigel, the author of *Zen in the Art of Archery*—to which her own *Zen in the Art of Flower Arrangement* is a companion volume.

Aldous Huxley is well-known as a novelist, essayist, and philosopher, the author of such works as *Brave New World* and the somewhat idiosyncratic *The Perennial Philosophy*, in which he explored common ground shared by the great religious traditions. After moving to the USA in 1947 he was closely involved with the Vedanta Society of Southern California until his death in 1963.

Philip Kapleau was, until his death in 2004, one of the West's most authoritative teachers of Zen. He underwent thirteen years of training in Japan before establishing the Rochester Zen Center in upstate New York. He wrote many influential books on Zen practice, including *The Three Pillars of Zen* and *Zen: Dawn in the West.*

Thomas Merton is perhaps the most widely known and loved Christian monk of the twentieth century. After entering the Cistercian monastery of Our Lady of Gethsemani, in Kentucky, he recounted his spiritual journey in *The Seven Storey Mountain*, which became a best-seller. However, it was only in later works such as *New Seeds of Contemplation* and *Zen and the Birds of Appetite* that his thinking, fertilized by Eastern influences, attained its full maturity.

Marco Pallis was born of Greek parents in Liverpool in 1895, educated at Harrow and Liverpool Universities, and served in the British army during the Great War. He wrote two books deriving from his experiences traveling in the Eastern Himalaya region and with Tibetan Buddhism: *Peaks and Lamas*, which was reprinted several times and became something of a bestseller, and *The Way and the Mountain.* Pallis also wrote many articles for the journal *Studies in Comparative Religion*, some of which are gathered together in his last publication, *A Buddhist Spectrum: Contributions to Buddhist-Christian Dialogue,* recently republished by World Wisdom in 2003.

John Paraskevopoulos is an executive officer with the Australian Department of Foreign Affairs in Canberra. He studied philosophy at the University of Melbourne before receiving ordination in the Pure Land tradition of Mahayana Buddhism in Kyoto in 1994. He is the author of several articles on Shin Buddhism and is a contributor to *Sacred Web.*

Whitall Perry was born near Boston in 1920. His early intellectual interests included Platonism and Vedanta and he traveled extensively in the Middle and Far East both before and after World War II, with a brief interlude of study at Harvard University. He was one of several Harvard students who came under Ananda Coomaraswamy's influence in the 1940s, and later became a close associate of Frithjof Schuon. His major work was the compilation of a magisterial compendium of spiritual doctrine, *A Treasury of Traditional Wisdom*, spanning the ages and drawing on all of the major mythological, religious, and initiatic traditions of both East and West.

Frithjof Schuon is best known as the foremost contemporary spokesman of the perennial philosophy and as a philosopher in the metaphysical current of Shankara and Plato. Born of German parents in 1907 in Basle, Switzerland, Schuon died in the United States in 1998. He wrote more than twenty books on metaphysical, spiritual, and religious themes as well as being a regular contributor to journals on comparative religion in both Europe and America. Schuon's writings have been consistently featured and reviewed in a wide range of scholarly and philosophical publications around the world, respected by both scholars and spiritual authorities.

Huston Smith is Thomas J. Watson Professor of Religion and Distinguished Adjunct Professor of Philosophy, Emeritus, Syracuse University. His many books include *Forgotten Truth: The Common Vision of the World's Religions*, *Beyond the Post-Modern Mind*, and *Why Religion Matters: The Fate of the Human Spirit in an Age of Disbelief*, as well as the classic *The World's Religions*. His discovery of Tibetan multiphonic chanting was lauded as "an important landmark in the study of music," and his film documentaries on Hinduism, Tibetan Buddhism, and Sufism have all won international awards.

Gary Snyder is a Pulitzer Prize winning poet, environmentalist, and teacher. Snyder was a major figure in the Beat movement and, after spending many years in a Japanese monastery, helped to make Zen more widely known in the West. His many books include *Turtle Island*, *Earth House Hold*, *A Place in Space*, *The Real Work*, and *The Practice of the Wild*.

Ian Watson lectured in religious studies at La Trobe University, Melbourne. He translated and edited many of René Guénon's articles, was joint editor of *Religious Traditions*, and a contributor to *Studies in Comparative Religion*.

BIOGRAPHICAL NOTE

HARRY OLDMEADOW is Coordinator of Philosophy and Religious Studies in the Department of Arts, La Trobe University, Bendigo, Australia. He studied history, politics, and literature at the Australian National University, obtaining a First Class Honors degree in history. In 1971 a Commonwealth Overseas Research Scholarship led to further studies at Oxford University. In 1980 he completed a Masters dissertation on the traditionalist or perennialist school of comparative religious thought. This study was awarded the University of Sydney Medal for excellence in research and was later published under the title *Traditionalism: Religion in the Light of the Perennial Philosophy* (2000). His principal intellectual interests include not only the traditionalist school of thinkers but the mystical and esoteric dimensions of the major religious traditions, especially Christianity, Hinduism, and Buddhism. He also has an abiding interest in the primal traditions of the American Plains Indians and the Aborigines of Australia. His latest works include *Journeys East: 20th Century Western Encounters with Eastern Religious Traditions* (World Wisdom, 2004) and *Abhishiktananda: A Christian Pilgrim in India* (forthcoming World Wisdom, 2007). He is also the editor of *The Betrayal of Tradition: Essays on the Spiritual Crisis of Modernity* (World Wisdom, 2005). Over the last decade he has published extensively in such journals as *Sacred Web*, *Sophia*, and *Vincit Omnia Veritas*. He currently resides with his wife on a small property outside Bendigo.

INDEX

Abhishiktananda, Swami, 165
Abraham, 196, 300, 307, 314
Advaita Vedanta, 58, 147, 151, 166, 175
Africa, 146, 249-251, 257, 271, 287, 293-294, 296, 304, 310-311, 314-315
Agni, 1, 165
Ahimsa, 144, 157-160, 163, 256, 296, 310
Amida Buddha, 188, 282, 304
Ancestors, 71, 298
Animals, 25, 37, 82, 95, 144, 154, 157-158, 210, 246
Annihilation, 42, 148, 176
Antitheology, 50, 56
Appearance, 8, 26, 32-33, 37, 122, 136, 143, 168, 246
Aquinas, Thomas, 36, 229, 262-263
Archetypes, 51, 63
Architecture, 193-195, 197, 327
Arendt, Hannah, 256, 264
Aristotle, 11, 13, 25, 57, 272
Art, 4-5, 29-32, 39, 41-42, 50, 84, 100, 112, 122, 140, 146, 191, 193, 195, 198, 206-207, 215, 217-219, 232, 235, 238, 258, 262-263, 268-269, 278, 282
Artist, 85, 106, 215, 217-219, 238, 243, 246, 283
Asceticism, 121, 141, 148
Ashram, 59, 170, 271, 291, 294-295
Asvaghosha, 177, 179
Atman, 30-31, 51, 53, 57, 61, 166, 175
Augustine, 23, 27, 36, 125, 232, 237
Axis, 88, 165, 196-198, 211, 214, 220

Banaras, 286, 290-291, 299, 301
Beatitude, 30, 33, 39, 150, 181
Beauty, 28, 97, 112, 180, 200, 208, 210, 212-214, 223, 231-232, 237, 246, 252,
Becoming, 12, 63, 73, 82, 94, 102, 145, 166, 175, 193, 207, 263, 268, 270
Beliefs, 45, 47, 96, 156, 232, 241, 252, 307
Bhagavad Gita, 1, 23-25, 33, 35, 42, 230, 298
Bhagavata, 142
Bible, The, 17, 53, 96, 221, 225, 295, 298, 319
Blake, 100, 231, 234
Bliss, 73, 148, 150-151, 161, 175, 179, 185-186, 188, 190
Bodhisattvahood, 72, 76-79, 81, 85, 92, 94
Boehme, Jacob, 104, 234, 269
Boethius, 26, 34, 37, 233
Bondage, 73, 139, 142, 145-146, 149-150, 154-156, 163
Brahman, 23, 31, 42, 147, 151, 166, 171, 173, 220
Brahmanas, 24-25, 36, 173
Brahmins, 141, 222, 295
Buddhahood, 77-78, 135, 137 175, 179, 183, 186-188

Buddhas, 48, 75-77, 86, 93, 131, 166, 180-181, 186-187, 199
Buddhists, 64, 76, 174, 182, 248, 288-289, 302, 304, 307, 310, 318

Caste, 4, 58, 91, 241, 254, 258, 295, 312, 314
Ceylon, 70, 76, 203-204
Chenrezig, 82, 86-87
Childhood, 133, 326
Children, 31, 52, 56, 101, 284, 286, 293
Chuang Tzu, 99, 103, 108, 110-112, 114-116
Circle, 113-114, 194, 196-198, 208-209, 214, 249
Cities, 196, 215, 291, 296, 303-304
Civilizations, 8-9, 21, 70-71, 196, 220, 249, 278
Competition, 75, 110-111, 297
Concentration, 15, 58, 74, 86 130-131, 144, 148, 159, 223, 280
Confucianism, 71, 95, 113, 116
Confucius, 95-96, 107, 116-117, 252
Contemplation, 40, 45, 47, 80, 85, 87, 191, 195, 209, 223, 249
Coomaraswamy, Ananda, 23, 50, 78, 140, 227, 229, 238, 242, 251, 267-269
Cosmography, 156,
Cosmology, 17, 272-273
Creatures, 40, 62, 73, 78, 80, 92-93, 95, 158, 220, 231
Cultures, 50, 244, 250, 259, 288, 297, 300-301
Cycle, 7, 17, 150, 195, 197, 210, 264, 296

Dalai Lama, The, 44, 86
Dance, 53, 82, 100, 107-108, 197-198, 252
Dante, 24-26
Dao De Jing, 278, 282
Daoism, 278
Darkness, 18, 30, 55, 67, 126, 128, 182, 213, 230, 274
Defilement, 139, 153
Deity, 1, 39, 139, 230, 234
Deliverance, 18, 73-76, 82-83, 86, 145, 181, 190, 198, 223
Delusion, 73, 80, 120, 131, 155, 171, 177, 180-181, 284
Desire, 60-61, 83, 102, 131, 133, 142, 160, 167, 175, 183, 186, 218-219, 245, 257, 268
Destruction, 184, 198, 220-221, 224, 254, 259, 313
Detachment, 62, 65, 159
Devotee, 84, 178, 181
Devotion, 1, 139, 160, 187, 230, 270
Dharmabody, 187-188, 190
Dharmakaya, 175-177, 179, 181, 186-188, 190, 200
Dhyana, 159, 170, 204, 235, 276
Dialogue-, 44-45, 263, 288-290, 298, 300-302, 305-306, 309-314, 317
Digambara, 143, 146, 155, 161
Diksa, 146, 166-169, 172
Dionysius, 26, 30, 40, 231, 233
Disbelief, 111, 311
Disciple, 23, 30, 41, 121-122, 135, 168, 172, 222
Discipline, 27, 72, 122, 136, 142,

152, 157, 160, 184, 217, 235, 273, 280-281
Dispositions, 47-48
Dissociation, 106, 149, 250-251
Dissolution, 37, 84, 175, 203, 217, 246
Dogen, 123, 131, 138, 281, 284
Dogma, 57, 62, 232, 235, 262
Dogmatism, 65, 293, 311
Doubt, 3, 21, 64, 169, 181, 187, 218, 235, 272, 292, 299, 314
Dragons, 213, 224
Dreams, 57, 143, 145, 286, 316
Dualism, 5, 9, 61, 75, 176, 250
Duality, 24, 58-60, 237
Duty, 160, 252, 256, 259, 267, 287, 306-307

Eckhart, Meister, 23, 25-26, 39-41, 43, 55, 64, 84, 231, 234, 236
Education, 25, 30, 91, 133, 160, 230, 238, 252, 291, 305-306, 308
Effort, 11, 16, 44, 48, 58, 61, 107, 114, 120, 130, 159, 182, 221, 273, 279, 281
Elements, 15, 35, 91, 130, 148, 153, 206, 211, 221, 259, 302
Eliot, T.S., 238-239
Elite, 6, 9, 14, 21, 71, 90, 144-145, 239
Emanation, 55, 144, 151, 178, 234-235
Emptiness, 120, 124-125, 127, 179-180, 200, 282
Energies, 87, 104, 129, 131-132, 274, 290, 307
England, 98, 146, 298, 305, 326
Enlightened, 40, 122-123, 126, 128, 137, 149-150, 156, 240, 267
Environment, 21, 33-34, 38, 44, 112, 146, 157, 187, 287, 303
Esoteric, 9, 21, 50, 54, 147
Eternity, 16, 27, 42, 151, 179, 190, 224, 232, 236, 246, 248
Ethics, 293, 295, 311, 315
Europe, 4, 28, 196, 230, 242, 308
Evil, 6, 41, 53, 55, 62, 75, 83, 113-115, 158, 182-184, 237, 243, 261-266, 268-270, 288
Evolution, 17, 20, 34
Exile, 144, 256
Exoteric, 9, 234

Faith, 3, 28, 56, 62, 104, 133, 148, 161-162, 174, 177-179, 183-186, 188-189, 231, 233-235, 237, 239, 241-242, 253, 262, 289, 295, 300, 302, 307, 309, 312-314, 316-318
Farmer, 114, 280
Farmers, 103, 281, 293
Fasting, 144, 159, 257-258
Fathers, 5-6, 236, 241, 266-267
Fengshui, 206, 209
Festival, 208, 221, 305
Fideism, 240, 242
Fire, 30, 165, 168, 195, 229, 265, 268, 283
Flesh, 33, 50, 54, 97, 127, 205, 211, 236, 261, 266, 268
Food, 112, 159, 161, 170, 229, 280, 294, 319
Forces, 131, 152-153, 156, 162, 195, 202, 206-207, 210, 212, 249, 253, 259, 289
Forgiveness, 159, 262-263, 265,

268-269, 314
France, 46, 308

Gandhian, 255, 266, 291, 293, 295, 298-299
Ganesh, 163
Ganges, The, 242, 300, 320
Gardens, 209-210, 212, 214-215, 221, 281
Gautama, 175, 283
Gnosis, 3, 24, 30, 106, 321
Godhead, 40-41, 236, 246
Gods, 27, 48, 143-144, 154, 214, 220, 224, 293
Goodness, 40, 45-46, 85, 96, 246, 317
Gospels, 26, 54, 83, 266, 298, 310, 312
Government, 239, 270, 291, 303, 305
Grace, 51, 61, 93, 166-167, 169, 171, 185, 253, 278, 280
Guénon, René, 8, 13, 50, 142, 163
Guru, 30, 57, 93, 168, 171-172, 203, 256

Habits, 15, 79, 89, 252, 288
Happiness, 44, 60, 161, 175, 180, 188, 211, 214, 233, 248
Harijan, 254, 257-258, 266-267
Healing, 62, 104-105, 255, 269, 319-320
Heavens, 74, 194-195, 197
Hell, 55, 60, 125, 154, 156
Hermes, 23, 26, 51
Hermit, 206, 213, 260
Hierarchy, 50, 63, 154, 197, 233, 316
Honor, 48, 86, 93, 110, 117, 319
Hope, 46, 57, 61, 81-82, 89, 103, 110, 167, 181, 184-185, 269, 284, 287, 300
Humanism, 26, 61-62, 85, 93, 253
Huxley, Aldous, 61, 245
Hymn, 55, 222, 293, 316

Ibn Arabi, 64, 232
Ideologies, 224, 301
Idolatry, 89, 94, 232, 245
Idols, 56, 230
Illusion, 18, 56, 75-76, 104, 145, 261, 275
Images, 5, 12, 198, 218, 308, 315, 319
Immortality, 28, 32, 53, 64, 100, 203, 213, 245
Impermanence, 53, 80-81, 151-152, 284
Incarnation, 74, 134, 143, 238
Indra, 143, 178, 224
Industrialism, 250
Industry, 4, 291, 294
Initiates, 89, 103
Initiation, 40, 86, 146, 157, 161, 166, 168-169, 171-172
Initiative, 71, 145, 177, 181-182,
Injustice, 258-259, 283, 294, 310
Insight, 6, 73, 90, 92, 102, 124, 128, 161, 204-205
Inspiration, 84, 106, 203, 205-206, 210, 220
Institutions, 23, 69-71, 92-93, 171, 270, 284, 288, 308
Intellect, 5, 12-13, 34, 39, 62, 127, 131, 133, 148, 187, 218, 231, 245, 282
Interfaith Dialogue, 300, 312
Intuition, 5, 12, 127, 150, 220,

260
Invocation, 86-87, 183-184
Islam, 9, 41, 147, 196, 229-230, 234, 306, 308

Jains, 139, 142, 145, 151-152, 154, 157-159, 162-163, 288
Japan, 70, 119, 136, 184, 198, 251, 254, 277, 280, 283, 298, 310
Jerusalem, 46, 193, 300
Jesus, 32, 53-54, 59, 73, 105, 240, 252, 265, 292, 298, 314, 319
Jews, 64, 262, 286, 288-289, 295, 301-302, 304-305, 308, 313, 316
Jiva, 149-150, 153-156, 162
Jodo Shinshu, 184, 186-189,
Joy, 44, 54, 73, 102, 123, 133, 144, 151, 155, 161, 180, 258

Kali Yuga, 223, 240
Karma, 35-36, 150, 153-156, 162, 176, 185
Kevalajnana, 139, 144-145, 148, 156
Knowing, 12, 15, 27, 31, 35, 39, 56, 140, 144, 148-149, 156, 158, 163, 199, 310
Koran, The, 230
Krishna, 50, 59, 61, 63
Krishnamurti, Jiddu, 50, 56, 58-59, 61, 282
Kyoto, 187, 277, 280

Laity, 141, 146, 157, 160, 163, 177
Lao Tzu, 95-96, 99, 104, 112, 116-117
Laws, 17, 150, 160, 198, 201, 217-218, 265, 288
Liberty, 4, 7, 32, 42, 91, 167, 255-256, 271, 308
Logic, 28, 149, 163, 251, 257, 264
Logos, 31, 41-42, 272
Lotus, 121, 175, 183, 209, 213-214, 316
Love, 28, 39, 45, 48, 52, 54, 60-61, 117, 131, 133, 167, 223, 230, 236, 253-254, 260, 263, 265, 268, 270, 283, 292, 310, 314-315, 317
Luther, Martin, 292, 299, 317

Madhyamika, 177, 180, 199
Magic, 29-30, 104-106, 110, 112, 214, 266
Mahaprajna, Acharya, 148, 160-161, 163
Mahayana Buddhism, 148, 174, 176, 179, 181, 280
Mantra, 139, 159, 168, 214, 223,
Marriage, 39, 54, 213, 250
Marx, Karl, 247-248, 252
Masters, 49, 119, 127, 132, 134-138, 180, 183
Materialism, 38, 54, 112, 293
Meditation, 44, 46-47, 57-58, 100-102, 115, 117-120, 131, 138, 156, 159, 170, 182, 184, 201, 204, 206, 208, 210, 280-281, 283, 318
Merton, Thomas, 45, 108, 199, 249
Metaphysics, 8-14, 17-18, 20, 22-26, 28-30, 33-35, 39, 42, 50, 57, 149, 164, 175, 177, 229, 233-234, 261, 272-273

Mind, 4, 6, 13, 15, 26, 28, 33, 37, 46-47, 57-58, 60, 80, 83-84, 89-91, 101-102, 104, 106-107, 109, 114, 119-121, 124-131, 133, 144-145, 150, 160-161, 165, 170, 179, 184-186, 199, 207, 210, 219, 225, 234, 249-250, 253-254, 267-268, 271-272, 277, 282, 288, 320
Missionaries, 230, 298
Moksa, 139, 142, 146, 149
Monastery, 45, 171, 280, 283
Monasticism, 166, 171, 147, 234
Monks, 72, 119, 141, 144, 160-161, 166-167, 171, 215, 230, 281, 299
Mountains, 45, 112, 199, 205-206, 210-212, 215, 277, 283
Mount Meru, 320
Mystery, 52, 80, 97, 166-168, 171-172, 200, 218-220, 269, 293
Mysticism, 5, 30, 93, 103, 106
Mystics, 53, 64
Myth, 28, 51, 55, 172, 194, 249

Nagarjuna, 64, 180
Naldjorpa, 87-88, 90, 92-93
Non-duality, 23-24, 42, 76-79, 84, 86
Nontheism, 140, 147
Non-violence, 144, 146, 156-158, 248-249, 252, 254-255, 257, 260-261, 263-264, 296, 299, 310, 314-315

Opposites, 26, 84, 113-114, 176, 211, 218
Orthodoxy, 28, 65, 91, 93, 141,

Painters, 112, 205, 219, 243
Painting, 112, 156, 205-207, 211, 215
Pantheism, 194, 233
Parliament of Religions, 286, 300, 306
Penance, 144, 162, 182
Philosophia Perennis, 26-27, 50
Pilgrimage, 38, 200, 230, 300-301
Plants, 154, 163, 188, 208, 210, 214, 246, 277
Plato, 25-26, 43, 64, 241, 243, 255
Platonism, 234
Plotinus, 23, 26, 97, 234
Poetry, 206, 208-209, 246
Politics, 248, 255, 257, 283-284, 291, 313
Polonnaruwa, 199-200
Prajna Paramita, 76-78
Prayer, 46-48, 163, 167, 221, 223, 295, 304-305, 318
Precepts, 184, 271, 289
Priest, 195, 260, 279
Priesthood, 104
Progress, 29, 62, 80, 234, 239, 241-242, 251, 264, 301
Psychology, 14, 19, 29-31, 161, 272-273
Pure Land Buddhism, 181, 184, 186, 282
Purity, 65, 79, 102, 155, 179, 186, 190, 200, 212, 242, 293, 314
Purusha, 67, 194, 197, 316

Quality, 81, 116, 147, 150-151,

153, 155, 185, 201, 246, 284
Quantity, 4, 153, 155, 249-250, 266

Race, 20, 62, 71, 110, 130, 295, 310
Racism, 310-311, 314
Ram, 297
Ramakrishna, 50, 223, 229, 234-235
Ramana Maharshi, 282
Recurrence, 35-36, 245-246
Reincarnation, 25, 35-36, 56, 154
Relativity, 18, 59, 80, 113-115, 177, 180
Religion, 4, 24, 27, 34-35, 39, 46-47, 50-52, 54, 57-58, 61-64, 71, 96, 104, 140, 146-147, 163, 191, 205, 230, 233-236, 238-239, 241, 252-253, 267, 272, 288, 293, 295, 297, 300-301, 303, 306-307, 310, 312-313, 316
Religious Tolerance, 229-230, 237
Religious Traditions, 44-47, 152, 286, 288, 295, 298, 300-305, 308, 310, 312, 316, 318
Renaissance, 3, 227, 250
Renunciation, 144-145, 156-157, 165-169
Revelation, 54, 77, 141, 144, 231
Rig-Veda, 169, 194
Rishis, 166-167, 171-172
Risis, 274, 276
Rites, 14-15, 27, 51, 64, 158, 168, 172, 195, 241, 292
Ritual, 25, 141, 146, 157, 168, 172, 197, 201, 241, 284, 305, 314
Round of Existence, 72-73, 77-78, 82-83

Sacredness, 158, 173, 220, 260
Sacrifice, 42, 165, 168, 194, 197, 232, 248, 258, 268
Sadhus, 144, 172
Sainthood, 85, 88, 90, 241
Saints, 5, 36, 63, 85, 105, 135, 204
Salvation, 40, 62, 78, 80, 89, 138, 184, 220
Samadhi, 46, 58, 122, 124, 235, 292, 297
Samsara, 150, 154, 174, 176-178, 180-181, 184-186
Sannyasadiksa, 166, 168, 171
Sannyasi, 165, 167-170, 172
Sanskrit, 23-25, 76, 78, 101, 142, 144, 154, 165, 183, 193, 224, 235, 237
Satyagraha, 253, 255, 259, 269-271
Scholars, 26, 29, 36, 42, 45-46, 95-96, 174, 212, 215, 289
Schuon, Frithjof, 163
Science, 3-5, 9-10, 19-20, 28-29, 57, 62-63, 111, 153, 161, 163, 220, 224, 234, 239, 249-250, 252, 272-276, 287, 300
Scriptures, 5, 41, 52, 142, 144-146, 149-150, 156, 159, 161, 168, 175, 189, 221, 224, 230, 233, 240, 305-306
Sects, 28, 143, 146, 148, 155, 187, 189, 229, 251
Senses, 10, 25, 30-31, 75, 96, 98, 102, 122, 131, 133, 169, 220-221
Shakyamuni Buddha, 134, 182

Shankara, 23-24, 32, 40, 43, 64
Sikhs, 286, 288, 298, 305, 309, 311
Silence, 34, 102, 170, 191, 199, 255-256
Simplicity, 107, 113, 117, 157, 160-161, 205, 222, 233
Sleep, 34, 115, 133, 158, 214, 223, 278, 280
Solitude, 45, 74, 84, 88, 96, 112, 169-170
Souls, 25, 139, 144, 150-151, 153, 166, 247
Space, 31, 34, 55, 85, 108, 150, 153, 162, 165, 193, 197-198, 202-203, 206-207, 215, 222, 246-247, 251, 256-257, 287
Speech, 63, 144, 157, 159, 171, 235, 314
Spirituality, 45, 63, 69, 79, 85, 89, 91, 139, 162, 188, 254, 300
Suffering, 73-75, 77, 81-84, 86, 132, 134, 144, 175, 180-181, 185-187, 190, 261-263, 265-266, 283, 317
Sunyata, 177, 180, 190, 199
Sutras, 148, 155, 177, 181, 185, 188, 260, 280, 284
Suzuki, D.T., 111, 118, 176
Symbol, 28, 81, 113-114, 154, 166, 194, 197-198, 205, 211-213, 246-247
Symbolism, 3, 5-6, 14, 25, 77, 82, 84, 142, 181, 187, 191, 196-197, 205, 208, 210-215, 286

Taoisms, 98-99
Taoists, 64, 97-100, 104, 108, 110, 113-114, 248
Tathagata, 179, 188-190
Theology, 24, 40, 50-51, 53-56 58, 73, 91, 104, 232, 234, 236, 292, 298
Tibet, 56, 69-72, 77, 82, 85-88, 92, 96, 198, 202
Tibetans, 73, 76, 86, 89, 93
Time, 3-5, 12, 15-16, 18-21, 28, 32-36, 38-41, 45, 47-48, 50, 53, 60, 63, 69, 71, 73-74, 77, 81, 86, 91-92, 97, 103-104, 106, 114, 117, 119-121, 124-125, 129-131, 134, 136, 138, 141, 144, 146, 148, 150, 153, 159, 162, 166, 168, 170, 176-179, 182-183, 185, 187, 193, 197-198, 202, 205-206, 208-209, 213-214, 218, 220, 222-224, 229, 232, 240-242, 244-248, 251-253, 255, 258-260, 264, 269-270, 280-284, 286-287, 291-292, 295-297, 299, 301, 304-305, 307, 315-316, 319
Tradition, 4, 14, 20-21, 23, 25, 27-28, 35-36, 44-45, 47-48, 50, 69, 71-73, 84-85, 87, 92-95, 118, 135, 139-144, 146-147, 151, 155, 159, 161, 165, 167-168, 170-172, 174, 176, 181-182, 188-189, 194, 197, 210, 224, 232-233, 235, 244, 252-253, 275, 279, 282, 289-290, 293, 295, 297-300, 304, 307-309, 311-312, 314, 316-318
Transcendence, 21, 51, 147, 163, 165, 170, 247, 293
Transformation, 42, 47, 56, 123,

194, 219, 290-291, 294, 318
Transmigration, 25, 36, 38, 150, 154, 163
Tyranny, 145, 255-256, 261, 264,

Ultimate Reality, 26, 80, 97, 120, 139-140, 149, 162, 174, 176, 180, 189-190, 247-248
Universities, 306
Untouchables, 243, 254, 257, 267, 293-295
Upanishads, 167, 172, 175

Vedas, 24-25, 141, 173, 236, 260
Visions, 87, 120, 225, 318
Void, 74, 77-78, 84, 94, 176, 180-181
Vows, 157, 160-161, 163, 170, 183, 187-188, 271

War, 33, 116, 133, 251, 286, 304-305
Work, 11, 13, 18-19, 21, 24, 43, 50, 56, 72, 74, 78, 85, 89, 98-99, 104-105, 109, 112, 115, 128-129, 133, 169, 177, 206-208, 217, 219, 232, 238, 243, 261, 277-285, 288, 290-291, 293, 301
Worship, 39, 54, 139, 146, 221, 248, 256, 258, 260, 300, 304-305

Yin-yang, 205-206, 210-212, 214-216
Yoga, 6, 19-20, 29, 62, 99, 101, 103, 106, 146, 159, 161, 235, 254

Zazen, 118, 120-122, 127, 129-130, 138
Zendo, 119, 132, 136

For a glossary of all key foreign words used in books published by World Wisdom, including metaphysical terms in English, consult: www.DictionaryofSpiritualTerms.org.
This on-line Dictionary of Spiritual Terms provides extensive definitions, examples and related terms in other languages.

Other books in the Perennial Philosophy series

The Betrayal of Tradition: Essays on the Spiritual Crisis of Modernity, edited by Harry Oldmeadow, 2005

Borderlands of the Spirit: Reflections on a Sacred Science of Mind, by John Herlihy, 2005

A Buddhist Spectrum: Contributions to Buddhist-Christian Dialogue, by Marco Pallis, 2003

The Essential Ananda K. Coomaraswamy, edited by Rama P. Coomaraswamy, 2004

The Essential Lord Northbourne, edited by Lord Northbourne and Joseph A. Fitzgerald, 2007

The Essential Seyyed Hossein Nasr, edited by William C. Chittick, 2007

The Essential Sophia, edited by Seyyed Hossein Nasr and Katherine O'Brien, 2006

The Essential Titus Burckhardt: Reflections on Sacred Art, Faiths, and Civilizations, edited by William Stoddart, 2003

Every Branch in Me: Essays on the Meaning of Man, edited by Barry McDonald, 2002

Figures of Speech or Figures of Thought: Collected Essays on the Traditional or "Normal" View of Art, by Ananda K. Coomaraswamy, 2007

A Guide to Hindu Spirituality, by Arvind Sharma, 2006

Islam, Fundamentalism, and the Betrayal of Tradition: Essays by Western Muslim Scholars, edited by Joseph E.B. Lumbard, 2004

Journeys East: 20th Century Western Encounters with Eastern Religious Traditions, by Harry Oldmeadow, 2004

Light from the East: Eastern Wisdom for the Modern West, edited by Harry Oldmeadow, 2007

Living in Amida's Universal Vow: Essays in Shin Buddhism, edited by Alfred Bloom, 2004

Paths to the Heart: Sufism and the Christian East, edited by James S. Cutsinger, 2002

Returning to the Essential: Selected Writings of Jean Biès, translated by Deborah Weiss-Dutilh, 2004

Science and the Myth of Progress, edited by Mehrdad M. Zarandi, 2003

Seeing God Everywhere: Essays on Nature and the Sacred, edited by Barry McDonald, 2003

Singing the Way: Insights in Poetry and Spiritual Transformation, by Patrick Laude, 2005

The Spiritual Legacy of the North American Indian: Commemorative Edition, by Joseph E. Brown, 2007

Sufism: Love & Wisdom, edited by Jean-Louis Michon and Roger Gaetani, 2006

The Underlying Religion: An Introduction to the Perennial Philosophy, edited by Martin Lings and Clinton Minnaar, 2007

Ye Shall Know the Truth: Christianity and the Perennial Philosophy, edited by Mateus Soares de Azevedo, 2005